THE IMAGINED CIVIL WAR

CIVIL WAR AMERICA

Gary W. Gallagher, editor

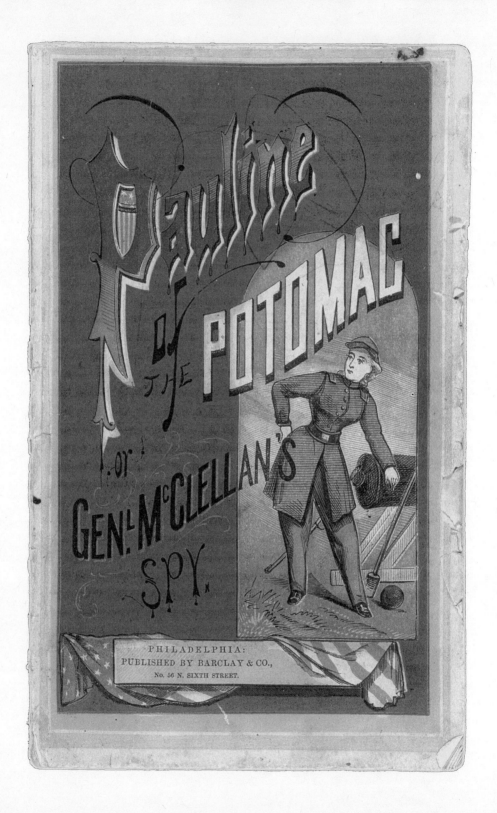

Pauline of the Potomac

or Gen.l McClellan's Spy.

PHILADELPHIA:
PUBLISHED BY BARCLAY & CO.,
No. 56 N. SIXTH STREET.

THE IMAGINED CIVIL WAR

Popular Literature of the North & South, 1861–1865

ALICE FAHS

The University of North Carolina Press

Chapel Hill & London

© 2001

The University of North Carolina Press

All rights reserved

Designed by Richard Hendel

Set in Bell and Madrone types

by Tseng Information Systems, Inc.

Manufactured in the United States of America

The paper in this book meets the guidelines for permanence

and durability of the Committee on Production Guidelines for

Book Longevity of the Council on Library Resources.

Library of Congress Cataloging-in-Publication Data

Fahs, Alice.

The imagined Civil War: popular literature of the

North and South, 1861–1865 / Alice Fahs.

p. cm.—(Civil War America)

Enlargement of author's thesis (Ph. D.)—New York University.

Includes bibliographical references (p.) and index.

ISBN 0-8078-2581-6 (cloth: alk. paper)

1. United States—History—Civil War, 1861–1865—Literature

and the war. 2. War and literature—Southern States—History—

19th century. 3. American literature—Southern States—History

and criticism. 4. Popular literature—Southern States—History

and criticism. 5. War and literature—United States—History—

19th century. 6. American literature—19th century—History and

criticism. 7. Popular literature—United States—History and

criticism. 8. War stories, American—History and criticism. 9. War

poetry, American—History and criticism. 10. Southern States—In

literature. 11. War in literature. I. Title. II. Series.

PS217.C58 F34   2001

810.9′358—dc21   00-055958

05 04 03 02 01   5 4 3 2 1

Page ii:

From *Pauline of the Potomac, or General McClellan's Spy*

(Philadelphia: Barclay and Co., 1862)

To Charlie & Mimi

CONTENTS

ILLUSTRATIONS

ACKNOWLEDGMENTS

It is a pleasure to acknowledge the many friends, family members, teachers, and colleagues who have provided me with support and encouragement in the writing of this book.

My deepest intellectual debt is to Thomas Bender. At New York University, Tom was an exceptional adviser, just as he is an exceptional teacher, thinker, and writer. The depth, breadth, and generosity of his intellect made the experience of being a student profoundly rewarding, and for this I thank him. I would not have become a historian without his inspiring example and constant support and encouragement. He is a rare mentor indeed.

I received other important help at NYU as well. This book began as a dissertation on New York book publishing during the Civil War. I was lucky enough to receive the thoughtful editorial guidance of Susan Ware throughout the entire dissertation process and Michael O'Malley's skillful suggestions on my final draft. And I learned much, too, from a group of friends including Marc Aronson, Sally Charnow, Jeanne Houck, Kathleen Hulser, Pat Kelly, Eliza McFeely, and Lola Van Wagenen. They were and are a wonderfully supportive cohort.

At the American Antiquarian Society, a Frances Hiatt Fellowship provided for residence at a truly remarkable research institution while I was completing my dissertation. Though I had previously heard of the legendary helpfulness of the staff of the AAS, I was nevertheless unprepared for the reality—the generosity with which staff members treat fellows, helping to create a tightly knit and wonderfully productive scholarly community. I was, needless to say, delighted to receive a second chance to do research at the American Antiquarian Society as a postdoctoral fellow with a Steven Botein Fellowship. I especially want to thank John Hench, Nancy Burkett, Joanne Chaison, Gigi Barnhill, Caroline Sloat, and Marie Lamoureux for their many efforts on my behalf. Not the least of the many pleasures of working at the AAS was getting to know other fellows and scholars in residence, including Steven Bullock, Scott Casper, Nina Dayton, Phyllis Hunter, Steve Nissenbaum, and Billy Smith. I also count myself lucky to have enlisted the research skills of Su Wolfe.

On the West coast, another remarkable research institution has become an important part of my life, and I am grateful to the Huntington Library for two research fellowships, including a William Keck Foundation Fellowship and a crucial year-long stint as a Barbara P. Thom Postdoctoral Fellow. I especially want to thank Roy Ritchie for his support and encouragement. He has created a welcoming scholarly community at the Huntington, which has become for me, as well as for many other scholars, an intellectual home away from home. I count myself lucky to have a group of Huntington friends from whose insights I have regularly benefited, including Joan Waugh, Stuart McConnell, Judith Jackson Fossett, Hal Barron, and Karen Lystra. Conversations at the Huntington with visiting scholars have been helpful too, including Sharon Block, Bob Bonner, Karen Halttunen, and Deb Harkness.

I want to express my gratitude as well for a Women's Studies Grant from Duke University, a Bibliographical Society of America Fellowship, and a McLean Contributionship Fellowship at the Library Company of Philadelphia. At Duke, Elizabeth Dunn and Lois Schultz were most helpful; at the Library Company, I appreciated the suggestions and wisdom of Jim Green and Phil Lapsansky.

At my own institution, the University of California at Irvine, I have been fortunate to share work with a number of colleagues. A faculty women's reading group including Marjorie Beale, Thelma Foote, Dorothy Fujita-Rony, Lynn Mally, Pat O'Brien, Tanis Thorne, Heidi Tinsman, and Anne Walthall offered helpful suggestions on two chapters of my work in progress. An interdisciplinary faculty reading group including Chris Beach, Michael Fuller, Susan Klein, Joe McKenna, Carrie Noland, and Kathy Ragsdale also provided useful criticism of my work. Bob Moeller, an exceptional colleague, friend, and critic, characteristically went above and beyond the call of duty by reading the entire manuscript and providing in-depth criticisms and suggestions. Jon Wiener, too, provided crucial encouragement throughout the process of writing. In addition, I benefited from the research assistance of Vivian Deno.

Friends inside and outside the academy have also been important sources of support, including Joan Ariel, David Blight, Ellen Broidy, Barbara Dosher, Jane Elkoff, Nina McDonald, Holly Poindexter, Linda

Schaub, George Sperling, Chris Wilson, and Ted Wright. Nancy John-son and her family offered extraordinary hospitality in Princeton while I worked at the Library Company. Jackie Ariail opened her home to me twice while I was working at Duke University. Both made research trips away from home a pleasure, and I appreciate their generosity.

I am grateful that Kate Torrey at the University of North Carolina Press took an early interest in my dissertation and that she and Sian Hunter have been so supportive of its transformation into a book. Thanks are also due to Pam Upton and Grace Buonocore for their skillful help with production and copyediting.

My deepest thanks go to my family. Before his death, my father was an indefatigable and vociferous supporter of my academic career, even when it meant my moving across the country from him at a difficult time. I appreciate his generous support, and I miss him. My sister has been a constant supporter of my work as well, and I continue to rely on her enthusiasm and encouragement. But most of all, I have found inspiration in the love and support of Charlie and of Mimi, who has grown up with this book. My dedication expresses how deep my debt is to them.

THE
IMAGINED
CIVIL WAR

INTRODUCTION

Now there may be those who would save me all trouble by the assertion that there has been no real poetry produced during the war. I hope to convince you that there has been a great deal of good readable verse, and some genuine poetry written during the past four years, under the inspiration of the times through which we have passed.

—*Oliver Wendell Holmes, "The Poetry of the War," 1865*

"The real war will never get in the books," Walt Whitman wrote in his 1882 *Specimen Days*. For years, historians and literary critics alike accepted Whitman's remark as a central truth of the Civil War: the war was the "unwritten war"—the title of Daniel Aaron's influential 1973 study—because no masterpiece resulted from this most dramatic of conflicts in American history. "The period of the American Civil War was not one in which belles lettres flourished," Edmund Wilson affirmed in his classic *Patriotic Gore*.[1]

This book starts from a different premise. Far from having been an "unwritten war," the Civil War catalyzed an outpouring of war-related literature that has rarely been examined: war poetry, sentimental war stories, sensational war novels, war humor, war juveniles, war songs, collections of war-related anecdotes, and war histories—literature that has often been designated, then dismissed, as popular. Appearing in newspapers, illustrated weeklies, monthly periodicals, cheap weekly "story papers," pamphlets, broadsides, song sheets, and books throughout the conflict, such literature was often widely distributed, sometimes to hundreds of thousands of readers in the North and to a smaller separate audience sometimes reaching thousands in the South.

In both the North and the South, popular war literature was vitally important in shaping a cultural politics of war. Not only did it mark the gender of men and women as well as boys and girls, but it also explored and articulated attitudes toward race and, ultimately, portrayed and helped to shape new modes of imagining individuals' relationships to the nation. Feminized war literature, for instance, explored the nature of new connections between white women and the nation in hundreds of stories, articles, and cartoons appearing in popular magazines and weeklies. Much of this literature demanded recognition for women's allegiance to the nation, arguing that white women's war-related experiences constituted authentic participation in the war—and in the "imagined community" of the nation—on a par with that of male soldiers. Similarly, illustrated weeklies explored the new, postemancipation connection between African Americans and the nation in stories and illustrations that featured black soldiers (but not, significantly, black women). Northern wartime boys' war novels portrayed boys' new allegiance to the nation through the medium of individualized adventures and exploits that emphasized the excitement of war. In a different key, war humor both north and south explored the limits and problems in the new links between individual and nation. All these different forms of popular war literature participated in a cultural conversation concerning the evolving relationships between diverse individuals and the nation in wartime.[2]

Popular war literature reveals that a discussion of the meanings of the war occurred across a much wider range of representations than is usually thought to be the case. A study of these wartime writings and illustrations forces us to expand our ideas of the cultural meanings of the war. Many writers have assumed, for instance, that Northern imaginative writers chose to avert their eyes from the subject of race in wartime and failed to center racialized themes in their fictions. African Americans "figured only peripherally in the War literature" of canonical writers such as Hawthorne and Melville, Daniel Aaron has noted. Yet the pages of popular literature reveal a very different picture: issues of race were omnipresent in the major Northern illustrated weeklies throughout the war, revealing an intense preoccupation with the changing status of African Americans in American life. Likewise, Confederate popular literature showcased numerous illustrations and poems concerning African Americans throughout the war. Popular literature also explored women's experiences of the war in ways not true of canonical literature. Turning to the pages of popular literature allows us, in short, a more inclusive view of literary representations of race and gender in wartime.[3]

Popular war literature also adds an important chapter to cultural histories of the war that have focused primarily on elites, canonical writers, and Northern and Southern intellectuals. By "popular" I mean a wide and inclusive range of Civil War literature that cannot be summarized simply with the label of "low" to distinguish it from "high" literature. The high-low dichotomy, shaped in the late nineteenth and early twentieth centuries as a way of categorizing and organizing cultural authority, is often retroactively applied to mid-nineteenth-century culture in ways that readers, writers, and publishers would not have recognized at the time. *Harper's Weekly,* for instance, which reached a broad audience of more than one hundred thousand readers during the war, was neither obviously "high" nor "low" in its content or its audience. Nor were the illustrated histories of Benson J. Lossing, who styled himself a "popular historian." Likewise, the Southern periodical the *Southern Illustrated News* was published in a cheap "story paper" format but was not therefore "low" literature; rather, it included work by some of the most prestigious poets in the South, such as Paul Hamilton Hayne. In other words, distinctions between "high" and "low" often obscure as much as they reveal within nineteenth-century literary culture.[4]

This is not to say that authors, readers, and publishers did not make hierarchical distinctions among literary forms. Louisa May Alcott, for instance, published under her own name in the prestigious *Atlantic Monthly* but used a pseudonym in publishing fiction in cheap story papers that she regarded as less respectable venues. Clearly she assumed—quite correctly—that the *Atlantic Monthly* had higher literary status than the *Flag of Our Union.* George William Curtis, political editor of *Harper's Weekly,* commented that the *Weekly* was "not altogether such a paper as [he] should prefer for [his] own taste" but also recognized that he could reach a broader audience through its pages than in "a paper of a different kind." The Southern periodical the *Magnolia Weekly* spoke of the "higher regions of literary art" and the "less reflective region of popular lore." All these commentators made hierarchical distinctions among literary forms, yet the fact remains that a broad range of literary forms defied easy categorization on a high-low axis during the war. Popular literature often occupied a "middle" status that incorporated elements of both high and low.[5]

"We must build up a popular literature of our own," the *Magnolia Weekly* asserted in 1863. This study examines literature that was intended to appeal to a wide public, from stories published in *Harper's Weekly* to war poetry in newspapers to cheap dime novels to song sheets. Much of this popular literature was published by obscure authors about whom little is known, or it was published anonymously, pseudonymously, or with initials that provide tantalizing—but often insoluble—clues to authorship. Taking its cue from such popular literary conventions, this study focuses less on authors than on published works. Further, as it is fundamentally interested in the multiple ways in which the war was imagined into being, it primarily concentrates on belles lettres, including poetry, short stories, novels, songs, and histories. It does not discuss drama, a popular art form during the war but rarely a popular form of literature. Nor does it consider personal reminiscences of the war or specialized religious, educational, military, and political war publications such as war sermons, textbooks, military guides, and partisan political pamphlets, though these were part of the larger print culture of the war as well. And although this study is attuned throughout to the racial politics of popular literature, it does not examine publications specifically devoted to emancipation, such as the American Anti-Slavery Society's *National Anti-Slavery Standard* or *Douglass' Monthly*.[6]

The "imagined war" of my title includes both published works and the creative acts of the writers, readers, and publishers who produced them. By "imagination" I mean to include both individual inspiration and the "imaginative dimensions" of events, or the "context of thought and expression that suffuses individual and social life." Part of this context was a public literary culture in both the North and the South in which literature was valued as a vital part of personal and civic identity. Early in the war, for instance, patriotic newspaper poetry by ordinary citizens was widely hailed both north and south as an appropriate response to the events of war. Declaimed on numerous public occasions, this public poetry was also part of a shared oral culture of rhetoric and oratory, or "democratic eloquence." Such public war poetry was part of a wider understanding of the war as a literary event: far from literature being separate from the experience of the war, it was accepted as an appropriate, expected, and often deeply felt part of that experience.[7]

If popular war literature was part of a shared public culture, it was at the same time a highly visible part of a shared commercial literary culture. In Northern cities, anyone who bought a newspaper at a newsdealer's shop or passed a railway bookstall saw—and perhaps purchased and read—cheap story papers and dime novels, many of which featured war stories. In rural areas, subscription canvassers for popular war histories brought the popular literature of war right to the doorsteps of hundreds of thousands of readers. Popular war songs, "piled up by the gross on counters" for sale, according to Oliver Wendell Holmes, were "dinned in our ears by all manner of voices until they have made spots on our ear-drums like those the drumsticks made on the drum-head." War literature was even available in saloons, one contemporary observer tells us. And in the South, popular war poetry and stories appeared in daily newspapers as well as several new Confederate journals.[8]

The economic, social, and cultural practices of this commercial literary culture are an important part of my story, for they not only helped to determine whether a work was published but also helped shape its content and reception. As my first chapter shows, the material conditions of publishing were strikingly different in the North and South at the beginning of the war. Not only did the North dominate all aspects of publishing economically, but it dominated literary taste, too—at least according to the many Southerners who decried this fact. At the outbreak of war many Southerners agreed that they had for too long been dependent on Northern books and periodicals and that their new nation demanded a new national literature as well. Yet by 1864 many commentators sadly agreed that they had been unable to achieve this goal. "Are we a literary people?" the *Southern Punch* asked; it concluded, "More in sorrow than in anger, we answer: it is to be feared we are not." [9]

The undeveloped state of Confederate publishing on the eve of the war, combined with the severe economic hardships of the conflict itself, including shortages in paper, ink, printing presses, and personnel (in short, everything needed to produce a successful publishing industry), meant that Southerners were unable to rise to the high hopes of the early war. Yet it was not only economic hardships that limited Confederate literary nationalism. Ironically, though the Confederacy broke free from the North politically, it was unable to break free of the North's literary influence. Spurred by the war, many Southern authors and publishers produced new stories, poems, and books. But Confederate literature tended to imitate Northern forms—indeed, the stridently anti-Yankee periodical the *Southern Illustrated News*, which prided itself on its "pure" and original Confederate literature, reprinted several war romances from *Harper's Weekly*, without attribution, as Southern stories.[10]

This was a particularly egregious and, to be fair, unusual example of literary thievery. But the fact that a Confederate periodical could publish a Northern war romance without changing more than a few names indicates a set of shared literary sensibilities that overrode even the divisions of war. Other indications of these shared sensibilities abound: both a Northerner and a Southerner claimed authorship of the popular poem "All Quiet on the Potomac," and Southern author Agnes Leonard based her popular poem "After the Battle" on a Northern story of the same title by Virginia F. Townsend. Many popular songs, such as "When This Cruel War Is Over" and "Who Will Care for Mother Now?," circulated widely in both the North and the South. Some songs, "written, composed and published by Yankees," were "palmed off upon the people as Southern productions," the *Magnolia Weekly* noted with dismay. Northerners and Southerners also read the same popular literature from England and Europe during the war, including Victor Hugo's *Les Misérables*, M. E. Braddon's *Eleanor's Victory*, and Bulwer Lytton's *A Strange Story*.[11]

This study explores the imaginative dimensions of shared Northern and Southern literary sensibilities by examining several themes and genres of popular war literature. It does not argue that there was a unified "American mind" discernible in popular war literature or a unified "American imagination"—both modes of approaching literature that are artifacts of an older, consensus-oriented school of American studies. But it does recognize that there was a set of shared rhetorics in popular war literature and argues that it is crucial to understand how Northern and Southern popular literary cultures were alike in order also to understand their differences.

The shared rhetorics of Northern and Southern popular war literature had everything to do with the specific cultural, social, and economic practices of commercial literary culture. At the start of the war authors, publishers, and readers all assumed that the war would be represented within an established set of literary categories drawn from an antebellum literary tradition characterized by a "dramatic rise in the number and variety of imaginative texts." That tradition included all the genres discussed in this study, from sensational novels to romances to sentimental poems to popular histories, all of which set up a number of assumptions about the way in which the war could and should be represented. Many of the specific conventions of war literature had also been shaped during the Mexican War of 1846–48, which inspired a number of dying-soldier poems, sensational novels, humorous verse, songs, and patriotic poetry that later provided a set of templates for Civil War literature. Indeed, several Civil War writers, including James Russell Lowell and William Gilmore Simms, had published war literature during that previous conflict.[12]

Only weeks after the start of war in 1861, illustrated weeklies such as *Frank Leslie's Illustrated Newspaper* began publishing columns labeled "war humor," "war romance," and "thrilling incidents of the war," all categories of thought that were both mapped onto the war and helped to produce its cultural expressions. As Charles Royster has commented, "Conventions of popular literature shaped many Americans' expectations when war began." [13]

We can see some of the assumptions behind these different genres of Civil War literature in an 1866 volume of "anecdotes and incidents" of the war that asserted that "the sober History, the connected Narrative, and the impassioned Story" were all appropriate means to "exhibit and commemorate" the events of war. The historian had "gathered together and woven into thoughtful chapters the documentary materials and official details of the Struggle," this volume asserted, while the "poet's genius [had] lent its inspiration to the charm of glowing and melodious rhyme," which would "not cease to be the keynote to warm the sympathies and rouse the heart to greater love of patriotism, freedom, and justice." At the same time "the pen of romance" appealed to "more gushing sensibilities" by providing "its most touching story of mingled pathos and horror," a "well-wrought tale of heart-trials." "All these have their appropriate place" and "their peculiar usefulness and adaptation," this commentary concluded, before asserting that its own usefulness would lie in providing yet another category of war literature in a volume of "the most *thrilling, racy and wonderful incidents*" of the war. Such commentary asserted the appropriateness of a spectrum of war literature ranging from the "official" to the "gushing" to the "racy." [14]

Just as literary tradition aided in imagining the war in discrete literary categories, so too did the economic and social practices of publishers, authors, and readers. Sensational literature, for instance, the subject of chapter 7, was marked as a distinctive genre of literature in a number of ways in the North. Not only was it priced cheaply at a nickel, dime, or quarter, but it was published in pamphlets with garishly colored (often yellow) covers and distributed widely by news agencies rather than bookstores. Stressing the "thrilling" and "exciting" aspects of war in stories of "hair's-breadth" adventures featuring both men and women, sensational literature was widely read but also widely criticized—the term "sensational" signified dubious morality to many commentators (making sensational literature the closest to twentieth-century ideas of "low" literature in this study). In short, a constellation of economic, social, and cultural factors including the physical appearance of a piece of literature, its price, its mode of distribution, its subject matter, and its reception by a reading public all determined sensational literature's distinctive niche within commercial literary culture.

This study takes its cues from such social, cultural, and economic practices in examining war literature by category. In doing so it is attuned to both the production and reception of popular literature, recognizing that the two are fundamentally intertwined. Southern publishers, for instance, both cajoled and berated their readers in order to gain their support, recognizing that the success of a new Southern literature rested on reader response. But reader support was not undiscriminating: Southern readers did not support Southern literature simply because it was patriotic to do so, although this was surely one motivation, but also because it met their needs for entertainment, news, and instruction. George W. Bagby, the editor of the venerable *Southern Literary Messenger*, which Edgar Allan Poe had edited in the 1830s, misread his public when he bitterly concluded that Southerners would support only Yankee literature. Many Southerners *did* support attempts at a more popular Southern literature, including the periodicals the *Southern Illustrated News*, the *Southern Field and Fireside*, and the *Magnolia Weekly*. Still, Bagby's complaint had some truth to it. The Southern periodicals that had the largest circulations during the war were those that imitated such Northern counterparts as *Harper's Weekly* and *Frank Leslie's Illustrated Newspaper*. In contrast, the *Southern Literary Messenger*, a more traditionally literary journal, failed in 1864.[15]

Although readers' choices and habits might ensure either profitability or failure for a given periodical, novel, or pamphlet, their perceived interests often also acted as a powerful determinant of the subject matter of popular literature. A number of authors and publishers not only noted the public's "all-absorbing interest" in the war but also energetically responded to that interest by producing new war stories and histories. In the South, the *Southern Field and Fireside* published a series of cheap war "novelettes" in pamphlet form. In the North, numerous subscription publishers sought to capitalize on public interest in the war by producing subscription histories of the conflict. Several publishers of "cheap literature" introduced series such as T. R. Dawley's "Camp and Fireside Library," whose first volume, *Incidents of American Camp Life*, reportedly sold fifty thousand copies in one week. So intense was the interest in popular war literature that even abolitionist James Redpath decided to become a publisher in 1863, producing a series of books that he called "Books for the Camp Fires."[16]

If readers' perceived interest in the war helped to produce war literature, war literature in turn served to direct and shape readers' responses to the war. Reader-response theory has taught us that reading is a creative act that allows individuals to construct their own meanings of literature. But such creativity is nevertheless profoundly transactional and conditioned. Any reader's engagement with a book is one that necessarily involves him or her in a cultural exchange (though admittedly a one-way transaction) with the producers of that book, including the publisher, author, and even previous readers who may have inspired its production. If reading is most often a solitary act, it is also, paradoxically, a profoundly social one.[17]

To what extent does this social aspect of reading, and of print culture more generally, mean that popular literature created the "fictive affective bonds" that some have seen as a precondition to nationalism? The case of the Civil War reveals that print culture was far from acting merely as a unifying force. Although there were numerous similarities between Northern and Southern literatures, it was not true that shared literary sensibilities, reading habits, and rhetorics necessarily indicated a shared *political* culture uniting North and South. Southern commentators, for instance, repeatedly asserted that their wartime literature was essentially different from the literature of the North—despite all evidence to the contrary. These repetitive published comments were themselves a performance of political difference that may have been the most distinctive aspect of Southern literary culture. As Drew Gilpin Faust has remarked, "The struggle for the achievement of nationalism often becomes itself the occasion of its fullest realization." In short, one major reason why Southern literary culture should be seen as different from Northern literary culture is simply because so many Southerners insisted that this was so. If print culture can produce fictive affective bonds, it can equally produce imagined differences.[18]

Just as the cultural practices of print culture created differences *between* the worlds of Northern and Southern print, so too the economic practices of print culture produced differences *within* the separate worlds of Northern and Southern literary culture. These differences undermine any simple notion that print culture created one shared sense of nationality in either section. Then as now, print capitalism worked in a complex dynamic of consolidation and differentiation, with drives toward homogeneity offset by countervailing drives toward distinction. On the one hand, publishers sought to align their publications with others of a similar nature, thus communicating to would-be buyers that they were purchasing an established type of literature. Northern subscription publishers of war histories, for instance, produced a distinctive physical style of literature in elaborate, gilt-decorated volumes that suggested the parlor-table respectability of their works. On the other hand, however, these same publishers worked hard in advertisements to distinguish their works from those of their competitors in order to convince potential book buyers of the unique and desirable qualities of their works. This alternation between homogeneity and difference was a fundamental rhythm within Northern and Southern commercial print culture.

The need to define difference in order to encourage sales helped to promote a proliferation of war literature in the North, where commentators noticed the spiraling quantity of war literature with some amazement. The New York–based trade journal of the book-publishing industry, for instance, commented in 1864 that though the country was "engaged in a civil strife which one would suppose would have the effect of draining and absorbing" or at least "restricting the domestic market," the opposite was the case. Instead of a "depression of the book business," the *American Publishers' Circular and Literary Gazette* said, "we have a greatly increased activity," with the war itself adding "a new and imposing department to our literature." Not only were book publishers issuing "military treatises of all kinds, original and republished," but they were also publishing "biographical publications, histories of the war, journals of officers, narratives, war-novels and war poems," among other publications. This variegated literature created not just one but a multitude of different imagined wars, complicating notions of what kind of national community was created through the auspices of print culture.[19]

This point can help us to reassess widely held assumptions concerning the cultural outcome of the war. Ever since the 1960s one of the reigning paradigms of Civil War historiography has been the idea that the Civil War produced a drive toward organization, centralization, and consolidation in the North that somehow changed the "national character." The seventh and eighth volumes of Allan Nevins's epic *Ordeal of the Union* announced this theme explicitly in their subtitles: volume 7 was "The Organized War"; volume 8, "The Organized War to Victory." "To organize armies, to organize the production of arms, munitions, clothing, and food, to organize medical services and finance, to organize public sentiment— all this required unprecedented attention to plan," Nevins wrote, "and an unprecedented amount of cooperative effort. The resultant alteration in the national character was one of the central results of the struggle." In his brilliant *The Inner Civil War*, George Fredrickson provided support for the idea of the "organized war" by demonstrating that Northern intellectuals and writers not only espoused new practices and theories of organization both during and after the war but also critiqued antebellum notions of individualism in favor of a new adherence and allegiance to the group. Fredrickson confined his analysis to a small but influential group of intellectuals, but other writers have assumed that a new adherence to ideologies of centralization, organization, and consolidation characterized a wide swath of Northern culture.[20]

In the realm of literary culture, however, the war was often interpreted as personal experience in such a way as to complicate emergent understandings of an organized or centralized nationhood. Sentimental war stories, sensational war adventures, boys' war stories, war humor—all show that popular literature portrayed a war whose importance was revealed at the individual level. Such literature catered to desire and fantasy, portraying personal experiences of the war as the basis of its most profound meanings. Further, these stories enacted direct relationships between individuals and representatives of the nation, with the nation understood in highly personalized terms. The 1862 *Pauline of the Potomac*, to cite just one example among many, portrayed the heroine Pauline meeting General Grant in his battlefield tent in order to discuss her spying for the Union. Such literature insisted that the shared experience of a new nationhood occurred at the individual level, forming the basis for a new, nation-based individualism.

This study traces the trajectory of the imagined experience of nationhood within popular war literature from the beginning of the conflict to its close, revealing that there were significant changes in the imagined connection between individuals and the nation. On the eve of the war most Americans related to their nation in profoundly localized and particularized ways. Whereas today we imagine the nation as a powerful abstraction, the state, at the time of the Civil War Americans understood the nation through "the more immediate and concrete social experiences of town and family." [21]

Given the particularized understandings of the nation that held sway at the beginning of the war, it struck many contemporary commentators as no less than amazing that both Northerners and Southerners achieved unity of purpose in the early days of the war. In both the North and the South, this early unanimity of purpose was expressed in a variety of forms of popular literature. Hundreds of poetic paeans to the flag written by ordinary citizens, for instance, appeared in newspapers and magazines. These early wartime invocations to the flag represented an attempt by individual writers to celebrate the nation as a newly abstract entity, one to be intuited symbolically through the flag rather than through more particularist associations.

The intensity of this early wartime fascination with abstract nationhood, however, did not last within the pages of popular literature beyond 1861: after that paeans to the flag appeared on a more episodic basis. In their place, popular literature increasingly explored the personal experience of war. Hundreds of poems and songs written in the first person, for instance, imagined the dying thoughts of soldiers on the battlefield. Hundreds more poems and short stories imagined mothers, sisters, and lovers on the home front who tearfully parted from their loved ones and then waited anxiously for news from the battlefield.

This sentimental and feminized war literature explored the felt tension between the needs of the nation and the needs of the individual. It is true that most Civil War popular literature, both north and south, was patriotic—that it developed no sustained critique of the war. It is also true that Civil War literature offers a striking contrast to the ironic, embittered war literature that developed during World War I, for example. Yet if Civil War popular literature by and large embraced the war as a cause, some categories of that literature demanded recognition for the tremendous cost borne by discrete individuals in that cause. Indeed, the felt tension between the needs of the nation and the needs of individuals became the chief energizing plot device in countless stories and poems. Some of this tension was explored directly in issue-oriented stories or poems that focused on the problem of whether a husband should enlist or whether a mother should allow a son to join the army. The answer was almost always yes, but the emotional tenor of such stories was far from celebratory. Instead, the main emotional focus of such stories was on the individual suffering— both emotional and physical—that war caused.

Such stories enacted the tension between individual desires and national needs in explicit patriotic tableaux. But such tension also permeated sentimental and feminized literature in less explicit but no less compelling ways. The numerous songs and poems that imagined soldiers' dying thoughts turning homeward to mother, for instance, expressed a deep cultural ambivalence about the new wartime relationships between home and nation. Likewise, feminized war stories that explored the devastation wrought in women's lives by the deaths of men may not have explicitly critiqued the war, but they nevertheless bemoaned the war's impact on individual women.

While several types of popular war literature explored the devastating personal impact of war, by the middle of the conflict other forms of war literature increasingly explored the liberatory potential of war for individuals. African Americans in particular occupied a dramatic, center-stage role throughout the conflict in the pages of the two most popular Northern illustrated weeklies, *Harper's Weekly* and *Frank Leslie's Illustrated Newspaper*. Song sheets, illustrated envelopes, popular novels, and stories also all explored the emerging story of black freedom during the war, thus revealing to what extent a fascination with black actions permeated a wide-ranging popular literature.

At first, *Harper's Weekly* and especially *Frank Leslie's* relied extensively on buffoonish, minstrelsy-based images in depictions of blacks. Yet in the months leading up to and following emancipation, particularly as more and more Northerners argued for the employment of black men as soldiers, such images gave way to illustrations that articulated and celebrated black manhood and even, occasionally, black heroism. That such portrayals were often tentative and halting, with potentially radical illustrations often deliberately undercut by accompanying text, should not obscure the substantial changes being wrought in popular images of African Americans for the duration of the war.

Just as the unfolding political and social realities of war affected these changing images, so too did changing cultural realities behind the production of popular literature. Responding to Northerners' intense interest in visualizing all aspects of the war, both *Frank Leslie's* and *Harper's Weekly* employed "special artists" at the front who sent back illustrations, often with accompanying commentary, to their employers. These "special artists"—including, most famously, Winslow Homer, Thomas Nast, A. R. Waud, Edwin Forbes, and Theodore Davis—represented a cultural economy that emerged briefly during the war and provided for a new set of perspectives on race and the war.

It was not only literature that dealt with African American freedom that imagined the war as liberatory. In a different key, Northern boys' war novels portrayed boy soldiers engaged in daring exploits that took them away from their families and that involved cunning as well as physical bravery, thereby enacting a new relationship between individual and nation. In this fiction, the nation facilitated the increasingly popular ethic of individual adventure—an ethic that carried over to the mass juvenile fiction of the postbellum era. Similarly, sensational novels such as *Pauline of the Potomac* and *Maud of the Mississippi* portrayed heroines who were lifted out of the domestic sphere to act as spies and even soldiers. In such stories and novels, the nation often existed as an instrument that helped to fulfill individual desires, especially by allowing transgressions of the normative roles associated with gender and age.

In this literature the imagined bonds between individual and nation did not just involve a relationship of loyalty and obedience. Rather, adventurous war literature enacted a form of literary citizenship promising that loyalty to the state would facilitate individual adventure. As expressed in popular literature, this cultural politics of identity was a far cry from the ideology of republicanism that emerged from the Revolution, with its more sober sense of the shared civic duties of virtuous citizens to uphold the Republic.[22]

Whether or not war stories celebrated the liberatory nature of war or explored its devastating impact, however, the focus of much popular war literature remained on the relationship between the individual and the nation in wartime. The sense that each individual had his or her own war story to tell fueled a steadily increasing number and variety of war fictions during the war. "No two persons see a battle alike; each has his own stand-point," the Northern author Charles Carleton Coffin remarked in 1863. "No other one will tell a story like his." A culture-wide sense that all war stories were valuable—whether at the home front or battlefront— also underlay the publication of numerous collections of "incidents and anecdotes" during the war, volumes that savored individual experiences of the war at the level of vignette, humorous sketch, or "pen-picture."[23]

To stress this focus on the individual is not to say, of course, that Civil War popular literature was free of typologies and stereotypes. On the contrary, popular war literature was highly typological, tending to represent characters through a constellation of well-established conventions of portrayal. Nowhere was this more immediately obvious than in representations of African Americans, which drew heavily from the imagery of minstrelsy on the one hand and from sentimental antebellum literature such as *Uncle Tom's Cabin* on the other. Likewise, the emotional range of Civil War popular literature derived from the conventions of the mid-nineteenth-century "melodramatic mode," with its focus on the intense dramatic significance of even the most ordinary of individual lives. The importance of melodramatic convention in structuring the imagined Civil War of popular war literature cannot be overstated.[24]

In both the North and the South, a number of writers and critics initially hoped that war would produce an ennobling literature worthy of the event. "Perhaps now for the first time we have in America the scenes, the personages, the events," the *United States Service Magazine* commented in 1864, from which would "spring the great American epic, as did the Iliad." Likewise, the new journal the *Round Table* explained from New York in 1864 that "it is generally fancied that great events bring out great expressions." After all, "in the minds of most men a certain dignified solemnity connects itself inseparably with the idea of war." The "gorgeous trappings of man and beast, the flapping of sanctified banners, the masses of moving humanity" were "all fraught with a high degree of something akin to sublimity." [25]

Yet unfortunately the war had produced a great deal of "trash" and "shoddy literature," including "the so-called 'Romances of the War' so much in vogue among magazines and 'story papers' during the two sorry years just past," the *Round Table* lamented. "Is this tremendous epic we are now living to bring forth naught but trash unutterable and bombast?" it asked. In the South, the *Southern Punch* commented in 1864, "It is said that the war will give a new impetus to Southern literature," but it received "these promises with skepticism." Describing Southerners as a "rude," "uncultivated," "untasteful people," it asked, "Wipe us out to-morrow, and where be our monuments of parchment or of marble?" [26]

The issue of the quality of Civil War literature has long troubled literary critics who have written about the war. Although the idea that the war produced no "great" literature first appeared during the war itself, it has also haunted twentieth-century appraisals of Civil War literature. Edmund Wilson, for instance, spoke of the "mediocre level of the poetry of the Civil War," complaining that the war drove "into virtual hiding the more personal kind of self-expression which had nothing to do with politics or battles, which was not concocted for any market and which, reflecting the idiosyncrasies of the writer, was likely to take on an unconventional form." Applying modernist aesthetic standards to war poems, Wilson almost inevitably found them lacking. Daniel Aaron, too, commented that though "one would expect writers, the 'antennae of the race,' to say something revealing about the meaning, if not the causes, of the War," with "a few notable exceptions, they did not." [27]

Yet looked at from a different set of angles, popular war literature *is* revelatory. The very fact that war poetry, for instance, was often "concocted" for the market should alert us to the complex synergy between patriotism and commerce during the war. Its existence also reminds us that the Civil War took place within a larger Victorian culture, both north and south, which valued poetry as part of significant public events. [28]

Moreover, popular war literature reveals that just as the war resulted in an expanded realm of political freedom, it also resulted in an expanded realm of imaginative freedom. Adventurous war stories, juvenile war literature, war romances, race stories, sentimental soldier poems, war humor—all these different forms of popular literature enacted individual relationships to the nation that together formed a diversity of interpretations of the war's meanings within American life. As African Americans freed themselves by fleeing to Union lines, as children played at being soldiers, as women on the home front confronted the often harrowing domestic realities of war, popular literature absorbed these social realities in works that themselves became part of the wider cultural reality of war. Together they created not a unified but a diversified nationalism, one that embodied a democratizing impulse both energized and constrained by the practices of commercial literary culture.

Popular Literary Culture in Wartime

Beat! beat! drums!—Blow! bugles! blow!
Through the windows—through doors—burst like a
*   force of ruthless men,*
Into the solemn church, and scatter the congregation;
Into the school where the scholar is studying:
Leave not the bridegroom quiet—no happiness must
*   he have now with his bride;*
Nor the peaceful farmer any peace, plowing his field or
*   gathering in his grain;*
So fierce you whirr and pound, you drums—so shrill
*   you bugles blow.*
*   —Walt Whitman, "Beat! Beat! Drums!,"*
    Harper's Weekly, *September 28, 1861*

"Men cannot think, or write, or attend to their ordinary business," Oliver Wendell Holmes reported from Boston in the fall of 1861. "They stroll up and down the streets, they saunter out upon the public places." War fever had produced a "nervous restlessness of a very peculiar character." An "illustrious author" confessed that he "had laid down his pen," unable to "write about the sixteenth century," while the nineteenth "was in the very agony and bloody sweat of its great sacrifice." An eminent scholar "read the same telegraphic dispatches over and over again in different papers, as if they were new, until he felt as if he were an idiot." In South Carolina, Mary Chesnut confided to her diary that she had "tried to rise above the agonies of everyday life" by reading Emerson. "Too restless," she concluded of her failed attempt in June 1861. "Manassas on the brain." [1]

In both the North and the South, war permeated the wide-ranging set of practices and beliefs that constituted popular literary culture. War changed what people read, what was available to read, and how, where, and with what expectations they read it. It altered the plans and prospects of publishers, pushing some to the brink of failure while giving new energy to a few well-positioned firms. It reshaped literary careers, forcing established authors to reconsider their writing plans, inspiring new authors to enter the literary marketplace, and deeply affecting what both found possible to imagine. Most profoundly, war catalyzed a rethinking of prevailing beliefs about the connecting links between literature and society and between individual and nation. In the South, war produced an urgent discussion of the place of literature within the larger project of nation building and of the role of the patriotic reader within a larger literary culture. In the North, an explosion of war-related popular literature and patriotic print goods, part of an expansive commercial culture of war, tightly bound the individual to the nation and yet, ironically, complicated attempts to fix the meanings of the war. Both north and south, war became not just an obsessive, all-consuming subject but also a mode of perception and way of life that disrupted and reorganized authors' and readers' conceptions of identity, nationhood, and even time itself. "How long it is since Sumter!" Jane Woolsey wrote to a friend from New York only three weeks after war began. "I suppose it is because so much intense emotion has been crowded into the last two or three weeks that the 'time before Sumter' seems to belong to some dim antiquity. It seems as if we never were alive till now; never had a country till now." [2]

The all-consuming nature of war was a subject frequently remarked on early in the war, both north and south. "Tonight," Kate Stone of Augusta, Georgia, recorded in her diary in May 1861, "we all gathered around" the fire to hear a friend "read the papers. Nothing but 'War, War' from the first to the last column. Throughout the length and breadth of the land the trumpet of war is sounding." "Town talk has but one topic these days," George William Curtis commented in the columns of *Harper's Monthly* during July and August. "The beat of the drum, the bugle-call, the shrill, passionate shock of martial music fill the air by night and day." Not only did "the bookshops have only placards of books of tactics and the drill," but "the windows glow[ed] with portraits of the heroes." The "photograph galleries are crowded with living soldiers looking at pictured soldiers upon the walls," while "the theatres revive old battle melodramas and invent new." Even "the piles of brick and rubbish in the streets are covered with posters bearing a charging Zouave for illustration, and with General Orders, and calls for recruits and notices of warlike meetings." [3]

Reading habits changed dramatically with the onset of war, a fact that numerous observers noted both north and south. Newspapers suddenly became an urgent necessity of life, with readers eagerly gathering at bulletin boards outside newspaper offices in order to read the news as soon as it was printed. In Boston, Oliver Wendell Holmes reported that one person he knew always went through the "side streets on his way for the noon *extra*,—he is so afraid somebody will meet him and *tell* the news he wishes to *read*, first on the bulletin-board, and then in the great capitals and leaded type of the newspaper." The newspaper was "imperious," according to Holmes. "It will be had, and it will be read. To this all else must give place. If we must go out at unusual hours to get it, we shall go, in spite of after-dinner nap or evening somnolence." "We haunt the bulletin board," Mary Chesnut concurred from Columbia, South Carolina, in 1862, while in New York, George William Curtis reported that "the crowds assemble daily before the bulletins of the newspaper offices, and the excitement of important news flutters along Broadway or Nassau Street like the widening ripples in water. You feel something in men's motions; you see something in the general manner of the throng in the street before you read it recorded upon the board or in the paper. There is but one thought and one question. The people are soldiers. The country is a camp. It is war." [4]

The ability of newspapers to satisfy the public's feverish desire for news on an hourly, not just daily, basis struck many contemporary observers as remarkable, signifying a fundamental shift not only in the nature of warfare but also in the very "manner of existence" itself. Already in the fall of 1861, Holmes mused that "new conditions of existence," including the railroad and telegraph, made this war "very different from war as it [had] been." From Memphis the *Southern Monthly* agreed, asserting in early 1862 that this war had no parallel in history, as "the railroad, the steamer, and the telegraph are a trinity which has killed all parallel. Mechanical ingenuity, in a thousand ways, has completely revolutionized war." One revolutionary aspect of war, said Holmes, was "perpetual intercommunication, joined to the power of instantaneous action," which keeps us "alive with excitement." No longer was the news delivered by a "single bulletin" or courier, as in the past; instead, "almost hourly paragraphs" made readers "restless always for the last fact or rumor they are telling." [5]

Such restlessness meant that initially during the war, reading the newspaper displaced other forms of literary culture. In November the *Southern Literary Messenger* commented, "In times like the present, very little interest is felt in literature. Nothing that does not relate to the war itself is read." The *Southern Monthly* concurred: "[The time is not] propitious to reading, or reflection, or study, as people's minds are filled with anxiety and expectation; and until this excitement shall subside, it cannot be expected that a different feeling will prevail." In the North, the trade journal of the book publishing industry noted a radically changed literary landscape, commenting, "The entire absorption of public interest by current events has caused a nearly complete cessation in the demand for new books, and publishers have in consequence discontinued their usual issues." There was abundant evidence of the truth of this remark: while in July 1860 the prestigious Boston publisher Ticknor and Fields, for instance, had had some thirty volumes in press, in July 1861 the firm had only four in production. Longfellow remarked on visiting Ticknor and Fields's "Old Corner" bookstore, "Nothing alive but the military. Bookselling dead." After a second visit he noted, "The 'Corner' looks gloomy enough. Ticknor looks grim and Fields is fierce. Business is at a standstill. So much for war and books." [6]

Books published during the spring of 1861, like George William Curtis's society novel, *Trumps*, tended to fizzle in the marketplace, and many projected books had to be put off. James T. Fields, editor of Ticknor and Fields, wrote to several of his authors to delay publication of their works: "The Times are so shaky," he wrote to Bayard Taylor, "we postpone 'The Poets' Journal' till autumn." To Thomas Wentworth Higginson he wrote that Higginson's *Outdoor Papers* must wait "till we see how McClellan is doing." The outlook for books was "hazy," he said; "the Trade is in a state of apathy I never saw approached." Metaphors of paralysis were common: the secession winter had "paralysed business for a time, utterly," James Perkins Walker of Boston's Walker, Wise and Company commented; the "national troubles" had "paralyzed all but military and periodical literature," *Harper's Monthly* agreed. In the South, William Gilmore Simms noted, "People here breathe nothing but war, & read none but military books now." [7]

Under the exigencies of war, literary careers were delayed or took unexpected turns, as the crisis affected what could be imagined as well as what could be published. In Charleston, the poet Henry Timrod wrote to a friend in September that he had "planned several poems of length during the present summer" but that "all of them, I am afraid, will remain the skeletons which they are as yet, until more peaceable times. The lyre of Tyrtaeus is the only one to which the Public will listen now; and over that martial instrument I have but small command." In Concord a worried Louisa May Alcott, who wished to submit a story to the *Atlantic Monthly*, reported in November that editor James T. Fields had told her "he has Mss. enough on hand for a dozen numbers & has to choose war stories if he can, to suit the times. I will write 'great guns' Hail Columbia & Concord fight, if he'll only take it for money is the staff of life & without one falls flat no matter how much genius he may carry." [8]

• • •

Alcott's comment suggested a developing reality of wartime popular literary culture. Just as Northerners and Southerners experienced the early disruptions of war in remarkably similar ways, so too authors and publishers in both sections rapidly responded to readers' all-absorbing interest in the conflict by producing popular war literature. But these efforts exposed deep economic and cultural divisions between the two sections, divisions that would only deepen over the course of the war. First and foremost was the fact that most major publishing firms and presses were in the North, not in the South. The 1860 census made the disparity dramatically clear: it counted 986 printing offices in New England and the middle states, with only 151 printing establishments in the South. Of these, the 21 presses in Tennessee produced the most work—yet Tennessee, with the only stereotype foundry in the South, fell under Union control early in the war. There were 190 bookbinders in New England and the middle states—but only 17 in the South. No printing presses were manufactured in the South, meaning that it would be difficult, if not impossible, to replace broken presses. The Richmond Type Foundry did advertise "Southern Type, Manufactured on Southern Soil," but it also acknowledged that it was "the only establishment of the kind in the South." At the same time there were only 15 paper mills in the South in 1861, which "could barely meet half the requirements Southern publishers placed upon them every day." There were no facilities in the South for making wood-pulp paper, which in the North became an important substitute for paper made from cotton rags during the war. The *Daily Richmond Enquirer*'s January 1862 advertisement for "Paper and Ink:—Wanted immediately" was a plaintive motif reiterated in many journals during the war. "Attention Everybody! Rags! Rags! Rags! I want to buy ten thousand pounds of well cleaned Cotton and

Linen Rags" was an advertisement placed by one printer in the *Southern Literary Companion* in June 1864. The Georgia firm of Burke, Boykin and Company advertised in verse for rags:

> Save your rags, and save your tags,
> Save your good-for-nothing bags—
> Bring them to this office, soon,
> Bring them morning, eve, or noon.
>
> Bring us scraps and cotton thread,
> Bring the night cap from your head,
> Bring the shirt upon your back,
> Bring us pieces white or black.[9]

On the eve of the war there were only a few established Southern book publishers, including West and Johnston and J. W. Randolph of Richmond; S. H. Goetzel of Mobile; Evans and Cogswell of Charleston; and Burke, Boykin and Company in Macon. Few other firms, except for religious publishers, were of any considerable size. Among the few established periodicals were the Richmond literary monthly the *Southern Literary Messenger*, established in 1834; the critical monthly *De Bow's Review*, first published in New Orleans in 1845; the weekly *Southern Field and Fireside*, first published in 1859 in Augusta, Georgia; and the *Southern Literary Companion*, begun in 1859 in Newnan, Georgia. Yet relatively few Southerners read these periodicals, instead depending on Northern books and periodicals for their reading matter.[10]

By the end of 1861, both the blockade of Southern ports and the end of federal mail service meant that Southerners no longer had access to the Northern literature on which they had long depended. Henry Timrod, for one, bemoaned the disappearance of literary culture as he had known it: "No new books, no reviews, no appetizing critiques, no literary correspondence, no intellectual intelligence of any kind! Ah! It is a weary time! To volunteer is now the only resource against *ennui*. The Camp is *life*. Thither flow exclusively all the currents of thought and action, and thither, I suppose, I must betake myself if I would not die of social and intellectual atrophy." Confronting cultural separation from the North, many Southern readers privately worried over the loss of Northern literature even as they proclaimed their sectional loyalty. "We take quite a number of papers," Kate Stone said in May 1861, listing among them the Northern journals *Harper's Weekly* and *Monthly*, the *New York Tribune*, and the *Jour-*

nal of Commerce. "What shall we do when Mr. Lincoln stops our mails?" Near Augusta, Georgia, Ella Thomas wrote in her diary in July, "The Blockade has prevented the importation of new Books and loyal as I am and wish to be I think that for a time this will prove a serious inconvenience." [11]

While privately readers worried about the impact of war on valued reading habits, publicly numerous Southern periodicals celebrated cultural separation from the North. "Now that Northern journals have become, as long ago they should have been, contraband articles at the South, it is hoped that the subscriptions for Southern literary journals will be rapidly increased," the *Southern Literary Messenger* said. "Literary journals of a high order must be sustained at the South, if we would have an actual and not a merely nominal independence of the North." "We must have a periodical literature," the *Charleston Courier* agreed. "The need is great and it is felt. Forced from our dependence on the North, we must see to it, that we meet this pressing demand with cheerfulness, earnestness, and liberality." The *Southern Monthly* stressed the importance of increasing the number of Southern book publishers, "by the sustainment of which alone are we to have a flourishing and healthy literature. It will be found that they go hand in hand, and when the one languishes, the other etiolates and withers." [12]

Many commentators stressed the connections between literary and political nationhood, arguing that nation building was a vital cultural as well as political project. "A nation cannot live upon bread alone," the *New Orleans Delta* commented in the fall of 1861. Although "the development of the South, up to this time, has been almost purely economical and political," the "destiny of the South will be but a crude and unfinished attempt" unless "along with her political independence she achieves her independence in thought and education, and in all those forms of mental improvement and entertainment which by a liberal construction of the word, are included in literature." Commentators celebrated the literary opportunities opened by secession and war: "We have risen to the dignity and importance of a nation," the *Charleston Courier* proclaimed in an article entitled "Literature in the South." "We are now treading the path to independence; we have begun a new career; unbounded prosperity and glory, such as our fathers never dreamed of in the wildest flights of their imagination, invite and stimulate our efforts and energies." [13]

Such comments envisioned war as an exhilarating opportunity finally to create an independent Southern literature. Calls for an independent Southern literature and the end of dependence on Northern print culture had been a familiar part of antebellum Southern literary culture, but many critics now agreed that the antebellum project had been a failure. One reason often cited was the disproportionate power of Northern cultural institutions. The literature that the South had been "able to claim for her own," the *New Orleans Delta* wrote, though "intrinsically rich and vigorous as much of it may have been, was wofully inadequate to cope with the literature arrayed against her. The pens and the presses, the books, the periodicals and the journals, the pulpits, the lecture desks, and the school rooms" of the North and of Europe were "openly or insidiously hostile to her institutions, her rights, her interests, her aspirations," and "placed her at a fearful disadvantage in the controversy she was compelled to maintain before the tribunal of public opinion." [14]

Yet few critics solely blamed Northern institutions for a perceived lack of Southern literary independence. What the *Southern Monthly* termed Southern "literary laziness" was also a culprit. Musing over the question of why the South was "dependent upon the north," Ella Thomas wrote in her journal, "We have plenty of talent lying latent in the South to make for us a glorious name. We have one great drawback—indolence—to contend against. Say what we may it is more this than indifference or anything else which prevents so many from improving their God given talent." [15]

If the "laziness" of would-be writers was partially at fault for the failure of Southern literary independence, the habits of readers were even more to blame. From the pages of newspapers and periodicals, Southerners reprimanded their compatriots for reading Northern literature and urged them to support Southern literature as a patriotic duty. "I trust though the present crisis has lost you Northern patronage," a "lady of Jackson, Mississippi" wrote to the *Southern Literary Messenger*, "it will not be long before Southerners, who have wasted their money to pay for the demoralizing trash, sent forth by the Northern press, will awake to a full sense of the duty they owe themselves and to Southern Literature." The South had for too long been tied to the "wheels of Northern publishers"; but now she trusted that "the Literary bonds will fall with the political ones, and that henceforth we may have the patriotism to sustain our own literature." Writing in the *Southern Field and Fireside*, Ella Swan scolded Southern women, accusing them of having "united with the entire North in supporting a literature at war with your dearest interests. Uncle Tom's Cabin, Dred Scott and other works as poisonous as the deadly Upas tree, have been freely circulated in your midst, while Southern authors have met with little encouragement at your hands. Are not Southern papers, periodicals and books as worthy of your patronage?" The *Southern Illustrated News* asserted that it did not "believe that the people of the South will ever again welcome a Northern periodical into their households—we cannot for a moment believe that they are so devoid of interest for the welfare of the rising generation—so lost to all reason and honor"; the *Charleston Courier* said simply, "Our patronage of magazines published at the North has heretofore been both a folly and a shame." [16]

As such comments made clear, the act of reading itself now took on a strongly ideological cast. Suffused with nationalistic aims, reading was less a private act than a vital part of a larger, public, patriotic culture. Furthermore, such patriotic reading involved not only what one did read but also what one did not; it demanded not just the embrace of Southern literature but also the repudiation of Northern literature—the two were intimately intertwined. Early in the war it was a commonplace to begin discussions of Southern literature with denunciations of Northern literature; Northern works pandered to popular taste; they were "trashy," "poisonous," "contemptible." Never one to shrink from hyperbole, the *Southern Illustrated News* in the fall of 1862 called "Yankee literature," with "a very few exceptions, the opprobrium of the Universe." Yankee books were "of the worst possible description," merely a "very bad imitation of the most indifferent class of English literature." Southern literature would come "in due time," and when it did, it would "in no way resemble the Yankee abortion." [17]

Despite these nearly universal public denunciations of "Yankee trash," however, many commentators expressed uneasiness over whether Southerners would ever give up their love of Northern literature, even under the conditions of civil war. While the *Magnolia Weekly* asserted, "We must build up a popular literature of our own, and it must be as far removed in style from that of our invaders as it is possible for it to be," it also acknowledged, "We have a most powerful *habit* to contend against." After all, perennial antebellum calls for an independent Southern literature largely had fallen on deaf ears. "Not one Southern book" had lain on the antebellum Southern parlor table, the *Southern Monthly* claimed in a scathing editorial in its inaugural September 1861 issue; instead the *Atlantic Monthly*, with "Harriet Beecher Stowe's last novel *continued*" and "Holmes' ingenious diatribes against our country," lay next to "the arrant *Harper*, with its Editor's Table, an essay on the value of the Union," while "on chair and sofa" lay "*Ledger* and *Mercury*, filled with the infectious and mephitic exhalations of Sylvanus Cobb, and others as innocent of ability as of decency." The *Southern Literary Messenger* agreed: "If the angel Gabriel had gone into very heart of the South, if he had even taken his seat on the top of the office of the Charleston Mercury and there proclaimed the immediate approach of the Day of Judgment, that would not have hindered the hottest secessionist from buying the New York Herald and subscribing for Harper's Magazine." The *Messenger* concluded, "Southern patriotism is, and has always been, a funny thing—indeed the funniest of things. It enables a man to abuse the Yankees, to curse the Yankees, to fight the Yankees, to do everything but quit taking the Yankee papers. Nothing less than a battery of 10-inch Columbiads can keep Southern patriotism away from Yankee papers. Even that is doubtful. We suspect that the animating impulse which will ere long carry the Army of the Potomac into Washington City, will, when it is analyzed, be found to be, merely the inappeasable desire of Southern patriotism to obtain a copy of Bonner's Ledger." [18]

Given this "just conception of Southern patriotism," the editor of the *Messenger* promised—tongue in cheek—that the magazine would attempt to appeal to its readers by combining "all of the most trashy, contemptible and popular features of *Harper, Godey, Frank Leslie,* the *Herald, Home Journal, Ledger, Yankee Notions, Nick Nax, Budget of Fun,* and the *Phunny Phellow.*"

> We shall have nothing but pictures. We shall have nothing but the latest news and the fashions. Diagrams of baby clothes, worked slippers, edgings, frills, cuffs, capes, furbelows, faraboves, and indeed all of the most interior and intricate feminine fixings, shall be supplied in much profusion. . . . We shall furnish each month not less than 1800 different photographic views of the proper way to do up the back hair. We shall devote eleven-ninths of each number to crochet work and fancy pincushions. Meantime we shall devote our entire space to riddles, charades, acrostics and questions in arithmetic. But the greater part of the magazine shall be given to little dabs of light literature *a la* Fanny Fern. Our exclusive exertions, however, shall be strained for the procurement of tales, stories, narratives, novels, novellettes, serials and serialettes. [19]

This was parody clearly meant to establish the grounds of Southern literary difference from Northern "trash." Yet it also suggested some of the complexities inherent in Southern attempts to establish a new national literature. Even as Southerners denounced Northern literature, it remained a powerful standard against which they defined their literature. According to the *Magnolia Weekly,* for instance, the "Northern weeklies abounded in stuff calculated to appease the cravings of the uncultured appetites" of the "vulgar rabble." The *Magnolia Weekly* sought instead to create "a style of literature which is at once useful and pure." "This is the true popular literature," it claimed. Yet such an attack on Northern literature did not so much dislodge its power within Southern cultural life as shift the terms on which that power was organized.[20]

One aspect of Southern literature that several commentators agreed might make it "useful and pure" was its depiction of slavery. Before the war, the *Southern Monthly* asserted, Southern poets and Southern novelists had failed to paint "in beauty" and idealize "into still higher fascination the domestic ties that breed elevating affections in our negroes" or to paint "the negro nurse, and the negro playmate, remembered by all of us with thrills of affection." "Had a Southern novelist" in the antebellum period "truly painted in as engaging a style" as *Uncle Tom's Cabin* "the real workings of our Biblical system of labor, and its truly Christianizing and elevating effects on the slave, the power of the misrepresentation" offered by Stowe "to mislead would have been checkmated," and the "baneful effect" of Northern literature would have been counteracted.[21]

The *Southern Monthly* argued for the importance of the institution of slavery not just within Southern life but within Southern literary culture as well. It thus made explicit linkages between Southern literary nationalism and slavery that in effect racialized and politicized the very definition of Southern literature at the outset of war. Southern literature, in this and many other accounts, carried a deeply political charge: seen by many observers as a critical component in the building of a new nation, it also had the task of defending the Southern "way of life"—always shorthand for the life of white Southern slaveholders. As many commentators in the early months of war continued to look back with bitterness on the powerful impact of *Uncle Tom's Cabin*, they assumed that a new Southern literature must continue to counteract what were perceived and represented as uniform Northern views. Thus it is not surprising that a number of journals continued to publish defenses of slavery, even after Confederate nationhood was established: in December 1861, for instance, the strongly proslavery *Southern Literary Messenger* began a series of articles by William H. Holcombe entitled "Characteristics and Capabilities of the Negro Race." These articles, like many proslavery manifestos of antebellum years, supported a modified version of polygenesis: "The negro is not a white man with a black skin," the series began, "but, if not a distinct species, at least a permanent variety of the human race." Attempting to find a biological justification for slavery in supposed Negro difference "from all other races of men," this series suggested that Southern wartime literature would continue to be preoccupied with justifications of slavery.[22]

Many commentators agreed on an agenda for Southern literature, but war quickly undercut their plans. Southern periodicals operated under a number of severe constraints during the war. Already in November 1861 the *Southern Literary Messenger* offered extended commentary on the difficulties of publishing in wartime. "In common with other Southern interests, and especially with publications, *The Messenger* has felt, and still feels, severely, the pressure of the war," it said. "While newspaper after newspaper has been suspended, and even the staunchest journals have been compelled to retrench and economise; while De Bow's *Review* is published but once in two months, *The Messenger* has steadily held its own, despite of bad ink, a scarcity of paper and of printers, a great falling off in contributions, and almost a suspension of payments." But "this cannot last," it concluded.[23]

Most dispiriting, the *Messenger* found, was the lack of wartime support from Southern subscribers. Before the war, the editors had "derived comfort from the assurance that the neglect of the Magazine" was "due not so much to Southern indifference to them, and to native literature, as to that habit of dependence on the North, from which nothing less than the horrors of war could ever have delivered us." But now "the war has come, Northern newspapers and magazines have been totally cut off, yet *The Messenger* is in no better plight than before." The publishers had "no more appeals to Southern patriotism to make. All they want is the money that is due them."[24]

The *Messenger*, like many other Southern publications, struggled for its existence during 1861 and early 1862. In April 1862 the editor confessed, "Never were we so 'put to it' for suitable contents for our Table. The Yankees have penetrated so far into the Confederacy—have menaced so many interior points, that our correspondents have had neither leisure nor inclination to furnish contributions." So "driven to the wall" was the magazine that the editor chose to print "some selections from old English writers." In the fall of 1862 it faced new problems, as "the government seized the paper mills in this city, and we failed to get paper" elsewhere. It published a double issue in the fall of 1862, a solution to publishing difficulties to which *De Bow's Review* also resorted. However, after publishing a quadruple number for May through August 1862, *De Bow's* suspended publication entirely except for one single issue in July 1864. As the editor, J. D. B. De Bow, explained in August 1862, "More than half of our subscribers are in Texas, Louisiana, Arkansas, and in parts of the other states held by the enemy, and to them, for some time to come, it may be our fate to be voiceless."[25]

Yet if the war undermined established periodicals such as the *Messenger* and *De Bow's Review*, it acted as inspiration for a new literature of war that appeared in daily newspapers throughout the South. Inspired by the war, for instance, numbers of ordinary citizens, both male and female, contributed a profusion of patriotic poetry to newspapers, a fact that many observers at the time found striking. In September 1861 the *Southern Monthly* noticed that "the daily journals of the South" had become the "depositories of much of that finished poetry generally reserved for the more careful monthly." The *Monthly* reprinted several of these, approvingly commenting that "as specimens of what our patriotism has called forth," the poems compared "favorably with the majority of fugitive pieces found in Northern periodicals." The *Messenger* also remarked on "the many excellent little poems which the war has called forth," and to rescue them from "newspaper oblivion," it offered its readers "a few specimens clipped from our exchanges." Two Richmond literati, Professor Chase and John R. Thompson, were making a collection of these poems, the *Messenger* informed its readers. In mid-1862, some of this collection became the basis for William G. Shepperson's *War Songs of the South*, intended to celebrate a new flowering of Southern literature.[26]

Shepperson, the correspondent "Bohemian" for the *Richmond Daily Dispatch*, argued that newspaper poems were compelling evidence of popular nationalism in the South—a nationalism arising from the people rather than from the government. They revealed a "spontaneous outburst of popular feeling" that gave "the lie to the assertion of our enemy that this revolution is the work of politicians and party leaders alone." Not only had many of the poems been written by women, whose "instinct" had "anticipated the logic of our statesmen," but many had also been composed by "soldiers in camp," and they possessed "all the vitality and force of the testimony of eye-witnesses to a glorious combat, or even of actors in it." Through "the Poet's Corner in the newspaper," these poems had "sped their flight from and to the heart and mind of the people." Such comments assumed that popular patriotic poetry was both an important indication and a creator of popular nationalism.[27]

Many Southerners highly valued this war poetry as an integral part of the war experience, copying favorite poems into their journals or pasting them into scrapbooks along with news clippings of important battles.

Mary Chesnut, for instance, copied lines from James R. Randall's stirring and enormously popular "My Maryland" in a January 1862 diary entry. Kate D. Foster, living near Natchez, Mississippi, pasted two newspaper copies of the famous "All Quiet along the Potomac Tonight" on the inside of the front cover of her diary. William Galt, a cadet at the Virginia Military Institute, copied "Maryland My Maryland" and "The Bonnie Blue Flag" in a wartime notebook. M. J. Solomons of Savannah, Georgia, created a scrapbook from a used account book — a sign of how severe the paper shortage was even early in the war — and into it pasted numerous poems from a variety of newspapers.[28]

Drawn from the "Poet's Corner" of a variety of newspapers, these poems revealed how the well-established newspaper "exchange" system worked to link Southerners at wide distances from one another. Under the exchange system, newspapers sent one another copies of their papers as a courtesy, with the understanding that reprints were allowable as long as they were credited. Thus one newspaper might draw poems and articles from a variety of sources, providing a window into a broader culture beyond the local arena. Certainly in the pages of Solomons's scrapbook, poems and news accounts are credited as being drawn from an astonishing array of sources, including the *Richmond Dispatch; Southern Advocate; Southern Field and Fireside; Richmond Daily Examiner; Natchez Courier; Charleston Mercury; Bowling Green (Kentucky) Daily Courier; Atlanta Intelligencer; New Orleans Picayune; Petersburg (Virginia) Daily Express; Savannah Republican; Atlanta Confederacy; Memphis Appeal; Montgomery Advertiser; Norfolk Day Book; Richmond Whig;* and *Southern Illustrated News,* among many others. Although Solomons probably did not have access to all of these newspapers herself, she nevertheless could, through the limited number of newspapers available to her, participate in a wider literary culture of war.[29]

The many scrapbooks kept by Southerners are an important indication of how precious the print culture of war was to a widespread Southern reading public, who were deeply involved in the project of creating a print memory of the war. It is important to note, too, that the newspaper, typically associated with politics rather than the arts, was at the center of this Southern literary culture of war. But many Southerners were also proud that, inspired by the war, and despite the many hardships associated with it, publishers were printing new books and even creating new periodicals. The *Southern Literary Messenger* commented with surprise and pleasure on new Confederate books in December 1861. "Yankee publishers having ceased to subsidize us with presentation copies of their trashy publications, we had closed the 'Book Notice' department for the war, as we supposed. In this, we are glad to find ourselves mistaken," the *Messenger* said, before reviewing new military publications printed by the Richmond firm of West and Johnston. The *Messenger* was especially pleased that, "at a time when paper and printing ink are so scarce and costly," these books were printed and bound "in a superior style." [30]

Several new periodicals were also founded during the first years of war. The first number of the Memphis-based *Southern Monthly*, published by Hutton and Freligh, appeared in September 1861. The spring of 1862 saw the founding of Joseph Addison Turner's idiosyncratic the *Countryman*, unique for being published on a plantation in Putnam County, Georgia, as well as for employing the fourteen-year-old Joel Chandler Harris as printer's assistant. Modeled after both the *Spectator* and the *Rambler*, the *Countryman* had a small readership, at one time reaching "a circulation of nearly two thousand copies," according to Harris. [31]

In the fall of 1862, as the military fortunes of the Confederacy ran high, so too did Southern literary ambition. In September Charles Bailie founded the Richmond-based *Magnolia: A Southern Home Journal*, which became the *Magnolia Weekly* the next year. In September, too, the Richmond publishers Ayres and Wade founded the most ambitious of the new Southern periodicals, the *Southern Illustrated News*, an illustrated weekly meant as an answer to such popular Northern weeklies as *Frank Leslie's Illustrated Newspaper* and *Harper's Weekly*. The most popular of the new Confederate periodicals, it reportedly sometimes printed some twenty thousand copies. A number of Southern readers and authors alike registered the founding of this new Southern publication as a significant event: nineteen-year-old Lucy Breckinridge, for instance, an avid reader who lived in Grove Hill, Virginia, noted in her diary on September 10, 1862, that she had just received "the first copy of *The Southern Illustrated News*" from Richmond. Twice more during the war would she note that she had been sent a copy of the *News*. [32]

Though war created severe difficulties for an established literary monthly such as the *Southern Literary Messenger*, it created opportunities for an upstart such as the *Southern Illustrated News*. As the *Southern Literary Messenger* ruefully noted, "a pictorial paper, started in this city not much more than a month ago, has already a circulation quadruple that obtained by THE MESSENGER after twenty seven years." The difference between the two publications was not so much an economic one—the *Southern Illustrated News* had great difficulties obtaining paper, too, for instance—as a

THE SOUTHERN ILLUSTRATED NEWS.

VOL. I. SATURDAY, SEPTEMBER 13, 1862. No. 1.

GEN. THOMAS J. JACKSON.

Major-General THOMAS JONATHAN JACKSON, or, as he is familiarly known, "STONEWALL" JACKSON, now engrosses as much of public attention as any other man engaged in the present struggle for Southern independence.

General Jackson was born in the town of Clarksburg, Harrison county, Virginia, in the year 1825. He is the son of Jonathan Jackson, who was born in what is now known as Lewis county, three miles north of Weston, its county seat. He was christened "Thomas," after his grandfather, Thomas Neal, and Jonathan after his own father. In early life, the father of the subject of this notice moved to Clarksburg to study and practice law with his cousin, Judge John G. Jackson. Shortly after commencing the practice of law, he married the daughter of Thomas Neal, of Wood county, by whom he had four children, two daughters and two sons, of whom THOMAS was the youngest.

Ere Thomas had entered his third year, the father and mother of these children died, leaving them without any estate for their maintenance.

Shortly after the death of his parents, Thomas was taken by his uncle to Lewis county, and he remained on the same farm with his uncle where his father was born until he arrived at the age of seventeen, at which period he was appointed a cadet in the West Point Academy. At the early age of sixteen, notwithstanding his minority, such was the generous sympathy of neighbors and acquaintances for a mere boy, manfully struggling to carve out a name and reputation for himself, he was ... of Lewis, who ... he resigned to accept an appointment of Cadet to West Point.

In 1842, he graduated at West Point with high distinction, and was immediately ordered to report for duty under the command of General Taylor, where he served until General Scott commenced his campaign in Mexico, when young Jackson was assigned to his command.

We find the following mention of our hero in "Gardner's Dictionary of the United States," (2d edition, published 1860.)

"Thomas J. Jackson, (Virginia,) cadet 1842—brevet second lieutenant 1st artillery, 1 July, 1846; with Magruder's battery in Mexico, first lieutenant, August, 1847; brevet captain "for gallant and meritorious conduct in battle of Contreras and Churubusco," 20 August 1847 (Aug. 1848); brevet major " for gallant and meritorious conduct in battle of Chapultepec," 13 September, 1847 (March, 1849); resigned 21 February, 1852."

In addition to the permanent promotions, he was brevetted major before he reached the city of Mexico. All of his promotions during the Mexican campaign, as will be seen by reference to the above, were for "gallant and meritorious conduct." It is a source of much gratification to the friends of this distinguished soldier, that the Army Register, and the actual history and facts of the Mexican war, do not furnish the name of another person, entering the war without position or office, who attained this high rank of major in the brief campaign and series of battles from Vera Cruz to the City of Mexico. In this particular, he had no equal in that war.

The severe service in the Mexican war and the climate of that country so impaired his health, that, shortly after the conclusion of peace, he resigned his position in the army, and sought and obtained a professorship in the Virginia Military Institute. Shortly after entering upon his duties as a professor, he married the daughter of Mr. Junkin, the Principal of the Washington College. She died, and he has since married Miss Morrison, of North Carolina. Like his second and illustrious kinsman, Andrew Jackson, he has no children by either marriage.

He continued to teach the arts of war at the Institute until the commencement of the present struggle. No sooner had the tocsin of war sounded, than he flew to the standard of his native State, with the same alacrity and zeal which have since that period characterized his whole career. He was commissioned colonel by Governor Letcher, and was immediately confirmed by the Convention of Virginia, then in session. He was the first colonel, and the first man, under the Provisional Army of Virginia, to take command of his troops.

A reputation, by his surroundings, brings to the surface materials, the existence of which was before obscured in humility and by the veil of native modesty. Circumstances make men, who, in turn, make circumstances. In ordinary times, as a general rule, the souls of men exhibit what force and fire they may contain, in those places where birth has placed them. Revolution rends this frame-work as if it were a cobweb, and exhibits to the world the man of merit, and allows him to appear in all his grandeur. The prejudice and bigotry of rank, fearing a depreciation of its own excellence, will rarely call into requisition or associate with worth below it; but those who obtain influence through the soul and force they carry with them, appreciate worth in others, and judge men by the true criterion. Hence, JACKSON, as is shown, having sprung from the same class of society with the soldiers who compose his army, appreciates them as equals, loves them, and associates with them.

Daunted by no danger, exhausted by no toil, caught by no stratagem, it is not to be wondered that he acquired the title of "STONEWALL."

THE BATTLE OF FALLING WATERS.

Col. Jackson commanded the forces of Harper's Ferry till the arrival of Gen. Joseph E. Johnston—a period of about a month. Gen. Johnston, after taking command, assigned to Col. Jackson the important duty of checking the Yankee General Patterson in his advance. That duty was performed to the entire satisfaction of Gen. Johnston and the country. In his official report of the battle of Manassas, Gen. Johnston said:

"On the 2d of July, General Patterson again crossed the Potomac. Col. Jackson, pursuant to instructions, fell back before him. In retiring, he gave him a severe lesson in the affair at Falling Waters. With a battalion of the 5th Virginia regiment (Harper's) and Pendleton's battery of field artillery, he engaged the enemy's advance. Skilfully taking a position where the smallness of his force was concealed, he engaged them for a considerable time, inflicted a heavy loss, and retired when about to be outflanked, scarcely losing a man, but bringing off forty-five prisoners."

Shortly after this affair, Col. Jackson was made a brigadier-general, and it was understood that the promotion was in consequence of his conduct at Falling Waters.

A few days afterwards, he stamped his name indelibly upon the pillar of his country's history by his participation in the battle of Manassas. The timely arrival of his brigade, it is believed, changed the fortunes of the day. It was at the battle of Manassas he gained the soubriquet of "STONEWALL," under the following circumstances:

At the battle of Manassas, overwhelmed by superior numbers and compelled to yield before a fire that swept every thing before it, Gen. Bee rode up and down his line, encouraging his troops, by every thing that was dear to them, to stand up and repel the tide which threatened them with destruction. At last, his own brigade dwindled to a mere handful, with every field officer killed or disabled. He rode up to Jackson, and said, "General, they are beating us back." His reply was, "Sir, we will give them the bayonet." Bee immediately rallied the remnant of his brigade, and his last words to them were: "There is Jackson standing like a stone wall. Let us determine to die here, and we will conquer. Follow me." His men obeyed the call, and at the head of his column, the very moment when the battle was turning in our favor, he fell mortally wounded.

BATTLE OF KERNSTOWN.

On Saturday, the 22d of April, General Jackson rapidly moved his little army from camp near Mount Jackson back to Cedar Creek, twenty-six miles, in one day, and camped there that night, making his headquarters in Strasburg, which was evacuated by the enemy the day before. Early the next morning (Sunday), he again moved forward, and his artillery opened on the enemy, near Kernstown, about 12 o'clock. An artillery duel was kept up until about 4 o'clock. In the afternoon, when the enemy's infantry advanced in force, and were met heroically by Jackson's brave little band. Three times the "stars and stripes" fell, and three times did our gallant troops drive the enemy headlong to the hill. The first brigade (the "Stonewall") finally came up, and again a fresh column of the enemy was driven back, leaving the side of the hill black with their dead.

No ... has been fought during the war ... under ... circumstances ... not exceeding 3,500 men—men had been on forced marches for weeks—the ranks thinned by the process of re-organization in front of the enemy—Jackson attacked 20,000 fresh troops, repulsed them again and again, and so crippled the dastardly foe, that he dared not, with all his numbers, follow him in his retreat. Notwithstanding the great disparity in their forces, the enemy themselves could claim nothing more than a "drawn battle."

We next hear of the untiring hero at Swift Run Gap, occupying a strong position, with daily skirmishes with the enemy. He remained in this position a short time, and then fell back to Staunton. In the meantime, the enemy had fallen back down the valley for the purpose of uniting the commands of McDowell, Banks and Fremont. Immediately after this movement on the part of the enemy, Jackson, with his forces, on the 7th of May, 1861, left Staunton, and, on the evening of the same day, the vanguard of his army encamped four miles west of Buffalo Gap, fourteen miles from Staunton. Gen. Johnson's forces had advanced to Shenandoah Mountain, in pursuit of Milroy, who was falling back before the united forces of Jackson and Johnson. Milroy is said to have had about 8,000 effective men.

BATTLE OF M'DOWELL.

On Thursday, the 6th, a bloody fight took place between Jackson's forces and the enemy under Gen. Milroy, at Sutlington Hill, near McDowell. After four hours' fighting, the enemy were completely routed and driven from all points. Gen. Jackson thus briefly and gracefully announced his victory:

"VALLEY DISTRICT, May 9, '61,
Via Staunton, May 10.

To General S. COOPER:

God blessed our arms with victory at McDowell yesterday.

T. J. JACKSON, Major General."

Fremont was expected to reinforce Milroy the day the fight took place, but did not arrive in time. Jackson captured in this fight 100 boxes ammunition, 500 Enfield rifles and Minie muskets, 60 to 75 cavalry saddles, and nearly 500 head of cattle, which had been stolen from the citizens living in the vicinity, by the Yankees. The loss of the enemy was supposed to be about 1,300.

After the fight the remnant of Milroy's army was reinforced by Fremont, and we hear nothing more from our gallant hero until

THE BATTLE OF WINCHESTER,

which was thus announced in an official despatch from Gen. Jackson:

"WINCHESTER, May 26.—During the last three days God has blessed our arms with brilliant success. On Friday, the Federals at Front Royal were routed, and one section of ar-

---

The first *Southern Illustrated News*, September 13, 1862.
(Courtesy of the Rare Book, Manuscript and Special Collections
Library, Duke University)

cultural one: the *Southern Illustrated News* offered a fresh viewpoint for the South, with a fresh combination of voices and features. Moreover, it was deliberately popular in a way that the more gentlemanly *Southern Literary Messenger* not only avoided but sometimes actively scorned. "We wish to pay our weekly visits to thousands of homes in our sunny Southern land," the *News* stated in its first issue, "homes that are lonely in the absence of loved ones in the army—and impart something of cheer to their loneliness. We shall send, far and wide, throughout our borders, carefully executed portraits of our distinguished leaders, that the people may know what manner of men they are, in bodily likeness, in the council and in the field. And we shall count, with something of confidence, upon furnishing our brave soldiers, in their summer bivouac and their winter cantonment, with a pleasant and not unprofitable companion." [33]

Imagining a Confederacy linked through its own readership, the *News* sketched a form of literary nationalism rooted most deeply in the war itself. Indeed, from the first the *Southern Illustrated News* concentrated primarily on the war, providing an eclectic group of war-related features including stories, profiles of generals, editorials on the war, humorous sketches of life in camp, reflections on women's home-front role, and war poems. The *News* commented with amazement on the number of poetic submissions it received: "We have lyrics enough, were they worthy of print," it said after being in print only eight weeks, "to supply the poet's corner for as many years. At a time when writing paper is preposterously high, and so constantly advances in price that it cannot, with any propriety, be called *stationery*, and when postage is a burden which might deter any one from needlessly cumbering the mails, we receive daily piles of poetical contributions." Unfortunately these "innumerous song-offerings" were "not remarkable for celestial fire," the *News* added, commenting, "The 'rebel' muse, we grieve to say, is so disobedient and wayward a child, so slip-shod a Sibyl, that she rebels against all the laws of rhyme, and cares less than nothing about her *feet*." [34]

As these comments revealed, the early reverence with which commentators treated the appearance of amateur war poems had dissipated by the fall of 1862: in January 1863, the *News* even predicted that in the "flour barrel full" of war poems it had received, "not one poetic expression or thought, coming from the heart would be found." The *Southern Literary Messenger* concurred, saying in July 1863, "We are receiving too much trash in rhyme." In September 1863 the *Magnolia Weekly* even ran a brief, pointed story in which a newspaper poet was exposed as nothing more than a "dandy clerk" and shirker. Newspaper war poetry was "all a hum-bug and imposture from beginning to end," according to this story. "Every man of us, thank God, is ready, heart and hand, to strike for his coun-try's cause, without the necessity of newspaper poets calling upon them to arise," it concluded. Nevertheless, the *Magnolia Weekly*, like other South-ern periodicals, continued to print a substantial collection of war poems, including dirges, narrative poems, ballads, and "national hymns," among others.[35]

Given the *News*'s avowedly popular purpose, it is perhaps surprising that two of the most revered antebellum literary names in the South—the poets William Gilmore Simms and Paul Hamilton Hayne—soon not only published poems in the *News* but also appeared on its masthead as regu-lar contributors. But there were compelling reasons for their willingness to appear in the pages of a weekly "story paper." First, cultural separa-tion from the North meant that Simms and Hayne could no longer pub-lish in Northern journals. Only two months before war had broken out, *Frank Leslie's Illustrated Newspaper*, sympathetic to the South throughout the secession crisis, had published a flattering profile of Paul Hayne. But with the onset of war Hayne not only lost his Northern audience for the duration but also, like his Southern compatriots, angrily denounced the "Northmen" as "ruffians," "robbers," and "invaders." [36]

Second, there were very few literary publications in which Southern poets and other writers could publish during the war, and even fewer still that promised to pay much to their authors, if anything at all. The *Southern Monthly*, for instance, simply told its readers that "when Southern readers enough pay for reading" the magazine, "the publishers will pay South-ern writers enough for writing it." The *Southern Literary Messenger* bluntly told one would-be contributor in July 1862, "The pressure of the times is such as to forbid any engagements with contributors. None receive com-pensation at this time." In contrast, the *Southern Illustrated News* did make promises of payment—although it did not always fulfill them, apparently. A plaintive letter from Hayne to a friend in May 1864 complained, "Since Jan. last the 'Illus. News' has paid me *not one* cent for the Poems of mine which have appeared in its columns"; he had expected to receive between fifteen and thirty dollars each for seven poems, most of them war poems. Still, Hayne admitted that he published with the *News* "almost entirely," as he was "constrained to work for *money*." Even the uncertain prospect of payment was a significant inducement for writers who had seen their literary livelihood cut off by war.[37]

Finally, the world of Southern literary publishing was small and inbred. Southern wartime literary publications tended to be edited by a small group of literary men who moved from publication to publication, often knew one another well, and published one another's work. John R. Thompson, for instance, had been the editor of the *Southern Literary Messenger* before the war, joined the staff of the *Southern Field and Fireside* for a brief period in 1860, and then later in the war worked as editor of the *Southern Illustrated News*, among other editorial duties. James D. McCabe was editor of the *Magnolia Weekly* in 1863, but after giving that position up in 1864, he was listed as a contributor to the *Southern Illustrated News* and the *Mercury*. George William Bagby of the *Southern Literary Messenger* also contributed to the *Southern Illustrated News*. And Paul Hamilton Hayne and William Gilmore Simms were listed as contributors to the *Southern Field and Fireside*, the *Southern Illustrated News*, the *Magnolia Weekly*, and the *Mercury*. In short, the exigencies of war encouraged a blending of voices within the pages of a story paper such as the *News*, as revered authors who had published in avowedly literary journals were joined by self-consciously popular authors and by first-time authors newly inspired by the war.[38]

By far the most important aspect of the *News* in its own reckoning was its claim to be "Illustrated." But here its ambitions far outreached its capabilities, emphasizing the extreme difficulties under which Confederate publications labored. The *News* promised to provide illustrations "honestly and faithfully drawn and engraved by competent and experienced artists." The first issue of the weekly, however, contained only one illustration, a small, crude engraving of Stonewall Jackson in the center of the first page. With a certain amount of defensive bluster, the *News* said, "We expect each week to increase the number of engravings, yet our aim shall be, not *number*, but *quality*."[39]

A central problem for the *News* was finding experienced artists and engravers in the South. The *News* may have promised illustrations, but it simply did not have the personnel to produce them: within only a few weeks of its first issue it advertised "Wanted Immediately—Two competent Wood Engravers." Admitting that "the Illustrated department of our paper is not yet complete," it nevertheless reassured its readers, "We hope in a few weeks to have a corps of competent Artists engaged solely in illustrating the pages of this journal with accurate and neatly executed wood cuts."[40]

Some months earlier, the *Southern Monthly* had had to admit defeat in its own quest to be illustrated. "With no small feeling of chagrin, and some of shame, we are forced to confess that a well-illustrated magazine *cannot* yet be produced in the South," it said in March 1862. "Good artists we can procure, but good engravers on wood are scarce among us, and even if they were more numerous, the wood itself is not to be had." A letter from a reader named Lucy complained, "The pleasant anticipations with which I opened the February number of your monthly were checked and my nerves experienced a violent shock when the things called *pictures* met my eyes." Calling them a "burlesque on the fine arts," Lucy assured the magazine that if these illustrations were indeed "'increased in number as the circulation of the Magazine increases,'" she would "exert what influence I may have to *diminish* its circulation as fast as possible." Under such circumstances, and meeting with "general condemnation," the *Monthly* decided it was "best to discontinue giving 'more of the same sort.'" Illustrating the magazine "'must wait upon opportunity' to do better," it concluded.[41]

Unlike the *Southern Monthly*, the *Southern Illustrated News* eventually did manage to "do better" by hiring several competent artists, including one who had been "actively and prominently engaged on Frank Leslie's Pictorial." Yet the illustrations in the *News* remained sparse and remarkably crude by Northern standards, their subjects usually portraits rather than scenes of action or battle, which were more difficult to engrave. Other illustrated periodicals faced similar problems. The *Mercury* of Raleigh, which advertised itself as "Beautifully Illustrated," published its first issue in April 1864 without any illustrations whatsoever, explaining that the ink it had purchased was of "such a very inferior quality" that it was impossible to work with. Such difficulties underscored a distinct and important difference between the popular literary culture of war in the North and in the South: whereas in the North the war was imagined visually in *Harper's Weekly, Frank Leslie's Illustrated Newspaper*, in dozens of other publications and forms of print ephemera, as well as in photographs exhibited in galleries such as Matthew Brady's New York gallery, in the South the literary war remained primarily a war of words, not pictures; of poetic images and oratorical flourishes, rather than painted or engraved representations.[42]

This was not for Southern lack of interest in a visual war: within a large city such as Richmond, newspapers advertised theatrical attractions such as Lee Mallory's "Pantechnoptomon," consisting of "War Illustrations Exhibiting the Soldier's Life in Camp, March, Bivouac, Battle." Mallory himself advertised that he needed "Sketches of Scenes and Incidents connected with our army, such as Views of Camps, Battle-Fields, Maps, etc.," and that "any drawings that will be interesting to the public, will be promptly acknowledged and paid for." In mid-1862 a "Confederate Reading Room" advertised "YANKEE PICTORIALS OF THE WAR giving all the scenes and illustrations of the recent great battles and portraits of the most promising actors." These had been "just received, by special order, through a party just arrived from the North." Monthly subscribers paid fifty cents, while a single admission—"good for all day"—cost ten cents.[43]

As this last advertisement revealed, war hardly annihilated interest in Northern periodicals, despite the expressed hopes of numerous Southern publications. Indeed, war may have intensified interest in Northern "pictorials." Not only were they virtually the only visual representations of the war available in the South, but they were so scarce as to be especially valuable commodities. Certainly numerous Southerners recorded the receipt of a Northern "pictorial" as a signal, noteworthy event.[44]

In a myriad ways Northern literature continued to hold power for Southern readers, writers, and publishers. The *Richmond Whig* advertised for "Northern Journals" in December 1862, saying that "any person arriving from the states north of the Potomac, and bringing Northern or European newspapers," would "confer a favor upon the Editors of the Whig by leaving or sending the same" to the *Whig* office. In the *Magnolia Weekly* in 1863, the columnist "Refugitta" (Constance Cary) confessed to missing "that charming Atlantic." Despite the blockade, and despite Southern calls for a boycott of Northern literature, at least one Richmond firm advertised both *Harper's Monthly* and the *Atlantic Monthly* for sale during the summer of 1863. The *Southern Illustrated News* was scandalized that "loyal citizens of the State and the Confederacy should encourage the sale of this pernicious trash." Yet the *News* itself secretly borrowed liberally from Northern periodicals for its own contents, republishing at least four *Harper's Weekly* war romances during 1863 and 1864.[45]

At the same time, though the *News* excoriated the "Yankees" at every opportunity, it nonetheless also sometimes measured its worth in a Northern mirror, professing to be jubilant, for instance, when *Frank Leslie's Illustrated Newspaper* gave it a negative notice. *Leslie's* had reprinted one of the *News*'s diatribes against the North, sarcastically commenting that "the South is going to have an art as well as a literature of its own" and noting that the *Southern Illustrated News* was "called illustrated, because it has one picture—an archaic portrait of 'Stonewall Jackson.'"[46]

Yet the *Southern Illustrated News* claimed to be delighted at this notice. "We ask no greater triumph," the *News* said, "than that of knowing we have excited the ire of these immaculate Yankees, the Harpers and Leslie, for with the advent of the 'Southern Illustrated Newspaper' they clearly perceive that the prospect for the circulation of their miserable sheets ever again in the South, is poor indeed. Hence, we welcome their criticism and abuse of us as a bright harbinger." The *News* even claimed, falsely, that "in New England and New York, the exigencies of the war, and the closing up of the Southern market, have well nigh extinguished authorship and its lights, from the little farthing candle of Mr. James Russell Lowell to the bright gas burner of Dr. Oliver Wendell Holmes." In contrast, "the publishing house of West & Johnston" had "issued more new books from original mss. during the past year, than any firm in Yankee land, not excepting our friends Sharper & Brothers of New York." The *News* concluded with satisfaction that "there has been a healthy stimulus given to literary production among us." [47]

It was true that war stimulated Southern literary production. By late 1862 the *Southern Illustrated News* reflected with some satisfaction (and a good deal of boosterism) on a changed literary world: "A Southern book, at one time, was a dreg in the market," the *News* said, but "now it immediately springs into popularity and is eagerly sought after." Southern authors had once "looked to the Harpers, the Appletons, and others of a like character, to publish their books for them," but now they relied on

> those enterprising merchants, Messrs. West and Johnston, who are extensively engaged in the publishing business. We have now upon our table a variety of military and other works gotten up in a very superior manner by these gentlemen. The typography will compare favorably with the Harpers, while the binding and general getting up is not inferior, and in many respects superior, to any work ever issued from the press of any Northern publishing house. Thus we will no longer be compelled to read the trashy productions of itinerant Yankees, worthless as their hearts are black; but will, in future, have Southern books, written by Southern gentlemen, printed on Southern type, and sold by Southern publishing houses.[48]

This was promotional rhetoric, of course. Not only was the West and Johnston list, consisting of mostly military books, minuscule by Northern standards, but there were other publishers operating in Richmond as well. Still, such a statement was an important indication of the considerable ambitions of many Southern authors, publishers, and periodicals.

In 1863 in particular, during an extended period of confidence in Confederate war fortunes, several new publications were established. The first issue of the humorous weekly the *Southern Punch* appeared in Richmond on August 15, and two other humorous periodicals, the Griffin, Georgia, *Bugle Horn of Liberty* and the Mobile, Alabama, *Confederate Spirit and Knapsack of Fun*, were announced during the summer and fall. At Christmastime the first issue of a new Richmond periodical, the *Bohemian*, appeared. In April 1864 William B. Smith began to publish the *Raleigh Mercury* after a hiatus of three years. In May the publishers of the *Magnolia Weekly* began a monthly periodical called *Smith and Barrow's Monthly*. The editors of such journals often talked of unrealistically ambitious plans for the future: the *Southern Punch*, for instance, planned to issue "a monthly supplement, consisting of a series of Historical Engravings, Equestrian Portraits of Generals, etc., printed on fine proof sheet paper, in the highest style of the art."[49]

By 1864, however, several commentators provided a more realistic assessment of the state of Southern popular literature. "It is useless to attempt to disguise the fact," the *Magnolia Weekly* stated, that "*in spite of our boasted desire to make our literary enterprises succeed, the combined circulation of all the literary journals in the South does not equal the circulation in the South of the New York Ledger, before the War.*" Not only had Southern periodicals not gained the audience they desired, but throughout the conflict war threatened their very existence. The *Southern Monthly*, located in Memphis, Tennessee, had alerted its readers in April 1862 that it had moved to Grenada, Mississippi, as the "occupation of Memphis by the Abolitionists" was "within the bounds of possibility." It promised, nevertheless, that the *Monthly* "will cease but with the Confederacy that gave it birth." Instead it ceased publication, forever, the next month. "But for the capture of Nashville by the Yankees, whereby the large stereotype foundry of that city was lost to us for the war," the *Southern Illustrated News* informed its readers in November 1862, "many valuable fresh books and new editions of old ones would have been brought out in a style highly creditable to the taste and enterprise of the South." Fear of invasion underlay a move by Charleston publisher Evans and Cogswell in 1864, but there was high irony in its choice of Columbia, South Carolina, as a safe haven.[50]

The war stymied the projects of numerous authors, as well. John R. Thompson collected poems for a volume of war poetry that he hoped would be published by a British publisher, but this project never came to pass. In January 1862 William Gilmore Simms wrote to several correspondents suggesting an elaborate plan for the publication of a "Library of the Confederate States," including "new works to be interspersed as prepared, and a wholesome variety to be sought in History, Biography, Statesmanship, Poetry & Fiction." But this plan remained only an idea. In mid-1863 the *Southern Illustrated News* announced that George William Bagby, the editor of the *Southern Literary Messenger*, was "collecting materials for two books, to be entitled respectively, 'Southern Heroes and Heroic Incidents,' and 'Humorous Anecdotes of the War.' " Neither book was published. In early 1865 the poet John Henry Boner wrote that he had been solicited to contribute to a volume compiled "from the writings of different authors of the confederacy—something, as I understand it, in the style of Griswold's 'Poets of America' " (a popular Northern anthology). But this project, too, never came to fruition.[51]

Several authors commented on the havoc war wrought with their literary careers. "My occupation utterly gone, in this wretched state of war & confusion, I have no refuge in my wonted employments," William Gilmore Simms lamented, adding, "Nobody reads nowadays, and no one prints. My desks are already filled with MS.S. Why add to the number?" Paul Hamilton Hayne remarked in 1864 that "all social, intellectual pleasures [had] been ruthlessly destroyed" by the war. "One cannot *think* calmly; the sympathies, fears, passions of the heart being abnormally excited, there is hardly any chance left for that cool, consistent mental action, essential to Artistic success." The poet James Wood Davidson, who fought with the Thirteenth Regiment S.C. Volunteers, simply said, "War is a very unliterary thing," telling a correspondent, "My lyric harp I rarely touch—One cannot easily carry a harp in addition to the usual outfit of a camp dweller!"[52]

In January 1863, four months after beginning publication, the *Southern Illustrated News* congratulated itself on having survived the difficulties it faced. At the time of its first issue, it commented, "Such was the scarcity of materials that the oldest, ablest, most widely circulated journals in the Confederacy were printed on dingy sheets, which in time of peace would hardly have passed muster as wrapping paper." At the same time "the printing ink then in use was of a quality which we doubt not so soiled the hands of every reader as to have left an indelible impression on every mind." Paper was "so scarce that many deemed it impossible to obtain enough to print a decent edition of a new paper." Moreover, "we had to ransack every State for artists and the materials which artists use—boxwood being then, as now, exceedingly scarce; so much so, indeed, that we had to *discover* some other wood to supply the deficiency." While the *News* had found the best supplies and artists that it could in the South, it had also "sent agent after agent into the lines of the enemy to purchase what could not be obtained at home" and in "more than one instance" had been "twiddled out of large sums by blockade runners."[53]

Still, even the enterprising *News* could not overcome the difficulties of war entirely. As problems with paper and ink supplies, machinery, and personnel became increasingly desperate during the war, it, like many other periodicals, sometimes suspended publication. Although the *Southern Literary Messenger* early in the war had boasted that it had not been forced to resort to double issues, in contrast to *De Bow's Review*, in fact it began to publish on a bimonthly basis in 1862. In October 1862 it informed its readers, "The present double number would have contained as much matter as the last, had not the government seized the paper mills in this city and we failed to get paper in North Carolina." In August 1864 the *Magnolia Weekly* explained to subscribers who complained of missing issues that in fact the *Weekly* had only been published three times during the last three months "owing to the calls made upon the employees of this office for military duty." Under the exigencies of war the *Southern Literary Messenger* was sold in January 1864 and published its last issue in June that same year. Most popular publications quietly folded with the defeat of the Confederacy.[54]

In April 1863 the *Southern Field and Fireside*, commenting that "the condition of the country [was] not favorable to literature," warned, "However violent may be our animosity against the North now, the possibility of our again becoming subservient to Northern pens, and Northern publications is not so unlikely as one might at first imagine." In August the *Southern Illustrated News*, indignantly noting the sale of "Yankee" magazines in Richmond, expressed a fear that "such was the slavishness of the South," that "the old patrons of the Yankee weeklies and monthlies would buy them at any price." In February 1864 the *Southern Punch* mentioned a letter from a correspondent who feared that " 'when this cruel war is over,' the Southern people will again patronise Yankee flash weeklies and monthlies" such as the *New York Ledger*, *Harper's Weekly*, and *Harper's Magazine*. The *Southern Punch* used this letter as the occasion for another spirited call for "literary independence" from the North. But in the event the letter writer was prescient. With the end of the conflict both Southern readers and authors returned, however ironically, to their dependence on Northern literature.[55]

• • •

The situation was far different in the North, which on the eve of the war boasted a mature literary marketplace capable of distributing a wide variety of literature to a farflung national market. While Southerners struggled to publish illustrated weeklies that sold a few thousand copies, *Harper's Weekly*, one of the most popular Northern publications of the war, advertised as early as June 15, 1861, that it had sold 115,000 copies of its previous number, what it deemed an "extraordinary circulation." The weekly *Frank Leslie's Illustrated Newspaper* reportedly had a circulation of 164,000 in 1860, while the weekly story papers *Flag of Our Union* and the *New York Weekly* both had circulations of roughly 100,000. The most popular story paper in the North, the *New York Ledger*, reportedly had a circulation of as much as 400,000. Although popular general-interest monthlies had smaller circulations than the weeklies, their circulations, too, dwarfed those of Southern periodicals. *Harper's New Monthly Magazine*, for instance, claimed an average circulation of 110,000 on the eve of the war, while the *Atlantic Monthly* reported a circulation of 32,000 in 1863. The circulation figures of the largest religious and women's magazines were also high, with *Godey's Lady's Book* claiming 150,000 subscribers by 1860 and the religious journal the *Independent* claiming 35,000 subscribers at the beginning of the war and 75,000 by 1863.[56]

In New York, the center of the Northern book publishing industry and the location of Harper and Brothers, the largest American publishing firm, the 1860 census counted 17 book publishers, with capital amounting to $3,121,000 and printed books reaching an annual value of $3,225,551. In addition, 81 book and job printing offices "produced work valued at $1,033,658." In Boston, 23 book and job printing establishments "produced a value of $699,522," while in Philadelphia there were "about 40 book-publishing houses," with book printing "executed by 42 establishments to the value of $2,377,400 annually." Cincinnati was another important center of printing and book publishing, with $1,503,000 the "product of 32 printing-houses." By comparison, the dollar figure attached by the census to all the printing and publishing of eleven Southern states was just $1,253,154.[57]

From the start of the war an abundance of Northern presses, paper, artists, and engravers made it possible to produce a wide array of periodicals, newspapers, books, and print ephemera related to the war. Although war initially caused a temporary paralysis of book publishing, it quickly became a catalyst for an extensive print culture of war, including a wealth of illustrated print forms simply not available to the less industrialized South. During the early weeks of war fever, for instance, Northern printers advertised a striking array of patriotic items that created visual emblems of the war for a broad public. Only a few days after the firing on Fort Sumter, E. Anthony of New York offered a photograph of "Glorious Major Anderson" for sale, saying that "EVERY PATRIOTIC AMERICAN SHOULD OWN THIS PORTRAIT." Abbott and Company offered a "beautiful UNION BUTTON containing Portraits of Washington, Martha Washington, Maj. Anderson, Goddess of Liberty, etc."; Cooper and Pond advertised a "Union Cockade"; Ross and Tousey offered Union pins, Union badges, Union rosettes, and Union envelopes; and Hatch and Company, "Practical Lithographers," offered "a handsome chromo lithograph" called "True Patriotism." Such advertisements underlined the fact that from the start of the war in the North, it was possible to connect buying a wide range of goods with being loyal to the nation.[58]

The public participated eagerly in this new patriotic culture. Demonstrating their adherence to the Union, men, women, and children decorated themselves with Union insignia, connecting their own bodies with the larger body of the nation. In New York, Abby Woolsey reported that "quantities of Union cockades were worn in the streets," and George Templeton Strong remarked that the city seemed "to have gone suddenly wild and crazy," with "every other man, woman, and child bearing a flag or decorated with a cockade." Some women wore a "Union bonnet," what Woolsey called a "fearful object of contemplation" composed of "alternate layers of red, white, and blue." "To Freedom's colors true," Lucy Larcom's poem "The Nineteenth of April, 1861" exclaimed, "Blooms the old town of Boston in red and white and blue."[59]

Ostentatious patriotic displays characterized the start of the war in the South, too, but there was a striking difference between the sections in the volume and diversity of patriotic goods available for sale. Early in the war in the North, for instance, patriotic envelopes printed with flags and a variety of cartoons and illustrations became a craze. "We have flags on our paper and envelopes, and have all our stationery bordered with red, white and blue," eighteen-year-old Caroline Cowles Richards of Canandaigua, New York, noted in her diary in May 1861. Such envelopes were initially popular because they provided individuals with a means of displaying — and sending — their patriotism, but within months patriotic envelopes had accrued an additional meaning as "collectibles."[60]

Numerous Northern printers and publishers advertised patriotic envelopes early in the war: in New York, H. H. Lloyd and Company advertised "Flag Envelopes" and "Union Envelopes," and J. G. Wells extolled his "Newest Styles Union Goods," including the "Bold Soldier Boy Envelope" and the "Peacemaker Envelope," whose design represented "a 76-pounder pouring forth grape, with the Stars and Stripes floating over it," and bearing the belligerent motto " 'Our Compromise.' " A journal devoted to post office affairs noted in May that a large proportion of the letters recently sent through the mails had been in envelopes with flag designs, and in June printers advertised an increasing crescendo of designs, with Charles A. Miller advertising "175 patriotic envelopes all different" on June 8; 300 patriotic envelopes on June 26; and "400 different styles of patriotic envelopes" by June 29. As demand for different styles of envelopes grew exponentially, several vendors began to stress their collectibility, offering collectors' albums in which to store and display them, such as the *Union and Patriotic Album Illustrated Envelope Holder* offered by J. M. Whittemore of Boston. In response to this new collectible market, printers produced more and more elaborate envelope designs, in some cases creating beautifully engraved sets of "camp scenes" that covered the entire face of an envelope and, ironically, made it impossible to mail.[61]

By mid-1862, the "rage for envelopes decorated with patriotic or other embellishments" seemed "to be subsiding." But while it lasted, this fad underlined a significant difference between North and South in the power to produce a war-related print culture. Patriotic envelopes were an early wartime fad in the South as well as the North—one among many indications of the cultural links between North and South, even in wartime. Yet Southern printers created only a few hundred different designs for patriotic envelopes over the course of the war, whereas Northern printers created at least ten times that amount, with literally thousands of such designs offered for sale, many of them extraordinarily intricate.[62]

As in the South, the public's all-absorbing interest in the war stimulated a new, war-related print culture. Although Southern publications celebrated being cut off from Northern culture as an opportunity to establish a new national literature, Northern popular publications initially worried over the loss of their Southern audience. Both *Harper's Weekly* and *Frank Leslie's* assumed during the secession crisis of winter 1860–61 that they could continue to appeal to a Southern as well as a Northern audience, with *Harper's Weekly* initially referring to "The Great Southern Movement" without taking a strong political stand against secession. As late as

Union envelopes.
(Courtesy of the American Antiquarian Society)

the end of March, the *Weekly* ran a poem titled "Let Us Be Friends," whose lines included:

> But if you *must* go, let us part like good friends—
>   It's hard on the heart that our Union should sever!
> Oh! Heaven conduct us to happier ends,
>   And keep us like brothers for ever and ever![63]

Frank Leslie's aimed for an even more Southern-leaning form of neutrality. In late February 1861, for instance, *Leslie's* took pains to assure its readers that "while the political bias of the other illustrated journals" had caused their "utter exclusion" from the South, the "wise conservative course" of *Frank Leslie's* had "opened its circulation to every section of the country." Further, the paper asserted that because its artists and correspondents were "cordially received in the South," only in the pages of *Frank Leslie's* could be found "correct representations of what [was] daily transpiring in that section of the country." Even after the onset of war, *Frank Leslie's* briefly attempted to maintain neutrality, with Leslie personally advertising in late April, "I shall be happy to receive from Officers and others attached to either Army, sketches of important events and striking incidents which may occur during the impending struggle which seems to threaten the country." Leslie promised not only to "pay liberally" for such sketches but also offered to send the newspaper free for a year to those who sent them. The commercial considerations of *Frank Leslie's*—a desire not to lose readership—initially dictated its political stance during the secession crisis; in contrast, for many Southern publications politics dictated a new definition of culture. Whereas such Southern publications saw politics and culture as inextricably linked, *Leslie's* initially assumed that politics could be separated from culture within its pages.[64]

In this assumption *Leslie's* was hardly alone. A bias against "partisanship," for instance, was an exceptionally strong convention within American Victorian literary culture: outside of the newspaper, partisanship was considered unsuitable for family reading. The most popular story paper in the North, the *New York Ledger*, had long disavowed politics in its pages in an attempt to create a "family" weekly. Looking back over his career as editor and proprietor of the hugely successful *Ledger*, for instance, Robert Bonner commented that "there were certain things that could not appear" in his publication. "If my reader came to the word 'libertine' in a story it had to go out," Bonner said. "So it was with politics. We did not print 'Abolitionist' or 'Democrat.' The paper was meant for the family, and it was neither sectarian nor political." Such commentary linked politics with the sexually scandalous.[65]

In this depoliticization of culture the *Ledger* was joined by many family journals and women's magazines such as *Godey's*, in which overt political discussion was deemed to have no place. Even after the start of the war, the popular Boston story paper the *Flag of Our Union* made explicit its abjuring of politics, explaining why "we avoid all record in these columns of the war in which our country is involved." "In these exciting times," it told its readers, "the public receive quite enough of such reading matter as administers to their patriotism—quite enough current intelligence of the most stirring nature." It would be the *Flag of Our Union's* part, it said, to "furnish, as we have always endeavored to do, only such agreeable entertainment as shall minister to the better feelings of our nature, such as shall be welcome in the domestic circle." The paper even suggested, "It will be a relief to our friends to turn to these columns for a calm hour's enjoyment, after the inevitable excitement and irritation attendant upon perusing the pages of the political press." Yet both the *Flag of Our Union* and the *Ledger* eventually published war fiction, war poems, and even occasional political commentary during the conflict, revealing how pervasive the popular culture of war became.[66]

Some story papers initially claimed to offer a refuge from the increasingly ubiquitous print culture of war, but illustrated weeklies such as *Frank Leslie's* and *Harper's Weekly* instead responded directly to readers' interest in the war. As Union feeling swept the North, it became clear not only that there was an exceptional demand for a visual war but also that the only visual war the public would accept, or for that matter that the weeklies now desired to offer, was one that explicitly aligned itself with the Union. Thus by May 4, two weeks after the war began, both weeklies had dramatically changed in tone and approach. *Leslie's* commented at length on the new devotion to the Union in New York—a story of transformation that might have described the changing views of *Leslie's* itself: "Oberon's wand could hardly have worked a more wonderful transformation than the lowering of the American flag at Fort Sumpter has worked upon the people of New York and upon the entire populations of the North, East and West. The moderate supporters became fast adherents—the hesitating became assured—the wavering firm—the indifferent were roused to action—party lost its distinctions—all lesser and greater considerations were merged in one grand overpowering sentiment—devotion to the Union!" In a city in which roving groups of men forced proslavery and pro-Southern journals such as the *Day Book* or the *Journal of Commerce* to display the American flag, *Leslie's* no longer attempted to cater to Southerners and instead devoted itself to becoming a commercial organ of patriotism for the North.[67]

Harper's Weekly announced its own new political stance in a ringing May 4 editorial that brought numerous protests from its remaining Southern readers. "Southerners have rebelled and dragged our flag in the dirt," the *Weekly* said. "The rebels have appealed to the sword, and by the sword they must be punished." Introducing the issue of slavery as central to the war, the *Weekly* nevertheless began by saying, "This is a matter which concerns the Southern States exclusively," asserting that though "we of the North have never liked slavery," the "bulk of us have believed that it was not our business to interfere with it where it existed." Thus the *Weekly* claimed that troops would not "march into the Southern States under an Abolition banner," but it also asserted, "If the South expect that our gallant volunteers are going to hunt the slaves who may run away as they approach, they labor under a delusion." Reminding its readers that wherever the army went "local, municipal, and State laws [would] be superseded by martial law" and that "the Fugitive Slave Act [was] not to be found in the Army Regulations," the *Weekly* concluded, "The practical effect of a war in the Southern States, waged by Northern against Southern men, must be to liberate the slaves. This should be well understood." [68]

Numerous Southern readers wrote to protest against this editorial, and on May 25 *Harper's Weekly* published "To Our Southern Readers," in which it responded to the letters—"complaining bitterly"—it had received from "Maryland, Kentucky, Tennessee, and other Southern States." Some of these letters were "from friends, and appeal to the Christian feelings and kindly disposition of the publishers," others were "simply abusive," and still others "threaten the proprietors of this journal with assassination." The issue that especially exercised the letter writers was the magazine's assertion that the war would "inevitably sooner or later become a war of emancipation." Noting that "some of our Southern friends accompany their abuse of this journal with a notice to the publishers to send it no more to their address," and further observing that in "Tennessee Vigilance Committees forbid its being sold" and "in Louisiana the Governor prohibits its distribution through the Post-office," the *Weekly* set forth a new, combative philosophy: "If the people of the South don't think they get the worth of their money when they buy *Harper's Weekly*, they would exhibit great folly in purchasing it. If they do, to proscribe *Harper's Weekly* is their loss. We do not propose, in publishing this journal, to stand indebted to any man's good-will for its success. We calculate to produce such a paper that it shall be every man's interest to buy it. If we fulfill our aim, our Southern friends merely cut off their own noses when they stop our circulation among them. It is purely their affair. If they think they can do without an illustrated record of the war we will not object. We have work enough to supply the Northern demand for *Harper's Weekly*." [69]

With this statement the *Weekly* explicitly set forth several aspects of a new wartime identity. It signaled its independence from a Southern readership, while simultaneously signaling firm loyalty to the Union for its Northern readers. It foregrounded the issue of slavery within popular print culture by refusing to modify its characterization of the war as a war of emancipation. Finally, by describing itself as "an illustrated record of the war," and by employing a newly belligerent tone, the *Weekly* aligned its own literary mission and style with the conflict, thus contributing to a new form of war-related literary culture in the North.

Both *Harper's Weekly* and *Frank Leslie's* now stressed their abilities to provide a visual war for the reading public. On April 20 *Harper's Weekly* printed a prominent "Advertisement" on its front page that begged "to draw public attention" to a list of "engravings which have been published in this journal within the past few weeks, as evidence of the fidelity and thoroughness with which they are redeeming their pledge to 'give a well-drawn, well-engraved, and well-printed illustration of every important event that occurs.'" In June *Leslie's* advertised its "unrivalled corps" of "artists in the field," claiming to receive "20 to 40 sketches per day" from its artists, many of them "military or naval officers." "From this immense mass of authentic matter," *Leslie's* said, "we select the most striking," thus creating the "only correct and authentic pictorial illustrations of the war." This last comment was especially revealing, indicating as it did that the most "striking" illustrations of the war were assumed to be the most "authentic." This was a widely shared assumption at the start of the war, as theatrical, stylized notions of the way war looked dominated the popular print culture of war.[70]

The illustrated weeklies saw their circulation increase dramatically in the early weeks of war. In contrast, with the exception of such publishers of military guides and manuals as D. Van Nostrand, most book publishers coped with a depression in their business during the early months of the conflict, as popular attention remained fixed on the war. In October 1861, for instance, the trade journal of the publishing industry announced that it would switch from a weekly to a monthly format until "the book business revives." In February 1862 the publisher George Palmer Putnam exhorted booksellers in an unusual ad to keep up their stocks of books, saying that he was well aware "that in these times Booksellers, as well as others, are not anxious to increase their stocks or engagements" but urging that a "constant though moderate supply of such books" of "PERMANENT VALUE, as well as of IMMEDIATE INTEREST and ATTRACTION, will prove both safe and politic and profitable, even though the war is not yet ended." Putnam in particular found that the war put an unbearable financial strain on his business, which had never fully recovered from the financial panic of 1857. "During the years of the war," his son later remembered, "the larger proportion of the town libraries throughout the country, whose incomes were dependent upon voluntary subscriptions, ceased buying books altogether." In a number of towns "the retail booksellers practically stopped business, and the younger men among them went to the war." The stress of these financial conditions forced the elder Putnam into an unusual publishing arrangement in 1862, whereby he temporarily put his business—all but war-related publications—into the hands of a younger subordinate, while he himself "permitted his name to be sent in to the President as a candidate for Collector of Internal Revenue." He was not alone: other publishers, too, found that the onset of war put an unbearable strain on their business. As James C. Derby tersely explained it in his memoirs, the firm of Derby and Jackson "had a prosperous career until 1861, when they discontinued business." [71]

Yet almost from the start of the war some book publishers and editors of monthly periodicals seized on the public's all-absorbing interest in war as an opportunity to produce an array of war-related literature. These publishers were joined by an increasing number of colleagues during the war; indeed, one of the important stories of Northern wartime popular literary culture was proliferation itself—the continually multiplying set of sources that represented the war.

Several publishers, for instance, began to produce print "records" of the conflict, collecting war documents, poetry, and war "anecdotes" and "incidents" into pamphlets and book-length volumes. Some Southerners also shared the goal of creating a print record of the war, as we have seen, but their efforts to "collect," say, Southern war poetry in book form met with insuperable barriers in the more undeveloped state of publishing in the South, not to mention the increasing chaos of the experience of war itself. The situation was far different in the North. If in the South those readers who wanted to "preserve" the print culture of the war had to create their own scrapbooks of war poems and articles, in the North readers could turn to a number of published sources for extensive print records of the conflict—sources that were, in effect, formalized scrapbooks of the war.

Only a few weeks after the start of war, for instance, *Frank Leslie's* itself began to publish an ongoing "Pictorial History of the War of 1861" as an appendage to its *Weekly*. Edited by E. G. Squier, who would soon take over from Frank Leslie as editor of the *Weekly*, the "Pictorial History" was a series of twenty-five-cent pamphlets of "mammoth size," published every two weeks. Each would provide a "complete epitome of the war," with "all the Facts, Scenes, Incidents and Anecdotes connected with it, arranged chronologically so as to form a cotemporary and permanent history of the time." With its reprints of illustrations from the *Weekly*, it would be "invaluable to families, for in its magnificently illustrated page even children can trace the course of events, while as a work of reference for all classes its value and importance will increase year by year."[72]

Leslie's advertisements for the *Pictorial History* revealed a number of assumptions about war-related print culture. First, its attempt to appeal to whole families as well as to all classes could only have been made in a home-front war in which print culture was widely recognized as part of, rather than tangential to, the war effort. According to the *Pictorial History*, it was important for all members of society, even children, to be informed about the war. Second, the assertion that Leslie's *Pictorial History* would be a "permanent" record of the war responded to the widespread belief that the war was of extraordinary importance in American life and should be "preserved" and commemorated appropriately for future generations. Last, the notion that the *Pictorial History* would increase in "value" year by year suggested, however obliquely, that there were commercial values attached to the literature of the war as a collectible. These beliefs in the importance of the war and its collectibility bled into one another within Northern literary culture, as the consumption and display of appropriate "permanent" patriotic objects became a way of expressing deeply felt beliefs about the nation, while simultaneously suggesting the central role of commercial print memory in maintaining and preserving that nationhood.

Even more ambitious than Leslie's *Pictorial History* as a "record" of the conflict was G. P. Putnam's the *Rebellion Record*, intended to be "a diary of American events," including "the patriotic POETRY of the time; a Digest of all verifiable FACTS; accurate copies of all essential documents, and a reliable transcript of all notable and picturesque INCIDENTS." To be edited by Frank Moore, who had previously produced the *Diary of the American*

Revolution, it was, like Leslie's *Pictorial History*, first "to be issued in handsome pamphlets of 48 pages," which would later be gathered in volumes as "a permanent digest for future reference." It, too, was marketed as a collectible: it "deserves to be well sustained," the *American Publishers' Circular and Literary Gazette* said, "as its value will no doubt increase as time progresses."[73]

Even more so than Leslie's *Pictorial History*, the *Rebellion Record* aimed to be inclusive, reprinting from a variety of newspapers and other sources "illustrative documents and narratives, rumors, incidents, poetry, anecdotes, etc.," plus "proclamations, general orders, speeches, etc., etc., North and South," in order to give a "comprehensive history of this struggle." Such inclusiveness had twin roots: first, within Victorian assumptions that all facts were potentially meaningful within a greater whole (even if that greater whole might only be discerned in the future); and second, within a Victorian material culture that celebrated the proliferation of objects as part of an expansive, possessive mode of relationship to the outside world.[74]

The *Rebellion Record* marked a possessive relationship to the war itself. Implicit within its conception, first of all, was the idea that every aspect of the war was important and worthy of recording: as George Palmer Putnam's son later remembered, "It was supposed, not unnaturally, that every detailed document connected with the events of the time would be of interest for later readers." The creation of the *Rebellion Record* also reflected Victorian optimism that the war could be made, quite literally, legible if enough "facts" connected with it were gathered together. Within the pages of the *Rebellion Record*, war could be doubly possessed: first by being contained within the pages of the *Rebellion Record* itself, and second by being purchased and read. Thus when the *Boston Transcript* recommended the *Record* for "those who would preserve and ponder the authentic chronicle" of the war and the *New York Times* recommended it in order to "preserve the great story of this great epoch," they also connected buying the *Record* with a full understanding of the war.[75]

The organization of the *Rebellion Record*, with its sections titled "Documents," "Poetry," "Rumors," "Incidents" and "Anecdotes," also revealed that from the start of the conflict authors and publishers conceptualized the war within familiar literary categories. Thus the *Rebellion Record* promised to present "the poetical and picturesque aspects, the notable and characteristic incidents" of war, "separated from the graver and more important documents." *Frank Leslie's Illustrated Newspaper*, too, organized the war into literary categories, including, in addition to its military subhead-

ings, "Anecdotes, Incidents, and Humors of the Times" a
of War." Such categories revealed that from the begin
was widely assumed that there *would* be "picturesque
"romantic" elements to the conflict.[76]

The *Rebellion Record*'s reprinted newspaper and p
revealed that, just as in the South, numerous amat
poets responded to the outbreak of war in verse. Va
mentators noted this outpouring with some amazement: Richa.
White, for instance, commented that "the excited feeling of the country
vented itself in verse to a remarkable extent," and *Harper's Monthly* observed that "the Poet's Columns in the newspapers [had] become almost
as formidable as those of General Scott." Yet there were subtle differences
in the cultural roles of Northern and Southern war poetry. Southern amateur war poetry became one of the keynotes of the literary war in the
South, in part because there was relatively little other war literature published. But Northern amateur war poetry, only a fraction of the outpouring
of popular war literature produced during the war, was less central to the
imagined war. Instead, an increasing number of professional publishers,
writers, and editors seized the publishing opportunities created by the war,
unhampered by the difficulties with paper supplies that immediately faced
the South and not yet facing the dramatically increased prices characteristic of later in the war. James T. Fields, for instance, who took over the
editorship of the *Atlantic Monthly* from James Russell Lowell shortly after
the war began, advertised the June 1861 number of the *Monthly* as "An
Army Number," with the claim, "The especial adaptation of the contents
of this number to the wants of the reading public at the present time has
induced a number of patriotic gentlemen of Boston to subscribe for 10,000
copies as a gratuitous donation to the officers and privates of the Army of
the United States." This was a grand gesture that Southern printers and
publishers could not possibly imitate.[77]

By July, two women writers, Mary J. Webber and Phebe Ann Coffin Hanaford, had published a collection of patriotic war poems called
Chimes of Freedom and Union. This slim volume contained verse by such
established antebellum writers as Oliver Wendell Holmes, John Greenleaf Whittier, Lucy Larcom, Rose Terry, Lydia Sigourney, Harriet Beecher
Stowe, Caroline A. Mason, Alice Cary, and Richard Henry Stoddard. At
the same time, a few enterprising book publishers in the North were quick
to produce patriotic volumes that created a highly decorative war. James T.
Gregory of New York, for instance, advertised two slim parlor-table vol-

of patriotism in July 1861. His *The Star Spangled Banner* was, he
 the neatest and prettiest literary and artistic production yet elicited
 the war." Illustrated by F. O. C. Darley and designed like a precious
volume of poetry, this work was soon followed by a companion volume,
Rodman Drake's *The American Flag*. Both of these works were part of a
varied group of books that Gregory already advertised as "War Publications," only months after the war had begun. "For selling in the Cars,
Steamboats, etc.," Gregory said, "there is nothing better in the market."
The idea that war might be an aesthetic and commercial project also lay
behind the publication of popular poet A. J. H. Duganne's "splendidly and
profusely illustrated" *Ballads of the War* in 1862, intended to be a "POETICAL
SOUVENIR" of the war. Duganne proposed to publish ballads serially, with
new ballads each month to "chronicle" new battles or other significant
events.[78]

A different sort of publishing opportunity was reflected in the increasing numbers of "memorial volumes" published early in the war to commemorate the deaths of officers. In December 1861, for instance, Charles B.
Richardson of New York published "a new and elegant gift book," *The
Fallen Brave*, described as "a biographical memorial of the American officers who have given their lives for the preservation of the union." Gilt-
trimmed and oversized, *The Fallen Brave* was a "precious volume — a tribute
fitting now, a beautiful monument hereafter." Presented as a parlor-table
book that, like other memorial volumes, would transform the parlor into a
shrine, *The Fallen Brave* revealed the easy fusion of commerce, patriotism,
and death within the Northern literary marketplace.[79]

Advertisements of *The Fallen Brave* as a "gift book" have a macabre air,
but they must be understood as part of a Victorian material culture that
celebrated the proliferation of objects, including books, as part of an expansive, possessive mode of relationship to the outside world. That possessive relationship was literally on display in the Victorian parlor, where
books often resided on the parlor table. A striking aspect of midcentury
Victorian culture was its reflexivity — an absorption with representations
of itself in forms of symbolic self-display. Related to the maturation of
a capitalist economy and the possibilities for consumption it offered an
emerging middle class, such reflexivity was expressed through a status-
oriented display of images and objects.

The editor James T. Fields, for instance, did not just build a library
of his favorite books — he collected an array of such appurtenances as

autographs, prints, authors' letters, and other memorabilia that were then prominently displayed in a library to which he took his many guests as if to a shrine. One visitor remembered "endless numbers of first editions, autographed volumes, presentation copies, and association copies," as well as "pictures, etchings, oils, crayons, on every available wall space that remained free." In addition, "prints, photographs, autographs and letters lay about in profusion." Like James T. Fields's library, Victorian parlors teemed with possessions, from plants and tapestries to prints and photographs to statuary and books. These not only proclaimed the refined taste of their owners but also marked a possessive relationship to the outside world. *The Fallen Brave* was part of this possessive relationship, providing links between the private world of the parlor and the public world through a gilt-decorated paean to patriotism.[80]

Northern parlor culture centered not only around books but also around music. The importance of songs throughout the Civil War, in both the North and South, cannot be overestimated. Sung around the piano or a cappella in parlors, at public gatherings, on the march by soldiers, and in camp, war songs, like war poetry, were widely understood to be an important part of a patriotic culture that united the private world of the parlor with a larger public world. Throughout the war, the "line between poems and songs was so extremely fine as to disappear in most cases." Poems were often put to music and printed as sheet music; conversely the lyrics of popular songs were often published individually in song sheets or collected in cheap pamphlets called songsters. During 1861 alone numerous such songsters, with titles such as *The Union Song-Book*, *The Stars and Stripes Songster*, and *The Flag of Our Union Songster*, were published and distributed widely. The author Charles Godfrey Leland said that he had heard "from a collector that during the first year" of war "two thousand songs were published upon it." Such song sheets and songsters were a major part of the expansive print culture of the early war in the North, and to a lesser extent, in the South as well.[81]

• • •

By 1862, as war, patriotism, and commerce fused within the Northern literary marketplace, publishers and authors began to produce a variety of new genres of war literature, including sensational war novels, war romances, war histories, and even war humor. The speed with which the war was transformed into a salable commodity was captured in humorous form by the writer Robert Henry Newell, who under the nom de plume Orpheus C. Kerr began to publish parodies of the excesses of Northern war-related print culture in newspaper columns and then books of war humor.

Harper's Weekly began to publish popular war stories in addition to its articles on the war. In 1862 alone, for instance, the *Weekly* published forty-six war stories, with thirty of these featuring Northern heroines on the home front and the remaining sixteen stories a variety of types including first-person accounts of war campaigns by male narrators, stories featuring Southern heroines, and adventurous "border stories" set in Kentucky and Tennessee. Other periodicals, including *Frank Leslie's, Arthur's Home Magazine, Harper's Magazine,* the *Atlantic Monthly,* and the *New York Ledger,* also began to publish war fiction, especially the soon-to-be ubiquitous "war romances." [82]

By 1862, representations of the conflict were being recycled and reshuffled from newspaper to weekly, and from weekly to pamphlet, in order to create new popular forms. *Frank Leslie's,* for instance, capitalized on its ability to recycle its own published representations of war into a proliferating variety of publications. By May of 1862 its war-related list included, in addition to *Frank Leslie's Pictorial History of the War of 1861, Frank Leslie's War Chart, Frank Leslie's War Maps, Frank Leslie's Portrait Pictorial* of "the Commanding Officers of the Union Army and Navy," and *Frank Leslie's Pictorials of Union Victories.* It also published *Frank Leslie's Budget of Fun* and *Frank Leslie's Heroic Incidents of the Civil War in America.*[83]

In 1862, as well, a number of Northern publishers began to make plans to publish histories of the war, even as it was still being fought. In late March 1862, for instance, George William Curtis, soon to be political editor of *Harper's Weekly,* wrote his friend Charles Eliot Norton that Fletcher Harper, the editor of the magazine, had asked him "to take into consideration" writing "a history or Chronicle of the War." It was to be "illustrated by the war pictures of the Weekly, a huge (in size) book for popular reading." Curtis seriously considered this project, but he ultimately decided that if he wrote about the Rebellion he would want to write "a proper history," which he felt could not be written "until we can know something of the secret annals of the conspiracy." [84]

Although Curtis decided against writing such a popular history, other writers and publishers seized the publishing opportunities created by the war. During early 1862, for instance, several subscription publishing firms began to contract with authors to produce richly illustrated popular subscription histories of the war. George W. Childs of Philadelphia, for instance, contracted with popular historian Benson J. Lossing early in 1862, clearly hoping to repeat the earlier success of Lossing's narrative sketchbook *The Pictorial Field-Book of the Revolution* (1850–52). By the spring of that year several publishers had announced subscription histories, and some already had canvassing agents in the field, taking orders for books that were still to be produced. In March 1862 Childs wrote that a subscription history of the war by popular historian Evert A. Duyckinck had just been announced and that one publisher, Virtue, had "canvassers already in the field" while another publisher, Johnson and Fry, was "getting ready to run them." Late May 1862 also found popular historian John S. C. Abbott hard at work on a subscription history for the Connecticut-based Bill brothers; by June he already had "*five* chapters ready for the printer." Eventually, more than three hundred thousand volumes of Abbott's history, the "largest sale of any book on the war," had reportedly been subscribed for among a farflung Northern audience in small towns and rural areas. Although in the South there was also interest in publishing war histories—and indeed, Richmond editor E. A. Pollard published his *The First Year of the War* in 1862—no Southern publisher could match the capabilities of Northern publishers to produce printed memories of the war even as it was being fought.[85]

Looking back over Northern "literature and literary progress" for the year 1862, the *American Annual Cyclopaedia* commented that the "continuance of the war" had "materially checked the enterprise of publishers, and caused the number of new works published to be greatly below that of some former years." But by the next year the *Cyclopaedia*'s tune had changed dramatically: "In no period of the past history of the United States," it announced, "has the literary activity of the country been so manifest as in the year 1863." Although the "price of paper" had "more than doubled, and the cost of printing and binding been greatly enhanced," at the same time that "the scarcity of skilled labor" had "rendered production difficult," the "number of newspapers, periodicals, and magazines" had "greatly increased, and the circulation of those previously established been much enlarged, and the number of new books issued surpasses that of any previous year." By 1863 and 1864, the market for war books in the North even extended to children: in the last two years of the war an extensive juvenile war literature, consisting of war stories stressing an adventurous boys' war, began to appear.[86]

If war had at first been a disruption to Northern popular literary culture, it increasingly instead fueled an entire subgenre of "war literature."

HARD TACK.

THE GUARD HOUSE.

Winslow Homer's *Life in Camp* cards.
(Courtesy of the American Antiquarian
Society)

The game of "Visit to Camp."
(Courtesy of the American Antiquarian Society)

As the trade journal of the publishing industry marveled in 1864, the war had added "a new and imposing department to our literature." Not only were publishers issuing "military treatises of all kinds, original and republished," but they were also publishing "biographical publications, histories of the war, journals of officers, narratives, war-novels, and war poems" and "political treatises and pamphlets without number." Though this list was imposing, it in fact failed to mention several types of war-related publications, including juvenile war literature, war humor, and war romances.[87]

Illustrations and ephemera, too, continued to be an important part of the print culture of the war. Currier and Ives produced numerous sentimental war-related lithographs, such as *The Soldier's Dream of Home*, distributed to a wide audience. Other printers produced "Pictures for the Times" including "Colored Lithographs of the Great Battles and Other Scenes and Incidents of the War." Winslow Homer, one of a corps of artists hired by *Harper's Weekly* to go into the field and produce sketches of the war from which engravings could be made, produced *Campaign Sketches* in 1863 and a series of collectible "souvenir" cards in 1864 depicting "Life in Camp," both for the printer L. Prang. Prang was one of a number of printers who produced such souvenir cards in wartime.[88]

Enterprising printers also produced paper soldiers and war games such as "The Game of the Rebellion," which promised to give "every person, Ladies, Gentlemen and Children, a chance to 'fight the rebels by their own firesides.'" One printer produced a war game called "Visit to Camp," with illustrated cards featuring figures including "The Sutler," "The Zouave," and "The Surgeon," and another produced a "snakes and ladders"–style game called "The Game of Secession." Other printers created colorful paper fans with war poems printed on them or embossed with the slogan "We Raise a Breeze To Cool the Heroes Brow." Still others produced red, white, and blue "'Union' Collars and Cuffs," as well as decks of Union playing cards, with one comprising "52 likenesses of Officers in the Union Army." In short, war offered numerous commercial opportunities for printers and publishers in the North, in striking contrast to the increasingly desperate situation of printers and publishers in the South.[89]

From the start of the war many readers, writers, and publishers in both the North and South assumed that the war was a literary as well as military event, one that would inspire a new linking of individual and nation within poem, song, and story. Few would have admitted that market considerations played an important role in both encouraging and limiting expressions of patriotism in poetry and prose. Yet by the end of the war many Southerners had made the discouraging discovery that it was difficult to achieve literary nationalism without the aid of a prosperous commercial literary culture. By contrast, many Northerners were dismayed to learn that within a thriving literary marketplace they could not easily separate patriotism from commerce.

The Early Spirit of War

Harp of the South, awake!
But not to sing of love,
In shady forest-bower,
Or fragrant orange grove;
Oh, no, but thy song must be
The wrath of the battle crash,
Inscribed on the cloud of war,
With the pen of its lightning flash.
—J. M. Kilgour, "Harp of the South Awake!,"
War Songs of the South, 1862

O brother bards, why stand ye silent all,
Amidst these days of noble strife,
While drum and fife, and the fierce trumpet-call,
Awake the land to life?

Now is the time, if ever time there was,
To strike aloud the sounding lyre,
To touch the heroes of our holy cause
Heart-deep with ancient fire.

—George H. Boker, "Ad Poetas,"
Rebellion Record, vol. 2, 1861

In the first year of war commentators in both the North and the South marveled at the outpouring of newspaper poetry inspired by the conflict. "Southern independence has struck the lyre as well as unsheathed the sword," the war correspondent "Bohemian" (William G. Shepperson) announced in the preface to his 1862 collection *War Songs of the South*. "That it has inspired many a song no less truly poetical than intensely patriotic, our newspapers amply testify." The Northern author Richard Grant White also noted that "the excited feeling of the country vented itself in verse to a most remarkable extent," writing in late 1861 that "newspapers which undertook to gather these effusions of popular sentiment together from various quarters, filled column after column with them, and sometimes page after page." "A single volume of ordinary size cannot contain a tithe of the songs which have already appeared and are daily appearing," Shepperson concluded.[1]

At the start of the war, it was widely assumed that poetry and song had an important patriotic role to play in the war. Numerous writers—both obscure and well known—produced poetry that asserted the communicative power of poetry in wartime. They wrote verse intended to inspire their compatriots to enlist in the war. They composed "national songs" intended to be new symbols of nationality. They wrote paeans to the national flag. They composed and recited poetry for soldier "benefits" and military ceremonies, including formal flag presentations. And they sent hundreds of verses to newspapers. In writing such verse, they treated poems as imaginative acts that not only reflected a new nationhood but actively called it into being. "These newspaper waifs have played no unimportant part in the actual drama which surrounds us," Shepperson said, praising their "wealth of patriotic sentiment." Assuming that poetry and song were a vital part of nation making, early wartime poets demonstrated an optimism concerning the power of representation that never entirely disappeared during the Civil War and that was only directly challenged during World War I.[2]

Both Northern and Southern poets sought to imagine a unified nationhood into being across such boundaries as occupation, class, and geography. They treated public verse as a persuasive means of creating not just a local but a widespread, all-encompassing community. As John Savage wrote in "The Muster of the North: A Ballad of '61,"

> The woodman flings his axe aside
> The farmer leaves his plough;
> The merchant slams his ledger lids
> For other business now;
> The artisan puts up his tools,
> The artist drops his brush,

And joining hands for Liberty,
    To Freedom's standard rush.[3]

According to Savage, war not only created a new union among men of different occupations but also obliterated divisions among nationalities. "Round the flag the Irish like a human rampart go," he said, while the "Teuton corps," as well as "Scots and Poles, Italians, Gauls," are "all aglow with pilgrim fire." Similarly, the war obliterated party divisions:

And in the mighty mustering,
    No petty hate intrudes,
    No rival discords mar the strength
Of rising multitudes.

"No party badges flaunting now,—no word of clique or clan"—confirmed Lucy Larcom's "The Nineteenth of April, 1861."[4]

Southern poets likewise imagined the war gathering men together into a unified whole. "The Voice of the South" addressed the separate states of the South in an attempt to enfold them into the new nation:

Nor shall Tennessee pause, when like voice from the steep,
The great South shall summon her sons from their sleep;
Nor Kentucky be slow, when our trumpet shall call,
To tear down the rifle that hangs on her wall!

Such poetry did not just reflect a new united nationhood; it attempted to imagine such unity into being rhetorically.[5]

Dozens of poems early in the war also sought to bind compatriots more closely to the nation at war through rallying cries to battle. Numerous Southern poets, for instance, both male and female, called to their countrymen to "arise" for battle. High wrought, passionate, defiant, this early Southern war poetry developed a set of familiar motifs as it asked countrymen to "advance" and "unsheathe" their swords in defense of their new country. Simultaneously drawing on and creating a shared language of war, this poetry especially celebrated the anticipated bravery of Southern manhood. "Uprise ye braves of Southern birth," one typical poem in the *Richmond Daily Dispatch* began in June 1861:

Uplift your flag on high,
And bear it through the battle's breeze
    To conquer or to die.
Let every scabbard be forsworn

And every sword flash out,
Till every foot of Southern soil
Resounds to freedom's shout.[6]

The popular poet Susan Archer Talley, "whose writings are always eagerly sought after," the *Southern Literary Messenger* claimed, published her "Rallying Song of the Virginians" in June as well:

Now rouse ye, gallant comrades all,
And ready stand, in war array;
Virginia sounds her battle call
And gladly we obey.
Our hands upon our trusty swords,
Our hearts with courage beating high;
We'll fight as once our fathers fought,
To conquer or to die![7]

Such "rallying songs" were rhetorical acts meant to draw a nation together. But they also allowed poets moments of individual assertion in the public sphere of the newspaper. As the Memphis poet Annie Chambers Ketchum wrote to a friend of her war song "Battle Call" in May 1861, "I could not resist the temptation to blow my individual bugle just a little." Her poem began with a set of already familiar tropes, as it called on "Gentlemen of the South" to "Gird on your flashing swords!"[8]

Ketchum was an established poet on the eve of the war. But many ordinary citizens also felt empowered by the patriotic demands of war to express themselves in poetry—often for the first time. As Oliver Wendell Holmes noted in 1865, war poems "were written by soldiers, by the wives, sisters, parents, children, friends of soldiers." Many of these were occasional poems celebrating specific companies, such as the June 1861 "To the Hawfield Boys of Alamance County, North Carolina," written by "L. L.," "an accomplished young lady of Raleigh, N.C." As such poems— and dozens of other "battle-calls"—revealed, one accepted literary role for women in wartime was to write patriotic verse supporting men in battle.[9]

But men, too, wrote these "cries" to battle. Numerous civilians published war poems in the popular press. Soldiers also sent war poems to popular weeklies such as the *New-York Mercury.* Even the poet Henry Timrod, who early in the war lamented that he had "small command" over the "martial instrument" demanded of a poet in wartime, by March 1862 had produced "A Cry to Arms," in which he called to his countrymen:

Come, with the weapons at your call—
   With musket, pike, or knife:
He wields the deadliest blade of all
   Who lightest holds his life.[10]

Such ubiquitous "calls to battle" explicitly attempted to create a unified nationhood. They did so by imagining a sharply gendered world with clear distinctions between masculine and feminine codes of wartime behavior. As the authors of *Behind the Lines: Gender and the Two World Wars* have remarked, war is a "gendering activity" that "ritually marks the gender of all members of a society." Certainly both Northern and Southern poems early in the war imagined a wartime world of exaggerated masculinity.[11]

Southern calls to battle, for instance, imagined a heroic Southern manhood by drawing on a variety of literary conventions and allusions. Some poems drew on classical examples of heroism: the high-flown "Patriotism," for instance, claimed that "The holy fire that nerved the Greek / To make his stand at Marathon" lived on "unquenched—unquenchable" in Southerners. Others compared Southern men to their Revolutionary forebears. John Overall's "Seventy-six and Sixty-one" was one among many poems that evoked the Revolutionary "heroes of the deathless past," asserting that "We build our altars where you lie, / On many a verdant sod, / With sabers pointing to the sky, / And sanctified of God." [12]

Numerous poems also drew on the myth of the Southern "cavalier." "The Virginians of the Valley" praised Virginians as "The knightliest of the knightly race / Who since the days of old / Have kept the lamps of chivalry / Alight in hearts of gold." [13] Annie Chambers Ketchum's "Battle-Call," dedicated "to her Countrymen, the Cavaliers of the South," also praised the "Brave knights of a knightly race," who would "Show to the minions of the North / How valor dares the fray!" Such evocations of Southern bravery constructed a nationalism centered not so much on allegiance to an abstract state as on a shared and inherited culture of manly bravery.[14]

Many early wartime Union poems also imagined a newly masculinized wartime culture, one that abjured feminized values. "Let not the child's voice be heard, nor the mother's entreaties," said Walt Whitman in his September 1861 *Harper's Weekly* "Beat! Beat! Drums!," as he, along with so many of his fellow Northerners, imagined a masculine war. Whitman would soon turn to more sentimental and emotive versions of manhood in his writings on wounded soldiers (see chapter 3). But in the first flush of war fever he, and many other poets, created exaggerated images of a hearty, robust masculinity. In his "Eighteen Sixty-one," which he submitted to the *Atlantic Monthly* in October, Whitman talked of "your masculine voice O year," imagining 1861 "not as some pale poetling seated at a desk lisping cadenzas" softly

> But as a strong man erect, clothed in blue clothes, advancing,
>   carrying a rifle on your shoulder,
> With well-gristled body and sunburnt face and hands, with a knife
>   in the belt at your side.[15]

Like Southern calls to battle, poems that called Northern men to arms explicitly and implicitly defined wartime codes of manhood. Sarah Warner Brooks's "On! Brothers, On!," for instance, imagined men "in the face of death, fearless and proud!," and John Clancy's "A Northern Rally" stressed the legacy of Northern "patriot blood":

> Like rushing tide down mountain side,
>   The Northern hosts are sweeping;
> Each freeman's breast to meet the test
>   With patriot blood is leaping.
> Now Southern sneer and bullies' leer,
>   Will find swift vengeance meted;
> For never yet, since foemen met,
>   Have Northern men retreated.[16]

If Southern poets characterized their countrymen as "cavaliers," Northern poets instead called on the strengths of Northern "Puritans" and "Mudsills," sometimes asserting the prowess of working men. "Northmen, come out!" called a poem by Charles Godfrey Leland:

> Give the pirates a roaring rout;
> Out in your strength and let them know
> How Working Men to Work can go.
> Out in your might and let them feel
> How Mudsills strike when edged with steel;
>   Northmen, come out![17]

In addition to the ubiquitous poetry celebrating Northern and Southern manhood, a few poems early in the war addressed the question of what women could do for the war. In the July 1861 *Southern Literary Messenger*, the poet "Cora" paid tribute to woman's fervent desire to participate in the war but also acknowledged the perceived limitations on her ability to do so:

> Soldiers! woman's heart beats high;
>   Fain would *she* your glory share,
> March through blood, to victory,
>   In a cause so just, so dear.
>
> But her feeble strength denies,
>   Though her heart is brave and true.[18]

In the North, too, several early wartime poems by women puzzled over women's relationship to the war. Caroline A. Mason's "The Will for the Deed" began by defining women's roles in contrast to those of men:

> No sword have I, no battle-blade,
> Nor shining spear; how shall I aid
> My Country in her great Crusade?

"I am a woman, weak and slight," the poem continued, "No voice to plead, no arm to fight, / Yet burning to support the Right." Concluding at this early stage of the war that nursing was not an option—"With oil and wine I may not go, / Where wounded men toss to and fro"—the narrator decided that she must stay with her child, reassuring herself that

> "They also serve, who stand and wait,"—
> Oh, golden words!—and not too late!
> My soul accepts her humbler fate.[19]

Augusta Cooper Kimball's "My Country," published in the *New York Tribune* only two weeks after the war began, also considered the question of what women might do for their country. "Yes, what may Woman do for thee!" Kimball exclaimed before also listing women's gendered limitations in time of war:

> her voice may not be heard,
> To rouse the apathetic mind with soul-impassioned word;
> Her small hand was not formed to aid the battle throng,
> Howe'er her heart may burn and bleed for all her country's wrong.

Kimball concluded, however, that "there's a power, all these above—she may in meekness wear, / And wield in humble majesty—the matchless power of Prayer."[20]

These early wartime poems offered extremely circumscribed solutions to the question of what women could do for the war, solutions that few Northern women would continue to accept beyond the first days of war. Even so, however, Kimball's poem is revealing for the assumption it made that women not only had a right to claim "my country" but had a special claim to power through prayer and suffering. "Deem it not weak, my country! this aid we bring to thee," Kimball concluded. In such a poem, women claimed a place in the imagined war.[21]

· · ·

Calls to battle were one poetic means by which Northerners and Southerners sought to imagine a unified nationhood early in the war. But numerous poets also attested to the importance and power of national symbols in poems and songs that praised the national flag or attempted to create new national hymns.

In the North, many observers felt that the American flag accrued a new depth of meaning as a symbol of nationalism in the early days of war. With what "intense feeling," Richard Grant White remembered in late 1861, had the "whole country" learned "that Major Anderson had struck his flag" when Fort Sumter "became untenable, and had evacuated, not surrendered, the post, raising his flag again and saluting it." In the days that followed, "the eye could hardly turn, north of the Potomac, without being gladdened by the sight of the American flag—how dear to us, we of this generation never knew till then!" The author Grace Greenwood agreed: "With what new splendor and sacredness has that banner been invested," she wrote during the summer of 1861, "since its transfiguration in the flame and smoke of Sumter! We had grown indifferent to the emblem of our nationality, as something seldom to be seen, except in tiresome Fourth-of-July parades."[22]

The religious quality of this transformed Unionism struck many observers. From New York, Hiram Barney commented on the "devotion which is whole hearted and religious like to the Union and the present Government," as "flags were displayed from all the church steeples." One stranger asked George Templeton Strong, who helped to organize the raising of a flag on New York's Trinity Church, "Are they really going to hoist the flag on the steeple, Sir?—Well, now, I tell you, that's the biggest *thing* that's been done in New York in my time!" Musing on the delighted public reaction to this event, Strong commented, "The ideas of Church and State, Religion and Politics, have been practically separated so long that people are specially delighted with any manifestation of the Church's sympathy with the State and recognition of our national life on any fitting occasion." Certainly it was true that in many churches, as Hiram Barney pointed out, "national airs were played on the organs and in some cases national anthems, such as 'The Star Spangled Banner,' were sung by the whole congregation."[23]

As these startled but approving reactions to a perceived new fusion of church and state in wartime indicated, the advent of war catalyzed reformulations and redefinitions of nationhood within Northern culture, including popular literary culture. Many popular poems, for instance, explored the idea of the flag as a symbol that for the first time united church, state, and home. "Let the flag of our Country wave from the spire of every church in the land," wrote the Reverend E. A. Anderson, whose comment was the inspiration for a poem on that subject. Written by "W.," "Our Flag" called for the flag to fly

From every hill, in every vale,
　Where freemen tread the sod,
And from the spires where freemen meet,
　For prayer and praise to God;—
Yes, on the church—no place too good—
Our country yet is free!

"God bless our star-gemmed banner," said another poem, "shake its folds out to the breeze, / From church, from fort, from house-top, o'er the city, on the seas."[24]

Many poems reprinted in the *Rebellion Record* during 1861 expressed a new appreciation and tenderness for the flag's history within American life—"Tis Freedom's standard, tried and proved on many a field of old"—said one, while another apostrophized the "Bright emblem of the mighty Past!," calling it "A costly, bright, and sacred thing!" Others conveyed a new appreciation for the expansive Unionism conveyed by the flag, which not only linked Northern states together but for the first time linked all of Northern society.[25]

Northern poets exhorted their countrymen to gather around the flag. As Edna Dean Proctor's "The Stripes and the Stars" urged,

From prairie, O ploughman! speed boldly away—
There's seed to be sown in God's furrows to-day—
Row landward, lone fisher! Stout woodman, come home!
Let smith leave his anvil and weaver his loom,
And hamlet and city ring loud with the cry,
"For God and our country we'll fight till we die"
Here's welcome to wounding and combat and scars
    And the glory of death—for the Stripes and the Stars!" [26]

Southerners, too, imagined gathering a nation together under the official Confederate flag, the "Stars and Bars," which had been adopted in March 1861. "Our Flag" evoked a farflung Confederate nationalism:

Fling it out, fling it out, in its glory and might,
    With the sky its colors blend;
Where'er there's a spot by the tyrant oppressed,
    Where'er a home to defend—
Where'er there's a weak despairing one,
    Where'er a soul to inspire.
Where'er they would yield to oppressor's foul rod,
    Where'er a bosom to fire.

Likewise, Cora Livingston's "The Confederate Flag" asserted that "This great flag of victory / Shall float far and wide," and "Stand by That Flag" urged, "Dim not a single star that decks / The Southern flag o'erhead, / And let its light ne'er cease to glare / But wider LET it spread!" All these poems asserted the importance of the national flag as a symbol uniting a farflung national community, at the same time that they implicitly created a rhetorical community of nationhood.[27]

Because there was no universal agreement early in the war on what the new Confederate national symbols were, such poems were also part of a public conversation regarding the nature of Southern nationhood. Southern poets did not necessarily agree, for instance, on whether the derivative-looking new Confederate flag retained the best of the "Star-Spangled Banner" or forcefully repudiated it. On one side of the issue, Theo H. Hill advised his fellow Southerners to "Tear down the flag of constellated stars!," arguing that "It flouts the breeze, / A flagrant-flaunting insult to the sky; / Disgraced at home—dishonored on the seas." Likewise, in "Away with the Stripes," "Kentucky" advised, "Ho! away with the stripes, the despots' fit flag! / The stars and the stripes are the bully's great brag." J. R. Barrick commented that the flag "to which we clung / In years agone, hath ceased to be / The pride on which we hung." And Mrs. E. D. Hundley's high-wrought May 1862 "Farewell, Forever, the Star Spangled Banner" counseled:

> Let tyrants and slaves submissively tremble
>   And bow down their necks 'neath the Juggernaut car;
> But brave men will rise in the strength of a nation
>   And cry "Give me freedom, or else give me war." [28]

Yet even as many writers rejected Northern national symbols in their attempts to create new symbols for the Confederacy, they drew on familiar motifs: a number of songs, for instance, rewrote the "Star-Spangled Banner" for the South, such as St. George Tucker's paean to "The Southern Cross," which would become the official Southern flag in May 1863. "Oh, say can you see," began Tucker's poem, "through the gloom and the storm, / More bright for the darkness, that pure constellation?" Similarly, "The Flag of Secession" began

> O, say can't you see, by the dawn's early light,
>   What you yesterday held to be vaunting and dreaming?
> The Northern men routed, Abe Lincoln in flight,
>   And the Palmetto flag over the Capitol streaming.

"The Northmen shall shrink from our warrior's might," the poem concluded, "And the Flag of Secession in triumph doth wave / O'er the land of the freed and the home of the brave." [29]

On the one hand, such poems and songs asserted Southerners' right to transform what had formerly been national symbols for Confederate use. Yet because such national symbols as the flag or "Star-Spangled Banner" remained of central importance in the North, popular Confederate writers ran the risk of imitating the very culture they repudiated, with their poems enacting the very dependence on Northern culture that they spurned. M. B. Wharton self-consciously reflected on this point in "The Starry-Barred Banner," set to the tune of the "Star-Spangled Banner," by carefully enumerating the new Southern flag's difference from the Northern flag:

> O, who ever knew so majestic a view
>   As yon flag now presents, that the pure breeze is kissing,
> It resembles, 'tis true, the old "Red, White and Blue,"

But its stars are more bright, while the stripes are all missing;
Still the *stars* are all there—those that seem to be gone
Were but false *Northern lights*, which all patriots disown.[30]

As such a poem revealed, the creation of a new Southern culture inevitably exposed the many continuing cultural links between the North and the South. These perceived links were often a source of frustration and annoyance: as the *Southern Literary Messenger* claimed in January 1862, "Every body wants a new Confederate flag. The present one is universally hated. It resembles the Yankee flag, and that is enough to make it unutterably destestable." [31]

· · ·

If "everyone" wanted a new national flag, so too did everyone want a new national song—in both the South and the North. Underlining their many cultural similarities, both Northerners and Southerners, for instance, published multiple versions of the "Marseillaise" in the early months of war. The "choir of the Broadway Tabernacle church, wishing to sing the *Marseillaise*, called upon the pastor to prepare a patriotic hymn," the Northern *Independent* reported. "Arise! Arise! ye sons of patriot sires!" began the resulting hymn, while the *New York Evening Post*'s May "Song for Battle," sung to the "air" of the "Marseillaise," also urged, "Arise, arise, ye brave, / And take your swords in hand." In the *Southern Literary Messenger*, "The Gathering of the Southern Volunteers," whose refrain was "To arms, men of the South, your country shall be free! / March on, march on, each heart resolved for death or liberty," was just one among many Southern "national songs" set to the tune of the "Marseillaise" in the early months of war.[32]

Many Northerners and Southerners agreed that national songs were an integral part of an appropriate war literature. Acting on this belief, both Northerners and Southerners sought to create new national songs in wartime. In the North, a self-appointed committee of prominent New York "gentlemen," having "observed the tendency to give poetic expression to the emotion which stirs the heart of the nation," in May 1861 offered to "award a prize of Five Hundred Dollars" for a new "National Hymn, set to music." As committee member Richard Grant White observed, a national hymn seemed "almost as indispensable an appanage of nationality as a national flag." Yet there were significant problems with the "Star-Spangled Banner," which "had been growing in favor in the loyal States from the beginning of the secession movement, and was played continually by all military and orchestral bands, and sung often at concerts and private musical gatherings." The "Star-Spangled Banner" was "almost useless" as a patriotic song, White contended, since the "range of the air, an octave and a half," put it out of the compass of ordinary voices"; the lines were "too long, and the rhyme too involved for a truly popular patriotic song"; and the rhythm was not only "complicated" but often "harsh and vague" — all criticisms that still obtain today. Though "loyal Americans" longed to sing when they "assembled in those dark days of the Republic which immediately followed the bombardment of Fort Sumter," there was "no song suited to them or to the occasion." [33]

The many newspaper poems published in the first weeks of war inspired White and his fellow members of the National Hymn Committee. Among these verses "really spirited compositions appeared with sufficient frequency, considering what a very rare production good lyric poetry is, to give color to the hope that from some poet of reputation, or from some other who had his reputation to make, the wished-for song would come." After advertising its contest, which was the "subject of newspaper comment throughout the country," the committee met with an outpouring of poetry, a "response, for the extent of which" it was "not prepared." Some "twelve hundred competitors appeared upon the field," as "manuscripts came from all quarters of the country." Most of these were from amateur poets: White noted the "reluctance of poets of high and long established reputation to enter upon such a competition." [34]

What should a national hymn include? In his late 1861 volume *National Hymns: How They Are Written and How They Are Not Written*, White explained that a "hymn for Americans" must "of all things proclaim, assert, and exult in the freedom of those who are to sing it." At the same time it should be "brimful of loyalty to the flag, which is our only national symbol, and for that all the dearer"; and its "allusions" should be to "our fathers' struggle for national existence." It should also have a "strong, steady, rhythmical flow," with "simple and strong" music with a "graceful and lively strength." A song that "fulfilled these conditions, and which superadded to their requirements the inspiration that would set them all at naught, or make them entirely superfluous, would pervade and penetrate, and cheer the land like sunlight." [35]

Perhaps not surprisingly, few hymns met these lofty standards. Most, according to White, were "of interest only to their writers," the "merest common-place, brief effusions of decent dulness, or fantastic folly." Conversely, those that did exhibit "a degree of poetic excellence" were rejected as not being "popular" enough in tone: a hymn by Richard Storrs Willis, for instance, was "too subtle to suit the emotions of large masses of men, who always feel in, so to speak, the most elemental manner." Not only did the committee award no prize, but it destroyed most of the submissions. The mass of the "rejected manuscripts," which filled a "vast washing-basket" five times, "were seized upon for incendiary purposes by the cooks of the gentlemen at whose houses the meetings took place." [36]

The National Hymn Committee may have failed to produce a national hymn in the first months of war, but its concerted efforts did underline the perceived importance of patriotic poetry and song in Northern public life. Its attempts also exposed a deep uneasiness in Northern culture concerning the wartime marriage of commerce and patriotism. Newspaper response to the contest was highly critical; the press was by turns outraged and satirical at the committee's expense — "eloquent upon the theme that great songs could not, and were not, and are not, and indeed, should not, be written to order," as George William Curtis, one of the members of the committee, commented in *Harper's Monthly*. Curtis pointed out that many great writers and musicians — from Mozart to Dickens — had produced "works of the highest genius" to order. But he recognized that the press felt that "a national song is the offspring of an emotion that can not be summoned for a price." [37]

Although patriotism and commerce often fused within the Northern literary marketplace — indeed, they often undergirded each other's development and expression — a powerful cultural fiction held that expressions of patriotism were beyond the reach of commerce. As the humorist Orpheus C. Kerr (Robert Henry Newell) wrote in late June in a piece published in the *New-York Mercury*, "The Rejected 'National Anthems,'" most "acknowledged poets" claimed that "the idea of bribing the muse to be solemnly patriotic was altogether too vulgar to be tolerated for a moment by writers of reputation." Yet as he dryly remarked, the fact that so many would-be poets had submitted verses to the contest indicated a "singular resemblance between Genius and other marketable commodities." "Genius may carry with it a seeming contempt for the yellow dross of common humanity," Kerr said, but "it has to pay its occasional washerwoman." [38]

A few humorists writing early in the war provided a satiric counterpoint to the hundreds of patriotic poems published in newspapers and journals throughout the North. Newell, for instance, satirized the rejected anthems of the "venerable committee," asking, "Must they *all*, therefore, be lost to the world?" before providing his own parodies, including a "National Anthem" by "Ralph Waldo E———."

> Source immaterial of material naught,
>   Focus of light infinitesimal,
> Sum of all things by sleepless Nature wrought,
>   Of which abnormal man is decimal.
>
> Refract, in prism immortal, from thy stars
>   To the stars blent incipient on our flag,
> The beam translucent, neutrifying death;
>   And raise to immortality the rag.

Tongue in cheek, Newell commented that "this 'anthem' was greatly praised by a celebrated German scholar; but the committee felt obliged to reject it on account of its too childish simplicity." [39]

The humor magazine *Vanity Fair* also satirized the "Rejected National Hymns," saying, "By special favor to Vanity Fair, on the part of the Committee, we are allowed to publish a few of the unsuccessful hymns." Its first offering was "A Psalm of Union; Or, What the Heart of the Zouave Said to Uncle Sam," which included the verse

> War is real! War is earnest!
>   And defeat is not our goal;
> "Mud-sill, thou to mud returnest,"
>   Is not true, upon the whole. [40]

Such satires caught the banality and even absurdity of much patriotic verse catalyzed by war, but they also highlighted the visibility and prominence of war songs within Northern culture early in the war. So prevalent were patriotic war songs that in March 1862 *Vanity Fair* published "A Hint to Poets: Showing How to Make a War Song," which provided fill-in-the-blank instructions for would-be war poets that drew on the conventionalized language of war:

> I.
> The air is glad with bannered life
>   And gay with pomp of stripes and stars!
> (Here, for the rhyme, you'll mention "strife,"
>   And happily allude to "Mars.")
> A nation musters to the field,
>   Truth to maintain and wrong to right!

(Here promise that the foe shall yield,
And promise it with all your might.)

II.

Rebellion rears its rampant head,
  And Hate lets loose the dogs of war,
(Here speak about the "gory bed"
  Where heroes are provided for.)
But while the hearts of freemen beat,
  And while their hands can wield the sword—
(Describe them pouring "leaden sleet,"
  And falling on the "traitor horde.")[41]

Like Northerners, Southerners early in the war also attempted to create "national songs"—indeed, this was a much more urgent project in the South than in the North, where, after all, the much-criticized "Star-Spangled Banner" was at least acknowledged as an unofficial national anthem. Yet although many Southerners considered a national song to be an important part of their new national identity, they, too, had difficulty in deliberately producing such a song. The poet Henry Timrod reported in 1861 that he had been asked to create a "warlike ode" set to music, but though he attempted to "write a national song," his work "failed to satisfy [him] and [he] destroyed it." Timrod took some comfort from the fact that "but the other day all the Yankee poets (and it cannot be denied that there are some noble ones among them) were trying, with the incentive of a prize of five hundred dollars before them, to manufacture a national hymn; yet they all signally failed."[42]

The need for a national song—and the failure to produce it—became a reiterated motif of Confederate periodicals during the war. "Now that we are separated forever from the fanatics of the North," the *Southern Illustrated News* urged in September 1862, "it behooves the literary men of our native South to put themselves energetically to the work of furnishing our people with a national anthem." But its own offering of a national song, James Barron Hope's "Oath of Freedom—A National Hymn," did not have the popular impact that the *News* desired. "Who shall write our national songs?" the *Magnolia Weekly* asked in 1863. "Nearly three years have elapsed since the birth of our nation, and we have produced but a very few respectable ballads, not one of which can be called 'National.'" Commenting that "there never was a time which offered finer opportunities for national song writing," the *Magnolia Weekly* demanded, "Do our

Bards draw no inspiration from their country's struggle for liberty? We hope that we may see, before the war is over, a collection of national songs, of which we may always be proud."[43]

But such was not to be. By 1864 the *Southern Punch* admitted that "that much talked of 'national song' [had] not yet been written." The poet Henry Timrod agreed. "A short while ago," he mused in January 1864, "everybody was calling for a national song. The few poets who are to be found in the Confederacy, were importuned to write one, and many attempts to supply the want were made, both by poets and poetasters, without the slightest success." Timrod did not blame poets for this state of affairs: "A nation does not choose its songs on the ground of poetical merit. In fact, it does not choose them at all." A song's "diffusion throughout a nation depends upon some fortunate conjunction of time, mood, association, and circumstance."[44]

Timrod's perceptive comment reminds us that while there were no agreed-on "national songs" during the war in either the North or the South, there *were* songs that were national in popularity, even if only briefly. As Timrod commented about James Randall's "My Maryland," "None, with the exception of 'My Maryland,' and that only for a little time, touched the heart of the people so deeply as to become one of its representative songs." In the North, "John Brown's Body," rewritten by Julia Ward Howe as "The Battle Hymn of the Republic," achieved a similar popularity.[45]

"The war had hardly begun," Oliver Wendell Holmes remembered in 1865, "when a strange song shaped itself on the lips of the thousands who were marching to the southern battle-fields. That song never finished itself. It began grand, noble, almost sublime,—it changed to doggerel and stopped, ashamed of itself, but never had any proper ending.

John Brown's body lies a mouldering in the grave,
　His soul is marching on!

These were the lines that thundered like the crack of doom in the ears of the proud rebels who had hung the old man up between heaven and earth." Expressing a deeply religious Unionism, the second verse proclaimed: "He's gone to be a soldier in the army of the Lord!" Yet it was true, as Holmes commented, that the later verses of the song, such as "They will hang Jeff. Davis to a tree!," did not carry forth this religious theme.[46]

"John Brown's Body" was a widely popular song—"so familiar that printed copies were hardly necessary," according to Holmes—but it did not attain the dignity of a "national hymn" until it was reshaped by individual imagination. In November 1861 Julia Ward Howe and some friends were returning from a review of troops outside Washington, D.C. on a road "nearly filled" with soldiers. "We presently began to sing some of the well-known songs of the war," she later remembered, among them "John Brown's body lies a-moldering in the grave." "This seemed to please the soldiers," she recalled, "who cried 'Good for you,' and themselves took up the strain." One of her companions, the minister James Freeman Clarke, said, " 'Mrs. Howe, why do you not write some good words for that stirring tune?' I replied that I had often wished to do this." The next morning, in the "gray of the morning twilight," the "long lines of the desired poem began to twine themselves in my mind." Using an "old stump of a pen" in the "dimness" of her hotel room, Howe "scrawled the verses almost without looking at the paper." They were published by the *Atlantic Monthly* as the "Battle Hymn of the Republic" in February 1862 and then widely copied throughout the North:

Mine eyes have seen the glory of the coming of the Lord:
He is trampling out the vintage where the grapes of wrath are stored;
He hath loosed the fateful lightning of his terrible swift sword:
    His truth is marching on.

I have seen Him in the watch-fires of a hundred circling camps;
They have builded Him an altar in the evening dews and damps;
I can read His righteous sentence by the dim and flaring lamps.
    His day is marching on.

I have read a fiery gospel, writ in burnished rows of steel:
"As ye deal with my contemners, so with you my grace shall deal;
Let the Hero, born of woman, crush the serpent with his heel,
    Since God is marching on."

He has sounded forth the trumpet that shall never call retreat;
He is sifting out the hearts of men before his judgment-seat:
Oh! be swift, my soul, to answer Him! be jubilant, my feet!
    Our God is marching on.

In the beauty of the lilies Christ was born across the sea,
With a glory in his bosom that transfigures you and me:
As he died to make men holy, let us die to make men free,
    While God is marching on.[47]

These were images of a powerful, martial God, of a triumphant, holy Unionism. Much commentary on "The Battle Hymn of the Republic" has stressed, rightly, the importance of biblical imagery in its creation, including especially Isaiah 63:1–6: "I have trodden the wine press alone; and of the peoples there was none with me: for I will tread them in mine anger, and trample them in my fury." The assumption has been that Julia Ward Howe was directly inspired by her knowledge of the Bible in the creation of her hymn.[48]

Yet the powerful imagery of being "a soldier in the army of the Lord" was widespread throughout Northern culture in the early months of war, present not only in "John Brown's Body" but in numerous newspaper poems as well, where poet after poet associated God's favor and blessing with the Union. "God for Our Native Land!" was a hymn sung on May 5 in New York, one of many poems and hymns using this phrase. "Freedom's God is o'er you," said Elizabeth D. Wright in a *New York Tribune* poem addressed to soldiers; "Our Union and Liberty! God and the Right!" affirmed a poem by David J. Dickson, while H. A. Moore asserted that "God leads our loyal host; / God is our people's boast," and concluded that "God leads the fight!" Numerous Northern poets also invoked the "Christian warrior," in both a martial and sacrificial mode. W. F. L.'s "Redemption," for instance, made an explicit connection between the soldier's sacrifice and Christ's sacrifice, commenting that "in each blood-drop from each breast, / See the red tide that Calvary pressed," and concluding that "nations rise/ Through sacrifice." In writing "The Battle Hymn of the Republic," then, not only did Julia Ward Howe draw deeply on her own reading of the Bible, but she also drew on an extensive popular culture in which biblical imagery was omnipresent. The composition of the hymn involved an intermingling of individual and collective imagination, as Howe built on popular forms.[49]

Southern poets were equally as confident as their Union counterparts that God was on their side; E. K. Blunt asserted in "The Southern Cross," for instance, that "On our side, Southern men, / The God of battles fights!" and George H. Miles's "God Save the South" proclaimed, "Let the proud spoiler know / God's on our side!" But the most popular Southern songs of the early war were not counterparts of these Northern celebrations of what Edmund Wilson called "the Union as religious mysticism"—they were instead defiant calls for vengeance. Here was a marked difference in the tonality of Northern and Southern early wartime patriotic poetry.[50]

Among popular songs, James Randall's "My Maryland" was "decidedly the most popular, for a season," of the "claimants to be a national song," the *Southern Punch* noted in 1864. Like Julia Ward Howe's "The Battle Hymn of the Republic," Randall's "My Maryland" was written "almost involuntarily" in the middle of the night on April 26, 1861. Randall, a New Orleans professor of English literature and the classics, found that he "could not sleep" after reading of the attack on Massachusetts troops as they crossed through Baltimore. "Some powerful spirit appeared to possess me," Randall remembered, and he "rose, lit a candle, and went to [his] desk," where "the whole poem was dashed off rapidly" under "what may be called a conflagration of the senses, if not an inspiration of the intellect." Like numerous other wartime poets, Randall also admitted that a desire for individual recognition fueled his effort: "I was stirred to a desire for some way of linking my name with that of my native State," he said.[51]

In 1865 Oliver Wendell Holmes offered a victorious Northerner's view of the differences between "John Brown's Body" and "My Maryland," which he recognized as the most popular songs of the early months of war. The two sections of the country had stood "face to face," he said, "each with a sword in its hand, each with a song in its mouth." "If one chooses to indulge the fancy which sees puritan and cavalier" in the "two parties at strife, the songs may help out the conceit," he continued. "One is a hymn, with ghostly imagery and anthem-like ascription. The other is a lyric poem, appealing chiefly to local pride and passion." "My Maryland" urged Maryland to "Avenge the patriotic gore / That flecked the streets of Baltimore, / And be the battle-queen of yore, / Maryland! My Maryland!" Characterizing the enemy as "Northern scum," it called to Maryland to reveal her "peerless chivalry" and to "gird thy beauteous limbs with steel." "Thy beaming sword shall never rust, Maryland!"[52]

"My Maryland" highlighted themes of vengeance that were already keynotes of Southern war poetry, just as it also helped to further disseminate these themes. When a "lady of Baltimore," Hetty Cary, set Randall's lyrics to the music of "Lauriger Horatius" (also the melody for "Tannenbaum, O Tannenbaum") in order to impress her patriotic glee club, she set in train events that would help "My Maryland" find "its way to the hearts of our whole people, and become a great national song."[53]

The expressions of vengeance in "My Maryland" were familiar to Southerners in a wide range of newspaper poetry. Southerners had long characterized "Yankees" as greedy and materialistic, characterizations that only intensified in wartime as Southern writers used such stereotypes not only to imagine an enemy in wartime but to create a national identity in opposition to the North. As "The Cotton States' Farewell to Yankee Doodle" put it,

Yankee Doodle's grown so keen
    For every dirty shilling—
Propose a trick, however mean,
    And Yankee Doodle's willing.

So Yankee Doodle, now good-bye,
    Keep the gains you've gotten—
Proud independence is the cry
    Of Sugar, Rice and Cotton.[54]

This was familiar rhetoric, but in wartime Southerners began to portray Northerners in far more brutish terms as well. In poem after poem, Southern writers characterized Northerners as "ruffians," "minions," "villains," "vandals," "vampires," "wolves," "robbers," and—in Randall's "My Maryland"—"scum." [55]

By 1862 the most sensationalized wartime poems, such as John Killum's "Old Betsy," went even further by warning of Northern violence against Southern white women:

Hear ye the yelp of the North-wolf resounding,
    Scenting the blood of the warm-hearted South;
Quick! or his villainous feet will be bounding
    Where the gore of our maidens may drip from his mouth.[56]

Likewise, the first-person narrator of S. Teakle Wallis's summer 1862 "The Guerrillas" reported:

Where my home was glad, are ashes,
    And horror and shame had been there;
For I found on the fallen lintel,
    This tress of my wife's torn hair! [57]

These sensationalized poems argued, first of all, that men must join in the public war effort in order to fulfill their private obligations to protect women. As one newspaper poem, "The South in Arms," put it, "Tis not the love of bloody strife, / The horrid sacrifice of life, / But thoughts of mother, sister, wife, / That stir their manly hearts." [58]

At the same time "The Guerrillas" imagined that such violence against women would result in a white brotherhood based on the desire for revenge among Southern men:

> By the graves where our fathers slumber,
>> By the shrines where our mothers prayed,
> By our homes, and hopes, and freedom,
>> Let every man swear on his blade—
>
> That he will not sheath or stay it
>> Till from point to heft it glow,
> With the flush of Almighty vengeance,
>> In the blood of the felon foe!
>
> They swore; and the answering sunlight
>> Leapt red from their lifted swords,
> And the hate in their hearts made echo
>> To the wrath of their burning words! [59]

With themes that anticipated the postwar creation of the Ku Klux Klan, this poem emphasized the importance of imagining the new nation as a defiant, heroic white brotherhood bent on vengeance.

"The Guerrillas" was more sensationalized than many early wartime poems, but its themes of proud defiance and vengeance ran through dozens of early wartime Confederate verses. Catherine Warfield's "Southern Chant of Defiance," for instance, encapsulated many of the patriotic themes of the early war, with its evocation of white Southern racial superiority over the North, its hymn to Southern defiance and violence, and its praise of Southern manhood.

> You can never win them back—
>> Never! never!
> Though they perish on the track
>> Of your endeavor;
> Though their corses strew the earth,
> That SMILED upon their birth,
> And blood pollutes each hearth-
>> Stone forever!
>
> They have risen to a man,
>> Stern and fearless;
> Of your curses and your ban
>> They are careless.

Every hand is on its knife,
Every gun is primed for strife,
Every PALM contains a life,
  High and peerless!

You have no such blood as theirs
  For the shedding;
In the veins of cavaliers was its heading:
You have no such stately men
In your "abolition den,"
To march through foe and fen,
  Nothing dreading!

Here was an embrace not only of defiance but of bloodshed as well. Such an expressed eagerness for bloodshed was a theme running through many early wartime poems, whose naive bloodthirstiness was all too soon fulfilled by the violence of war.[60]

•   •   •

Well before any deaths in battle had occurred, popular poetry in both the North and the South had imagined and celebrated both the masculinity of the warrior and his Christian sacrifice. Thus when actual deaths occurred, they were initially represented within a set of well-worn conventions, many with deep roots in antebellum culture. During the 1840s and 1850s, individuals' deaths had been mourned by family and friends in increasingly intricate public rituals of mourning requiring special clothing, stationery, and behavior. Now, with the start of war, officers' deaths were perceived to be of national importance, requiring not just commemoration by family and friends but national commemoration. Within Northern popular literary culture, an elaborate martyrology grew up around the early wartime deaths of a small group of officers in the summer and fall of 1861. Newspaper poems, patriotic envelopes, engravings, illustrations in weekly newspapers, and elaborate memorial volumes all celebrated officers' wartime deaths as redemptive sacrifices in the nation's cause.[61]

The early wartime death of Elmer Ellsworth, for instance, provoked an impassioned popular literary response. Ellsworth was already famous when the war started for the electrifying antics of his Chicago Zouaves, a militia unit. Dressed in their trademark red caps, sashes, and baggy red pants, the Zouaves had become a craze throughout the North in the summer of 1860 as they traveled from city to city displaying precision drilling and challenging local militias to gymnastic competition. The *New-York Mercury* caught the exhilarating, circuslike flavor of their exhibitions in a humorous sketch: "[A fellow] who can climb a greased pole feet first, carrying a barrel of pork in his teeth—that is a Zouave. A fellow who . . . can take a five-shooting revolver in each hand and knock the spots out of the ten of diamonds at 80 paces, turning somersaults all the time and firing every shot in the air—that is a Zouave." Although the Zouaves' colorful uniforms were later to make them fatally easy targets on the battlefield, in the high spirits of the early war their dash and brio, their colorful exhibitionism, were much admired as an appropriate approach to war. Ellsworth was an image of what many expected the war to be—the glittering, dazzling, show-uniform side of the military. Indeed, many felt as though they had known Ellsworth intimately because of his celebrity.[62]

When Ellsworth was killed in Alexandria in May 1861 as he sought to confiscate a Confederate flag from a hotel keeper, many mourned the loss of a hero—even though Ellsworth had never been in battle. Speaking of Ellsworth and of Theodore Winthrop, another early wartime casualty, Louisa May Alcott wrote, "Tho I never saw either I mourned over their loss as if they were my own brothers." Certainly an extensive popular culture of mourning sprang up in the weeks after Ellsworth's death, as poems, engravings, and patriotic envelopes commemorated his death.[63]

A number of early wartime poets, for instance, responded to Ellsworth's death with poems that sought to create a shared national culture of mourning. "So young, so brave, so early called," began the poem "To Ellsworth":

> We mourn above his laurelled bier;
> His name on every heart enrolled,
> To friends, and home, and country dear.

"Weep, weep, Columbia!" began the elegy "Elmer E. Ellsworth":

> Death, with traitorous hand,
> Has slain a Hero, quenched a manly flame;
> Cast heartfelt sorrow o'er a throbbing land,
> And carved, for future years to read, a name,
> On the grand altar of our Country's fame.

"Strew roses o'er his corpse," the poem instructed. "Chant, O ye Land, the soldier's burial hymn / O'er Ellsworth's bier; and as ye sadly turn, / With falt'ring voice, and eyes with teardrops dim, / Swear ye that Retribution's torch may burn / In every breast!" Several poems asserted that from such

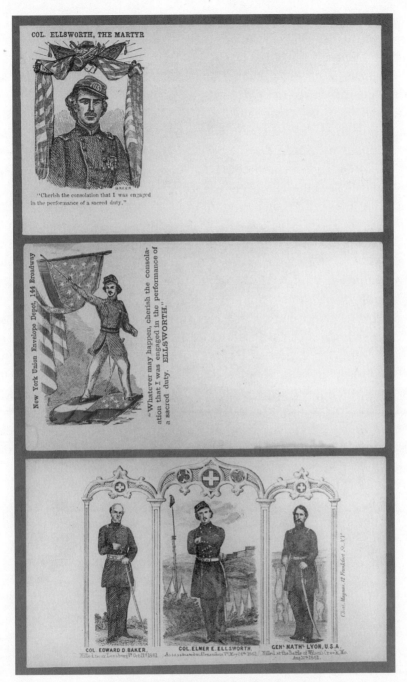

Elmer E. Ellsworth envelopes.

(Courtesy of the American Antiquarian Society)

death came a birth of patriotism: "Weep o'er the heroes as they fall," instructed Charles William Butler. "O'er Ellsworth's early tomb, / And by his dark, funereal pall, / Bid patriot life-buds bloom."[64]

Such idealized images of mourning had less to do with Ellsworth than with a perceived need early in the war for heroes who would be symbols of nationhood. As the memorial volume *The Fallen Brave* put it, "Rome embalmed in eternal benediction the memory of her Curtius,—shall we be less grateful to a Ward, a Lyon, a Baker, an Ellsworth, a Winthrop, a Lowe, a Cameron, a Haggerty, or the other noble officers who have reckoned their lives as naught in the hour of our country's peril?" Clearly the answer was no. With "every effort" employed "to make it worthy by pen and pencil of the illustrious dead," *The Fallen Brave* offered praise to officers who formed an early wartime pantheon of death. Other memorial volumes, too, such as *The Patriot's Offering: or the Life, Services and Military Career of the Noble Trio, Ellsworth, Lyon and Baker*, commemorated fallen officers. Pointedly, martyrology had no place for privates at this stage of the war.[65]

Early wartime memorial volumes revealed a strong connection between death and commerce within the Northern literary marketplace. *The Fallen Brave* even suggested that with war and a harvest of death came future marketing possibilities, as other bodies might also receive commemoration in gilt-decorated objects: "If the present volume meets the public approval, which it honestly seeks, it will be followed in time by a second, embracing sketches of future martyrs to the cause of constitutional freedom." Although editor John Gilmary Shea never published such a volume, in 1862 he did advertise *The Victims of the Rebellion*, a "Biographical Memorial of Officers Killed in Defence of the Union," which he promised would be published in "semi-monthly Numbers, price 25 cts. Each."[66]

A number of publishers perceived and acted on the commercial opportunities to be found in early wartime death. Publisher James T. Fields of Ticknor and Fields, for instance, participated in the popular culture of martyrology by publishing the posthumous works of novelist Theodore Winthrop. Winthrop had been unable to find publishers for his fiction before the war, but his literary career briefly received new energy when, with the outbreak of war, he became a military correspondent for the *Atlantic Monthly*. His June "Our March to Washington" was flavored with the high spirits of the early days of war: "It was worth a life, that march," he exclaimed of the New York Seventh Regiment's march down Broadway. He talked, too, of a night march near Washington on a "night inexpressibly sweet and serene," but in the fashion of new soldiers he confessed, "After

I had admired for some time the beauty of our moonlit line, and listened to the orders as they grew or died along the distance, I began to want excitement." He reveled in small soldierly discomforts such as being caught in the rain, feeling that he was "receiving samples of all the different little miseries of a campaign." In his last sketch, the posthumously published "Washington as a Camp," he buoyantly summarized a day in camp: "It is monotonous, it is not monotonous, it is laborious, it is lazy, it is a bore, it is a lark, it is half war, half peace, and totally attractive, and not to be dispensed with from one's experience in the nineteenth century." [67]

After Winthrop's death at Great Bethel on June 10, his friend George William Curtis eulogized him in the *Atlantic Monthly*, characterizing Winthrop's writing as "charming by its graceful, sparkling, crisp, off-hand dash and ease." Winthrop, Curtis said, had been but "a lovely possibility before he went to war." His life, "like a fire long smouldering, suddenly blazed up into a clear, bright flame, and vanished." [68]

Yet Curtis shied away from transforming his friend into an icon, saying, "I do not wish to make him too much a hero." For many in the North, however, the mere fact of Winthrop's early death established his heroism. Acting on intense public interest in Winthrop, Fields acquired Winthrop's unpublished works from his family and released the novel *Cecil Dreeme* in October 1861, advertising that "Major Winthrop's brilliant contribution to the *Atlantic Monthly*, and his early death on the field of battle, [had] established his reputation as a writer and a hero." Fields published four more works by Winthrop during the war, each of which achieved respectable sales of several thousand copies. Ironically, only through death in war was Winthrop able to achieve the literary success that had eluded him in life. [69]

If wartime memorial volumes revealed a close connection between wartime death and commercial literary culture, they also revealed a profound link between death and a fervent Unionism. The elaborate mourning rituals that commemorated the deaths of fallen heroes became a means of linking Northerners symbolically to one another early in the war. *The Last Political Writings of General Nathaniel Lyon, U.S.A.*, for instance, a volume that commemorated the death of Lyon at Wilson's Creek, Missouri, in August 1861, provided readers with an elaborate depiction of Lyon's funeral ceremonies. A passage of thirty pages vividly portrayed the funeral cortege that had carried Lyon's coffin from city to city for public viewing before burial, reassuring the reader that "the whole proceedings were conducted with that solemnity and good taste which were due to the memory of the departed soldier." Among the many civilians who "gazed upon the coffin" were "hundreds of ladies"; it was "a refreshing sight," the book said, to see "tender-hearted women weeping as they passed through—a just tribute to the memory of the soldier."[70]

Popular poetry was often a part of this funereal ritual. In New York, the volume noted, one woman placed a poem titled "To the Lion-Hearted Gen. Nathaniel Lyon" on his coffin. In addition, published poems celebrated Lyon, with one asserting that his name would be "immortal," engraved on "history's brightest page," and "fame's glowing portal." Another, titled "Half-Mast," imagined that "on thy martial bier / The tears of grateful millions flow." Such poems and commentary provided Northerners with images that confirmed and celebrated their expressive support of Union.[71]

Southerners, too, participated in an early wartime culture of martyr-ology, although within a constricted literary marketplace their means of expression were more limited, usually involving newspaper poems rather than the elaborate gilt-decorated volumes available to Northerners. Still, the short-lived *Southern Monthly* began a column called "Necrology" in October 1861, intended "to enshrine the memories of those brave patri-ots who [had] fallen upon the field of battle, or those who [had] yielded their lives on the altar of their country." And if Northerners wept over Elmer Ellsworth, Southerners mourned his killer, James W. Jackson, who had been shot by troops accompanying Ellsworth. The *Southern Field and Fireside* poem "Jackson, Our First Martyr," for instance, talked of Jackson as a "Martyr patriot":

Yes! he hath won a name,
Deathless for aye to Fame,
Our flag baptised in blood,
Away as with a flood,
Shall sweep the tyrant band,
Whose feet pollute our land.[72]

Likewise, in "Jackson, the Alexandria Martyr," William H. Holcombe apostrophized Jackson, "O type of our impetuous chivalry!," who pos-sessed "fierce, heroic instincts to destroy / The insolent invader." James W. Simmons's "The Martyr of Alexandria" imagined a shared culture of mourning, as "A nation gathers round thy bier, / And mourns its friend." In addition to such poetry, by early 1862 the *Richmond Whig* advertised a new memorial volume for sale, *The Life of James W. Jackson, the Alexandria*

Hero, the Slayer of Ellsworth, the First Martyr in the cause of Southern independence. But it was only with the 1863 death of the other Jackson—Stonewall Jackson—that Southerners produced an outpouring of mourning poetry to rival that of Northern publications.[73]

• • •

As deaths in actual battles mounted, and as it became clear that the war would last far longer than had initially been assumed, the popular literary response to wartime death began to shift and expand, however. To be sure, in the wake of the July 1861 victory at Bull Run, or Manassas, Southerners initially expressed an often giddy sense of triumph in an outpouring of poems. The broadside poem "Hurrah for Jeff. Davis," written by "a Lady Rebel," gloated, "We've whipped them some five or six times," and the broadside poem "Bull Run" gleefully suggested that the battle should be called "Yankee Run." In a more solemn vein, Susan Archer Talley proclaimed

> Now proudly lift, oh sunny South,
>   Your glad, triumphal strains,
> From fair Virginia's verdant hills
>   To Texas's sandy plains.
> Now glory to our Southern bands,
>   That crushed the Northern foe,
> That swept away their gathered hosts,
>   And laid their banners low.

Numerous other Southerners, too, registered their delight over Manassas in celebratory verses. "Now glory to the 'Lord of Hosts!' oh, bless and praise His name," wrote Mary Bayard Clarke, "For he hath battled in our cause, and brought our foes to shame."[74]

Yet increasingly in the wake of battlefield deaths, both Southerners and Northerners began to produce more somber forms of popular literature. A number of Northern poets responded to the defeat at Bull Run with a sense of desolation: "Help lips white with anguish to take up His prayer," wrote Alice B. Haven in her "Bull Run, Sunday, July 21st." Sarah Helen Whitman's "After the Fight at Manassas" began:

> By the great bells swinging slow
> The solemn dirges of our woe,

By the heavy flags that fall
Trailing from the bastioned wall,
   Miserere, Domine![75]

These were not surprising responses by Northerners to their unexpected defeat at Bull Run. But by the end of 1861, the tone of much Southern war literature had changed as well. The high spirits, the cockiness
that characterized much early wartime poetry were increasingly complemented, if not replaced, by a mood more dark and restrained. As "Christmas Day, A.D. 1861" put it,

No festive garlands now we twine
   For walls all echoless;
No viands rare and costly wine
   Our vacant boards oppress;
The empty chairs at every hearth,
With sad suggestions banish mirth.

The poet "Libertina" asked, "Can the Glory of War Atone for Its Misery?" and answered:

Not all the pageantry of war,
The gleaming sword, the glittering star,
The laureled hero's gallant tramp,
The panting steed's impatient stamp—
Not the ten thousand giddy charms
That sound a nation's call "to arms,"
Can atone for the sundering of *one* heart.[76]

Both north and south, popular writers also measured the great distance
they had traveled from the beginning of the war. Gertrude Grant's elegiac
"One Year Ago," written for the *Atlanta Southern Confederacy* in May 1862,
remembered the fervor with which Southerners had greeted the war:

Scarcely has one twelvemonth gone by
Since thousands, at their country's cry,
With bounding hearts and spirits high,
   Rushed out to meet the foe;
We waved and cheered them to the fray,
And bade them "God speed" on their way—
'Twas in the smiling month of May,
   One year ago.

Now, however, all had changed. "Where now is all that martial band— / Those soldiers brave, those heroes grand," she asked before answering her own question: "Many a lonely forest grave, / O'er which the drooping yew trees wave, / Is all that's left of those so brave / One year ago." [77]

• • •

Early in the war patriotic poetry was an important part of a shared public culture of war. The Southern poet Mary Bayard Clarke, who wrote her "The Battle of Manassas" "in the cars while on [her] way to the encampment of the 14th," found that before she had "had time to do more than copy it out fairly" the poem was "seized by an officer" who "took it to his camp and read it" to his fellow officers. Not only did they give her "three cheers," but they requested the "liberty of publishing it" and sent it to the *Richmond Enquirer*. Printed also as a broadside by the editor of the *Raleigh Standard*, it was "sold for the benefit of the sick soldiers of the 14th." Clarke commented that she "had applications for" the poem "from all parts of the Confederate States." Such poetry was an expressive part of the shared public experience—and performance—of war. [78]

In the North as well as the South, numerous newspapers printed poems that urged citizens to unite themselves to the nation at war. As *Harper's Monthly* noted in July 1861, "The Poets' Columns in the newspapers have become almost as formidable as those of General Scott." Poem after patriotic poem celebrated a fusion of individual and national interest, imagining the war creating a new Union out of diversity in the North, and a new blood brotherhood among whites in the South. In the wake of the first wartime deaths, the bodies of "martyrs" were represented as a symbolic means of imagining a unified national body, both north and south. [79]

Yet the popular interest in poetry celebrating a unified, abstract nationhood shifted dramatically after the first months of war. Increasingly, commentators found in the personal experience of war itself the real "poetry of war." Young men found "in themselves, and quite unsuspectedly, so much that is the very substance of romance and the music of poetry," *Harper's Monthly* noted in September 1862. "It is not given to all," Charles Congdon wrote, "to weave the eternal lyric verses." But the "soldier, in the far-away camp and thinking of his home," the "statesman, by whose prudence we are to be saved," the "mother, giving her loved ones to the land—the rich man and the poor man, each offering all—the child, raising his tiny flag and saluting it with his young, fresh voice—*all* these are poets—patriots, if you will—yes, patriot-poets!" [80]

Increasingly, the lived, personal experience of war became the subject of war literature. Although "war-songs" and "battle-calls" were published throughout the conflict, they were supplemented with an extensive literature that insisted instead on the primacy of the individual experience of war. Remembering this shift in emphasis in 1864, the *Atlantic Monthly* writer Mrs. Furness looked back in wonder on the early spirit of war. "We entered gayly on our great contest," she wrote. "At the first sound from Sumter, enthusiasm blazed high and bright. Bells rang out, flags waved, the people rose as one man to cheer on our troops." But this was before the harrowing realities of battle reshaped both Northerners' and Southerners' understanding of war. "When we saw our brave boys, whom we had sent out with huzzas, coming back to us with the blood and grime of battle upon them, maimed, ghastly, dying, dead," she commented, "we knew that we, whom God had hitherto so blessed that we were compelled to look into the annals of other nations for misery and strife, had now commenced a record of our own. Henceforth there was for us a new literature, new grooves of thought, new interests." [81]

The Sentimental Soldier

These Hospitals, so different from all others—these thousands, and tens of twenties of thousands of American young men, badly wounded, all sorts of wounds, operated on, pallid with diarrhea, languishing, dying with fever, pneumonia, etc., open a new world somehow to me, giving closer insights, new things, exploring deeper mines than any yet, showing our humanity, (I sometimes put myself in fancy in the cot, with typhoid, or under the knife,) tried by terrible, fearfulest tests, probed deepest, the living soul's, the body's tragedies, bursting the petty bonds of art. To these, what are your dramas and poems, even the oldest and tearfulest?
—*Walt Whitman*, Correspondence, *March 19–20, 1863*

"Oh! it is great for our country to die," began a poem published in the *Boston Transcript* on May 28, 1861; "Bright is the wreath of our fame; glory awaits us for aye." "It is well—it is well thus to die in my youth, / A martyr to freedom and justice and truth!" proclaimed the narrator of the October 1861 *Southern Monthly* poem "The Dying Soldier." At the start of the war, numerous popular poems in the North and South offered variations on the classical adage *dulce et decorum est pro patria mori*, imagining the subordination of individual interests to the needs of the nation. Diarists, too, approvingly noted the patriotic sentiments of such literature: Caroline Cowles Richards of Canandaigua, New York, for instance, reported in May 1861 that it seemed "very patriotic and grand" to hear departing soldiers singing " 'It is sweet, Oh, 'tis sweet, for one's country to die.' " [1]

Yet by 1862, and then in increasing numbers as battle deaths mounted during 1863 and 1864, popular poems that asserted the importance and individuality of the ordinary soldier began to act as a counterpoint to poetry that stressed the subordination of individual interests to the needs of country. Sentimental stories and songs also focused intently on the individual experiences of the ordinary soldier on the battlefield and in the hospital, especially imagining that soldier's thoughts at the moment of death.

Even as the mass movements of armies increasingly defined the war and the outcome of battle was increasingly mass slaughter, sentimental literature often explicitly fought against the idea of the mass, instead singling out the individual soldier as an icon of heroism. This popular insistence on the individual, personal meanings of the war was far more prevalent than is usually recognized, and it militated against developing ideas of the war as new forms of system and organization in American life. Writing about Northern intellectuals, for instance, George Fredrickson has suggested that during the war "a process of natural selection was occurring which was giving more relevance to impersonal efficiency than to pity or compassion." At the same time, because "there were clear limitations to what could actually be accomplished for the relief of the wounded and dying, a stoical and fatalistic sense of the inevitability of large-scale suffering was also being inculcated. Implicit in both developments was a challenge to those antebellum humanitarians who believed that sympathy was the noblest of emotions and that all suffering for which human beings could be held responsible was unacceptable and called for immediate relief." [2]

Fredrickson's comments provide an acute analysis of the experiences of many Northern intellectuals, especially those who sought to systematize the care of wounded soldiers under the auspices of the Sanitary Commission. Yet within a wide-ranging popular literature and among a broad reading public, a sentimental insistence on the importance of sympathy and individual suffering increasingly became the most potent mode of discussing and coping with the wounding and killing of soldiers during the war.

The sentimental soldiers of this popular literature were not "realistic" in the modes later developed by late-nineteenth-century social realism, with its insistence on the primacy of "fact" and a mimetic depiction of social conditions. Rather, these literary soldiers were highly conventionalized and typologized, presented within a framework of sentimentalism that insisted on the primacy of emotion and sentiment as a form of "reality." Both a popular mode of thought and language of expression in mid-nineteenth-century America, sentimentalism emphasized the central importance of emotion in the individual's life. For sentimentalists powerful feelings structured individual identity, but not as the bursts of solitary rapture or the intimate communion with nature earlier celebrated by English romantics, or, in a different key, by American transcendentalists. Sentimentalists celebrated sympathy, not self-communion; they portrayed experiences of emotion as social events rooted in human relationships, legitimized through being witnessed by or communicated to another.[3]

It was because sentimentalism stressed the social—and potentially transformative—nature of emotion that antebellum sentimental literature often included deathbed scenes in which a character's impending death had a powerful impact on the lives of witnesses. The most famous of all antebellum sentimental deathbed scenes, for instance, Little Eva's lingering death in *Uncle Tom's Cabin*, was portrayed as a profoundly social act, with one after another of the characters in the novel receiving guidance and inspiration through their last contact with her. Her death was conceived of as deeply spiritual, as well: *Uncle Tom's Cabin* was written within an explicitly Christian framework—what one scholar has called the "Sentimental Love Religion" of sacrifice, suffering, and redemption that in the mid-nineteenth century increasingly offered a stirring, personalized alternative to the sometimes grim rigors of Calvinism. Within this emotive religion the bodily sufferings and deaths of little Eva and, especially, Uncle Tom were crucial elements of a redemptive Christian national parable, in which the exercise of a sacred domesticity was imagined as being able to redeem the nation from the sin of slavery. A vast antebellum popular literature shared Stowe's concern with the Christian-influenced themes of sacrifice, suffering, and redemption—especially through the vehicle of the suffering body.[4]

With the coming of war, the wounded, dying, and dead bodies of soldiers became the vehicle for a new sentimentalism that fused patriotism and Christianity. Walt Whitman, who became a hospital visitor in Washington, D.C., in 1862, reflected on the experiences and deaths of soldiers in letters, notebooks, and articles, as well as a group of poems ultimately published in 1865 as *Drum-Taps*. His poem "A Sight in Camp in the Day-Break Grey and Dim," for instance, explicitly associated the dead body of a soldier with Christ: after examining, outside a hospital tent, a corpse with "a face nor child, nor old, very calm, as of beautiful yellow-white ivory," the narrator directly addressed the body:

Young man, I think I know you—I think this face of
    yours is the face of Christ himself;
Dead and divine, and brother of all, and here again he lies.[5]

Sentimentalism provided a way of making sense of the bodily sacrifices of soldiers within an explicitly Christian framework. It also allowed wartime writers to cope with a central problem posed by the war: the shocking anonymity of suffering and death undergone by ordinary soldiers far from home. This was an aspect of war that many Americans found unbearable: they simply could not accept that soldiers' suffering and death would go unsung and unmourned. As George William Curtis noted in *Harper's Monthly* in June 1862, during the first year of war there had been many "leaders" in the army whose "heroic names and acts" were "repeated and remembered with joy and pride." But Curtis reminded his readers that there were many "unnamed heroes" as well, who "marched with no less lofty purpose" and who fought "with the same bravery" as their leaders. "When we count our treasures," Curtis urged, "let us remember the unnamed, the devoted sons and brothers and husbands and lovers, who have obeyed the call of their country" and "have marched to battle and to death, knowing that their fall must be unknown to all but those whose homes it would darken, and whose hearts it would break." In March 1862 the *Southern Monthly* also urged its readers to remember the "unlaureled heroes," who "fall undecked with victory's splendors." Both north and south, writers not only asserted the importance of remembering *all* "fallen soldiers" during the war but implicitly and explicitly assigned literature a central role in accomplishing this task.[6]

Many writers during the war also expressed their indignation that soldiers' deaths occurred among strangers or that soldiers might be nameless or unknown in death. The idea that there might be "unknown soldiers" as an inevitable aspect of warfare only took hold in the wake of World War I; the Tomb of the Unknown Soldier was dedicated in 1921. During the Civil War, in contrast, many writers protested against the idea that soldiers were alone or even anonymous when they died. Whitman, for instance, wrote at length to his mother in 1864 of "one poor boy" who "groaned some as the stretcher-bearers were carrying him along—& again as they carried him through the hospital." Though "the doctor came immediately," it "was all of no use," for the soldier had died at the hospital gate. "The worst of it is too," Whitman said, that he was entirely unknown—"there was nothing on his clothes, or any one with him, to identify him—& he is altogether unknown—Mother, it is enough to rack one's heart, such things—very likely his folks will never know in the world what has become of him— poor poor child, for he appeared as though he could be but 18."[7]

The Soldier's Grave. This Currier and Ives print offered a means
of personalizing and commemorating soldiers' deaths.
(Courtesy of the Library Company of Philadelphia)

Louisa May Alcott, too, registered indignation and sorrow at the solitary death of a soldier in her 1863 *Hospital Sketches*. Her narrator, Nurse Tribulation Periwinkle, had just gone to get a drink of water for a patient, but when she came back, "something in the tired white face caused [her] to listen at his lips for a breath." Nurse Periwinkle continued,

> None came. I touched his forehead; it was cold: and then I knew that, while he waited, a better nurse than I had given him a cooler draught, and healed him with a touch. I laid the sheet over the quiet sleeper, whom no noise could now disturb; and, half an hour later, the bed was empty. It seemed a poor requital for all he had sacrificed and suffered,— that hospital bed, lonely even in a crowd; for there was no familiar face for him to look his last upon; no friendly voice to say, Good bye; no hand to lead him gently down into the Valley of the Shadow; and he vanished, like a drop in that red sea upon whose shores so many women stand lamenting. For a moment I felt bitterly indignant at this seeming carelessness of the value of life, the sanctity of death.

For both Alcott and Whitman, it was a cultural affront that wartime death occurred outside the framework of sentimental norms that emphasized a tender, emotive parting from family and friends.[8]

Many of the most popular poems of the war attempted to provide exactly that tender, emotive death. "Somebody's Darling," for instance, first published in the South but reprinted widely both north and south, counseled the reader/witness to take a final, tender parting of an anonymous soldier who had just died in the hospital:

> Kiss him once for *somebody's* sake;
>   Murmur a prayer, soft and low;
> One bright curl from the cluster take—
>   They were somebody's pride, you know.[9]

Likewise, John Reuben Thompson's popular "The Burial of Latané," first published in the *Southern Literary Messenger* of July and August 1862, imagined a tender funeral among sympathetic strangers for a slain Confederate captain:

> A brother bore his body from the field,
>   And gave it into strangers' hands, that closed
> The calm blue eyes, on earth forever sealed,
>   And tenderly the slender limbs composed:

Strangers, yet sisters, who, with Mary's love,
Sat by the open tomb, and weeping, looked above.

As with Whitman's "A Sight in Camp in the Day-Break Grey and Dim," the poem made an explicit connection between the body of the dead soldier and the body of Christ.[10]

Many wartime poems softened the brutal realities of war by aestheticizing death. "Somebody's Darling," for instance, lingered over the dead soldier's features:

Back from the beautiful, blue-veined face
    Brush every wandering, silken thread;
Cross his hands as a sign of grace —
    Somebody's darling is still and dead![11]

"Beautiful Lines" painted the "sorrowfully impressive" scene of a soldier's death through pathetic fallacy:

We smoothed the bed, and softly laid him there,
We turned back from his brow his curly chestnut hair;
And while the wind outside went raging past,
While leafless trees bent, groaning, to the blast,
We laid his trusty musket by his side —
He grasped it, held it to his heart — AND DIED![12]

A number of Southern poems aestheticized soldiers' deaths by setting them within a pastoral landscape. Northern poems, in contrast, rarely utilized this device, no doubt because Union soldiers' deaths usually took place on "foreign" soil. "The Dying Soldier," for instance, first printed in the *Southern Field and Fireside*, imagined a pastoral death in fulsome language:

Lay him down gently, where shadows lie still
And cool, by the side of the mountain rill,
Where spreads the soft grass its velvety sheen,
A welcoming couch for repose so serene.[13]

In the poem "Missing," as well, a lushly conceived landscape was the setting for a dead soldier, whose still form offered a striking contrast to the sounds and motion of springtime life around him:

In the cool, sweet hush of a wooded nook,
    Where the May buds sprinkle the green old mound,

And the winds, and the birds, and the limpid brook,
    Murmur their dreams with a drowsy sound;
Who lies so still in the plushy moss,
    With his pale cheek pressed on a breezy pillow,
Couched where the light and the shadows cross
    Through the flickering fringe of the willow?
        Who lies, alas!
So still, so chill, in the whispering grass?

In this poem, the site of the "missing" soldier's death was a "secret" that was "safe with the woodland grass." If the manner of the soldier's remote, isolated death meant that expressions of sympathy could not be provided by other people, it did not mean that sympathy for the soldier was lacking. Instead, nature itself provided a tender, emotive death for the soldier, as "The violets peer from their dusky beds, / With a tearful dew in their great, pure eyes," while "The lilies quiver their shining heads, / Their pale lips full of a sad surprise." [14]

Hundreds of popular songs and poems during the war grappled with the fact of mass, anonymous death by creating idealized deaths for soldiers. While numerous poems sought to aestheticize the dead body of the soldier or the site of his death, far more poems and songs gave voice to dying soldiers' thoughts. "Dying soldier" poems had been published during the Mexican War, too; D. W. Belisle's "The Dying Soldier to His Mother" was but one example of war poetry that ventriloquized dying soldiers' thoughts. But during the Civil War this sentimental poetry exploded in popularity. Published throughout the war in both the North and the South, these poems and songs were ubiquitous, with songs in particular sometimes selling hundreds of thousands of copies. In October 1864, for instance, an ad in *Harper's Weekly* claimed that the song "Who Will Care for Mother Now?" had in "less than one year attained the unprecedented sale of over half a million copies." [15]

These "dying soldier" poems have traditionally been dismissed as "mere" sentimentality, but that view obscures the importance of these poems within Civil War culture, allowing little means of analyzing the meanings of the war they shaped both north and south. It is useful to note that at the time of the war, even as a number of Northern intellectuals questioned the efficacy of sentimental humanitarianism, several commentators asserted the cultural value of these sentimental poems. In an 1865 lecture entitled "The Poetry of the War," for instance, Oliver Wendell

Holmes reflected on the "ballads and sentimental pieces which are numbered by the thousand" and are "piled up by the gross on counters" for sale. "There is a genuine and simple pathos in many of them," he concluded. "I do not know whether it sounds scholarly and critical and all the rest, but I think there is more nature and feeling in some of these [songs] than in very many poems of far higher pretensions and more distinguished origin." Holmes told his audience, "If I should read the familiar lines 'Dear Mother, I've come home to die,' and could read them as they ought to be read, you may be very sure that the light would trouble a good many eyes before it was finished." [16]

Holmes's comments give important clues to the significance of these poems and songs for a Civil War audience: not only did they ventriloquize the dying thoughts of soldiers, thereby countering the brutal anonymity of death, but they also allowed a form of communication between the imagined soldier and his listener—in reality a reader on the home front. These poems imagined the soldier as an emotive and sympathetic figure, but they also, by implication, imagined the listener/reader on the home front as similarly emotive and sympathetic. Thus these poems imagined tight links between home front and battlefront, links that were in fact usually broken by the soldier's death far from home.

Dying soldier poems did not so much deny the deaths of soldiers as perform the difficult cultural task of making those often anonymous deaths appropriately meaningful. It was widely assumed during the war that soldiers' deaths held great meaning; the idea that such deaths might be senseless only fully emerged in the wake of World War I. Yet it was also widely assumed that for soldiers' deaths to be meaningful that meaning needed to be expressed; it was only through the creation of appropriate representations—whether funeral rituals, monuments, or poems—that the fallen soldier could be appropriately memorialized. In other words, the inverse of the Victorian obsession with self-representation was the fear that a lack of such representation threatened nonexistence.[17]

Thus it makes sense that in a war of unprecedented slaughter, in which ultimately more than six hundred thousand men died, there were an unprecedented number of poems, too, that over and over again imagined the dying thoughts of soldiers. The task of making soldiers' deaths meaningful was one that required constant effort; the sentimental meaning of the soldier's life could not simply be generated once but needed to be re-created over and over again. Hundreds of dying soldier poems were the result, both north and south.

Many of these began with a brief account of a soldier's death from a newspaper and then elaborated on that account in the poem that followed. "You'll Tell Her, Won't You?," for instance, published in the *Richmond Dispatch* of October 4, 1862, prefaced the poem with a brief quotation from a witness who had described a soldier's last moments. "Shot through the lungs," the soldier "clasped a locket to his breast and moved his lips till I put down my ear and listened for his last breath—'You'll tell her, won't you?'" The witness commented, "Tell who or what I could not ask, but that locket was the picture of one who might be wife, sweetheart, or sister." This quotation was presented as the inspiration for the poem that followed—a common device for poems and songs throughout the Civil War.[18]

The subsequent poem, however, no longer accepted the soldier's whispered last moments but instead imagined an eloquent dying speech for him:

You'll tell her, won't you? Say to her I died
    As a brave soldier should—true to the last,
She'll bear it better if a thought of pride
    Comes in to stay her, the first shock o'er past!

You'll tell her, won't you? Show her how I lay
    Pressing the pictured lips I loved so well;
And how my last thoughts floated far away,
    To home and her, with love I could not tell.

You'll tell her, won't you?—not how hard it was
    To give up life—life for her sake so dear;
Nay, nay, not so! Say it 'twas a noble cause,
    And I did die for it without a tear.

You'll tell her, won't you? She'll be glad to know
    Her soldier stood undaunted, true as steel,
His heart with her, his bosom to the foe,
    When the blow struck no human power could heal.

You'll tell her, won't you? Say, too, we shall meet
    In God's Hereafter, where our love shall grow
More holy for this parting, and more sweet,
    And cleansed from every stain it knew below.[19]

This poem touched on a number of motifs that underlay "dying soldier" poetry during the war: the concern for a loved one at home; the desire for and memory of home itself; the soldier's acceptance of death, because it had been in a "noble cause"; the desire to communicate his last thoughts to his loved one; and his assurance that his sacrifice would receive a heavenly reward. All of these were considered appropriate deathbed or dying thoughts, and they were reiterated in numerous poems during the war. In this poem, as in many others during the war, such imagined thoughts acted as an explicit form of compensation for the difficult truth that the dying soldier often had no time to compose the well-wrought sentences and final thoughts that were considered an appropriate part of Victorian death.[20]

Like so many dying soldier poems, "You'll Tell Her, Won't You?" concentrated not on the martial identity of the soldier but on his identity as an individual tied to family and home. Indeed, surprisingly few battle poems achieved real popularity during the war, despite the fact that numerous Civil War readers enjoyed—apparently without ever understanding its bitter irony—Tennyson's 1854 ballad "The Charge of the Light Brigade," with its galloping lyrics of a doomed British cavalry brigade during the Crimean War:

Cannon to right of them,
Cannon to left of them,
Cannon in front of them
    Volleyed and thundered;
Stormed at with shot and shell,
Boldly they rode and well,
Into the jaws of Death,
Into the mouth of hell
    Rode the six hundred.

Several poets imitated Tennyson's ballad, and numerous poets wrote battle poems during the war, but no ballad or poem of comparable popularity emerged during the war to celebrate the heroics of battle. The most popular Civil War poems and songs, on the contrary, were those that turned away from battle and imagined the thoughts of individual soldiers.[21]

Among those imagined thoughts, by far the most prevalent involved the soldier's mother. In 1865 Oliver Wendell Holmes commented that he had "obtained from several vendors" in Boston and in New York "copies of

THE
Dying Confederate's Last Words

1.

Dear comrades on my brow the hand of death is cast,
My breath is growing short, all pain will soon be past;
My soul will soar away to that bright land of bliss,
Far from the pain and woe of such a world as this.

2.

I left my home and friends to battle with the foe,
To save the Southern land from misery and woe;
I gave my life my all (oh! not to win a name,
Or have it e'en enrolled upon the scroll of fame.)

3.

Not so, I only wished a helper brave to be
To save the glorious South from cruel tyranny;
My soul with ardor burned the treacherous foe to fight,
And take a noble stand for liberty and right.

4.

But oh! how weak is man! It was not God's decree,
That I should longer live a helper brave to be,
Before another day I shall be with the dead,
And 'neath the grassy sod will be my lonely bed.

5.

And should you see the friends that nurtured me in youth,
Tell them I tried to walk the ways of peace and truth;
O! tell my mother kind the words that she has given,
Have led her wayward child to Jesus and to heaven.

6.

Farewell! farewell! my friends my loving comrades dear,
I ask you not to drop for me one bitter tear;
The angels sweetly stand and beckon me to come,
To that bright land of bliss that heavenly realm my home.

MARYLAND.

"The Dying Confederate's Last Words," by Maryland,
was one of many poetic broadsides published during the war.
(Courtesy of Rare Books and Manuscripts Department,
Z. Smith Reynolds Library, Wake Forest University)

the songs most largely sold to soldiers and others." There was "one little fact" about these "that must find its way to every heart": "What thought was most constantly present with those who were hurrying to the conflict, who were fainting on the march, who were bleeding on the battle-field, who were languishing in prisons? These were the men who were doing the hardest work that falls to manhood. And out of thirty-three songs lying before me, selected by different vendors as the most popular according to their sales, no less than fourteen find their inspiration in the sacred name of *mother*." [22]

"Mother Would Comfort Me," a song with words and music by Charles Carroll Sawyer, was a typical example of this genre. As was true of many Civil War songs, it began with an explanatory note: "A soldier in one of the New York regiments, after being severely wounded, was taken prisoner; and after lying in the hospital for a number of days, he was told by those who were in attendance that 'they could do no more for him,' that he must die. For a few moments the poor fellow seemed in deep thought; reviving a little, he turned slowly toward those near him, and after thanking them for the kind manner in which they had treated him during his sickness, a sweet smile pased over his pale face, and with a firm voice he said, 'Mother would comfort me, if she were here.' These were his last words." [23]

The song itself elaborated on this theme, ventriloquizing the dying soldier's thoughts and especially stressing the soldier's loneliness, his distance from home, and the fact that he was "unknown":

Wounded and sorrowful, far from my home,
Sick among strangers, uncared for, unknown;
Even the birds that used sweetly to sing
Are silent, and swiftly have taken the wing.
No one but Mother can cheer me today,
No one for me could so fervently pray:
None to console me, no kind friend is near—
Mother would comfort me if she were here.[24]

The reiteration of thoughts of mother reminds us that the Civil War occurred within a widespread maternalist culture that celebrated soldiers' connections to their mothers as an appropriate feminization of their characters. The emphasis on mother was an intertwined social and cultural reality: soldiers often spoke and wrote of their mothers, at the same time that it was widely perceived that it was appropriate that they do so. In a small "Hospital Note Book" that Walt Whitman carried with him, for instance, he noted about a "poor unfortunate boy" shot for desertion on June 19, 1863, that "he was very fond of his mother"; "he tried to get away to see his mother"; and again, "he was dotingly fond of his mother." Numerous other hospital visitors also noted soldiers' concern for their mothers.[25]

During the war the concept of manliness included feminized components that late in the century would be excised from new concepts of masculinity. On appropriate occasions it was considered manly to show emotion, even to cry, for instance; indeed, in a wide variety of popular poems weeping was presented approvingly as a tribute to a dead comrade. At the same time, within a culture of domesticity that tightly bound not just women but also men to their homes, the soldier's imagined longings for home were also deemed highly appropriate and represented not only in poems and songs but also in numerous popular engravings. "I'm thinking of my distant home, / That Eden spot of earth to me, / And something comes across my eyes / I do not care my men should see!" were lines of Viola's "By the Camp Fire," published in 1863 in the *Southern Illustrated News*. The widely reprinted Currier and Ives engraving *The Soldier's Dream of Home* showed a soldier sleeping on the ground while thinking of his wife and children on the home front.[26]

Caroline A. Mason's much reprinted poem "The Soldier's Dream of Home" also imagined a soldier longing for his wife and three children:

Oh, my very heart grows sick, Alice,
    I long so to behold
Rose with her pure, white forehead,
    And Maud, with her curls of gold;
And Willie, so gay and sprightly,
    So merry and full of glee;
Oh, my heart *yearns* to enfold ye,
    My "smiling group of three!"[27]

Soldiers as well as civilians were moved by this poem. One soldier wrote to Mason that his own family was an "almost exact copy of the picture you have painted." "Such lines as yours," he said, "carry with them many a blessing as they are read by the exiled soldier—self exiled as many of us are, away from home, kindred and friends, especially from the dear ones of his heart."[28]

Expressions of such longings for home, but especially for mother, were part of a shared popular literary culture both north and south. In February 1863, for instance, *Frank Leslie's Illustrated Newspaper* published "A Sol-

The Soldier's Dream of Home.
(Courtesy of the American Antiquarian Society)

dier's Letter," which began, "Dear Mother—in my lonesome tent, / With battle-whispers on the air, / I weave some pleasant dreams of home, / And wish myself a moment there." The next year, the same poem was published in the *Magnolia Weekly* as Southern in origin; the contributor of the poem said that "the following beautiful and touching lines were enclosed to his mother by a young Lynchburger," who was represented as having composed the poem in May 1863 shortly before "his fall in battle."[29]

Striking about the shared emotive manly universe of such poetry was the virtual absence of representations of fathers. At the beginning of the war much popular poetry and prose spoke with reverence of Revolutionary forefathers and the need to emulate them, but sentimental soldier literature rarely mentioned actual fathers. Indeed, in many popular poems soldiers' fathers were imagined to be dead, so that the imagined social universe of the war sidestepped the patriarchal authority invested in family altogether. There was a compelling reason for this: war demanded that soldiers be loyal to a new patriarchal authority, the state, as expressed in the popular enlistment poem "We Are Coming Father Abraham, Three Hundred Thousand More." As another poem put it, "Would you be a soldier, laddy? / Come and serve old Uncle Sam! He henceforth must be your daddy." With the state imagined as a new "father," the family was redefined in sentimental soldier poetry as the province of republican mothers who "gave" their sons to the state.[30]

It was mothers, not fathers, who were imagined in popular poetry to have authority over their sons' enlistment in the war, as in *Harper Weekly's* March 1862 "Mother, May I Go?" by Horatio Alger Jr.: "I am eager, anxious, longing to resist my country's foe: / Shall I go, my dearest mother? tell me, mother, shall I go?" And Oliver Wendell Holmes confessed to "some weakness about the eyes" in reading Nancy A. W. Priest's "Kiss Me, Mother, and Let Me Go," an enlistment poem reprinted in numerous collections during the war.[31]

A soldier's entire career could be charted through popular poems and songs that affirmed his connection to his mother. One of the most popular songs of the war, for instance, was "Just before the Battle, Mother," which imagined a soldier's thoughts turning to his mother the night before a battle:

> Just before the battle, Mother,
> I am thinking most of you,
> While upon the field we're watching,
> With the enemy in view. . . .
>
> Farewell, Mother, you may never
> Press me to your heart again;
> But O, you'll not forget me, Mother,
> If I'm number'd with the slain.[32]

In addition, from early in the war numerous popular songs imagined a soldier's dying thoughts turning to his mother, including Charles Carroll Sawyer's "Who Will Care for Mother Now?" ("Soon with angels I'll be marching, / With bright laurels on my brow, / I have for my country fallen, / Who will care for mother now?"); "The Dying Volunteer" ("Come mother, dear mother, oh! come to me now; / My soul wings its flight, I would see thee once more, / Again I would feel thy dear hand on my brow"); "The Dying Soldier or Kiss Me Good Night Mother" ("But mother, your kiss turns the darkness to light; / Kiss me good night, mother, kiss me good night,"); "Is That Mother Bending o'er Me?" ("Is that mother?—Is that mother bending o'er me, / As she sang my cradle hymn— / Kneeling there in tears before me? / Say! my sight is growing dim."); and Henry C. Work's "Our Captain's Last Words" ("Strangers caught his parting breath, / Laden with the murmur 'mother' / Last upon his lips in death. / 'Mother!' 'Mother!' / Last upon his lips in death"). Many of these songs circulated both in both the North and the South.[33]

With their frequent evocation of a physically passionate attachment to mother that recaptured the experience of infancy and childhood, such songs imagined soldiers as boys rather than men. As Oliver Wendell Holmes commented in 1865, "These were *boys* then who fought our battles, boys at heart, if not always, as they often were, in years and growth." Many soldiers during the Civil War were literally boys: according to estimates made by Bell Irvin Wiley, for instance, approximately 1.6 percent of Union soldiers were under eighteen years old. Still, the point remains that, according to Wiley, "the great mass" of Union soldiers, approximately 98 percent, "were neither very old nor very young, but fell in the eighteen-to-forty-five group." James M. McPherson has commented that the median age of soldiers was 23.5. Yet imagining soldiers as "boys"—a usage, tellingly, that arose during the war—was so commonplace during the conflict that it suggests a distinct cultural unease with the idea of soldiers as full-grown men separated from the maternalist culture of home.[34]

Although numerous wartime accounts, including soldiers' own letters, make clear that a social reality of the war was soldiers' intense longing for home, a simultaneous cultural reality was a culture-wide denial that those who fought for their country should be defined as men. Such denial is suggestive, indicating perhaps a widespread fear that soldiers as "men" were a frightening entity, especially in a mass that subordinated their individuality to national needs. Sentimental literature operated in contradistinction to this wartime development, creating domesticated individual soldiers characterized by tenderness of feeling and yearnings for home. Such literature emphasized that those who fought in the war were not professional soldiers but "citizen-soldiers," with the emphasis on "citizen."

Certainly many sentimental writers during the war preferred to find the essence of American manhood not on the battlefield but in the hospital, a site where men often were perceived as "boys" and where an inevitable process of reduction took place. Eben Hannaford, for instance, who published "In Hospital after Stone River" in the January 1864 *Harper's Monthly*, remembered his experience recovering from a wound in a hospital as a process of infantilization. Describing the weeks of his recovery in the hospital, he evoked the "infantile weakness" of his condition and "the utter prostration of all the powers of mind and body that form the glory and the strength of manhood." When a male nurse sang the "Battle Cry of Freedom," he found that early wartime memories "came surging back over my poor, weak, disordered brain, in a wild, sweeping rush of feeling, which I was powerless, utterly, to control." [35]

Yet it was precisely the powerless condition of soldiers in the hospital that many sentimental writers celebrated as the essence of American manhood. Whitman, for instance, wrote, "I find the best expression of American character I have ever seen or conceived—practically here in these ranks of sick and dying young men." To Ralph Waldo Emerson, Whitman wrote in January 1863, "I desire and intend to write a little book out of this phase of America, her masculine young manhood, its conduct under most trying of and highest of all exigency," and added that in Washington he saw "America, already brought to Hospital in her fair youth." [36]

For Whitman, as Betsy Erkkila has pointed out, the hospital became a metonymic figure for the nation at war. But as was true for many other sentimental writers, the nation at war did not mean the "traditionally masculine polarity of militarism, violence, and aggression" but instead was closer to the "traditionally feminine polarity of nurturance, compassion, and love." It was precisely because the hospital "softened" the aggressive masculinity associated with war that so many observers found their ideal of manhood in the hospital: it was a commonplace during the war, as William Howell Reed pointed out in his *Hospital Life in the Army of the Potomac*, that "suffering subdues and softens any nature, however rough; and that there is an influence all the time in the hospital to bring out what is purest and noblest in the heart." "Many a soldier," Reed said, "is like a September chestnut,—the outside is hard, and sharp, and shut up; but the inside is soft, and sweet, and good." [37]

Because he clung to these sentimentalized ideals in wartime, it has sometimes been suggested that Whitman was little more than a holdover from a feminized antebellum culture of sentimentalism supplanted during the war. But this view underestimates the continuing hold of a powerful sentimental culture during the war. It also wrongly presupposes that the war was primarily understood as "masculinized" in its own time, when in fact ideas of the Civil War as a "masculinized" war only coalesced in the 1880s and 1890s. Finally, this view ignores the outpouring of literature— whether poems, songs, stories, or books—during the war that celebrated a sentimentalized soldier. As the 1864 *Notes of Hospital Life* argued, "our army is no 'Corporation without a soul'" but instead "a collection of beating hearts, throbbing pulses, and straining nerves, which ask and need our love." The poem "Dying in the Hospital," published in July 1863 in the *Con-*

tinental Monthly, was one of many wartime verses that asserted the soldier's yearning for love:

> I am dying, mother, dying, in the hospital alone;
> With a hundred faces round me, not a single one is known;
> And the human heart within me, like a fluttering, wounded dove,
> Hungers with a ceaseless yearning for one answering word of love.[38]

The idea that the individual soldier in the hospital needed the love and tenderness of those on the home front became a commonplace during the war. In an 1864 *New York Times* article, for instance, Whitman wrote, "The American soldier is full of affection and the yearning for affection. And it comes wonderfully grateful to him to have this yearning gratified when he is laid up with painful wounds or illness, far away from home, among strangers. Many will think this merely sentimentalism, but I know it is the most solid of facts." [39]

At the same time, numerous writers noted that hospitalized soldiers displayed a tenderness that sometimes surprised them. William Howell Reed, for instance, noted, "It is surprising to see what tender spots there are in the hearts of some of our roughest men," and recounted the time a female nurse sang "a plaintive little song, 'Just before the battle, mother,' then the most popular song in the army, and reproduced in a hundred different ways by the soldiers or by the bands." There was "perfect stillness in the ward, the melody melted into that exquisite air, 'I'm lonely since my mother died.' Nearly every man had raised himself on his elbow to catch these notes. Some were wiping their eyes, and others, too weak to move, were hiding their emotion, which still was betrayed by the quivering lip, and the single tear as it fell, but was not wiped away." [40]

The author of *Notes of Hospital Life* also argued for the tenderness of the soldier: "It is often asserted that the sight" of "constant suffering and death, so hardens and accustoms the men to the fact, that they do not appear to feel it in the slightest degree. My own observation has led to a directly opposite conclusion." [41]

Thousands of soldiers' wartime letters, plus the reminiscences of hundreds of hospital visitors, indicate that the hospitalized soldier's tenderness, yearning for love, and longing for home were "the most solid of facts" during the war. What is of interest here, however, is not so much that the wounded soldier in hospital yearned for affection but that the literary figure of that same wounded soldier became, much like the figure of the dying soldier on the battlefield, an icon of American nationalism. This was not a nationalism located in the subordination of the individual to the demands of the Union or Confederacy, as early in the war; rather, this was a tender, individualized nationalism that located the very essence of the nation's meaning in the individual bodies of wounded soldiers.

Louisa May Alcott's *Hospital Sketches* created such an icon in the depiction of the lingering death of John, a "brave Virginia blacksmith." Published in 1863, Alcott's "sketches" were drawn from a collection of letters detailing her six weeks of experience as a nurse at the Union Hotel Hospital in Georgetown. First published in the *Commonwealth* before being reprinted in book form by James Redpath, her letters attracted a great deal of notice: as Alcott noted with delight in her journal, "Much to my surprise they made a great hit, & people bought the papers faster than they could be supplied." Alcott's sketches captured public attention at a time when interest in the hospitals was growing, reflected in a wide variety of popular literature. As Whitman noted in 1864, "As this tremendous war goes on," public interest "gathers more and more closely about the wounded, the sick, and the Government hospitals." [42]

In Alcott's fictionalized *Hospital Sketches* the sentimental drama of the dying soldier took center stage in a way that readers found immensely appealing. The centerpiece of the book was "A Night," a chapter in which the narrator, Tribulation Periwinkle, witnessed the lingering death of John, represented as an ideal type of American manhood, combining both feminized and masculinized traits. "A most attractive face he had, framed in brown hair and beard, comely featured and full of vigor," with a mouth "grave and firm, with plenty of will and courage in its lines," and a smile "as sweet as any woman's." [43]

At first, however, Nurse Periwinkle did not recognize John's tender side and found his obvious manliness disquieting. She "was a little afraid of the stately looking man, whose bed had to be lengthened to accommodate his commanding stature; who seldom spoke, uttered no complaint," and "asked no sympathy." It was only when John inadvertently revealed his feminized, tender side, through crying, that Periwinkle responded to him fully. "I had forgotten," Periwinkle said, "that the strong man might long for the gentler tendance of a woman's hands, the sympathetic magnetism of a woman's presence, as well as the feebler souls about him." Noticing John looking "lonely and forsaken," she saw "great tears roll down and drop upon the floor." Now she was able to respond to him not as a self-sufficient man but as a boy: "My fear vanished, my heart opened wide and took him in," and she gathered "the bent head in [her] arms, as freely as if he had been a little child."[44]

Periwinkle's account stressed John's boyish qualities: although he was almost thirty and "the manliest man" among the patients Nurse Periwinkle cared for, he also said " 'Yes, ma'am,' like a little boy"; and "his eyes were child's eyes, looking one fairly in the face." As Periwinkle's account made clear, it was only through recognizing John's powerless, enfeebled, boyish qualities that she could fully celebrate him as a soldier. Afraid of the manly man, she was tender and compassionate with the homesick, yearning boy. It was this side of the soldier that her readers celebrated, too: as a surgeon at the Union Hospital wrote to her, "These papers have revealed to me much that is elevated, and pure, and refined in the soldiers' character, which I never before suspected. It is humiliating to me to think that I have been so long among them with such a mental or moral obtuseness that I never discovered it for myself."[45]

Imagining John as a sentimental soldier allowed Alcott to create a meaningful death for him, one in which he settled his affairs by having Periwinkle write a farewell to his family; said good-bye to a comrade by kissing each other "tenderly as women"; and, after suffering greatly at the last, saw "the first red streak of dawn" and "seemed to read in it a sign of hope of help, for, over his whole face there broke that mysterious expression, brighter than any smile, which often comes to eyes that look their last." This last evocation of the dawn, a conventional mode of rendering sentimental death, allowed Alcott to suggest that John's sufferings might be the vehicle to ultimate redemption, thus keeping John's death within the parameters of the "sentimental love religion."[46]

At the same time, imagining John as a sentimental soldier allowed Alcott, like other sentimental writers during the war, to claim possession of the soldier through special knowledge of his real nature and needs. This possessive relationship to the soldier was a theme running through the writings of sentimental authors, who claimed knowledge of the tender, often elevated qualities of the soldier that neither the government nor sometimes even soldiers themselves possessed. As Whitman wrote, "I know what is in their hearts, always waiting, though they may be unconscious of it themselves."[47]

This sense of special knowledge empowered witnesses to soldiers' suffering, who responded to the widespread sentimental belief that the suffering body should "speak" or communicate its pain in public by publishing, or attempting to publish, their hospital experiences. Hannah Ropes, for instance, a nurse who was Louisa May Alcott's superior at Union Hotel Hospital, hoped in the winter of 1862 that the *Boston Advertiser* would send her "a *good price*" for excerpts from her journal. Also in late 1862, Charles Edward Lester, a prolific antebellum writer of popular biography and history who had been visiting hospitals in Washington, D.C., sent the Philadelphia publisher G. W. Childs a proposal for a book "on a subject which nobody has treated to any extent." To be called "Heroism in the Hospital," his proposed work "would abound in scenes of personal heroism in the midst of sufferings indescribable." Lester planned to speak of "*1st the heroism of soldiers during painful operations*—which by the concurrence of our veteran surgeons exceeds all they ever before witnessed in civil or military or believed to be possible," and "2—The heroism of the Soldier *dying from wounds, operations, or disease.*"[48]

The "main object of the work," he said, "will be to carry the brave & suffering soldier's *heart*, back to his home—to show how deep and unquenchable is the *amour patriae* in the young hero's breast." Yet it would "by no means be a book of horrors," he reassured his publisher. "It will rather be characterized by tenderness of sympathy." If he was "not entirely deceived," Lester said, "Heroism in the Hospital" could be "made a popular book." After all, he concluded, "Heroism & feeling will forever be the most attractive features of popular books, & this little work I speak of has both in abundance."[49]

The idea that stories of suffering soldiers might be popular points not just to the highly commercialized nature of the wartime literary marketplace in the North but also to the confidence on the part of a number of writers that representations of the war would be popular with a widespread reading public. This confidence also underlay a wide-ranging book project that Walt Whitman proposed to James Redpath in late 1863. After the success of Alcott's *Hospital Sketches* the previous summer, Whitman proposed "a book of the time, worthy the time—something considerably beyond mere hospital sketches—a book for sale perhaps in a larger American market—the premises or skeleton memoranda of incidents, persons, places, sights, the past year." Whitman especially had "much to say of the hospitals," including "many hospital incidents" that would "take with the general reader." He concluded, "[My book] should be got out *immediately*. I think an edition, elegantly bound, might be pushed off for books for presents etc. for the holidays, if advertised for that purpose. It would be very appropriate. I think it a book that would please women. I should expect it to be popular with the trade."[50]

Neither Ropes nor Whitman published their proposed books during the war. But there is at least anecdotal evidence to indicate that Alcott's book appealed to a variegated reading public who found in it reflections of the sentimental war they desired. Henry James Sr. responded to this aspect of Louisa May Alcott's *Hospital Sketches* when he wrote to tell her "how much pleasure" he had taken in her "charming pictures of hospital service" and "how refreshing he found the personal revelation there incidentally made of so much that is dearest & most worshipful in woman." James's comment reveals how important the responses of the witness to suffering were within literary sentimentalism, which involved two sets of relationships: that between the sufferer and witness to suffering, and that between author/narrator and audience.[51]

At the same time, at least one intriguing piece of evidence suggests that soldiers themselves sometimes enjoyed Alcott's representations of their hospital experiences. The nurse Amanda Akin Stearns recorded in her diary of December 6, 1863, that "when evening came" she sat next to one of her soldier patients "to keep him from feeling lonely and dispirited" at a time when "thoughts of home came very sweet and its comforts seemed very far off." She then "read aloud a chapter from Miss Alcott's 'Hospital Sketches,' which seemed to entertain a number very much, particularly my sensible John," who said "he did not see where such an interesting book came from; he had not been able to get such and would like to buy it." Such a comment raises the possibility that soldiers' own views of their hospital experiences may have been shaped by wartime popular literature.[52]

Sentimental literature discussing the hospitalized soldier redefined heroism during the war, moving heroism from the battlefield to hospital. A. S. Hooker's "Hospital Heroes," published in 1863 in *Frank Leslie's Illustrated Newspaper*, denied that "all the heroes" were on the battlefield, instead asserting that "our hospitals are full of heroes," who "uncomplaining die." As Mrs. H. (Anna Morris Ellis Holstein) wrote in her 1867 *Three Years in Field Hospitals of the Army of the Potomac*, Union soldiers endured "suffering with a heroism which exceeds even the bravery of the battle-field." William Howell Reed, too, noted this "harder heroism of the hospital."[53]

Moreover, such literature ascribed heroism to the ordinary soldier, not to the officers that had been celebrated in early wartime literature. Lester, for instance, titled one of his chapters "The Real Heroes of the War—The

Rank and File in the Hospital." Alcott, too, chose an ordinary soldier to become her iconic hero of the war. She consoled herself "with the thought that, when the great muster roll was called, these nameless men might be promoted above many whose tall monuments record the barren honors they have won."[54]

As the anonymous female author of the 1863 *Notes of Hospital Life* wrote, "at the opening of the war" she had thought "that the finer feelings of our nature were exclusively the property of the higher classes." But two years as a nurse in a military hospital, "where men appear mentally as well as physically in 'undress uniform,'" had shown her "the utter fallacy of such a theory." Now, in fact, she did "not hesitate to affirm" that she had "seen there as much unwritten poetry, tender feeling, aye, and love for the beautiful" as she had "ever witnessed among the same people gathered together at any time, or in any place." She dedicated her volume "to the Privates of the Army of the United States; whose daring in danger; patience in privation; self-sacrifice in suffering; and loyalty in love for their country, have given to the world a noble example, worthy of all imitation." Another nurse simply said, "The heroes are in the ranks."[55]

This literary process of redefining heroism occurred in both the North and the South. In 1863 the *Southern Punch* printed "Private in the Ranks," a poem that claimed "Deserving most, too oft forgot, a high-toned nation's thanks" was "one of nature's noblemen—the private in the ranks." In another piece the *Southern Punch* protested against the use of the phrase "common soldiers" to "distinguish the rank and file, from uncommon soldiers—officers." "Let us have no more of this," the magazine urged. "These 'common soldiers' constitute the flower and chivalry of the South." And in Augusta Jane Evans's *Macaria*, near the end of a lengthy account of the hospital death of a young private named Willie, the narrator urged that her compatriots remember that "we are indebted for Freedom" to the "uncomplaining fortitude and sublime devotion of the private soldiers of the Confederacy, not less than to the genius of our generals and the heroism of our subordinate officers." If early in the war the martyred officer had seemed emblematic of nationhood, increasingly during the war popular literature insisted on a democratization of heroism—and by extension a democratization of the nation itself.[56]

In "The Hero without a Name," the Confederate poet W. S. Hawkins reflected on his own wartime shift in ideas of what constituted heroism, writing, "I loved, when a child, to seek the page / Where war's proud tales are grandly told," before mentioning such boyhood heroes as Sir Launcelot and Light-Horse Harry. "But little I hoped myself to see," the narrator continued, "a spirit akin to these stately men." "Yet, I've seen in the wards of the hospital there, / A hero, I fancy, as peerless of soul." This hero, a wounded soldier and "a pale-faced boy," suffered "through the day's long pain and gloom," yet "he never makes a moan!" The narrator concluded,

> And somehow I think, when our lives are done,
>   That this humble hero—without a name—
> Will be greater up there, than many a one
>   Of the high-born men of fame.[57]

Adulation of the ordinary soldier occasionally crossed both class and ethnic lines. Northern hospital visitors and nurses who "discovered" the ordinary soldier sometimes wrote of Irish or German soldiers, for instance, though they maintained ethnic stereotypes in their writing, particularly in associating Irish soldiers with what one author labeled "Irish humor." Alcott wrote humorously of caring for a "withered old Irishman, wounded in the head," who offered her the blessing "May your bed above be aisy darlin', for the day's work ye are doon!" Likewise, she spoke of a "big Prussian, who spoke no English," with whom she shared an "irrepressible laugh" after together taking care of a recalcitrant fellow patient. William Howell Reed, too, spoke of "a young German, a noble fellow," who "had been in every battle of the Army of the Potomac." Within him were "smoldering those old fires of liberty which had allured him to this country, and finally into the strife; and he was there fighting for a cause which he believed to be his cause, as it was the cause of every oppressed people on earth."[58]

Praise for the ordinary soldier in popular literature sometimes crossed ethnic lines, but such adulation rarely crossed racial lines, even though African American soldiers were a vital military presence in the North after 1862. Walt Whitman was one of the few hospital observers who mentioned his care of and interest in black soldiers. In an 1864 *New York Times* article he claimed, "Among the black soldiers, wounded or sick, and in the contraband camps, I also took my way whenever in their neighborhood, and I did what I could for them." However, in a letter to his mother he was more candid: "I went once or twice to the Contraband Camp, to the Hospital, etc. but I could not bring myself to go again—when I meet black men or boys among my own hospitals, I use them kindly, give them something, etc.," but "there is a limit to one's sinews & endurance & sympathies." Certainly Whitman did not provide the detailed, individualized accounting of black soldiers that he provided for white soldiers. The individualized sentimental soldier was coded as white in Northern popular literature.[59]

Popular literature rarely had a place, either, for "bad" soldiers; such individuals appeared only as a strange rupture in texts that otherwise clung to the notion of the "worthy" soldier. Alcott's *Hospital Sketches*, for instance, suggested the possibility of "bad" soldiers, but only as momentary contrasts to her noble blacksmith John, not as subjects in their own right. Railing against John's impending death, Alcott commented that "such an end seemed very hard for such a man, when half a dozen worn out, worthless bodies round him, were gathering up the remnants of wasted lives, to linger on for years perhaps, burdens to others, daily reproaches to themselves." Yet these "worthless" bodies did not appear elsewhere in her text, which otherwise maintained the fiction of her subjects' worthiness. The sentimental soldier was above all pure of heart; other soldiers existed as little more than ruptures in otherwise seamless narratives.[60]

· · ·

For countless writers during the war, it was not the soldier marching with his regiment or fighting alongside his comrades who fired the imagination but rather the lonely, isolated soldier, sometimes in extremis. Poems about picket guards, for instance, were among the most popular soldier poems of the war both north and south, and yet they imagined a soldier away from his regiment rather than as a member of it. The Northern poem "The Picket-Guard," for instance, also often called "All Quiet along the Potomac Tonight," spoke of the "quiet along the Potomac to-night, / Where the soldiers lie peacefully dreaming":

> There's only the sound of the lone sentry's tread
>   As he tramps from the rock to the fountain,
> And thinks of the two in the low trundle-bed,
>   Far away in the cot on the mountain.
> His musket falls slack; his face, dark and grim,
>   Grows gentle with memories tender,
> As he mutters a prayer for the children asleep, —
>   For their mother, — may Heaven defend her![61]

A Southern version of this poem, Carrie Bell Sinclair's "All Quiet along the Savannah To-night," also imagined a Confederate sentinel whose "visions of loved ones flit over his soul" as he wandered "back home in his dreams." As was true of so many sentimental soldier poems published during the war, both "The Picket-Guard" and "All Quiet along the Savannah To-night" made clear that the soldier retained a primary connection to home.[62]

"The Picket-Guard" also stressed the soldier's extreme vulnerability:

Was it moonlight so wondrously flashing?
It looked like a rifle: "Ha! Mary, good-bye!"
And the life-blood is ebbing and plashing.

Likewise, a separate "The Picket Guard," published in March 1862 in the *Richmond Dispatch*, imagined a guard "at his lonely post" who felt "the foe's first deadly brunt" and died. Such poems were part of a popular litera-ture that vicariously embraced the violence of war, as Charles Royster has pointed out. But this embrace did not necessarily mean a shallow cele-bration of violence; rather, the many sentimental soldier poems published in wartime sought to comprehend and make sense of the violence of war individual by individual, and life by life—a task that grew ever more for-midable over the course of the conflict.[63]

Such a task required a form of imaginative sympathy that deepened the war's meanings for observers, as they found in the bodies of wounded and dying soldiers a new and revelatory way of comprehending country. In sentimental soldier literature, it was not an abstract notion of country that made the individual deaths of soldiers meaningful but the reverse: the suffering and deaths of soldiers themselves provided a new way of under-standing a previously abstract nationhood. "For herself the lesson of the day had not been unfolded in vain," commented a character in Alice B. Haven's "One Day," a *Harper's Magazine* story of one woman's visit to an army hospital. "She had seen all now. Loss, suffering—weary hearts, brave, hopeful hearts—" and, in the death of one soldier, "the drama's close." She knew that this suffering and loss "was but a tithe of the crimson harvest of War; that all over her country, in the dull walls of city hospitals, in the white tents pitched by wood and coast and stream, such scenes were daily transpiring. Her country!" she concluded. "Not only in the portion to which we are learning to limit our devotion, but in that where the wind of all this whirlwind was sown, strong men were bearing the anguish of pain and death, and women the heavier burden of suspense and breaking hearts; and she went out of the sunshine of her own undimmed life into the shadow of theirs, and so fulfilled the law of Divine sympathy and love." In doing so, she, like the authors and readers of sentimental soldier poetry, became in imagination a sentimental soldier herself.[64]

The Feminized War

Ah he kissed me, when he left me;
And he told me to be brave,
"For I go," he whispered "darling,
All that's dear on earth to save."

So I stifled down the sobbing,
And I listened with a smile;
For I knew his country called him,
Tho' my heart should break the while.

—*"Ah! He Kissed Me When He Left Me,"*
words by Mrs. Cornelia D. Rogers
and music by Lillia Dowling, 1863

Within weeks of the start of war a number of stories and vignettes stressing the vital role of women in the war effort began to appear in newspapers and popular magazines both north and south. Articles, illustrations, and stories emphasized the importance of women's domestic labor for the war effort, whether in preparing and packing provisions, sewing uniforms and havelocks (cloth pieces attached to soldiers' caps to protect them from the sun), or knitting socks and mittens for soldiers. In the North, the frontispiece of the June 29, 1861, *Harper's Weekly* was an engraving of women "making havelocks for the volunteers." In a poem titled "Stockings and Mittens," *Harper's Weekly* evoked "a thousand needles" that "glisten with the loving of remembering eyes." *Arthur's Home Magazine* commended an "army of knitters" in militarized language that itself served to link battle-front and home front, while exhorting women not "to fail to knit a pair of good yarn stockings" for the soldiers. All these works stressed women's special domestic role in the war.[1]

In the South, too, popular literature stressed the domestic contributions women could make to the war. A poem by the Southern writer Mary J. Upshur began, "Knitting for the soldiers! How the needles fly!," and "A Southern Woman's Song" urged "Quick, quick, quick, / Swifter little needle go; / From our home's most pleasant fires / Let a loving greeting flow." In addition to calling for contributions for soldiers, throughout the war Southern commentators urged women to weave and wear homespun rather than buy cloth from the North. "Oh, yes, I am a Southern girl / And glory in the name," began Carrie Bell Sinclair's "The Homespun Dress; or, the Southern Girl," before proclaiming,

> We scorn to wear a bit of silk,
>   A bit of Northern lace,
> But make our homespun dresses up
>   And wear them with a grace.

As the *Southern Monthly* summarized women's domestic role in December 1861, "Woman has a mission in this work as well as man, and while his strong arms are fighting, let her be brave, and thoughtful for the soldier's comfort, and if the shouts of victory come not as soon as wished for, still let them, with their sweet smiles, nimble fingers, and labors of love, find courage in their undertaking."[2]

Other writings stressed the central importance of women in supporting men's enlistment, sometimes explicitly drawing parallels to the actions of Revolutionary mothers. As the Northern *Arthur's Home Magazine* commented in November 1861, "Our American mother has mused wonderingly over that heroism of Revolutionary times which armed the son, and set him forth, to fight in the battles of his country. Admiration filled her heart—there was something saintly in the words, 'Our Revolutionary Mothers.' But, she did not feel strong enough for a like trial." Now, however, women were learning to be like their Revolutionary forebears: "There are few homes from which has not gone out a son, and few of these in which a reluctant heart is left behind. Our mothers are equal to their high duty, and strong enough for any sacrifice their country, in this hour of its trial, may demand." The April 20 *New York Times* approvingly reported an "incident" in a New York store in which "a matronly lady," after helping her son, a "fine youth of about nineteen years," to buy all the articles necessary for his equipment as a soldier, remarked, "This, my son, is all that

I can do. I have given you up to serve your country, and may God go with you! It is all a mother can do." Not only was the mother's remark made with "evident emotion," but "tearful eyes followed this patriotic mother and her son, as they departed from the place."[3]

Such emblematic portrayals revealed that at the outset of the war the ideology of republican motherhood continued to be an important means of imagining women's participation in the war. Early wartime feminized literature informed readers that women's appropriate role in the war was to sacrifice their sons for the sake of country, a gendered construction of patriotism that continued to be popular during the war. "The Southern Mother," for instance, a poem published in the March 1863 *Magnolia Weekly*, imagined a mother willingly sending her fourth, and last, son to war after his three brothers had died in battle. Likewise, the December 1863 poem "The Patriot Mother," published in the *Southern Illustrated News*, imagined a mother saying, "Go forth, my son, and bear a mother's blessing / Who proudly bids thee for thy country go!" "Our Mothers Did So before Us," another Southern poem urged. In the North, several enlistment poems and songs were composed as "conversations" between mothers and sons, with one *Harper's Weekly* poem, "Go, My Boy, Where Duty Calls You," an explicit answer to a previously published poem, "Mother, Can I Go?"[4]

Such literature revealed more about the culture of which it was a part than its propagandistic aims might at first suggest. As Mary Poovey has commented, texts "always produce meanings in excess of what seems to be" their "explicit design." In the case of wartime feminized literature, many of these "excess meanings" had to do with the creation of a distinctive, sentimentalized form of patriotism.[5]

The "evident emotion" and "tearful eyes" mentioned in the *New York Times* vignette, for instance, remind us that the Civil War took place within a widespread sentimental culture that valued the expression of feeling. In an extensive feminized war literature that explored women's home-front experiences, women's emotions, especially their tears, were often portrayed as giving appropriate value to men's actions, marking the transition of men from the private to the public realm and from being at home to being in the service of their country. "My tears are the tribute of anxious devotion," commented the narrator of the Confederate broadside poem "The Southern Matron to Her Son," "[but] I would not withhold thee from duty and fame."

Though my heart, may in parting, with sadness overflow,
Yet undaunted go forth to meet the invader,
   I would not detain you, oh no, my love, no![6]

In the North, Virginia F. Townsend's November 1861 series of war sketches called "Home Pictures of the Times" highlighted the tearful patriotism of women from several walks of life as they learned to sacrifice their men to the war. In one sketch, a young sister at first told her brother, "Oh, Walter, I can't let you go to the war!" But after her brother urged her to "be brave now as the sister of a soldier should, and tell me I shall go with a 'God bless you!,'" she was able to sacrifice him. Though "great tears" were "hanging down her fair cheeks," the "'God bless you!' was faint but steadily spoken." In a second sketch in the same series, a mother, "poor and old," put her "feeble arms" around her only son, and "the sobs shook her gray hair." Yet at the son's urgings — "Come now, mother, give me a real, hearty, cheerful good bye" — she "swallowed down her sobs, and drawing down the sunburnt face to her lips, she said, with a tremulous smile, 'God bless you, my precious boy!'"[7]

Such sentimentalized patriotism highlighted the idea that women, and especially mothers, personalized the nation both north and south, that they acted as a connecting link between the private and the public realm. Indeed, no sight was "more expressive," affirmed Samuel Osgood in *Harper's Monthly* in 1863, than "the good mother seated at the window from which floats the household flag, and watching intently the passing regiment, and waving her handkerchief to some friend or kinsman. The sight of her and her daughters brings the whole country nearer to us, and the great continent seems to rise before us in living personality, and to speak with her voice, and to glow with our affections. The nation seems to live in the person of its queen, and here every patriotic woman does a great deal to animate and impersonate the whole government."[8]

For departing soldiers, women and home were the most effective connection to the flag and nation. "There is a reverence for our flag amounting almost to worship; yet without some human face or word to go with it, the flag is a very insufficient incentive, and the good soldier feels its power far more when he receives the silken banner at the hands of some fair woman, and sees her cheering face wherever he marches, and hears her encouraging voice above all other music. In some way every soldier is enabled to interpret his country by some such personal association," Osgood said, "and so give it a place in his fancy and affections, as well as in his reason and conscience."[9]

Early in the war women in both the North and the South provided such "personal associations" by presenting flags to companies of volunteers in ceremonies that were often commemorated in occasional poetry. The poet "Cora's" "To a Company of Volunteers Receiving Their Banner at the Hands of the Ladies," for instance, published in the July 1861 *Southern Literary Messenger*, exhorted soldiers to guard "this fair banner—sacred trust," saying that woman's "eager eyes, / Rest upon and follow you." In late 1862, a writer in the Georgia periodical the *Countryman* agreed with Samuel Osgood that women performed an important role early in the war by making such flag presentations, commenting that "in receiving their colors, youthful warriors were inspired with firm resolution, and many a well-kept vow did they make as they took in keeping the flags delivered by the fair ones of their acquaintance; wrought by their hands; consecrated by their touch; hallowed by being associated with them in conception, construction, and presentation. He who went to the field was strengthened and buoyed up when he remembered the words of encouragement that came from the lips of the women of his home." Commemorated in newspaper poetry and commentary in periodicals, flag presentations by women ultimately made their way into popular fiction as well.[10]

Women's perceived ability to personalize the flag, and therefore the nation, also underlay the widespread popular success of John Greenleaf Whittier's 1863 *Atlantic Monthly* ballad "Barbara Frietchie." Based on an apocryphal incident, "Barbara Frietchie" told of an old woman in Frederick, Maryland, who defied Stonewall Jackson himself by flying the Union flag from her window even after his troops had shot and "rent the banner with seam and gash":

> She leaned far out on the window-sill,
>> And shook it forth with a royal will.
> "Shoot, if you must, this old gray head,
>> But spare your country's flag," she said.

Widely copied in newspapers throughout the North, made into a popular song, and the subject of numerous illustrations, "Barbara Frietchie" was one among many cultural indications that women were perceived to provide a compelling emotional connection to nationhood.[11]

Sometimes, however, that emotional connection was more astringent in nature. In addition to the many poems and stories celebrating mothers'

"Barbara Frietchie."
(From L. P. Brockett and Mary C. Vaughan, *Woman's Work in the Civil War: A Record of Heroism, Patriotism, and Patience,* 1868)

wartime role in sacrificing sons, numerous prescriptive enlistment fables, poems, songs, and cartoons turned to their daughters, portraying young women renouncing and chastising those men who refused to enlist. Often this literature emphasized young women's own earnestness and heroism even as it revealed men as cowards. T. S. Arthur's "Blue Yarn Stockings,"

SCENE, FIFTH AVENUE.

"Scene, Fifth Avenue," *Harper's Weekly*, August 30, 1862.
(Courtesy of the Henry E. Huntington Library and Art Gallery)

published in December 1861 in *Harper's Monthly*, featured a heroine who
"drank in with every breath the spirit of heroism and self-sacrifice." When
a suitor laughed at her work of knitting socks for the soldiers, she showed
him the door: "If you are not sufficiently inspired with love of country to
lift an arm in her defense," Katie Maxwell told her admirer before dis-
missing him, "don't, I pray you, hinder, with light words even, the feeble
service that a weak woman's hands may render. I am not a man, and can
not, therefore, fight for liberty and good government; but what I am able
to do I am doing from a state of mind that is hurt by levity." Likewise, Kate
Sutherland's "The Laggard Recruit," published in *Arthur's Home Magazine*

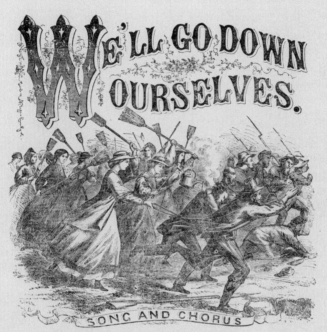

"We'll Go Down Ourselves," by Henry C. Work, 1862.
(Courtesy of the Rare Book, Manuscript and Special
Collections Library, Duke University)

in January 1862, featured two young heroines who shamed an admirer for not enlisting: "If we ladies cannot fight for our country, we can at least organize ourselves into a band of recruiting sergeants, and bring in the lukewarm and the laggards. The test of favor now is courage. Men who stay at home, court our smiles in vain." [12]

In the South, too, early wartime poems imagined women renouncing men who would not be soldiers, or sometimes even announcing that they would prefer men's death to their cowardice. As the female narrator of Alexander Meek's July 1861 *Richmond Daily Dispatch* "War Song" proclaimed:

> Rather would I view thee lying
> > On the last red field of life,
> 'Mid thy country's heroes dying,
> > Than to be a dastards' wife! [13]

The May 3, 1861, broadside "Address" echoed these themes, as it imagined a Southern woman saying,

> I'd never own,
> My looks were on a coward thrown;
> Love to a poltroon I'd ne'er give,
> But rather bid him *die* than live! [14]

Much feminized war literature in both the North and the South thus imagined women as the vehicle through which men's patriotism could be encouraged, expressed, and valorized. This is a point made in a different context by Robert Westbrook, who has argued that during World War II the figure of the pinup girl served to personify "what men were fighting for," part of "the cultural construction of women as objects of obligation" in order to persuade men to fight. Similarly, during the Civil War the figures of the patriotic mother and daughter became a way of imagining personal obligation to the state. [15]

However, not all Civil War literature representing the experiences of women concentrated on women simply as vehicles for male patriotism. Indeed, it is important to distinguish among different types of feminized understandings of the war within popular literature, for while much literature concentrated on women as a means of personalizing the nation for men, it also concentrated on the wartime home-front experiences of women themselves, finding in them a major drama of the war.

The point here is not that such home-front stories and poems eschewed patriotism in any way. In many of these stories and narrative poems plots revolved around women's need to learn to sacrifice their men for country, thereby subordinating their own needs to the larger needs of the nation. Yet these works primarily focused on women's feelings and emotional struggles as a valid, indeed central, story of the war. In doing so, they were sustained, particularly in the North, by a commercial literary culture in which literature exploring women's concerns had been a major form of cultural production before the war. In both sections, war literature representing women's experiences drew on the intertwined languages of sentimentalism and melodrama, with their central assumption that both ordinary and extraordinary events were charged with intense emotionality and significance. As Peter Brooks has written, the pervasive nineteenth-century "melodramatic mode" insisted on the "dramatics and excitement discovered within the real," including the emotions of everyday life.[16]

Many poems and songs, for instance, created narrative dramas centered around women's emotional struggles and sacrifices in allowing their men to go to war. On the one hand, these poems and songs urged women "to repress their grief, lest they weaken soldiers' resolve," as Drew Gilpin Faust has pointed out. "So I stifled down the sobbing" was a typical line in Mrs. Cornelia D. Rogers's popular Northern song "Ah! He Kissed Me When He Left Me." Yet at the same time that this literature urged women to repress their emotions, it paradoxically accentuated women's emotional struggles in doing so. Numerous narrative poems created emotional dramas in which mothers had to choose whether to allow their sons to go to war. The outcome was never in doubt, but the focus of these poems was on women's emotions, not on the glory of country. One poem and song widely popular in both the North and the South, "I Have Kissed Him, and Let Him Go," reached out to readers, especially mothers, by inviting them to share a mother's terrible dilemma:

He's my own boy, and this is my plea:
    Perhaps it is foolish and weak;
But mothers I'm sure will have pity on me,
    And some word will tenderly speak.
The light of my home—my tears fall like rain—
    Is it wonder I shrink from the blow—
That my heart is crushed by its weight of pain?
    But I've kissed him, and let him go.

Commenting that some "feel a strange pride / In giving their country their all," this narrator ultimately denied feeling such pride after sending her son to war: "But oh, sitting here, this desolate day, / Still there comes no feeling of pride." This poem demanded an acknowledgment of war's emotional cost to women.[17]

Magazine fiction also focused intently on women's feelings and emotional struggles as an important story of the war. In the December 1861 *Southern Monthly*, the heroine of "A True and Simple Tale of 1861" struggled with her new husband's request that she consent to his enlistment: "My consent! Oh, Charles, do not ask *me* to decide; for how can I give you up? Oh never, never. Why this hard lot?" Eventually, however, Ella did consent to let her husband go, "though the thought is agony." Likewise, *Harper's Weekly*'s October 1861 "Red, White, and Blue" featured a heroine who reacted with bitter anger when her fiancé told her he had enlisted. "You love your own glory better than you love me!" she accused. After breaking off her engagement, Caroline underwent a "wild, inward war," nursing "an insane sense of wrong, born of her defective education as a woman — of her ignorance." But after her lover's departure for the front, she began a new education, first by changing her reading habits: "on her table now, in place of romances," she put "newspapers and books pertaining to the various struggles for liberty in other countries, and all manner of patriotic addresses." She was "learning a new lesson. It filled her soul with sorrow and perplexity, but it elevated and enlarged it." After having a patriotic epiphany in church, then waiting in agony to hear whether her beloved had survived a battle, her education was complete: when he returned to her, she simply told him, "I was wrong, and you were right; but I sinned through ignorance. Life has wider meanings to me now. This war has been my education." She now "put mere personal ends away and flung her sympathies into the common cause." [18]

The idea that war was educational for women dominated numerous stories in which women learned the patriotic lesson that they must sacrifice their personal interests for the sake of the nation. Yet this overt, didactic patriotic lesson was only one of several lessons of such fiction, which also taught that women's emotions and personal experiences were a centrally important aspect of the conflict and that their sacrifices for the nation might even secure a personal love interest. A number of stories also made clear that the granting or withholding of women's love was a life-and-death matter, and represented women as having enormous power over men's well-being, whether in battle or in hospital. In "Jessie Underhill's Thanksgiving," published in *Harper's Weekly* in December 1862, the hero lay "sick, wounded, dying"—until hearing that the woman he thought had rejected him actually loved him. "It was like a draught of immortality, an elixir of life to me," he told her later. "I grew better under the very eyes of the surgeon, who had told me I was a doomed man." [19]

The withholding of a woman's love had the opposite effect in the *Weekly's* November 1862 "A Leaf from a Summer." In that story a soldier faced an amputation hopefully because he had a letter from his beloved "next to his heart"; afterward, contrary to the surgeon's expectations, he indeed "began to rally." But after receiving a letter telling him that his shallow lover had changed her mind and would not "marry a cripple," the hour quickly came "when they lowered him into the earth, and fired their volleys over him." As the narrator commented, "his enemy had struck him unarmed and unaware." As such popular fiction revealed, the war only intensified a long-standing literary connection between love and war: numerous stories claimed not only that women's love was vital to a successful war but also that love itself equaled war in its power to kill men. [20]

In the North, such war romances became a staple not just of *Harper's Weekly*—there were fifty-six published in the *Weekly* during 1862 and 1863 —but of numerous other monthlies and story papers, too. Even one of Henry James's earliest works of fiction, "The Story of a Year," was a war romance. By early 1864 one Northern magazine had had enough: in January the new wartime journal the *Round Table* roundly condemned the "so called 'Romances of the War' so much in vogue among magazines and 'story papers' during the two sorry years just past." These romances, the *Round Table* acerbically commented, had "but one thread of a plot to hang the incidents upon." They began with a heroine initially objecting to a lover's enlistment, "weeping 'bitter tears' upon his coat collar and murmuring—always murmuring—'I cannot spare you *now!*' " After his enlistment there followed news of a battle, in which the hero was "reported killed, or there would be no little wholesome agony to depict." Finally, at the end of the story he miraculously returned, so that the plot ended "with a wedding on the part of the couple, and a yawn on the part of the reader." This "tissue of flimsy plot, dreary platitude, and sickly sentiment," the *Round Table* complained, "floods the market of to-day, and gives us a healthy fear of opening most of the popular magazines." [21]

There was little risk of flooding the market in the South, where not only were there many fewer venues for such fiction, but even those journals publishing war fiction produced it on a more and more episodic basis under the hardships of war. Still, there were many notable congruities between Northern and Southern popular portrayals of a woman's war. The most remarkable evidence of such cultural similarity was the *Southern Illustrated News's* reprinting of four war romances—without attribution, and in some cases without even a change of title—from *Harper's Weekly* during 1863 and 1864. All these stories focused on the revelatory power of the war for women in matters of love. In "The Heart of Miriam Clyde," for instance, the heroine understood the strength of her love for the hero only when she heard he was wounded. "Suddenly the truth grew plain," the narrator commented, before providing a happy ending in which the wounded hero recovered. Southern war romances by Southern writers echoed these themes as well. Margaret Stilling's July 1863 "Love versus Pride," published in the *Southern Illustrated News*, also featured a heroine who "realized, for the first time, how truly she loved" the hero only after he was wounded. This story, too, ended happily with the recovery of the hero, though he was "a cripple for life." [22]

Not all war romances recounted miraculous returns or hospital-bed weddings, however. Indeed, despite the caustic criticisms of the *Round Table*, war romances were an indication that women occupied a far more varied and complex position in the imagined war than the *Round Table* critic was willing to acknowledge. As early as the fall of 1861, some essays and stories began to insist that a central meaning of the war was women's domestic suffering, the price they paid for personalizing the nation for men.

This cost took many forms. In the fall of 1861 a range of Northern works began to stress the economic costs of men's enlistment to women of the "laboring classes," especially as the loss of men in battle began to register on the home front. *Frank Leslie's Illustrated Newspaper*, for instance, ran an illustration titled "Distributing Relief to the Families of the New York Volunteers" in its September 7 issue and commented, "One of the most terrible effects of war is the misery and desolation it carries into our homes." In particular, it noted, "Women who have never known what it is to receive a favor are compelled by starving children to turn suppliants." Chastising the "indifference of the public to the sufferings of the wives and children," *Leslie's* hoped that its illustration would "quicken the benevolent impulses of the public" and reminded them that "the least they can do is to alleviate the privations of the bereaved families." [23]

Two Northern war stories published during this period also stressed the disastrous economic consequences of war for women, whether of the laboring classes or precariously situated on the margins of the middle classes. Carry Stanley's "The Volunteer's Wife," published in October 1861 in *Peterson's Magazine*, suggested that women of the laboring classes literally could not afford to be patriotic: "Many a wife and mother, in the laboring classes, held fearful watches" in the days of patriotic enthusiasm following Fort Sumter, the narrator commented. "To them, poor souls! their country was an abstraction, their husbands and sons the only reality." Enlistment was a practical matter: as the hero, George Campbell, told his wife, Margaret, "There is no chance for getting work I don't know when; and you'll be taken care of as a volunteer's wife, besides getting my pay." [24]

Yet the thrust of the story was to reveal that men's enlistment put women at terrible economic risk. At first Margaret, though "dreadfully poor," managed to survive on the pay George sent her. But after the news reached her that George had been killed in battle, "she began to look her future in the face, and thought she saw nothing but starvation before her." Only the miraculous return of her husband saved her from death.[25]

A second story emphasizing how precarious a woman's economic position could be in wartime was "The Tuberose: A Story of the War," published in November 1861 in *Harper's Weekly.* As in other enlistment stories, the heroine's tears were evoked as a sign of the value of both her and her lover's sacrifice: at their parting Jesie "choked the rising sob, the tears only crept slowly down the pallid cheek as with a sweet, sad smile she gazed up at him." After her lover's departure, Jessie, who in the past had been able to support herself with "a trifling sum" from "a few scholars," suddenly found that she could not make a living because her pupils were out of town. She was reduced to selling flowers on street corners, and her problems only increased when she heard that Edward had been taken prisoner, for " 'Hope deferred maketh the heart sick:' and the chill air which Jessie was so much exposed to penetrated beneath her thin shawl, and racked her slight form with pain." Finally, "she found herself unable one morning to rise" and "closed her eyes with a sad longing to be at rest—to be in the world where parting and sighing are unknown—to be where wars and rumors of wars can not reach." At this moment, however, Edward returned from the war, with an arm in a sling. Significantly, he was "wounded more painfully than by the sabre-thrust he had received" to find that Jessie had had to sell flowers to live.[26]

Both of these stories suggested the intriguing possibility that a class-based feminized critique of the war, centered on the figure of the soldier's lover or wife, was developing as early as late 1861. But though poems, stories, and illustrations throughout the war would explore its painful impact on women, including women of the laboring classes in the North, rarely did such literature directly critique the war itself. Instead, numerous stories, poems, and articles in both sections found an important central meaning of the war in women's domestic heroism, especially their suffering. Even commentators sympathetic to the economic plight of soldiers' wives tended to valorize their hardships: in her editorial "Soldiers' Wives," for instance, published in the *New York Ledger* in November 1862, Fanny Fern (Sara Parton) commented on "what an immense amount of heroism among this class passes unnoticed, or is taken as a matter of course."[27]

Writing of the wife of the poor soldier, "who in giving her husband to her country, has given everything," Fern imagined her "as the lagging weeks of suspense creep on, and she stands bravely at her post, keeping want and starvation at bay; imagination busy among the heaps of dead and wounded, or traversing the wretched prison dens, and shuddering at the thought of their demoniac keepers; keeping down her sobs, as the little daughter trustfully offers up her nightly prayers 'for dear papa to come home;' or when her little son, just old enough to read, traces slowly with his forefinger the long list of killed and wounded, 'to see if father's name is there;' shrouding her eyes from the possible future of her children, should *her* strength give out under the pressure of want and anxiety; no friend to turn to, when her hand is palsied for labor." When "the history of this war shall be written," Fern concluded, "let the historian, what else soever he may forget, forget not to chronicle this sublime valor of the hearthstone all over our struggling land."[28]

Many writers made clear that the unbearable passivity of women's role, in which the chief war work allowed them was intense feeling, itself caused enormous suffering. "Oh! what was the untold agony of those weary months that followed, day after day, and no news from the army," wrote Southern author Margaret Stilling in "Love versus Pride"; "day after day, and he might be wounded, or even dead! No wonder her cheek grew paler, and even her health declined." At the same time, however, authors argued that women's agonized waiting was a form of wartime valor. "They used to tell us," "Refugitta" (Constance Cary) wrote in the August 1863 *Southern Illustrated News*, "that what required most courage was to walk into a battle-field, and die amid its thunders. We waiting women at home can tell a different tale," she concluded.[29]

Feminized war literature consciously highlighted the "gifts" that women "lay" or "sacrificed" on the "altar of freedom"—expressions that appeared widely in feminized literature both north and south. Many stories not only insisted that women's suffering formed an important story of the war but also set up a moral economy in which women's suffering was seen as at least equal to, if not greater than, that of men. In the South, the popular poem "The Brave at Home" asserted that the "wife who girds her husband's sword" and who was "doomed nightly in her dreams to hear / The bolts of war around him rattle, / Has shed as sacred blood as e'er / Was poured upon the field of battle!"[30]

In the North, several writers made a point of quoting from Elizabeth Barrett Browning's 1861 poem "Parting Lovers":

Heroic males the country bears;
But daughters give up more than sons;
Flags wave, drums beat, and unawares
You flash your souls out with the guns
And take your heaven at once!

But we—we empty heart and home
Of life's life, love![31]

The narrator of Northern author Louise Chandler Moulton's 1863 "One of Many" claimed that women's domestic suffering, related to the passivity of their wartime role, was actually greater than the wartime suffering of men: "Honor to the brave who fight and conquer, or fight and fall! But is theirs the hardest fate? Do not those suffer more who can not lose in action their fear and anguish?—who must count slow hours, shudder at tidings of onward movements, live on fragments of newspapers?"[32]

Other writers set up explicit reciprocities of suffering in stories and poems that envisioned a tight link between home front and battlefront, between soldiers and those they left behind. If war demanded the ultimate sacrifice—life—from men, then much popular literature also argued that it demanded the same sacrifice from women. A much repeated trope in the North during the war, for instance, was the idea that every bullet killed or wounded twice, once on the battlefront and once on the home front.[33] As the narrator of "One of Many" commented, "Is it not true that every bullet shoots double, and the shot which flies farthest makes the sorest wound?" In the anonymous "My Absent Soldier," which appeared in *Harper's Weekly* in May 1862, the narrator imagined that if her husband were killed,

I could not bear such anguish, love,
　　For all that I could do;
I know my widowed heart would break,
　　And *I* should perish too!

Likewise in Julia Eugenia Mott's poem "Within a Year," published in *Peterson's Magazine* in July 1862, when "the fatal tidings came" of a lover's death, the heroine also died: "she heard it, mutely, and fell forward prone / Upon the floor—so white and deathly still, / With features rigid as the sculptured stone."[34]

In the South, too, writers imagined a tight link between the fate of soldiers and the women who loved them. In the 1863 *Magnolia Weekly* story "Waiting," lovers who had had a misunderstanding were reconciled in the hospital where he was a wounded patient and she a nurse. But after he died, she "did not move. All through the deepening twilight she sat there," and when a surgeon passed by he discovered that she had "reached the Happier Land." In the 1863 poem "A Picture," when a mother realized that her son had died in battle, "The moon that night shone with double grace / O'er the mother's corse, the soldier's face." And in Augusta Jane Evans's 1864 novel *Macaria; or, Altars of Sacrifice*, the heroine Irene mirrored both the wartime wounding and death of her beloved father as she sat watch over his corpse: her "face was chill and colorless as death, the eyes were closed, and a slender stream of blood oozed slowly over the lips, and dripped upon the linen shroudings of the table."[35]

As such poems and stories suggested, the idea that a soldier's death (or even the possibility of his death) also killed a woman, or that a soldier's wound also wounded a woman, was treated not as metaphor but as literal truth in much popular literature during the war. If, as Elaine Scarry has argued, the wounding and destruction of bodies is a central goal of war, it is also central to claims of participation in war. Certainly during the Civil War many writers claimed that wounds and their accompanying suffering provided a direct connection to the higher meanings of the war, whether political or religious. The poem "Our Wounded," for instance, published in the *Continental Monthly* in October 1862, invoked the "sublimity of suffering":

Wounded! O sweet-lipped word! for on the page
　　Of this strange history, all these scars shall be
The hieroglyphics of a valiant age,
　　Deep writ in freedom's blood-red mystery.

For men it was through wounds, and with blood as "ink," that the history of the war would be written.[36]

A feminized war literature reversed this formula: it was through writing about the war that women's own wartime wounds could be claimed. And war killed and wounded women on the home front, this literature argued, even if the injuries were invisible or the causes of death misunderstood. The July 1862 *Harper's Weekly* story "Wounded," for instance, presented an extended discussion of this point between a husband and wife. Reading from the newspaper to his wife, the narrator reported "six hundred and forty-three wounded" in the latest battle; his wife simply responded, "If that were all!" and when her husband expressed puzzlement, she elaborated, "A great many more were wounded—a great many more." From "every battle-field," she continued, "go swift-winged messengers that kill or wound at a thousand miles instead of a thousand paces; bullets invisible to mortal eyes, that pierce loving hearts. Of the dead and wounded from these we have no report. They are casualties not spoken of by our commanding generals."[37]

A case in point was Mrs. Harley, the wife of a soldier who had recently recovered from a wound: "His eyes were bright, his lips firm, his cheeks flushed with health. You saw scarcely a sign of what he had endured." But "how different with Mrs. Harley! It touched you to look into her dreamy, absent eyes, on her patient lips and exhausted countenance." Yet her husband did not seem to notice her condition. "Did he not know that she had been wounded also? That two balls left the rifle when he was struck, one of them reaching to his distant home?" When he was finally alerted to his wife's pain, Harley himself offered a commentary on the gendered difference in wounds: "Our wounds, so ghastly to the eyes, often get no deeper than the flesh and bone. The pain is short, and nature comes quickly to the work of cure with all her healing energies. We suffer for awhile, and then it is over." Women's wounds, however, were both more serious and longer lasting, with only a slow healing, and "often through abscess and ulceration. The larger number never entirely recover."[38]

"Our wounded!" the story concluded. "If you would find them all you must look beyond the hospitals. They are not every one bearded and in male attire. There sat beside you, in the car just now, a woman. You scarcely noticed her. She left at the corner below. There was not much life in her face; her steps, as they rested on the pavement, were slow. She has been wounded, and is dying. Did you notice Mrs. D—— in church last Sunday? 'Yes; and now I remember that she was pale, and had an altered look.'

One of our wounded! Do you see a face at the window? 'In the marble-front house.' Yes. 'It is sad enough, what in-looking eyes!' Wounded!" Here was a different sort of face than that of the patriotic mother at the window portrayed by Samuel Osgood in *Harper's Monthly.* Yet as the story "Wounded" insisted, this sad face personalized the nation, too, and must not be forgotten.[39]

That women's wounds — represented as deeper and more profound than those of men — were at the emotional center of the nation was a point made pictorially by Winslow Homer in his June 14, 1862, illustration for *Harper's Weekly* titled "News from the War." Homer pictured war news in a variety of settings, including soldiers communally reading *Harper's Weekly*; soldiers eagerly reaching for the *Herald* as it was tossed from a newspaper train; a "special artist" from one of the papers sketching two soldiers; and a soldier delivering news for the staff by horseback. At the still center of all this activity, the point of repose that drew and kept the eye's attention, was a solitary woman seated at her parlor table, bent in agony over a letter held in her left hand. This illustration, simply titled "Wounded," told two stories: not only that she had just received news of the wounding of a beloved but that she was now wounded too. The fact that she was surrounded by the icons of domesticity — her workbasket on the parlor table, a birdcage in a corner, an ivy vine — only underlined the message that war had invaded Northern homes to create great suffering.

In the South, "Refugitta"'s May 1863 "Implora Pace" created an uncanny poetic echo of Homer's illustration. "She is sitting in the twilight, / All her work is laid aside," the poem began.

> In her hand she clasps a paper,
>   And again, and yet again,
> Reads with straining eyes the record,
>   In whose centre burns one name.
>
> 'Tis a list of dead and wounded!
>   His—God help her!—mid the first
> Dead and far away!—her darling!
>   Ah! her heart is like to burst.

Southern writers rarely claimed that women's wounds were the equivalent of men's, in contrast to Northern authors. Yet their fictions and poems nevertheless created striking portrayals of the wounds war inflicted on women.[40]

Winslow Homer, "News from the War," *Harper's Weekly*, June 14, 1862.
(Courtesy of the Library of Virginia)

In late 1862 and 1863, as the war became more brutal, more harrowing, Antietam and Fredericksburg began to figure in feminized war stories, registering on women's consciousness in the dreaded word "killed" in a newspaper. At the same time, some stories began to suggest solutions to a desperate new dilemma: as women did not in fact die when their men died, what should they do with the rest of their lives? In the next few years, solutions emerged in feminized literature involving both an embrace of work outside the home and a newly expansive view of domesticity.

Northern stories in particular increasingly imagined women embracing war work after the deaths of their beloved men. A turn to work concluded Louise Chandler Moulton's July 1863 "One of Many," in which the heroine's beloved died of wounds received at Antietam. After his death, "Margery Dane found her work," the narrator commented. "She is a nurse in a hospital." "I think she will live while her country has need of her, and then she will not be sorry to go to her love and her rest." Striking about this conclusion was that it imagined Margery's life after the loss of a lover, after the loss of domesticity as she had known it. Indeed, it was the death of her lover, and therefore of home as she had imagined it, that triggered her finding "her work." [41]

The connection between the death of a beloved and the turn to work on the part of middle-class women also underlay Rose Terry's "A Woman," published in the *Atlantic Monthly* in December 1862. In that story a childish bride, Josey, criticized by another character in the story as a "giggling, silly little creature" and a "perfect gosling," learned to be a "true woman" after the death of her husband in battle. She reassured the narrator that she was not going to die: "If I could, I wouldn't, Sue; for poor father and mother want me, and so will the soldiers by-and-by." Soon "she got admission to the hospitals" and "worked here like a sprite; nothing daunted or disgusted her." By the end of the story she was recognized as a "true heroine" as well as a "true woman." War had allowed her to fulfill her womanhood, even while decimating her home.[42]

As these stories revealed, by late 1862 and 1863 an increasing number of Northern popular articles, illustrations, and stories reflected approvingly on women's nursing, which had been controversial earlier in the war. A two-page illustration titled "Our Women and the War" in the September 6, 1862, issue of *Harper's Weekly*, for instance, exemplified this shift in public opinion: the *Weekly* explained that its picture, featuring two prominent vignettes of nurses, showed "what women may do toward relieving the sorrows and pains of the soldier": "This war of ours has developed scores of Florence Nightingales, whose names no one knows, but whose reward, in the soldier's gratitude and Heaven's approval, is the highest guerdon woman can ever win." Though approving of nursing—indeed, an October 1862 *Harper's Weekly* cartoon now made fun of women too frivolous-minded to nurse—the *Weekly* also suggested that women nurses should be anonymous, with names "no one knows."[43]

In contrast, however, much feminized popular war literature—including, most famously, Louisa May Alcott's 1863 *Hospital Sketches*—placed nurses center stage in the war, with their experiences and concerns at the heart of numerous stories. Moreover, many of these writings made clear that nursing allowed women to be as heroic as soldiers. As the protagonist of Virginia F. Townsend's August 1862 "Hospital Nurse" said, "If I die in this work—why, I shall only follow the noble company of men and women who have sacrificed their lives for their country." The nurse in Bella Z. Spencer's July 1864 "One of the Noble," published in *Harper's Monthly*, had just heard of the death of her husband in battle, yet "with a heroism worthy of immortality she carried relief to the suffering, ignoring the suffering in her own heart." When she died at the end of the story, the narrator commented, "America has received no purer or nobler sacrifice than that of her young, unselfish life." [44]

Much Northern popular war literature drew a crucial connection between women's wartime suffering and their turn to work. Harriet Beecher Stowe addressed that connection in "The Chimney Corner," published in the *Atlantic Monthly* in January 1865. She "had planned," she wrote to a friend in November 1864, "an article gay & sprightly wholly domestic but as I began & sketched the pleasant home & quiet fireside an irresistable impulse *wrote for me* what followed an offering of sympathy to the suffering & agonized, whose homes have forever been darkened." [45]

Stowe passionately addressed the women whose husbands, sons, or lovers had been killed in the war: "What can we say to you, in those many, many homes where the light has gone out forever?" "The battle-cry goes on, but for you it is passed by! the victory comes, but, oh, never more to bring him back to you! your offering to this great cause has been made, and been taken; you have thrown into it *all* your living, even all that you had, and from henceforth your house is left unto you desolate!" She asked, "But is there no consolation?" In answer, she offered the twin consolations of patriotism and Christianity. "There remains to you a treasure," she told the bereaved mother — "the power to say, 'He died for his country.' In all the good that comes of this anguish you shall have a right and share by virtue of this sacrifice." Equally she offered the consolation of a Christianity that affirmed the "treasures" that "come through sorrow, and sorrow alone." The report of every battle "strikes into some home; and heads fall low, and hearts are shattered, and only God sees the joy that is set before them, and that shall come out of their sorrow." In offering this consolation Stowe expressed a fundamental tenet of mid-nineteenth-century American Protestantism, with its promise of salvation through suffering.[46]

Recognizing, however, that such consolation did not answer the question of what women should do with the rest of their lives, Stowe urged bereaved women, after a period of suffering she recognized as "natural and inevitable," to seek out benevolent work: "We need but name the service of hospitals, the care and education of the freedmen," among other possibilities, including, especially, work among the soldiers. "Ah, we have known mothers bereft of sons in this war, who have seemed at once to open wide their hearts, and to become mothers to every brave soldier in the field. They have lived only to work,—and in place of one lost, their sons have been counted by thousands." Through such work, Stowe made clear, women could construct a new domesticity to replace family homes shattered by war: "In such associations, and others of kindred nature, how many of the stricken and bereaved women of our country might find at once a home and an object in life!"[47]

At almost the same moment that Stowe wrote her consolation to bereaved Northern women, a Southern author who used the pseudonym "Lora" meditated on the same issues in the pages of the *Southern Field and Fireside.* Like Stowe, "Lora" had "attempted to rally [her] energies" to "commune" with her readers through the columns of that journal, as she "was accustomed to do in the peaceful days that have long since gone by." But the "grim spectre war with his attendant train of crushed and bleeding humanity, of smouldering ruins, and desolated homesteads, of weeping and wailing, and anguish," had come "between my vision and the virgin page, until my heart falters, and my hand fails, nerveless and impotent."[48]

"How are we women of the South to evolve comfort out of this chaos?" Lora asked; "how derive strength to do and suffer to the end in the cause of truth, justice and freedom?" Like Stowe, Lora acknowledged the importance of women's war work: "We know that our energies must still be consecrated to the work of strengthening the hands of those who toil through blood, suffering and weariness, in the erection of the great and glorious temple of liberty." And like Stowe, too, she called for an understanding of the Christian rewards of suffering: "by a process of gracious transformation, the bitter tears in the christian's life" may become "radiant jewels." "Blessed are they that mourn," she concluded; "to such not only is comfort promised, but an exceeding and eternal weight of glory."[49]

Unlike Stowe, however, Lora did not expatiate on the importance of work outside the home as a way of finding a new home and object in life. As Drew Gilpin Faust has pointed out, Southern writers did not embrace women's work outside the home, including nursing, to the same extent as Northerners during the war, marking a significant difference in gender ideologies between the two sections. To be sure, a number of Southern writers praised Southern women's domestic contributions to the war effort. "The women of the South have covered themselves with glory in our present struggles for independence," said one typical article. "There is no labor which they have not shown themselves ready to perform, no sacrifice which they have not hesitated to make."[50] "All over the country, woman is *at work*," said another commentator. "She sews or knits, spins or weaves."[51]

Only a few authors, however, made more radical claims for the importance of women's work. In the character of the wise older woman "Mrs. Poynter," for instance, an anonymous author in the *Southern Illustrated News* praised women's work in the Treasury Department, saying that it did her "heart good to see" more than "fifty ladies, young and old, all writing away at desks." In the hospitals, especially, woman was "what she ought ever to be—a ministering angel to the suffering." "These are times when women must learn to take care of themselves," she argued, saying that "it's not woman's mission to be shut up at home, away from doing public good, and taught that such uselessness is *refinement*." [52]

The heroine of Augusta Jane Evans's *Macaria*, too—a novel that by the end of 1864 had reportedly sold some twenty thousand copies, making it a rare Confederate best-seller—especially embraced work outside the home as a cause suited to single women. "Mothers and wives are, in most instances, kept at home," Irene stated, but she had "nothing to bind" her at home or to prevent her from taking up the "sacred duty" of work as a nurse to "aid the cause." After the death of the soldier she loved, Irene expatiated on the theme of single usefulness, saying that married women, "occupied with family cares and affections—can find little time for considering the comfort, or contributing to the enjoyment of any beyond the home-circle." In contrast single women, though not so happy as their married sisters, had the "privilege of carrying light and blessings to many firesides—of being the friend and helper of hundreds." [53]

In their avowals of the importance of women's work outside the home, however, both Augusta Jane Evans and the anonymous author of "Mrs. Poynter's Reflections" were in the minority among Confederate popular authors, who tended to adhere instead to a conservative domestic ideology. As Faust has pointed out, a number of Southern reviewers of *Macaria* questioned Evans's embrace of single women's usefulness outside the home, finding her narrative "too much at odds with traditional models and expectations." To the self-imposed question "What Can Woman Do?" more common was the answer of "A. V. S." in the *Southern Illustrated News*. Woman's "true, only proper sphere" was as the "brightener of man's existence," while her proper place was in "that *home* which she can so well beautify and adorn." Rejecting the "strong-minded woman of the North" in the "stern character of lecturer upon the rostrum and stage," this author maintained adherence to an antebellum ideology of domesticity. [54]

However, the maintenance of that ideology came at great cost to Southern women. In an increasing crescendo during the war, Southern writers published pleas and prayers for peace that took note of women's anguish. The poet M. Louise Rogers, who contributed frequently to the *Southern Illustrated News*, spoke in "Our Country" of the "sad tale" to tell "of the cries and the widow's moans, / The mother's wail, / And a sister's sobs and piteous tones." Asking "When will it end?," Rogers called on "Our Father God" to "Let dove-eyed Peace brood over our land and main, / And oh! give us back our loved ones again." As another poem, "A Prayer for Peace," entreated,

> Peace! Peace! God of our fathers, grant us Peace!
> Unto our cry of anguish and despair
> Give ear and pity! From the lonely homes,
> Where widowed beggary and orphaned woe
> Fill their poor urns with tears.

One woman wrote a similar plea in her diary. Catherine Edmondston's late 1863 "A Prayer for Peace" began:

> By our sundered household ties
> Widow's wail and children's cries
> By the boding care and fears
> Stretching into future years
> By the loneliness of greif
> Greif and tears without releif
> By the sorrow & distress
> Of the wife's last fond caress
>
> . . . .
> Grant us Peace! [55]

More and more, late wartime feminized literature in the South reflected the fact that homes had become little more than sites of grief and loss. As the *Southern Field and Fireside* poem "The Old Year's Dirge" put it in early 1865,

> Bitterly, bitterly,
>   Tell of each orphan's cries,
> Tell of each mother's woe,
> Tell of each hope's death blow;
> Tell of all the tearful eyes,
> And of grief that never dies.

Despite such cries of anguish, however, most Southern popular literature—in contrast to many women's private diary entries—did not follow
through by disavowing or even questioning the war. A case in point was
Margaret Junkin Preston's long narrative poem *Beechenbrook; A Rhyme of
the War*, whose publishing history is also a reminder of the severe disruptions to literary culture caused by the war. Written at night "by the
light of the fire" during the winter of 1864–65, *Beechenbrook* was printed
in an edition of 2,000 copies "in the *plainest* manner—dark paper—dim
type," with "stitched brown paper covers," in the early spring. But after
only 50 copies had been sent out of Richmond, the city fell, and the remaining 1,550 copies were destroyed by the fires that also destroyed much
of the city. Reissued in Baltimore in 1866 and dedicated "To every Southern woman who was widowed by the war," *Beechenbrook* sold well, going
through a total of eight printings.[56]

What Preston called her "little ballad story" testified to the unbearable
sacrifices demanded of white women from the beginning of the war. The
very first line of the poem, "There is sorrow at Beechenbrook," focused
on the emotional struggles faced by the heroine, Alice, in allowing her
husband to enlist. Thereafter, the poem followed Alice and her husband
through the trials of war, including the burning of her house by Yankees.
When Alice ultimately learned that her husband had been killed in battle,
she was filled with despair:

> Break, my heart, and ease this pain,—
> Cease to throb, thou tortured brain;
> Let me die,—since he is slain,
>   —Slain in battle!

"'Tis thus through her days and her nights of despair, / Her months
of bereavement so bitter to bear, / That Alice moans ever," the poem
commented. But while *Beechenbrook* demanded that readers recognize the
"tempests that roll / Their desolate floods through the depths of her soul,"
it also emphatically denied that Alice disavowed the cause of the Confederacy as a result of her tragic personal experience. "Is the cause of her
country less dear to her now?" the poem asked.

> Does the patriot-flame in her heart cease to stir? . . .
> Does she stand, self-absorbed, on the wreck she has braved,
> Nor care if her country be lost or be saved?

The answer to these questions was an emphatic no, as Alice claimed "that her glorious South MUST BE FREE!" Like *Macaria*, *Beechenbrook* affirmed a heroic—and sacrificial—patriotism.[57]

With the loss of the Confederacy in April 1865, however, Margaret Junkin Preston's own diary told a different story and provided a striking contrast between public expressions of patriotism and private expressions of doubt and despair. After hearing of Lee's surrender, she asked, "Why then all these four years of suffering—of separations—of horror—of blood—of havoc—of awful bereavement!" "Why these ruined homes—these broken family circles—these scenes of terror that must scathe the brain of those who witnessed them till their dying day! Why is our dear Willy in his uncoffined grave? Why poor Frank to go through life with one arm? Is it wholly and forever in vain? *God only knows!*" Doubts that could not easily be expressed within the medium of public poetry, with its underlying prescriptive and patriotic aims, could not be repressed within the privacy of a journal.[58]

• • •

How could grief-stricken women make sense of the war? Several works of late wartime feminized literature in the North, just as in the South, recognized that work outside the home was not enough—or was not available—to provide consolation for all women. Instead, these works sought to provide women with religious consolation in the form of answers to their prayers, bright visions of their dead lovers, or even an imagined new heavenly home. The young writer Elizabeth Stuart Phelps, for instance, whose own fiancé was killed in the war, published an extended cry of agony in her January 1864 *Harper's Magazine* story "A Sacrifice Consumed." In that story Ruth, a poor and lonely needlewoman, "overtaxed" with "toil and desolation," had despaired before the war of ever finding domestic happiness—bowing "her face in her hands," she had "cried out, sharply," "Alone, all alone! No home, no love—always, always!" When, to her surprise, she received a proposal of marriage from a dry-goods clerk she had long been fond of, "a new world opened to the little seamstress. Her day's toil seemed short and easy. The light and air were strangely fresh and beautiful."[59]

Her happiness, however, was short lived; John enlisted for the war—as in other feminized war stories, after she had given permission, looking at him with eyes that were "tender, liquid, filled with no vain regret, but pure as those of a martyr"—and was killed at Antietam. The remainder of the story dealt with her overwhelming grief, calling on the reader to recognize her own heroism. "There are heroes who take their lives in their hands—their young, happy lives, all bright with dream of an unknown success," who "face death with a smile, and we do them honor." "But there are martyrs at humble firesides who give up more than this. 'They empty heart and home of life's life-love;' who yet go back to their desolate days from which all the beauty, all the fragrance, all the song, has departed, and take them up bravely, working in lowly trust till the Rest comes." At the end of the story, "One met her who had himself wept and struggled alone on the hill-sides of Judea for her," and Ruth "lived very patiently at the foot of the altar where the ashes of her sacrifice lay," her consolation the knowledge that "God had accepted it for the blessing of her country, herself, and John."[60]

Like Phelps, the author of the anonymous 1864 *Ruth: A Song in the Desert* recognized women's anguish late in the war and hoped, by her "little narrative, to reach a few of her sisters in sorrow." Her story began, rather than ended, with the news of the death in battle of the heroine's lover, Frank. "How could she take up these weary hours and days which must make her future," the narrator asked, "remembering what they might have been, and how he could have blessed them and made them bright?" The answer came in a religious vision of Frank, her dead lover, who came in a "glory of light" and counseled her to embrace suffering for God's sake. Ruth "saw, by the deathless love in his eyes," that Frank "would not leave her to toil alone."[61]

The desire to reach out to sorrowing women was also the impetus behind Elizabeth Stuart Phelps's 1868 novel *The Gates Ajar*, which she began to write late in the war. In her 1896 memoirs, Phelps remembered that during the two years that she wrote her book "the country was dark with sorrowing women. The regiments came home, but the mourners went about the streets." The "drawn faces of bereaved wife, mother, sister, and widowed girl showed piteously everywhere." It was these bereaved women who inspired Phelps: she did not think "so much about the suffering of men" but instead "would have spoken" to the women—"the helpless, outnumbering, unconsulted women; they whom war trampled down, without a choice or protest; the patient, limited, domestic women, who thought little, but loved much, and loving, had lost all."[62]

It seemed to Phelps that "even the best and kindest forms of our prevailing beliefs had nothing to say to an afflicted woman that could help her much." After all, "creeds and commentaries and sermons were made by men, and "what tenderest of men knows how to comfort his own daughter when her heart is broken?" Doctrines themselves were no more than "chains of rusty iron, eating into raw hearts," and "the prayer of the preacher was not much better; it sounded like the language of an unknown race to a despairing girl."[63]

Reacting against what she perceived as an unfeeling, masculinist religion in her attempt to "comfort some few" of the women "whose misery crowded the land," Phelps created a feminized theology that incorporated the ideology of domesticity. Rejecting the idea that heaven was "indefinite," a place "where the glory of God was to crowd out all individuality and all human joy from His most individual and and human creatures," Phelps instead sketched a domestic heaven in which human loves "could outlive the shock of death" and where the beloved forms of home could be re-created in spiritual form. A bereaved young woman whose beloved brother Roy had been killed in battle was comforted by her aunt Phoebe, herself widowed: "Do I think you will see him again? You might as well ask me if I thought God made you and made Roy, and gave you to each other. See him! Why of course you will see him as you saw him here." By the end of the novel Phoebe herself, dying, looked forward to the comforts of heaven, including the home that her husband, John, might "be making ready for her coming." Indeed, Phoebe's last words made clear to readers that her vision of heaven had been realized: "It was quite dark when she turned her face at last towards the window. 'John!' she said,—'why, John!' "[64]

• • •

"*What do women know about war?*" was the rhetorical question that "Fleta" posed in the popular Northern story paper *The Flag of Our Union* in January 1865. "What do they *not* know," she answered: "What drop in all the bitter cup have they not tasted?—what ball strikes home on the battle-field that strikes not hearts at the hearthstone as well?" Women knew about war, she argued, "who steadily crush back the blinding tears, and whisper through white, brave lips, 'Go,'" or "who wait in vain for the letter that never comes—who search, with sinking hearts, and eyes dark with anguish, the fearful battlelists." Chastising those who would ask such a question, she concluded, "Let the desolate homes, the broken hearts, and the low wail of agony that God hears on his throne, make answer!"[65]

In both the North and the South throughout the conflict, a feminized war literature put white women center stage in the war, demanding recognition not only of women's contributions to the war effort but also, as the war wore on, of their intense suffering. In doing so, such literature did not displace the importance of men in the conflict, but it did sometimes ask for equal recognition of women's sacrifices, thus contributing to the diversity of claims to the war's meanings to be found in the pages of popular literature. Ultimately, it was through women's individual, anguished experiences that they were most closely aligned to the nation, this literature argued: as Elizabeth Stuart Phelps claimed of her heroine in "A Sacrifice Consumed," she would "love her country all the more for what it had cost her." [66]

Kingdom Coming

THE EMANCIPATION OF POPULAR LITERATURE

The white people fancied that we could not fight,
But they saw their mistake when they gave us a sight,
For in the great charge of the colored brigade,
'Twas the boldest they say that ever was made.
For in the great charge of the colored brigade
'Twas the boldest they say that ever was made.
— *"Pompey's Contraband Song,"*
Words and music by J. Ward Childs, 1864

In early 1865 a Southern author named Mrs. Howard reflected resentfully on the easy living she imagined to be slaves' lot in wartime. In an essay titled "Plantation Scenes and Sounds" published in the *Southern Field and Fireside,* Howard commented on "how little" slaves "realize what distress and misery are pervading this land." After all, "rations are served to them the same as ever," so that the slave husband and father "can eat his bread in peace and quietness." Entirely ignoring the realities of slavery, including the hardships and disruptions that war caused in slaves' lives, Howard argued that unlike his master, the slave was not "compelled to separate from those he holds dear—he has not like him to brave all dangers and all weathers for his country's sake." Nor did slaves "know or understand" the "trials of the soldier's wife." Their "midnight dreams are not made terrific by visions of blood shed and of death. They have neither son nor husband a mark for the pitiless peltings of musket balls. They are not called upon to grieve that their darlings are exposed to hardships, discomforts and dangers such as have never been dreamed of before in our fair land." [1]

In claiming the wartime sufferings of white men and women, Howard participated, as we have seen, in an extensive popular literature exploring and valorizing sentimental soldiers' and women's experiences of war. But in deliberately fantasizing the "easy lives" of African Americans in wartime, Howard also participated in a wider discussion of race in wartime popular literature both north and south. In the South, popular stories, poems, and cartoons throughout the war created fantasies of satisfied slaves who wanted nothing more than to remain with—or return to—their masters. In the North, in contrast, from the start of the war a widespread popular literature including popular songs, envelopes, stories, cartoons, and novels embraced changes in African Americans' status during the war—although usually only if they seemed to benefit the condition of Northern whites. Still, in the wake of emancipation, a few popular works emerged that, however briefly, radically reconsidered the racial politics of Northern culture.

• • •

If within the writings of Northern literati African Americans "figured only peripherally," as Daniel Aaron put it in *The Unwritten War*, the pages of Northern popular literature told a profoundly different story. African Americans occupied a highly visible role in wartime popular literature. In June 1861, as slaves began the dramatic process of freeing themselves by coming into Union lines, two major Northern popular magazines explored this important social change with interest. Both *Frank Leslie's Illustrated Newspaper* and *Harper's Weekly* praised General Benjamin Butler's action in designating former slaves as "contraband" of war to prevent their being returned to their former owners. *Harper's* commented that Butler's "refusal to surrender fugitive slaves to their masters" was "equally sound in law and sensible in practice," and *Leslie's* praised General Butler's "sagacity," saying that his actions had "increased the dilemma of the Secessionists to a remarkable degree."[2]

The designation of escaped slaves as "contraband" represented a challenge to slaveholders' authority that many Northerners clearly relished. Depictions of "contrabands" began to appear in a wide variety of popular cultural forms. A number of printers early in the war, for instance, produced "contraband envelopes" that celebrated slaves' escape to Fort Monroe. One, printed in several different versions, depicted a master with bull whip calling out "Come back here, you black rascal" to an escaping slave, who in return thumbed his nose at his former master, saying, "Can't come back nohow, massa, Dis chile's CONTRABAN'." At the right of the envelope was Fort Monroe, the former slave's destination. Another envelope titled "Contraband of War" made the point that "contrabands" could be employed as laborers in the army by portraying a group of black men with pickaxes and other tools volunteering their services to Butler: "Massa Butler," one of them was depicted as saying, "we's just seceded from Harper's Ferry, whar we larn'd de trade ob making TRENCHES and FORTIFICATIONS." Yet another envelope depicted the discomfiture of an "F.F.V." (an abbreviation for "First Family of Virginia," widely used as a sarcastic shorthand for slaveholders during the war) as General Butler held him at swordspoint. "One of the F.F.V's after his Contraband," the caption read. "General Butler 'can't see it.'" The New York–based *Weekly Anglo-African*, an African American periodical published during the war, also printed advertisements for a "Zouave and Slave Envelope" featuring the banner "Slaves Contraband of War" and picturing a slave master attempting to retrieve a slave, while a Zouave held him off at the point of a bayonet.[3]

Yet if many Northern publications celebrated former slaves' new status as "contrabands" under the control of Union troops, this did not necessarily represent a change from antebellum versions of racism. In an article titled "The Contrabands at Fortress Monroe" in the November 1861 *Atlantic Monthly*, Edward L. Pierce reported that the word was "applied familiarly to the negroes" and that many African Americans were puzzled by it. "What d' ye call us that for?" he reported being asked. Indeed, there is every indication that the term "contraband" caught on rapidly precisely because it provided a means for Northerners to continue thinking of escaped slaves as property, without disturbing antebellum racist preconceptions. As Pierce wryly observed, "The venerable gentleman, who wears gold spectacles and reads a conservative daily, prefers confiscation to emancipation." Certainly numerous illustrations of "contrabands" on envelopes drew from antebellum racist imagery, especially minstrelsy: one, for instance, depicted a black in minstrel costume (including striped trousers and stovepipe hat) saying, "I'm Just From Dixie's Land." Another portrayed a black man and black woman dancing together, both drawn with hugely exaggerated lips, saying, "Bress de Lor, we am Contraban."[4]

Redefining former slaves as "contrabands," then portraying them as minstrels, was in part a strategy of containment. It reassured white Northerners that even in freedom African Americans remained no more than property and that familiar images from minstrelsy retained their currency in wartime as a mode of imagining blacks. Such linguistic and visual strate-

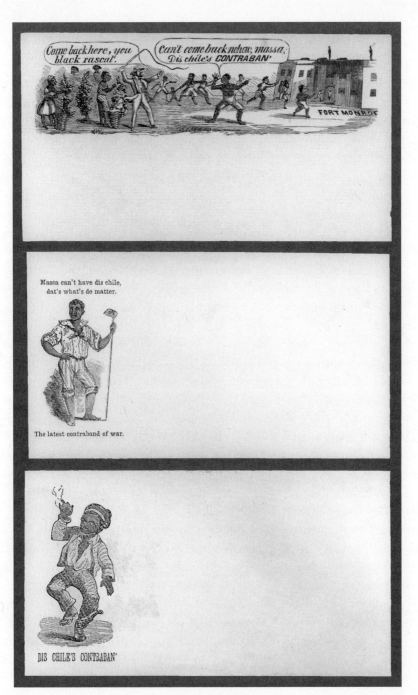

Contraband envelopes.
(Courtesy of the American Antiquarian Society)

gies in effect forestalled thinking of African Americans as free human beings.

They also framed the emerging wartime narrative of black freedom and participation in the war in relation to white concerns and fears. Arguments in favor of black emancipation, for instance, often revolved around its destructive impact on Southern slaveholders or its power to elevate the status of poor whites. In the pages of much popular literature black emancipation was as much about whites as about blacks; it had as much to do with maintaining or gaining new white freedoms as with gaining black freedom. Such literature created a set of narrative dependencies that had important implications for incorporating blacks into an imagined nationhood, as it offered only a circumscribed vision of how freedmen and freedwomen would become part of a new national family.[5]

Yet as much as defining African Americans as "contrabands" and portraying them as minstrels was a strategy of containment, it was also true that such imaginings introduced many layers of instability and complexity into wartime discussions of blacks. As Eric Lott has noted about antebellum minstrelsy, "No doubt its makers' purposes, though various, amounted to a hegemonizing effort, coincident with Democratic party policy, on behalf of things as they were: racist self-assurance, then sectional compromise, then white-supremacist Unionism." Once "off and running," however, minstrel acts contained contradictory "resonances and images," including "racial disdain as well as paranoid racial fantasizing," that could not so easily be contained. Likewise, defining African Americans as contrabands did not so much fix an image of blackness during the war as introduce additional layers of reference and complexity to older, already multilayered images.[6]

The fact that images of blacks were multilayered early in the war was not lost on Northern observers. An 1862 novel introduced a black character by describing him as "the Sable Brother—alias the Son of Ham—alias the Image of God carved in Ebony—alias the Oppressed Type—alias the Contraband—alias the Irrepressible Nigger—alias the Chattel—alias the Darky—alias the Cullud Pusson," thus providing a neat linguistic summary of simultaneously coexisting stereotypes of blacks. A popular song titled "The Intelligent Contraband" imagined one African American soliloquizing:

I'se de happiest darkey whatever you did see,
I'se been so ever since I heard

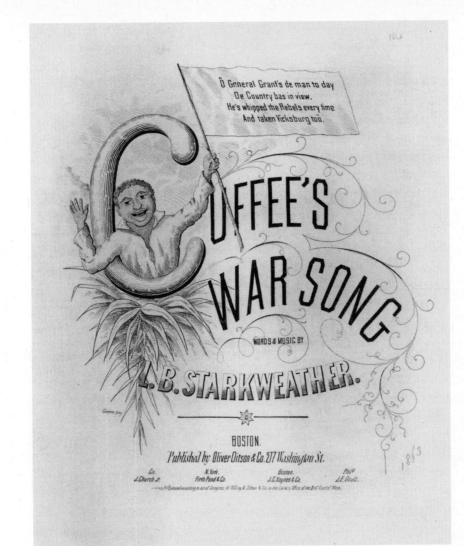

"Cuffee's War Song."
(Courtesy of the Rare Book, Manuscript and Special
Collections Library, Duke University)

Dat I was to be free!
I was born way down in Dixie's land
Where dey used to call me Sam.
By golly, now de white folks say
I'm a 'telligent contraband.[7]

One early wartime *Harper's Weekly* cartoon titled "Contraband of War" provided an ironic reflection on the power of linguistic categories to shape social realities, as it depicted one "Contraband Article" talking to another, saying, "Dis chile been mor'n sebenty yeahs one ob de cullud race, an' ben called a *niggah*, a *chattels*, an *institution*, an' now he's a *contraban'*. I s'pose de out-cum will be dis niggar will lose his position on de face ob de airth altogeder—dat's so!" There is more than a hint here of many white Northerners' wish—expressed not just by virulent racists but also by abolitionists such as James Redpath heavily involved in wartime colonization schemes—that African Americans would simply disappear from American life and that redefining them as "contrabands" would hasten the process.[8]

If the term "contraband" was meant to stabilize images of blacks as property, however, the progress of the war itself dramatically undercut this project. At first "contrabands" were depicted as only those African Americans who came into Union lines. But with the evacuation of Beaufort, South Carolina, by slave masters in December 1861, the idea of "contrabands" in Northern popular literature widened to include those slaves who were left or stayed behind. These "contrabands" were often portrayed with ambivalence, if not downright disapproval, because of their new relationship to whites' property. *Leslie's*, for instance, described "the spectacle presented by the 'emancipated contrabands'" in Beaufort, South Carolina, after the departure of slave masters. "Sambo, Dinah, and the picaninnies" were "lords of all they surveyed," and "it was evident that honesty had not been one of the lessons inculcated by the Southern chivalry, for every one of the colored persons were loaded with some articles which they had never paid for." Indeed, *Leslie's* concluded, "In our Artist's visit to Beaufort we have narrated the terrible picture of devastation presented to his sight wherever he entered any of the deserted houses. Mirrors smashed, pianos gutted, beds ripped open, carpets covered with filth, in a word, a foul pandemonium had been created in a few hours by these unhappy wretches, whose only idea of possession was to destroy what they could not steal. This, in fact, is quite sufficient to show on what a volcano every community rests which has slavery for a basis."[9]

Harper's Weekly likewise ran an illustration of African Americans in possession of white property in Beaufort. Its January 1862 "Scene in the Parlor of Mr. Barnwell's House at Beaufort, South Carolina" portrayed African Americans lounging on chairs and sofa, sitting on top of both the mantel and the piano, wearing their owners' clothes, and, symbolically, playing "Dixie's Land" upside down. While this illustration celebrated the inver-

"Scene in the Parlor of Mr. Barnwell's House at Beaufort,
South Carolina," *Harper's Weekly*, January 18, 1862.
(Courtesy of the American Antiquarian Society)

sion of power occurring in the South, it also presented crudely stereotyped physical portrayals of African Americans.[10]

Despite such ambivalence concerning African Americans, however, numerous songs and cartoons, with their enjoyment of slave masters' disempowerment, were an important medium through which emancipation began to be imagined as a positive good early in the war. Such literature concentrated as much or more on inversions of a previous order, and on white humiliation and discomfiture, as on black freedom. A double cartoon in *Frank Leslie's* during January 1862, for instance, showed on the left a "slave running from his Master" toward a sign marked "Canada" under the caption "As It Used To Be." On the right, a companion cartoon titled "As It Is" showed "the Master running from his slave" toward a sign marked "Beaufort."[11]

The early 1862 popular minstrel song "Kingdom Coming," by Henry C. Work, ventriloquized slaves' thoughts after their master had fled:

Say, darkeys, hab you seen de massa
Wid de muffstash on his face,
Go long de road sometime dis mornin'
Like he gwine to leab de place?

He seen a smoke, way up de ribber,
Whar de Linkum gumboats lay;
He took his hat, an' lef berry sudden,
An' I spec he's run away!

Chorus:
De massa run? ha, ha!
De darkey stay? ho, ho!
It mus' be now de kingdom comin',
    An' de year ob Jubilo!

The third verse of "Kingdom Coming" imagined blacks moving into the masters' parlor:

De darkeys feel so lonesome
Libing in de log house on de lawn
Dey move dar tings to massa's parlor
For to keep it while he's gone
Dar's wine an' cider in de kitchen,
An' de darkeys dey'll hab some;
I spose dey'll all be cornfiscated
    When de Linkum sojers come.

In the pages of much popular literature early in 1862, slaves laughed at masters, outwitted them, put on their clothes, sat on their furniture, drank their liquor, and turned the social framework upside down. Although the emphasis in such literature remained on the destruction of white property and Northerners' glee at the breakdown of slaveholders' power, depictions of slaves actively and overtly subverting slavery were important links in a developing narrative of the wartime transformation of black identity.[12]

While much Northern popular literature early in the war celebrated the disempowerment of slave masters, portraying contrabands as the visible signs of that disempowerment, other literature argued for emancipation on the grounds that it would empower common whites, both north and south. In January 1862, for instance, Charles Godfrey Leland published the first issue of a new monthly magazine, the *Continental Monthly*, whose rallying cry was "Emancipation for the sake of the White Man." Leland had previously been the editor of the *Knickerbocker* but had felt that publishing his political views in that conservative and little-read magazine was "like pouring the wildest of new wine into the weakest of old bottles." With the help of author and financial backer James Roberts Gilmore, Leland began his own political monthly magazine instead, "devoted to the Republican cause."[13]

That Leland was a conservative rather than radical Republican was obvious from the first. The inaugural issue of the *Continental Monthly* built on arguments made familiar by Hinton Helper's influential 1858 *The Impending Crisis*. As Leland explained, Helper had seen "that the poor white man of the South was being degraded below the negro, and that industry and capital were fearfully checked by slavery." But whereas Helper "desired the freedom of the slave for the sake of the poor white man in the South," Leland wanted more—"Emancipation" "for the sake of *all* white men." "Nowhere on the American continent is the white laborer free from the vile comparison and vile influences of slavery," Leland said, echoing a free labor argument initially popularized by the Free Soil Party. For the *"sake of all, and for that of men in comparison to whose welfare that of the negro was a mere trifle,"* Leland argued, slavery must be eradicated. With such arguments underpinning his new magazine, Leland made clear that both Northerners' and Southerners' definitions of white manhood were threatened by slavery, with emancipation the only feasible mode of maintaining a whiteness currently under siege. In this view emancipation, paradoxically, had virtually nothing to do with black freedom.[14]

Yet in vocally supporting emancipation, even on these limited grounds, the *Continental Monthly* was briefly in the vanguard among mainstream periodicals. At least this was how it seemed to abolitionist Thomas Wentworth Higginson, a frequent contributor to the *Atlantic Monthly*. Writing to editor James T. Fields in January 1862, Higginson complained that "the thing that troubled" him the "most" about the February issue of the *Atlantic* was "the absence of a strong article on the war, especially as January had none." Higginson reported, "I see men buying the 'Continental' for its strong emancipatory pieces, and they are amazed that the 'Atlantic' should not have got beyond Lowell's 'Self-Possession.' For the 'Atlantic' to speak only once in three months, and then *against* an emancipatory policy, is humiliating." Higginson concluded, "Public sentiment is moving fast, even if events are not, and it is a shame that life should come from the 'Knickerbocker' and not from the 'Atlantic.'"[15]

The *Continental Monthly*'s editorial viewpoint circulated widely in 1862 through the medium of a popular book published in June by the *Continental Monthly*'s financial backer, James Roberts Gilmore, who wrote under the pseudonym Edmund Kirke. *Among the Pines* was a collection of articles Gilmore had published under that title in the *Monthly* from January through the spring, and it sold widely during the summer of 1862, reaching total sales of thirty-four thousand—an excellent sale for books at this time—by December. The appeal of *Among the Pines*, according to the *American Publishers' Circular and Literary Gazette*, was "its sketches of Southern life, society, and scenery, and especially of slave life," written with "considerable graphic power, and often with a dramatic intensity which approaches the 'sensational.'" It was also "animated with a strong anti-slavery sentiment," although "the most prejudiced reader could not call it fanatical." [16]

Among the Pines offered Northern readers the satisfaction of witnessing the degradation of Southern common whites firsthand, which only emancipation would change. At the same time, however, it emphasized the subversive tendencies and intelligence of many Southern male slaves, thus providing links to the popular cartoons and songs that portrayed an inverted world order in which slaves outwitted or thumbed their noses at their masters. Gilmore presented the emancipation arguments of the *Continental Monthly* in dramatic form, offering recollections of his Southern travels that he insisted were true to life. However, they not only bore an uncanny resemblance to the editorial pages of the *Monthly* but also struck contemporary observers as "pure fiction from beginning to end." [17]

In the inaugural sketch, set near Charleston, South Carolina, "Edmund Kirke" and a native African slave named Scipio were forced to put up for the night in a "one-story log cabin, tenanted by a family of POOR WHITES." The narrator emphasized their extreme poverty and degradation: the daughter, who wore a "soiled, greasy, grayish linsey-woolsey gown," had "bare, dirty legs and feet, and her arms, neck, and face" were "thickly encrusted with a layer of clayey mud"; there wasn't "a morsel to eat or drink in the house"; and the family owned only a "big wooden bowl" and a "half dozen pewter spoons" with which to eat. Portrayed as entirely ignorant ("New York! whar's that?"), scornful of the Northern work ethic ("I reckon I'd ruther be 'spectable than work for a livin'"), and deeply prejudiced, they would not allow Scipio to eat with them. "'No, sar! No darkies eats with us. Hope ye don't reckon *yerself* no better than a good-for-nothin,' no-account nigger!'" In the present case, the narrator observed, "it struck me that the odds were on the side of the black man. The whites were shiftless, ragged, and starving; the black well clad, cleanly, energetic," and "much above the others in intellect." [18]

It was Scipio who then articulated the "degraded white" argument characteristic of the *Continental Monthly*. "Dey won't work 'cause dey see de dary slaves doin' it, and tink it am beneaf white folks to do as de darkies do. Dis habin' slaves keeps dis hull country pore."

"Who told you that?" I asked, astonished at hearing a remark showing so much reflection from a negro.

"Nobody, massa, I see it myseff."

The narrator spelled out the conclusion: although the "great mass" of Southern blacks were "but a little above the brutes in their habits and instincts," a "large body" were "fully on a par, except in mere book-education, with their white masters." The narrator's time spent with Scipio led him "for the first time to the opinion, that real elevation and nobility of character may exist under an ebony skin." [19]

This was one of the central arguments of *Among the Pines*—that most Northerners badly misjudged and underestimated slaves. Yet this was an argument made as much from fear as from an appreciation of blacks' "elevation and nobility of character," for Gilmore also stressed African Americans' capacity for subversion, violence, and revolution. "I *know* it to be a *fact*," the narrator said, "that there exists among the blacks a secret and wide-spread organization of a Masonic character, having its grip, password, and oath," and organized for the purpose of obtaining freedom for the black man. The existence of this society was not "positively known" by whites, however, for "the black is more subtle and crafty than anything human." As long as the black man was given freedom, he would "have no incentive to insurrection," and "the avenging angel shall pass over the homes of the many true and loyal men who are still left at the South, and the thunderbolts of this war will fall only—where they should fall—on the heads of its blood-stained authors." But "if this is not done," the narrator warned, "after we have put down the whites we shall have to meet the blacks" and wade "knee-deep in the blood of both." This "catastrophe" would "make the horrors of San Domingo and the French Revolution grow pale in history." [20]

Such a passage revealed a deeply ambivalent view of African Americans, an ambivalence to be found over and over again in the pages of popular literature during the war, which often stressed the "volcano" on which slavery rested. In story after story, illustration after illustration, positive images of blacks—sometimes quite different from antebellum images—were offset by more negative images. Thus even when Gilmore first envisioned Scipio as a preacher, saying, "How well his six feet of manly sinew would grace those pulpit stairs," he then immediately imagined that "if that didn't *pay*, how, put into the minstrel business, he might run the white 'troupes' off the track"—a brief passage that simultaneously invited the reader to reimagine an "elevated" free black as a minstrel while also suggesting that in that occupation he would be driving whites out of business. A doubled consciousness of blacks enabled whites to maintain older stereotypes even while looking ahead to the possibility of new social realities for African Americans.[21]

* * *

Ambivalence in popular representations of African Americans remained a constant during the war, but the nature of that ambivalence kept shifting under the pressure of war's unfolding events. Thus, in the spring of 1862, when General David Hunter first recruited African American troops in South Carolina in part to offset Southerners' military use of slaves' labor, the Democratic-leaning *Frank Leslie's* reflected on this event with qualified approval, reassuring its readers that the new "Negro Brigade" was not meant "to degrade the Anglo-Saxon race by putting the sons of Ham beside the sons of Alfred and the countrymen of Washington and Shakespeare, but to warn the rebels of the danger they run in bringing that peculiar element into play." At the same time, *Leslie's* itself self-consciously called into play a variety of racial stereotypes to contain the radical implications of the deployment of black troops. It called the new troops "the Black Brigade, or the Darkey Division—Contraband Conquerers—The Sable Sharpshooters" and "The Negro Minstrel Military." It further reinforced the connection between minstrelsy and black soldiering by reminding its readers that "in the Northern popular mind every contraband is associated with a white row of ivory, 'yah! yah!' and a banjo," which were supposed to be "the 'make-up' of that 'sable race' that forms the 'peculiar institution' of our Republic." And it described the parting of black families in terms that continued to view African Americans as entertainment: "Our Artist declares that nothing could exceed the grotesque mixture of tragedy and comedy exhibited by the dusky recruits and their relatives; some, forgetting that they were always exposed to be torn apart for ever at the will of a merciless Legree, howled over a temporary and profitable absence, undergone at the option of the chief party concerned. So unreasonable has oppression made this race!" An accompanying illustration showed a black woman reaching out to embrace a soldier and another weeping into a handkerchief. It is well to remember that black women's "unreasonable"

Robert Smalls, in *Harper's Weekly*, June 14, 1862.
(Courtesy of the American Antiquarian Society)

tears were in white women considered an appropriate response to men's departure for war.[22]

Though *Leslie's* sought to contain the radical implications of black soldiering with such references to minstrelsy, its very self-consciousness about those references revealed to what extent war was disturbing established notions of African Americans. In May and June 1862 that ongoing disturbance registered in a remarkable set of images that for the first time entertained the possibility of black heroism in the war. After a famous wartime incident, widely reported in newspapers, in which Robert Smalls and his crew, all African Americans, piloted the Confederate steamer the *Planter* out of Charleston into Union waters, both *Frank Leslie's* and *Har-*

per's Weekly published illustrations that created radically new images of African Americans. Under the heading "Heroes in Ebony" *Frank Leslie's* printed an engraving, drawn from a photograph, that showed the crew of the *Planter* looking forthrightly, even jauntily, into the camera. With three of the men confidently standing with hands on hips, with the fourth resting his arm on the American flag, and with all of them well dressed in suits and vests, this engraving presented African American men without the usual racialized shorthand of exaggerated, cartoonlike features common to other wartime illustrations of blacks. These were "gallant men of color," *Leslie's* informed its readers in accompanying text. Likewise, *Harper's Weekly* printed a portrait of the *Planter's* captain, Robert Smalls, drawn from a photograph "sent us by our correspondent at Hilton Head," which also presented Smalls dressed in suit and bow tie, steadily gazing into the camera. Quoting from the Democratic *Herald*, *Harper's Weekly*, too, commented on the "gallant and perilous service" of these men.[23]

Of vital importance in allowing these men to be perceived as heroes within the Northern popular press was the fact that they had performed a feat understood to be "heroic" within established conventions emphasizing individual "daring." Heroism, by accepted mid-nineteenth-century definition, necessarily involved the actions of individuals. Indeed, this love of the individual hero lay behind the mid-nineteenth-century popularity of Shakespearean protagonists. Thus it was the sense that the *Planter's* captain had individually initiated an act of daring, combined with the perception that this had been a military act directly humiliating to the Southern navy, that allowed these four men to be represented in terms that matched wartime depictions of white heroes.[24]

Particularly striking in these portrayals was the use of photographs instead of cartoonlike images; no doubt it was the perception that these were individual acts of daring that allowed the employment of photographs to represent these men, but conversely the very use of photography served to present African American men in a new, individualized way to a Northern popular audience. In contrast, contrabands, who were either depicted as undifferentiated groups or as "types," were never represented as heroic within the Northern press, despite the fact that their escapes into Union lines clearly often involved acts of daring.

The depictions of the "gallant" crew of the *Planter* signaled a new trend in wartime depictions of African Americans: the insistence that black men could be as "gallant" as whites. Such depictions were politically opportune, as an increasingly wide spectrum of commentators argued for the military necessity of employing black troops. Yet the use of doubling remained an important strategy in portraying blacks: positive images of black men, whether war heroes such as the *Planter's* crew or black soldiers, were often accompanied by images or commentary that reintroduced more familiar negative racialized imagery. Thus, at the end of its brief text celebrating the *Planter's* black heroes, *Frank Leslie's* commented, "In another part of our paper we have shown how our troops punish treacherous and murderous negroes." Likewise, on the same page of *Harper's Weekly* that carried an illustration of Robert Smalls, the weekly ran a cartoon titled "Feeding the Negro Children under Charge of the Military Authorities at Hilton Head, South Carolina," with the commentary "Poor little creatures! they are realizing for the first time that they are human beings, and not of the same class in animated nature as dogs and hogs." [25]

In the summer and fall of 1862, a wide variety of popular publications began to argue for blacks' employment as soldiers, an argument that after Lincoln's preliminary Emancipation Proclamation on September 22 was inextricably bound up with the prospect of emancipation for African Americans. There is no question that in much popular literature many of the initial reasons given for arming blacks, and for supporting emancipation, had a racialized cast that primarily emphasized benefits to whites. "Why are negroes exempt from the burthens of the war?" *Leslie's* asked in September. "Why are black men alone allowed to remain at home in peace and quiet, while the white men of the land are called into the ranks and sent to dig, suffer, fight, and die perhaps on Southern soil? One of the victims of the first collision between the citizens of Boston and the British soldiery was a negro." The right of blacks to be equal victims of the war was one of the few black rights that some Northerners became increasingly enthusiastic about, as shown by the popularity of the early 1864 poem "Sambo's Right to Be Kilt" (see chapter 6).[26]

Yet popular publications also provided positive, if qualified, depictions of black troops in training in 1862. The logic of arguing for the employment of black troops hardly allowed otherwise; after all, arguments claiming that blacks were ineffective soldiers would not be persuasive. Thus on August 30 *Leslie's* published a sketch and commentary by one of its special artists, Crane. His "object" had been "to witness the drill, bearing, and present condition of the 1st Regiment S.C. Volunteers, or, 'Nigger Brigade,' as some unpoetically term it." After witnessing "the parade entire," as well as "the company drills in the Manual of Arms," Crane acknowledged his "complete surprise at the discipline and even *vim* evinced by the rabble crowd." This evidence of "vim" became a motif over the next year in a campaign to persuade the public of the efficacy of employing black troops. In March 1863, for instance, *Harper's Weekly* printed a piece titled "Negroes as Soldiers," which reprinted comments from Thomas Wentworth Higginson on the First South Carolina Volunteers. "Nobody knows anything about these men who has not seen them in battle," Higginson said. "I find that I myself knew nothing. There is a fiery energy about them beyond any thing of which I have ever read, unless it be the French Zouaves. It requires the strictest discipline to hold them in hand." An accompanying two-page illustration by Thomas Nast of "A Negro Regiment in Action" visually underlined this point by showing blacks charging forward with great vigor into rebel ranks. Likewise, in March 1863 *Harper's Weekly* printed an engraving drawn from a photograph of one Jim Williams, an escaped slave who had joined a Union scouting party, singlehandedly captured two rebels, and shot a guerrilla scout. The piece reported that General M'Arthur, "who appreciates true bravery without regard to color, holds him in the highest estimation." To drive the point home, the piece concluded that in Louisiana "a force of ten thousand able-bodied negroes could be raised within thirty days if any effort were made for that purpose."[27]

George Fredrickson has argued that such commentary did not replace "the old stereotype of the docile and inferior 'Sambo'" with a "radically new image of self-reliant and intelligent blacks in uniform." The Sambo image was "merely modified" during the war as various commentators—including, in his diary as well as various published writings, T. W. Higginson— ascribed the success of black troops to their "submissiveness." Although Fredrickson is right in his analysis of the politicians and intellectuals who are his subjects, the pages of popular literature reveal that there was a popular wartime appreciation of the courage of black soldiers. Popular literature, in fact, did not tend to stress the submissiveness and docility of black soldiers. At the same time, however, such literature, whether in essays, illustrations, or fictions, employed a number of strategies to contain the implications of black soldiering and black freedom. Through these representational strategies popular literature denied blacks full membership in the nation.[28]

Foremost among such strategies in *Harper's Weekly* was the frequent assertion of white control of blacks, whether exhibiting "fiery energy" or not. Thus the *Weekly* included an engraving of a stern, upright white officer in the background of its illustration of "A Negro Regiment in Action." The

"Emancipation Day in South Carolina,"
Frank Leslie's Illustrated Newspaper, January 24, 1863.
(Courtesy of the American Antiquarian Society)

white officer's pose was to be a familiar one in engravings of black troops and white officers, in which only whites carried themselves fully erect. Likewise, *Harper's Weekly*'s front-page illustration for March 14, 1863, was "Teaching the Negro Recruits the Use of the Minie Rifle," which showed an upright white officer pointing ahead while an earnest black recruit followed his gaze.[29]

A second strategy was ridicule. Increasingly both *Harper's Weekly* and *Frank Leslie's* avoided the overtly racialized, crudely exaggerated visual representations of blacks that had characterized the first year of the war. Yet *Frank Leslie's* nevertheless often ridiculed blacks and black soldiers in textual commentary that provided a nervous counterpoint to illustrations that seemed to suggest more radical interpretations. *Harper's Weekly*, too, continued to run occasional derogatory cartoons of African Americans.

The January 24, 1863, *Frank Leslie's* illustration of "Emancipation Day in South Carolina" was a prime example of this ambivalent style of representation. Visually, this illustration was notable for its wartime radicalism, as it portrayed a black color sergeant publicly addressing his troops while holding the American flag. A remarkable, symbolic linkage of black soldiers with American nationhood, this illustration was also notable for its relative lack of exaggerated racial stereotyping.

However, the text explaining this image reasserted racial stereotypes even while calling them into question. "Whatever our readers' politics may be," this text began, "they cannot fail to feel a stern satisfaction in the simple fact that within a few miles of that 'most erring of sisters,' Charleston, Emancipation-day, as it is called, was celebrated with great pomp, and that one of the chief rejoicers on the occasion was our old acquaintance, Sambo, who, generally speaking, is always accompanied by the inevitable banjo." The text initially seemed to call into question such minstrel-derived images, saying, "Thousands take their notion of Indians from Cooper's imaginary Uncas, and other impossible Redskins, and just as many build their ideal of a colored person on George Christy's inimitable caricature. Two-thirds of our boarding-school misses believe that a contraband is a dark gentleman with a triangular collar of some two feet high, in new pumps and broadcloth, a set of white ivory, a fine tenor voice, a rather handsome banjo and a remarkably bad hat." A logical next step was to acknowledge that such "impossible" notions of minstrelsy did not define blacks. But this *Leslie's* did not do. Instead, it simply continued by saying, "But we must return to our sketches of some of their doings," with the "their" now referring to two referents merged into one: minstrel blacks and black soldiers.[30]

Such oscillations in popular images of black soldiers—especially between positive visual images of black soldiers and nervous, negative accompanying text—pointed not just to the flexibility and adaptability of older racial stereotyping in wartime but also to the dynamism of new discussions of African Americans in American life. Part of this dynamism in popular literature must be attributed to the variety of new voices appearing in major periodicals during the war. Responding to Northerners' intense interest in all aspects of the war, for instance, both *Frank Leslie's* and *Harper's Weekly* employed "special artists" at the front who sent back illustrations and written reports to their employers. These "special artists"—including, most famously, Winslow Homer, Thomas Nast, A. R. Waud, Edwin Forbes, and Theodore Davis—represented new perspectives emerging within popular literary culture, as war allowed them a cultural authority they would not otherwise have had. The war, in other words, produced new cultural conditions that allowed for changing representation of African Americans within American life.[31]

African American authors and publishers, too, contributed to the changed popular literary culture of war. In 1864, for instance, William Wells Brown republished his earlier 1853 antislavery novel *Clotel; or the President's Daughter* under the new title *Clotelle: A Tale of the Southern States* with the African American publisher Thomas Hamilton of New York. The abolitionist-turned-publisher James Redpath of Boston also published a version of this new *Clotelle* in 1864 as part of his "Books for the Camp Fires" series. Brown also contributed directly to the new literature celebrating black heroism with his 1863 *The Black Man: His Antecedents, His Genius, and His Achievements*, which included a discussion of Robert Smalls.[32]

• • •

It was only in the aftermath of the Massachusetts Fifty-fourth's fight at Fort Wagner on July 18, 1863, however, that popular images of black soldiers began to shift dramatically toward a forthright celebration of black courage and especially black manhood. As Louisa May Alcott wrote of Fort Wagner in her November 1863 *Atlantic Monthly* story "The Brothers," "Through the cannon-smoke of that black night the manhood of the colored race shines before many eyes that would not see, rings in many ears that would not hear, wins many hearts that would not hitherto believe." Yet as W. E. B. Du Bois would later note, there were deep ironies in this celebration of black manhood. "How extraordinary, and what a tribute to ignorance and religious hypocrisy," he wrote in 1935, that "in the minds of most people, even those of liberals, only murder makes men. The slave pleaded; he was humble; he protected the women of the South, and the world ignored him. The slave killed white men; and behold, he was a man!"[33]

If we turn to popular literature, we find an additional layering of the ironies that Du Bois noted. Increasingly in 1863 and 1864, popular literature explored the idea that the war brought a fundamental transformation to black male identity. Some popular war literature made this transformation literal in "before-and-after" illustrations that showed African Americans as slaves and then as soldiers. Yet the very idea of transformation, as Kirk Savage has noted, allowed a doubled consciousness of African Americans as both slave and free, rooted both in the past and in the future. The trope of transformation allowed the past always to be implicit in the present, a form of doubling that became a primary mode of discussing African American participation in the war.[34]

Harper's Weekly's July 4, 1863, illustrated essay "A Typical Negro," for

SEQUEL TO
"KINGDOM COMING."

BABYLON

IS FALLEN!

SONG AND CHORUS.

WORDS AND MUSIC BY

HENRY C. WORK.

CHICAGO:
PUBLISHED BY ROOT & CADY, 95 CLARK STREET.

Entered, according to Act of Congress, A. D. 1863, by Root & Cady, in the Clerk's Office of the District Court for the Northern District of Illinois.

"Babylon Is Fallen!," words and music by Henry C. Work, 1863.
(Courtesy of the Rare Book, Manuscript and Special
Collections Library, Duke University)

instance, presented three portraits based on photographs "of the negro
Gordon, who escaped from his master in Mississippi, and came into our
lines at Baton Rouge on March 1st." The first of the three portraits showed
Gordon seated in a chair, "with clothes torn and covered with mud and dirt
from his long race through the swamps and bayous"; the second "showed
him as he underwent the surgical examination previous to being mustered

"A Typical Negro," *Harper's Weekly*, July 4, 1863.
(Courtesy of the American Antiquarian Society)

into the service—his back furrowed and scarred with the traces of a whipping"; and the third portrait showed Gordon standing upright "in United States uniform, bearing the musket and prepared for duty." Striking about this triptych of portraits was that the portrait of Gordon's scarred back was much larger than the other two, suggesting that the most dramatic and compelling aspect of Gordon's identity was his scourged body rather than his new identity as a soldier. Such an image drew on the conventions of antebellum abolitionist literature in which the naked black body became the sign of slavery that white viewers visually "owned." [35]

If images of transformation paradoxically prevented that imagined transformation from ever being complete, so too stories of black soldiers in battle tended to circumvent the implications of a new black manhood by refusing to imagine the continuing lives of black men. Rarely, indeed, did popular literature attempt to imagine the continuing life of a black soldier. Instead, the imagined popular trajectory was straight to death, as encapsulated in the 1864 "Stephens's Album Varieties," one of several collectible series of "album cards" produced during the war. Titled "The Slave in 1863. A Thrilling Series of the Great Evil," these were twelve "splendidly litho-

Stephens's Album Cards, 1863.
(Courtesy of the Library Company of Philadelphia)

graphed" cards that summarized the life of a slave, including "The Slave in the Cotton Field; The Christmas Week; The Slave; The Parting; 'Buy Us, Too'; The Lash; Blow for Blow; In the Swamp; Free; The Union Lines; The Soldier of the Republic; 'Make Way for Liberty'; Victory; He Died for Liberty."[36]

In poems and stories about black soldiers, heroic death became a dramatic and also convenient way of celebrating black manhood without a sustained imagination of black participation in American life, just as the deaths of "tragic mulattoes" in antebellum novels had been a powerful narrative device that circumvented any sustained imagining of a mixed-race society. The prominent poet Phoebe Cary's "An Incident at Fort Wagner," for instance, imagined a dying black soldier saying to a white soldier, "I'm done gone, Massa; step on me, / And you can scale the wall!" Several stories of black soldiers, including Louisa May Alcott's November 1863 *Atlantic Monthly* story "The Brothers" and the April 1864 *Harper's Weekly* story "Tippoo Saib," also ended with the deaths of their black protagonists at Fort Wagner.[37]

At the same time, these stories provided an ironic twist on W. E. B. Du Bois's maxim that it was the killing of white men that made black men "men" in the eyes of whites, for both of these stories celebrated the reverse: blacks' avoidance of killing whites they had once known intimately. In doing so, these stories expressed a profound ambivalence about the fact of blacks killing whites, even while celebrating black manhood and heroism. In Alcott's "The Brothers," for instance, the former slave Bob, now a contraband working in the hospital where the female narrator Miss Dane was a nurse, was assigned to help her in caring for a rebel prisoner suffering from fever. As the title indicated, this Confederate prisoner was in fact Bob's half brother, a man "whose life had been none of the most righteous, judging from the revelations made by his unconscious lips," and whose "blasphemous wanderings" and "ribald camp-songs" had made the narrator's "cheeks burn." Over the course of the story the narrator learned that this white half brother had raped Bob's wife; yet when Bob considered murdering this hospitalized brother in the dramatic climax of the story, the narrator was able to convince him not to, offering the hope that his wife, Lucy, still lived, though in fact the ravings of his rebel half brother suggested (as indeed proved to be true) that she had committed suicide.[38]

Bob's manhood was of a higher order than that of his white brother, the narrator made clear: the rebel "captain was a gentleman in the world's eye, but the contraband was a gentleman in mine." And part of that manhood ultimately derived from his choosing—for a second time—not to kill his rebel half brother when they later faced each other in battle at Fort Wagner: instead, as a fellow African American soldier explained, Bob "flung away his gun, give a leap, an' went at that feller as if he was Jeff, Beauregard, an' Lee, all in one." Although Bob had flung away all weapons in this last, desperate fight, his rebel brother was not so magnanimous: instead, Bob's fellow soldier saw Bob "git the sword straight through him an' drop into the ditch." "Poor old feller!" his comrade commented. "We said we went in to live or die; he said he went in to die, an' he's done it."[39]

At the end of the story Alcott created a split image of black soldiers, allowing Bob's comrade the chance to kill that she did not allow Bob himself. As he remembered, after Bob had been killed, "I managed somehow to pitch that Reb into the fort as dead as Moses." Apparently Alcott was only comfortable portraying black killing if it was in retaliation or involved strangers. A fundamental discomfort often underlay whites' portrayals of black soldiers killing whites they had known.[40]

Certainly this reluctance to portray black killers of whites extended even to a story specifically intended to celebrate the heroism of African Americans at Fort Wagner. As the narrator of the April 1864 *Harper's Weekly* "Tippoo Saib" commented about Robert Gould Shaw's leadership at Fort Wagner, "We all know who led that assault. A nation mourns, a nation glories, over the hero who there won himself a name that shall not be forgotten while his country holds a memory, a tongue, a pen." But less well known were the heroic actions of some of the individual African American soldiers at Fort Wagner, a situation the story hoped to change: "No nation mourns, no poet sings, no history, save this rude tale, will chronicle the closing scene of another life as brave, as devoted, as earnest, as beautiful to those who have eyes to read the hearts of men as that of his hero-leader." [41]

This imagined hero was the former slave Tippoo Saib, who "was neither handsome, nor accomplished, nor gently bred." Rather, he was "a middle-aged negro of Congo descent, and formed after the ultra type of his race, with misshapen skull, immense lips, close-curled wool, and a skin as nearly black as human skin was ever tinted. He was heavy both of motion and intellect, and entirely ignorant of almost every thing a man should know." Nevertheless, the narrator challenged, "At the end of my story deny, if you dare, that he was a hero." [42]

In this story of black soldiering, the key to the heroism of Tippoo Saib lay in his loyalty and love for "good" whites. Some years earlier, Tippoo Saib had made a fateful choice in deciding against escaping to the North in order to stay and care for his master's "bright-haired child," saying, "He'd ha ben glad to lay down his life, ef so be 'twould ha' done lilly Missy any good." In making this choice, Tippoo "with a deep groan closed his mental eyes upon those alluring dreams of liberty and manhood that had for one brief moment seemed within his grasp." As in most wartime stories, loyalty to whites was praiseworthy — yet not enough to achieve manhood. [43]

Yet Tippoo was to get a second chance to achieve his manhood. Years later, after escaping to Union lines during the war, Tippoo became a soldier and at Fort Wagner was "foremost in that wild charge, dauntless in the front of that dauntless band." The writer had no trouble imagining Tippoo killing Confederate soldiers in the anonymity of battle, saying that he had sent "three of his opponents to their doom." But the climax of the story came when, just as in Alcott's "The Brothers," Tippoo faced a Confederate officer whom he recognized as "Captain Fernald, his former master." Remembering "his own enslaved youth and manhood," the "bitter passions of his strong nature rose within him," and he "tightened with savage vigor the hand that still held uplifted the gleaming bayonet." But even as Tippoo's "savagery" was evoked here, the restraining hand of white "civilization" was brought into play.[44]

"Before the blow could fall," another memory "shot athwart the vengeance of Tippoo's mood." As in *Uncle Tom's Cabin* with its depiction of Little Eva, the figure of a white child was evoked as a sign of purity that "tamed" the "savagery" of African Americans. Remembering his little white mistress, "with golden curls flowing back as she ran, with white arms uplifted to his embrace, with rosy lips that asked no better than to press themselves upon his swarthy cheek," Tippoo suddenly dropped his "arm with its deadly weapon" and instead "hoarsely cried, 'Go 'long Mas'r, I won't kill lilly Missy's fader." As in "The Brothers," such magnanimity was not reciprocal: "The white man with an oath drew the revolver from his belt, and with deliberate aim discharged its contents full into the generous heart that had so faithfully garnered and so well repaid the one love that had illumined his gloomy life." [45]

With both "The Brothers" and "Tippoo Saib" ending in the deaths of their protagonists, it was clear that some of the "manhood" so widely celebrated after Fort Wagner came not just from blacks killing whites but from the sacrificial deaths of blacks themselves for the sake of whites. Northerners were only too willing to celebrate the manhood of black soldiers who no longer had any manhood to exercise.[46]

Yet by 1864 indications of more substantial changes in representations of African American men could also be found in Northern popular literature. In July 1864, a year after its illustrated depiction of Gordon's transformation from slave to soldier, *Harper's Weekly* ran another transformation series, this time a diptych emphasizing the contrast between a seated "Escaped Slave" and a manly, upright "Escaped Slave in the Union Army." "Are these not affecting pictures which are here presented to us?" urged the text: "On the one side, the poor fugitive oppressed with the weariness of two hundred long miles of dusty travel," with "his meagre covering of rags about him"; on the other side, "the soldier crowned with freedom and honor." [47]

The format of this transformation scene was similar to the earlier depiction of Gordon, but there were nevertheless crucial differences. Not only did the emphasis on the scourged black body disappear, but the text itself deliberately focused on black heroism, asking, "Can we not at length have faith in that heroism which has been so gloriously illustrated at Wagner and Olustee and Petersburg?" Moreover, the text linked black heroism to

membership in the nation in a new way, saying that the nation was obligated to protect black soldiers just as black soldiers had protected the
nation. Such text represented an imaginative shift from aligning African
Americans primarily with slavery to aligning blacks primarily with black
manhood and membership in the nation. A doubled consciousness of African Americans remained, but its balance was shifting.[48]

At the same time, some stories, such as *Harper's Weekly*'s October 1864
story "Little Starlight," began to lift the taboo against representations of
former slaves killing their masters. In that story, "Little Starlight" was the
nickname of "a negro urchin" who had escaped to Union lines, whose appearance, like so many depictions of African Americans, was described as
"comical in the extreme" in a way that also suggested Little Starlight's
"barbarity." As the narrator noted, "He had fastened to the right shoulder of his ragged coat—a swallow-tailed blue of unknown antiquity—an
immense epaulet, probably plundered from the baggage of some rebel officer; while a silken sash of flaring crimson was twined round his waist in a
manner at once striking and barbaric, with a long end that trailed behind
like the gaudy tail of some variegated tropic bird." Told by a white character that he was free, for "the President's Proclamation has made you so,"
Little Starlight replied, "I doesn't feel it in de *bones* yet; I nebber will till I
git on to *him*, you know." "Him" was his old master, "Cunnel Billy," whom
Little Starlight expressed a desire to kill.[49]

The question of whether Little Starlight would kill his former master
formed the dramatic centerpiece of the story. "You surely would not kill
your old master?" a white character asked. But Little Starlight simply answered, "Wouldn't I? Yah! yah!," and then "began to fumble among the
various knives and pistols which adorned his person," explaining, "I seed
him lick my ole mudder till de blood flew. Jis' lemme on to him, mass'r, and
you'll see de blood fly yourse'f. Yah! yah! I'se a awful cuss, I is." The white
listener "shuddered at the intensity of passion that lurked in his tones."[50]

Yet despite this evocation of white reluctance to imagine blacks killing whites, the story allowed Little Starlight his wish. When he finally
met "Cunnel Billy" in battle, his "rushing bayonet gored the breast of the
officer." At the end of the story, Little Starlight himself lay dying, but
he could celebrate the freedom that the President's proclamation had not
been enough to give to him: "It am ebening now, an' de sun am setting,
mass'r," he told a white listener. "But I hears de big drum ob de sky rollin'
de rebellie ob de Lord. De day am breakin' for dis chile, mass'r; for *I'se got*

THE COLORED VOLUNTEER
MARCHING INTO DIXIE.

The Colored Volunteer.
(Courtesy of the Library Company of Philadelphia)

it at last!" Little Starlight had achieved freedom through having killed his white master.[51]

Little Starlight did not survive the story, however, a crucial narrative device that contained the imagined violence of blacks. Yet one immensely popular wartime novel revealed that by early 1864 some Northerners at least were ready to read books about black heroes that did not necessarily end with their sacrificial deaths. Still, even that book, John Townsend Trowbridge's *Cudjo's Cave*, underlined the importance of a doubled consciousness in imagining blacks' place in American life, as the book celebrated one "noble" black protagonist while killing off his "misshapen" double.

Cudjo's Cave was directly inspired by emancipation, Trowbridge later remembered, "written with great rapidity in the summer and autumn of 1863" and published in December. As Trowbridge explained, "The country had been but slowly awakening to a consciousness of the truth that the slave was not only to be freed; he was also to cease to be a merely passive occasion of the contest, and to become our active ally. Too many calling themselves patriots still opposed emancipation and the arming of the blacks, and clung tremblingly to the delusion that the Union and slavery might both be preserved. The idol-house of the old prejudice was shattered, but not demolished." Feeling the "old heat" of antislavery beliefs "fevering" him, Trowbridge therefore "flung" himself "upon the writing of as fiery an antislavery fiction as [he] was capable of compassing." "I was impatient to hurl my firebrand into the breach."[52]

As its title suggested, the book was indeed about a cave—an imagined cave deep in the Tennessee wilderness in which two runaway slaves, Pomp and Cudjo, lived. Like many authors during the war, Trowbridge was fascinated by the Unionist struggle in Tennessee and hoped that his romantic invention of a cave would pique Northern readers' curiosity. "Wishing to bring into it some incidents of guerrilla warfare and of the persecutions of the Union men in the border slave States, I cast about for some central fact to give unity to the action, and form at the same time a picturesque feature of the narrative. The idea of a cave somehow suggested itself, and I chose for the scene a region where such things exist." Trowbridge confessed that the "art of the book suffered" from the "disadvantage [he] labored under of never having visited the region [he] described, or studied the dialect of the people."[53]

The resulting novel was a sensationalist work that careened from one violent adventure to another. Trowbridge admitted that *Cudjo's Cave* contained sensational elements: it was a "partisan book, frankly designed to fire the Northern heart," and it "contained scenes of violence such as I should never, under other circumstances, have selected as subjects for my pen." But Trowbridge defended such sensationalism in wartime: "I adapted, but did not invent them; the most sensational incidents had their counterparts in the reign of wrath and wrong I was endeavoring to hold up to the abhorrence of all lovers of the Union and haters of slavery and secession." [54]

Despite the book's title its hero "was not Cudjo," though Trowbridge said, "I no longer shrank from giving a black man that role." Rather, the "real hero, if the story had one, was the proud and powerful, full-blooded African, Pomp, whom I afterwards carried into the third and last of my war stories, The Three Scouts." It was certainly true that *Cudjo's Cave* presented Pomp as a hero, but what is also striking about the book is the way in which the narrative constructed a deliberately split image of blacks. Pomp and Cudjo were the rescuers of a young Quaker schoolmaster, Penn Hapgood, who had "sunk into a swoon" after being beaten, tarred, and feathered for his abolitionist views. In Hapgood's delirium he imagined his rescuers as two halves of a black servant he knew named Toby: Pomp was "Toby the Good," and Cudjo was "Toby the Malevolent." While the good Toby (Pomp) argued, "We can't leave him dying here," the bad Toby (Cudjo) said, "What dat to me, if him die, or whar him die?" [55]

When Hapgood awoke from his delirium, having been carried to Cudjo's cave by these two, he recognized the "twin Tobys of his dreams. And what a contrast between the two! There was Toby the Good, otherwise called Pomp, dignified, erect, of noble features; while before him cringed and grimaced Toby the Malign, alias Cudjo, ugly, deformed, with immensely long arms, short bow legs resembling a parenthesis, a body like a frog's, and the countenance of an ape." [56]

Trowbridge sincerely meant for his book to combat Northern racial prejudice: when Penn Hapgood asked Pomp, "Why have you never escaped to the north?" Pomp answered, "Would I be any better off there? Does not the color of a negro's skin, even in your free states, render him an object of suspicion and hatred?" Penn "sadly" agreed, while "contemplating the form of the powerful and intelligent black, and thinking with indignation and shame of the prejudice which excludes men of his race from the privileges of free men, even in the free north." [57]

But despite this statement, Trowbridge unwittingly reinscribed the very prejudice he so passionately criticized. In creating Cudjo, he suggested that many slaves had been so debased by slavery as to be barely human. Whereas Pomp's features "lighted up with intelligence and sympathy," when Cudjo laughed, he showed "two tremendous rows of ivory glittering from ear to ear" and looked more "like a demon of the cave than a human being." When Cudjo died at the end—a dramatic death in which, after being shot himself, he dragged a cruel overseer down an embankment so that they both drowned in the river below—it was a solution to a dilemma that Trowbridge had portrayed as insoluble: how uneducated slaves would be integrated into free society.[58]

Yet Pomp, for all his cardboard, one-dimensional nobility, was a significant wartime invention, both a fighter and a leader. He and a group of white Unionists fought together against the rebels, and "instinctively they accepted his lead." His heroism may have been racialized—he was "swift and stealthy as a panther," for instance, and his "haughty self-assertion which would have been offensive in a white man, was vastly becoming to the haughty and powerful black"—but he was nonetheless a clear attempt to imagine a black military hero and, as such, a new wartime departure from antebellum norms of black heroism. Significantly, too, he was not killed at the end. "Have you read the newspaper stories of a certain negro scout," the narrator asked at the conclusion of the novel, "who, by his intrepidity, intelligence, and wonderful celerity of movement, has rendered such important services to the Army of the Cumberland? He is the man." [59]

Cudjo's Cave met with immense, even startling success in late 1863 and early 1864, in part attributable to the tactics of its publisher. J. E. Tilton, "a young and enterprising firm," according to Trowbridge, used "considerable ingenuity and no little audacity in advertising it." Not only were "pictures of the cave" on envelopes and posters, but Trowbridge remembered "a bookseller's window" with a "pile of the freshly bound volumes erected in the similitude of a cave." But readers did not only respond to the book's sensationalism; they also responded to its antislavery politics. As Elizabeth Boynton of Crawfordsville, Indiana, wrote to her soldier lover in February 1864, "I sometimes shudder when I think what an *horrible* institution 'American Slavery' *is*—how long before we can say *was*—I have just finished that new story 'Cudjo's Cave' and I wonder how men with any minds can think for an instant that slavery is aught but a *curse*." [60]

By the end of the war, the evocation of the achievement of black manhood through soldiering had become a commonplace in popular literature. In April 1865, for instance, *Harper's Weekly* ran a cartoon titled "A Man Knows a Man," portraying a white and black soldier, each on a crutch and with only one leg, shaking hands. The caption was "Give me your hand, Comrade! We have each lost a LEG for the good cause; but, thank GOD, we never lost HEART." Yet despite this overt acknowledgment of the manhood of black soldiers, the narrative strategies used to describe their actions, as we have seen, most often circumscribed and sharply limited the implications of such manhood in American society, whether through imagined white control of black actions, ridicule, or, most often, death.[61]

• • •

Popular literature in the South sustained an entirely different set of fantasies about African Americans and their relationship to soldiering in 1863 and 1864, imagining black men refusing to fight, kidnapped by Yankees, and always eager to return home in order to "belong to somebody." The *Southern Illustrated News* ran a cartoon in March 1863 showing Lincoln holding out a rifle to "my Dear Old Friend Sambo," saying, "Course you'll fight for us, Sambo," while in fact "Sambo" stood with his arms crossed and his back turned against Lincoln's entreaties. Two stories published in popular literary magazines fantasized that slaves were eager to run away from Yankees, not from slavery. "Nights on the Rapidan," published in March 1864 in the *Southern Illustrated News*, told the story of the slaves Hannibal and Jim, who had been to Gettysburg with their masters. Described in the reductive shorthand of racism as "grinning and rolling his eyes," Hannibal explained that in Gettysburg he "lost Mauss' Henry" and was taken up by "a mighty nice man wid a white choker and black clothes," who "said he would take care of us, an' bring us to the promised lan' of Canaan" and "tole us to return thanks for our 'mancipation." After a "camp meetin'" in which Jim "cried right out, and shouted glory," the story suggested Northern antislavery women's lascivious natures by commenting that "all de ladies cried an' shook hands with us again an' a'most hugged us, till we were real shamed." After this meeting, the antislavery minister told Hannibal that "dis chile was a chosen wessel, and was fit to carry the word of God to all my brudders." Indeed, Hannibal said that "it would be long to tell you all de places we went to, and the lots of apple butter we got, and the prayers an' exortions." But "all dis while," Hannibal reported, he and Jim were thinking "how mighty bad Mauss' Henry an' Jim's Maussa must be doin' widout us. An' besides dat, I had promised de ole Mauss, an' Miss Mary, down in Alabama, dat I would fetch Mauss' Henry home safe if I was alive."[62]

Not only did this story imagine continued slave loyalty in the face of

ONE GOOD TURN DESERVES ANOTHER.

"One Good Turn Deserves Another,"
Southern Illustrated News, March 14, 1863.
(Courtesy of the Rare Book, Manuscript and Special
Collections Library, Duke University)

emancipation, but it also imagined that these slaves escaped from Union lines in order to return South—the reverse of what actually happened during the war. One night Jim and Hannibal "pressed two mules" and "franked de pickets." "Lor bress you," Hannibal said, "dis nigger can frank a Confed picket any time, let alone an abolish one." "But Hannibal," another character in the story asked, "why didn't you and Jim think of staying in that country where the ladies all shook hands with you, and the apple butter was so plenty?" As Hannibal explained, "We had learn a deal about dat Canaan, as dey call it, an' how poor culled pussons is used dere at Washington"; they knew "'bout all de meanness of de abolish. An' so when we were prayin' an' returnin' thanks our very loudest, I was sayin' all dat while to myself: 'No, mister, you don't fool dis chile.'" These slaves were too smart to want anything but a return to slavery.[63]

The white fantasy that slaves would prefer at all costs to escape from Yankees and return to slavery reached its apotheosis in the sensational story "The Scout of Albado; or, Vengeance Is Mine: A Tale of Retribution," published in a series of installments in the *Southern Field and Fireside* during the late fall of 1864. At the heart of "The Scout of Albado" was a profound denial that slaves would willingly become soldiers. In an opening scene, the heroic white scout of the story's title captured a Yankee in the wilderness, only to be "astonished" to find "the woolly head and inky face of a negro, surmounting a full suit of Yankee blue." Indeed, the text reiterated, the scout "was almost paralyzed with astonishment, for a negro soldier was a far less common object than now." Yet as the text made clear, this Yankee soldier had only become a soldier under duress and certainly had not been made a man by his soldiering. Instead, under the "stern countenance" of the white scout, the black soldier "fairly sunk upon the ground and grovelled in the very abasement of terror": "Please God, Mar's, don't fire. Fore de Lord dey made me go wid 'em." "Shrieking out his frantic supplications," the slave "threw himself down at the very feet of the Scout."[64]

The text lingered at length over the physical abasement of the black soldier, calling into play the racist shorthand that signaled blacks' debased humanity: "Writhing in his terror the sooty defender of the old flag presented in his appearance a strange mixture of the tragic and the comic. Mortal dread was stamped too keenly in every lineament to excite a laugh, and yet, with his coarse animal features distorted with fear, his great, senseless eyes rolling frantically about, and the tears, hot and salty, coursing down into his huge, open mouth, the whole expression was such a grim caricature of the griefs of our own humanity that it would have been hard to restrain a smile at its absurdity." Here the threat of black soldiering was effectively dismissed through ridicule.[65]

It turned out that this slave, Sam, had been forced to become a soldier: "When dey kill ole marster an burn de house dey tuk all us boys to de camp an say dey would make us fine sojers for de ole flag an all sich, an dey wouldn't mine me 'tall, dough I tell 'em nigger ain't gwine to fight." Forced into battle, Sam had instead run away: "As soon as I hear de balls come along an say *zee-ip! zee-ip!* all about dar I say dis no place for Sam and takes out mighty peart." As a result, the Yankees had punished him severely, and in a scene that deliberately echoed both abolitionist litera-ture and war literature picturing slaves' scourged backs, Sam "exposed his back cut up in the most sickening manner with the lash." The narra-tor underlined this reversal between North and South: "True to their vile nature, the negro's pretended friends had scourged the poor wretch with a merciless severity that could find no parallel save in those mendacious and highly seasoned stories they write of the South." [66]

The sensationalist climax of "The Scout of Albado" came when Sam faced the Yankee who had whipped him and now threatened him in a fight. When Colonel Weaver "raised his sabre" to cut Sam down, Sam put "into practise [sic] the skill he had learned from the Yankee drill master, parried the blow and then with one furious lunge drove the bayonet into his assail-ant till the point came out between the shoulder blades." The point was clear: the training slaves received from Yankees would be turned against Yankees, not Southerners. As a major in the story commented, Weaver had "fallen by the very hand he taught the use of arms and would have turned against us. Some may deem it chance," but he instead believed that this was "RETRIBUTION." [67]

In the moment that Sam turned violently against the Yankees, a dif-ferent side of racial stereotyping came into play in the text, part of the doubling that incessantly accompanied representations of African Ameri-can men. The flip side of Sam's debased, cringing, fearful nature was his savagery, which the violence of war called forth: though Colonel Weaver stretched out his arms "for mercy," Sam was "frenzied with his triumph, and with all his savage nature aroused by the sight of blood, the African whirled the gun in the air" and "brought its heavy, iron shod butt swoop-ing down upon him, crushing his scull [sic] into a thousand fragments." The release of such "savagery" implicitly raised the question of whether Sam's violence might also be exercised against Southerners, too, but the text reverted to ridicule in order to minimize this threat. When Sam returned from killing Colonel Weaver, a Confederate major watching him "could barely restrain a smile" at the ludicrous sight Sam made, having decked himself in all of Colonel Weaver's finery, including a "rich crimson net silk sash," a "handsome sword," a "pair of polished spurs" that "glittered on his naked heels," and a "regulation hat and plume" on his "woolly head." He "approached the officers in a state of unimaginable pomp and self-glorification. His goggle eyes rolled rapturously in his head, and from ear to ear his huge mouth was on the grin, disclosing a range of ivories that seemed to join in the general expression of entire complacency and self satisfaction." This description was reminiscent of the description of Little Starlight in *Harper's Weekly* and a reminder of the linkages between Northern and Southern forms of racism.[68]

Driving the point home that African Americans not only preferred but often yearned for slavery, in the denouement of the story, a Confederate victory resulted in the capture of other "negro troops" who were "nothing loth" to be made "prisoners and sent off to their respective masters, from whom they had been stolen, amply satisfied with their experience of Yankee liberty and equality, and crazy to exchange the musket for the hoe and the camp for the cotton field."[69]

If African American men desired nothing more than to return to slavery in the pages of Southern popular literature, African American women, too, begged to return to their masters. "The Contraband's Return," for instance, published in the *Richmond Whig* on May 26, 1864, by "Hermine," portrayed "old Aunt Rebecca" pleading to be allowed to return to slavery after having escaped North:

> I never knew the old plantation
>   Was half so dear a place to me,
> As when among that Yankee nation
>   The robbers told me I was free!
> But when I looked around for freedom,
>   (We thought it something bright and fair)
> Hunger, misery and starvation
>   Was all that met us there.

Each of the verses of the poem detailed the cruelty of Yankees. Not only did they force Aunt Rebecca's son to be a soldier, but they expected him to kill his "young master." But as in Northern war stories, "poor Phil" could not kill a white he had known intimately, and in retaliation the Yankees, who in a process of inversion were the true "more than cruel masters," killed him instead:

Before him once, in line of battle,
　　He saw our fine young master Jim,
Then dropped poor Phil his Yankee musket,
　　He would not, could not, fire on him;
For they had played, been raised together,
　　Young master Jim had cried for Phil—
The Yankees gave the onward order,
　　But my poor boy stood still.

And then his more than cruel masters,
　　White men, with hearts and deeds all black,
Struck him down with gun and sabre,
　　And left him dying on their track.

At the same time, Yankee soldiers had ruined Aunt Rebecca's daughter Judy, as well:

Oh! missus, my old heart is broken,
　　My lot all grief and pain has been,
For little Judy, too, is ruined,
　　In their dark camps of sin!

The poem concluded with Aunt Rebecca's plea to be allowed to return to slavery:

O, Massa William, see me kneeling!
　　O, missus, say one word for me!
You'll let me stay? Oh! thank you, massa;
　　Now I'm happy! now I'm free!
I've seen enough of Yankee freedom,
　　I've had enough of Yankee love!
As they have treated the poor negro
　　Be't done to them above.[70]

As "The Contraband's Return" made clear, freedom for the slave was actually a form of slavery, while only slavery allowed true freedom. This paradoxical understanding that true freedom for African Americans could only be found in slavery also underlay two popular poems found in scrapbook collections of newspaper poetry made by Southern readers during the war, both of which imagined female slaves refusing offers to be free. "A Southern Scene from Life" imagined a conversation between a young white child and her "mammy" in which the mammy not only insisted that she wanted nothing to do with emancipation but also affirmed a racial order in which whites were superior to blacks:

"Oh! mammy, have you heard the news?"
Thus spoke a Southern child,
As in her nurse's aged face
She upwards glanced and smiled.
"What news you mean? my little one,
It must be mighty fine,
To make my darling's cheeks so red,
Her merry blue eyes shine."

"Why Abram Lincoln, don't you know
The Yankee President,
Whose ugly picture once we saw,
When up to town we went;
Well he is going to free you all;
And make you rich and grand,
And you'll be dressed in silks and gold,
Like the proudest of the land.

A gilded coach shall carry you
Where'er you wish to ride,
And, mammy, all your work shall be
Forever laid aside."
The eager speaker paused for breath,
And the old nurse said,
While closer to her swarthy cheek,
She pressed the golden head;

"My little Missus, stop and res,
You's talkin mighty fas,
Jes look up dere, and tell me what
You see in yonder glass?
You see old mammy's wrinkly face,
As black as any coal;
And underneath her hankercher
Whole heaps of knotty wool.

Kingdom Coming : 187

My baby's face is red and white,
Her skin is soft an' fine,
And on her pretty little head
De yeller ringlets shine.
My chile, who made dis difference
'Twixt mammy and 'twix you?
You reads de dear Lord's blessed book,
And you can tell me true.

De good Lord said it must be so,
And honey I for one,
Wid tankful heart will always say
His holy will be done.
I tanks Mass Linkum all the same,
But when I wants for free,
I'll ask the Lord of glory,
Not buckra man like he.

And as for gilded carriages,
Dey's nothin' tall to see:
My massa's coach, what carries him,
Is good enough for me,
An' honey, when your mammy wants
To change her homespun dress,
She'll pray like dear ole Missus
To be clothed with righteousness.

I've heard dis talk afore, Missus—
It all sounds mighty nice,
But I nebber b'lieve a word dey say,
It's all a mean dewice.
I'de rudder my old Missus sarve
An nus Young Missus too
Dan go to Yankee lan an starve
As foolish niggers do." [71]

Likewise, the poem "Philanthropy Rebuked. A True Story," reiterated
these themes by imagining a female slave rejecting an offer made by a
Northerner to "Come flee this land ob bondage, and go along with me, /
Where you, and where your children, will evermore be free." Again, the
female slave was imagined to prefer slavery over freedom:

Now, Massa, dis is berry fine, dese words youv'e [*sic*] spoke to me,
No doubt you mean it kindly, but ole Dinah won't be free,
I 'spect your home's a happy one—I hope it may be so,
But I'se better in de cotton-field den 'mong your hills ob snow.

Ole Massa's berry good to me—and though I am his slave,
He treats me like I'se kin to him—and I would rather have
A home in Massa's cabin, and eat his black bread too,
Den leave ole Massa's children, and go and lib wid you.

. . . .

I know I shall not suffer when I'm wrinkle old and blind,
For Massa's children will be good—I nursed 'em like dey'se mine,
And Missus will take care ob me—she's good and kind to all—
Though I'm Dinah in de cabin, and she Missus in de hall.

If nature made me to be free—now Massa ain't I right?
Do you think I would be what I am? Don't you think I would be
     white?
But for what I was intended, neither you nor I can say;
I only know I'se satisfied, and will not go away.

I've heard young massa tellin' how dese abolishers talk,
Till dey 'suade de nigger from his home, den make him toe de chalk.
Now'f you be one ob them go 'way, for Dinah's gettin' old,
And won't go wid you though you fill her pockets wid your gold.

De only freedom dat I want, is dat I'll hab in heaven,
De only hopes dat cheers my life are dem de Lord hab given;
And when He calls for Dinah she am prepared to go,
Till den she'll lub ole Georgia, with her cotton fields like snow.[72]

As a number of Southern popular poems argued, slave women's very identity was founded on their closeness to whites. Susan Blanchard Elder's "The Old Mammy's Lament for Her Young Master," published in the *Southern Literary Messenger* late in 1863, imagined a slave woman who missed her "dear young massa" who had "gone to war." "And oh! it makes my heart so sore," she said, "To think how long a time 'twill be / Before I see his handsome face / A peepin' in my cabin door." In Southern popular literature African American women appeared as "Dinah" or "Mammy," nurturing figures who not only did not desire freedom but chastised those whites who suggested that they might want anything other than slavery.[73]

Mulattoes, whether male or female, almost never appeared in such literature, for reasons suggested by Hazel Carby in analyzing the figure of the mulatto in late-nineteenth-century literature. As Carby has said, the mulatto "had two narrative functions: it enabled an exploration of the social relations between the races," and "it enabled an expression of the sexual relations between the races, since the mulatto was a product not only of proscribed consensual relations but of white sexual domination." Confederate literature, however, worked to mystify the power relations of slavery by maintaining the fiction that no such sexual or social relations existed. Thus the mulatto almost never figured in Confederate literature.[74]

Northern Civil War literature, on the other hand, frequently turned to the figure of the mulatto. Several stories during the war operated as explorations of the boundaries between white and black, with female figures as sexualized boundary markers. The *Harper's Weekly* June 1864 story "Why It Could Not Be," for instance, explored the evolving love story between a soldier blinded in battle and the nurse who cared for him and whom he did not realize was African American. "I valued Rose's kindness beyond all the rest," the soldier narrator commented. "One word of hers, one touch of hers, made me happy." The story even allowed the two would-be lovers an unknowing kiss, as the wounded soldier "pressed kisses on her lips." But when he eventually asked Rose to marry him, she simply told him that though she loved him, "God has placed a barrier between us: I can never be your wife." At first he thought that barrier must be his physical appearance: "Am I so unsightly a thing that you shrink from me with loathing?" But of course the underlying irony of the story was that it was he who would shrink from her when he later recovered his sight and discovered that Rose was a quadroon. Indeed, the story offered no hesitation in the soldier's rejection of Rose once he had discovered her racial heritage: "How beautiful she was! Yet her beauty—the sad beauty of her race—lay between us like a curse." The story made the necessary rejection explicit: "Had I heard Rose Peyton's voice, and, turning, looked upon a woman deformed and scarred, but *white*, I should have opened my arms and cried, 'Hide here; your soul is beautiful, and I love you.'" But because Rose was of mixed race, "the Rose I loved was not there for me; she lived no more." Indeed, "God had said it could not be." The narrator concluded, "I would give my sight again, and live blind forever," only "not to know the secret Rose strove to hide from me—only not to know that the only woman I ever loved was a quadroon."[75]

"Why It Could Not Be" marked a sexualized boundary between the races by asserting that intermarriage between a Northern white man and an African American woman was an impossibility. A few other Northern wartime stories explored interracial sexual relationships in a more sympathetic key, however. A more radical discussion of love and marriage between whites and blacks, for instance, was Louisa May Alcott's "M. L.," published in Boston's *Commonwealth* in January and February 1863, immediately following the Emancipation Proclamation. That the postemancipation climate of the war allowed for a more radical rethinking of sexual relationships between the races, albeit briefly and only in a specialized publication such as the *Commonwealth* (in which Harriet Beecher Stowe had initially serialized *Uncle Tom's Cabin*), was shown by the publishing history of this story, which Alcott had written before the war but had failed to get published. Indeed, in 1860 she had written in her journal that her story had been rejected because "it is antislavery and the dear South must not be offended." In 1863, however, this situation had changed. The *Commonwealth*, an "immediate-emancipation" weekly that had been started by abolitionist Moncure Conway, was willing to print Alcott's story.[76]

"M. L." developed the well-worn theme of the talented and compelling "tragic mulatto," in this case the gifted musician Paul Frere (the name itself reminding readers that he was their "brother"), who passed as a "Spaniard" in white society. With a more compelling and noble spirit than the shallow society around him, he attracted the interest of a similarly noble white woman, and the story was careful to stress the depth and spirituality of their love as well as their mutual passion. But after their engagement, a malicious and small-minded woman exposed the fact that Paul had once been a slave, a crisis that in most "tragic mulatto" stories would have led inexorably to the hero's death. The real radicalism of Alcott's story came from the simple fact that not only did the hero continue to live, but the hero and heroine married and flourished together. Indeed, Alcott sketched a picture in which, after suffering initially from the snubs of friends, Paul and Claudia were invited to reenter the society that earlier shunned them. "Slowly all things right themselves when founded on truth," the narrator concluded in this hopeful race fable. "Time brought tardy honors to Paul, and Claudia's false friends beckoned her to come and take her place again," but this time Claudia refused to rejoin society, saying with a "smile of beautiful content," "I cannot give the substance for the shadow." [77]

"M. L." was unusual in attempting to imagine, however briefly, the consequences of an interracial marriage and in denying "natural" social boundaries between the races. But "M. L." appeared in a specialized publication, not one that reached a wide audience. More common were popular stories and novels that, even when highly sympathetic to black freedom, reinscribed boundaries between the races through plots that killed mulattoes who occupied new social positions. The 1863 postemancipation novel *Peculiar, a Tale of the Great Transition*, for instance, written by editor and schoolbook author Epes Sargent, was explicitly sympathetic to black freedom—and, more radically still, to black equality in Northern life. Advertised by its publisher as "a new and striking American novel" that "cannot fail to command an extraordinary sale," *Peculiar* featured a fugitive slave named "Peculiar Institution" and a convoluted plot that began in the antebellum period but took its characters into the Civil War.[78]

One of *Peculiar*'s several subplots was a love story between a white man and a slave meant to confront white fears of "amalgamation." In this subplot William continued to love Estelle after discovering that "in spite of her fair complexion" she was actually a slave. Though at first, he confessed, "such was the influence of education, of inherited prejudice, and of social proscription, that when she told me she was a slave, I shuddered as a high-caste Brahmin might when he find that the man he has taken by the hand is a Pariah," he overcame this reaction and experienced a "strange rapture" when "nature had proved stronger than convention." After their marriage, however, Estelle was recaptured by her master—and died at his hands. This imagined death, like the deaths of "tragic mulattoes" in a number of wartime stories, provided a graphic, negative answer to the question of whether a biracial society was possible in America.[79]

Yet like several short stories written in 1863 and 1864, *Peculiar* also argued strongly for black equality through the figure of a black male. Introducing Peculiar, Sargent offered a critique of clichéd representations of blacks, noting that "there was nothing in the negro's language to indicate the traditional slave of the stage and the novel, who always say 'Massa,' and speaks a gibberish indicated to the eye by a cheap misspelling of words." "Let us give the black man a fair field," a white character named Vance urged: "Let us not begin by declaring his inferiority in capacity, and then anxiously strive to prevent his finding a chance to prove our declaration untrue." Vance carried such arguments to the White House, in a chapter that pictured him trying to convince Lincoln to dedicate himself unreservedly to emancipation and to allow Vance to raise a black regiment. The book concluded with a celebration of the courage of black soldiers at Milliken's Bend in June 1863: "The 'chivalry' came on, expecting to see their former bondsmen crouch and tremble at the first imperious word; but, to the dismay of the Rebels, they were met with such splendid bravery, that they turned and fled, and the Illinois men were saved." [80]

Leading those black soldiers, and dying in the attempt, was Peculiar. As in so many other Northern stories and novels of the war, the achievement of black heroism was, ironically, most easily imagined through sacrificial death. Nevertheless, the imagination of black heroism within popular literature marked a new phase in representations of African Americans.

• • •

It is hard to gauge the impact of *Peculiar*. Its publisher, G. W. Carleton, clearly hoped for a smashing success with its publication. "The sale of this book bids fair to be something enormous," he predicted in November 1863, and in December he advertised the "Sixth Thousand Now Ready." But there is little indication that *Peculiar* achieved the best-seller status Carleton desired. Still, one Indiana reader made clear that the novel had had a tremendous impact on her. "You have doubtless noticed criticisms upon a new book called 'Peculiar,'" Elizabeth Boynton wrote to her soldier fiancé in March 1864. "I read it last week and it has given me more intense views of that most enormous evil of the nineteenth century, American Slavery, than I have ever had before — and when I closed the book" and "thought of all the evils attendant upon slavery I thanked God that I had been called on to give him who is dearer to me than all else, to a war that will eventually produce its overthrow." [81]

By 1864, when Boynton wrote to her soldier lover, changes in representations of African Americans were obvious in major periodicals such as *Frank Leslie's Illustrated Newspaper*. In January 1864, *Leslie's* printed a two-page illustrated spread titled "The Negro in the War," which portrayed African Americans "On Picket," "In the Trenches," "Cooking in Camp," as "Scouts," at the "Govrnt. Blacksmiths' Shop," "Washing in Camp," "Driving Govt. Cattle," "Building Roads," "Unloading Govt. Stores," as a "Teamster of the Army," and at the "Battle of Milliken's Bend." In accompanying commentary, *Leslie's* said that "the negro will ever figure as a prominent feature in the present civil war." Saying that African Americans "have been caricatured in some cases and more fairly treated in others," it claimed that the "gallantry of the men who fought at Milliken's Bend, who rushed to the assault of Port Hudson and Fort Wagner, will stand as proudly in American history as the defence of the fort on the Delaware in the Revolution." [82]

This was a major shift from visual portrayals of African Americans in *Leslie's* early in the war. Although the weekly claimed that "it is not our part to discuss questions of political bearing, but simply to portray living history," in fact *Leslie's* portrayal of "living history" was a vital part of the cultural politics of the war. As Northern periodicals embraced changes in the status of African Americans that Southern periodicals continued to deny, they also embraced a new diversified nationalism in the public space of popular literary culture. That embrace was admittedly tentative, conditioned, and incomplete—but it nevertheless marked a transformative moment in American cultural politics. An expanded realm of imaginative freedom was a major result of the politics of emancipation during the war.[83]

This is not to argue, however, that all forms of popular literature participated equally in changed perceptions of blacks. On the contrary, even in the major illustrated weeklies cartoons and columns of "contraband humor" acted as counterpoint to new images of African Americans featured elsewhere in the same issues. Such humor was part of a larger popular literature that found much to mock in the war.

The Humor of War

Come all ye jolly volunteers
  Who have been into the wars,
I will tell you my sad story,
  And how made a son of Mars.

My age is twenty-five or more,
  And I never liked to fight;
So when this cruel war began
  I just kept out of sight.

The conscript guard they dodged about,
  And I tried to do the same;
They wanted to put me in the front,
  Do you think I was to blame?

— *"A Conscript's Troubles,"* The Punch Songster, *1864*

"I am in a star-spangled state of mind, my boy."
— *Orpheus C. Kerr [Robert Henry Newell],*
  Orpheus C. Kerr Papers. Second Series.

Only a few minutes before Abraham Lincoln announced the preliminary Emancipation Proclamation to his cabinet in September 1862, he read aloud an extended passage from a popular book of war humor by Artemus Ward, the pseudonym of author Charles Farrar Browne. Secretary of War Stanton later recorded his disgust with what he saw as Lincoln's inappropriate levity:

He was reading a book of some kind, which seemed to amuse him. It was a little book. He finally turned to us and said: "Gentlemen, did you ever read anything from Artemus Ward? Let me read you a chapter that is very funny." Not a member of the Cabinet smiled; as for myself, I was angry, and looked to see what the President meant. It seemed to me like buffoonery. He, however, concluded to read us a chapter from Artemus Ward, which he did with great deliberation, and, having finished, laughed heartily, without a member of the Cabinet joining in the laughter. "Well," he said, "let's have another chapter," and he read another chapter, to our great astonishment. I was considering whether I should rise and leave the meeting abruptly, when he threw his book down, heaved a sigh, and said: "Gentlemen, why don't you laugh? With the fearful strain that is upon me night and day, if I did not laugh I should die, and you need this medicine as much as I do." [1]

This was not the first—or last—time that Lincoln indulged in reading work by popular war humorists to high-ranking members of government. On the evening of March 17, 1865, for instance, Lincoln's "melancholy features grew bright" as he read to Charles Sumner "with infinite zest" from a pamphlet collection of the letters of Petroleum V. Nasby (the pseudonym of David Ross Locke). "For the genius to write these things," Sumner reported Lincoln saying, "I would gladly give up my office." Likewise, Lincoln "used to read and quote" from the "Papers" of Orpheus C. Kerr (Robert Henry Newell) on "all occasions, fit or unfit." [2]

Lincoln's enjoyment of war humor did not mark him as unusual in the North, despite some cabinet members' disapproval; on the contrary, it simply marked him as the foremost participant in an extensive popular culture of war humor. Pieces by Artemus Ward, Petroleum V. Nasby, Orpheus C. Kerr, and Miles O'Reilly in the North, as well as Bill Arp in the South, were first published in newspapers or magazines, exchanged and reprinted widely by newspaper editors, and then collected into books. Comic war songs, war cartoons, broadsides, and humorous journals such as the North's *Phunny Phellow* and *Frank Leslie's Budget of Fun*, as well as the Confederate *Southern Punch*, *Hard Tack*, and *Bugle Horn of Liberty*, all marked the belief both north and south that there was much that was entertaining in war. Several publishers produced books of humor aimed specifically at soldiers, such as the 1864 Confederate *Camp Jester or, Amusement for the Mess* or the Northern *Sojers' Comic Almanac for 1863*. In 1863 the *Southern Illustrated News* mentioned that editor George W. Bagby

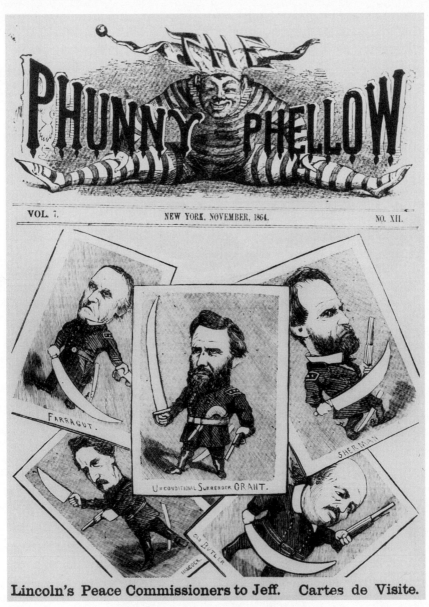

The Phunny Phellow, November 1864.
(Courtesy of the Brown University Library)

Southern Punch, August 15, 1863.
(Courtesy of the Rare Book, Manuscript and Special
Collections Library, Duke University)

Sojer's Comic Almanac for 1863.
(Courtesy of the Library Company of Philadelphia)

Go it, skedaddler, what a queer sight,
To see a brave (?) soldier run off from a fight;
Whenever you hear there's a sign of a battle,
Your kneepans and toes together do rattle.
The best friends you have they are now getting soured,
On seeing you are such an absolute coward.
519

T. W. Strong, New-York.

Comic valentine.

(Courtesy of the Library Company of Philadelphia)

was collecting material for a book to be called "Humorous Anecdotes of the War." Although this work was never published, it, along with other humor books and columns labeled "Humors of the War" in illustrated weeklies, revealed that war humor was an expected literary response to the war.[3]

In inviting laughter at the war, war humor was notable among genres of war literature for standing at a critical distance from the war, a distance not possible in earnestly patriotic or sentimental literature. Those genres maintained the fiction that all soldiers were brave, that battle was glorious, that battlefield death was heroic—that war, in short, was intrinsically noble. War humor, in contrast, emphasized the fear, incompetence, cupidity, avarice, and racism of those involved in the war effort. Rather than universalizing the war as noble, war humor found in the particulars of war much that was ridiculous and even despicable. Among the print ephemera of war in the North, for instance, were humorous soldier valentines that created a series of mocking portraits of drunken soldiers and cowardly officers. Accompanying one crude cartoon of a drunken Union soldier leaning against a lamppost was the following verse:

> My friend, your picture here you see,
> A *patriotic warlike Soldier*, yes, sir'ee!
> *You* love your country, and are its sworn defender,
> But love your *Cocktails*, and glory in a *bender*.
> With an army such as you to fight to slaughter,
> Jeff. Davis need not fear on land or water.[4]

If some war humorists expressed dissatisfaction with soldiers, others expressed soldiers' own dissatisfaction with the war. The 1864 Confederate *Punch Songster*, for instance, included several comic songs bemoaning the fate of those who wanted to avoid conscription. "The Conscript's Lament," a song that had been performed at the New Richmond Theatre, commented, "I'll tell you boys, in Richmond the times are getting tight, / For all young men who have no mind to go to the field and fight." "I Am Sick, Don't Draft Me, 'I have got a Doctor's certificate,' " was the title of a comic broadside.[5] Likewise, the 1863 "He's Gone to the Arms of Abraham," a Northern "comic war ballad," imagined a young girl singing

> My true love is a soldier
> In the army now today,
> It was the cruel war that made him
> Have to go away;
>
> The draft it was that took him,
> And it was a "heavy blow,"
> It took him for a Conscript,
> But he didn't want to go.

"Should he meet a rebel," the song continued, "I hope he may have courage / To 'take care of number one.'" "For what's the use of dying / Just for Jeff or Abraham?"[6]

War humor provided a means of registering dissatisfaction with the war, often through the mouthpieces of humorous characters. But it had other uses as well, including avowedly patriotic uses. A number of war humorists created comic characters whose own absurd opinions and prejudices were meant, through the device of exaggeration, to expose either narrow-minded resistance to the war or aspects of wartime culture that might threaten the nation. As the humorist Robert Henry Newell commented, "the flaws in patriotism, statesmanship and general public pretension, which most seriously menace the stability of a nation," must be "exaggerated" in humor "in order that they may find adequate reprehension in the popular understanding." Newell himself exaggerated what he saw as "flaws in patriotism" through his invention of the eccentric character Orpheus C. Kerr and the hapless Mackerel Brigade to which he belonged, whose comic, bumbling exploits at the front he published in a series of letters to the *New-York Mercury*. Similarly, David Ross Locke invented the racist Butternut character Petroleum V. Nasby with a specific patriotic purpose in mind: he sought to support Lincoln's administration by exposing the small-minded hypocrisies of Ohio Copperhead Democrats. Charles Farrar Browne also spoofed the absurdities of small-town patriotic culture through the character of Artemus Ward. And in the South, Charles H. Smith's invention of the yeoman farmer Bill Arp provided a means of supporting the Confederate war effort while also criticizing some of its failures and excesses.[7]

The work of these Civil War humorists, whose humor was widely read, often quoted, and frequently exchanged among newspapers, forms the main subject of this chapter. The war humorists shared several features. Each began work on a newspaper—Charles Farrar Browne (Artemus Ward) in Cleveland; David Ross Locke (Petroleum V. Nasby) in Hancock County, Ohio; Robert Henry Newell (Orpheus C. Kerr) in New York, on the *New-York Mercury*; and Charles H. Smith (Bill Arp) in Rome, Georgia. Their emergence from the world of the newspaper is significant for a number of reasons. First, it reminds us that their humor was deeply politicized, for most newspapers remained party organs at this time. Second, not only were newspapers avidly read during the Civil War, but they also, through an extensive exchange system linking newspapers to one another both north and south, provided a medium by which writers such as the war

"Grafted into the Army," words and music by Henry C. Work, 1862.
(Courtesy of the Rare Book, Manuscript and Special
Collections Library, Duke University)

humorists were highly attuned to culture and politics at both the local and the national levels. Indeed, it was the interplay of local and national politics—the ways in which local culture and politics, as well as the accidents of everyday life, reshaped national goals and aspirations—that provided the basis for most of their humor.[8]

Each of the humorists invented an eccentric character who became a mouthpiece and who operated as a window into an entire imagined world of war. Artemus Ward described the wartime activities of Baldinsville, Ohio; Petroleum V. Nasby chronicled the doings of Wingert's Corners, Ohio; Orpheus C. Kerr wrote of the comic misadventures of the Mackerel Brigade in war; and Bill Arp wrote of Confederate life in Rome, Georgia. Often portrayed as speaking or writing in dialect, with numerous misspellings (a form of nineteenth-century humor we have lost patience with), these characters commented in short set pieces on the conduct of the war. In doing so, they followed in the stylistic footsteps of popular antebellum humorists such as Seba Smith, the creator of Jack Downing, or James Russell Lowell, who had invented Hosea Biglow during the Mexican-American War (and who would resuscitate Biglow, with less success, during the Civil War). At the same time, however, Civil War humorists vitalized the genre of popular humor in a way that had significant impact in the postbellum period for such humorists as Mark Twain.[9]

This Civil War humor was not unpatriotic, but it did offer a vision of wartime society that most popular patriotic and sentimental literature elided. It exposed failures in the war effort, and it also acknowledged the existence of those who were disgruntled with or even actively working against the war on the home front. It created a wartime world of dissonance rather than a world of harmonious patriotism. Although it did not constitute a literature of bitter disillusionment like that produced in England in response to World War I, it nevertheless criticized wartime culture in pointed terms. Wartime humor underlines the fact that a diversity of interpretations of the war could be found in popular literature.

Robert Henry Newell, for instance, devoted himself in his humorous Orpheus C. Kerr letters to puncturing prevailing heroic ideas of war. As he wrote in 1871, "Much of general mankind's lamentable alertness for war is, and always has been attributable in a great degree to the dazzling glare, heroic glow, and miraculous splendor of achievement romantically associated with march and battle, in the common mind." In a series of brilliant war satires in the *New-York Mercury* beginning in 1861, Newell instead pointed out the "plain, often ludicrously incongruous realities of all that dazzling glare of steel and gold, heroic glow of patriotic ferocity, and miraculous splendor of strategical and personal achievement, which, through traditional imagination, have so long made all peoples the ready military sacrifices of some people." Newell collected his satiric war letters into three books, the first one published in 1862, the three together apparently selling upwards of fifty thousand copies—a highly respectable sale for the time. Newell remained a columnist for the *New-York Mercury* throughout the conflict, a telling sign of his continuing wartime popularity. In addition, his pieces were frequently reprinted in newspapers and magazines such as *Frank Leslie's Budget of Fun*. Even some Southern magazines reprinted Newell's satires. The Yankees "are compelled to deride their own follies," the *Southern Literary Messenger* commented in 1862 before reprinting an Orpheus C. Kerr sketch. Saying that "a friend" had "received through the blockade a copy of the latest work of 'Orpheus C. Kerr,' " the *Southern Illustrated News* reprinted one of Newell's pieces on its front page in May 1864. Southern journals no doubt found in Newell's criticisms of Northern war culture hopeful (as well as humorous) signs of the possible failure of the North.[10]

The name Orpheus C. Kerr was a play on "office seeker"—wordplay that must have seemed amusing in 1861, when Lincoln was beset by legions of office seekers in his new government. Through the character of Kerr and the hapless Mackerel Brigade to which he was imagined to belong, Newell mocked war-related culture, including the popular war literature that is the subject of this book. His humor exposed Victorian sentimentalism, gentility, and commercialism as a set of interlocking beliefs and practices that defined the style of the war effort and even contributed to its failure.

From early in the war Kerr skewered the inflated rhetorics and falsified patriotism that he found almost everywhere he looked within war culture. Over and over again Newell attacked the rhetoric of heroism and nobility that surrounded the war, including the Victorian fascination with death and bloodshed. "I have just returned, my boy, with my fellow-mercenaries and several mudsills from a carnival of gore," the character Kerr wrote early in the war. "I am wounded—my sensibilities are wounded, and my irrepressibles reek with the blood of the slain. These hands, that once opened the oysters of peace and toyed with the bivalves of tranquility, are now sanguinary with the *red juice of battle* (gushing idea!), and linger in horrid ecstasy about the gloomy neck of a bottle holding about a quart. Eagle of my country, proud bird of the menagerie! thou art avenged!" With an anticlimax typical of Newell's approach, this letter concluded with the revelation that the Mackerel Brigade had killed a chicken, not the enemy.[11]

In Kerr's letter of September 8, 1861, he revealed a society so enraptured with the theatrical performance of a heroic, lofty style of war that its members often forgot actually to fight it. He reported that the Mackerel Brigade had been ordered to "go instantly to the rescue" of a regiment rumored to be under attack at Alexandria. But the rituals of patriotism that surrounded the early war stopped the company in its tracks. "Just as we were ready to march," Kerr said,

> a distinguished citizen of Washington presented a sword to the colonel from the ladies of the Capital, and made an eloquent speech. He spoke of the wonderful manner in which the world was called out of chaos at the creation, and spoke of the Garden of Eden, and the fall of our first parents; he then went on to review the many changes the earth had experienced since it was first created, and described the method of the ancients to cook bread before stoves were invented; he then spoke of the glories of Greece and Rome, giving a full history of them from the beginning to the present time; he then went on to describe the origin of the republican and democratic parties, reading both platforms, and giving his ideas of Jackson's policy; he then gave an account of the war of the Roses in England, and the cholera in Persia, attributing the latter to a sudden change in the atmosphere; he then went on to speak of the difficulties encountered by Columbus in discovering this country, and gave a history of his subsequent career and death in Europe; he then read an extract from Washington's Farewell Address; in conclusion, he said that the ladies of Washington had empowered him to present this here sword to that ere gallant colonel, in the presence of these here brave defenders of their country.

Shortly after this speech, Kerr commented drily, "Starvation commenced to make great ravages in the regiment." [12]

This passage was only one among many in Kerr's three wartime books of humor that portrayed a wartime society addicted to an inflated war rhetoric. Satirizing the sentimental approach to wartime death found in popular literature, for instance, Newell imagined the captain of the Mackerel Brigade advising his troops, "Should any of you happen to be killed in the coming battle, let me implore you to *Die without a groan*. It sounds better in history, as well as in the great, heart-stirring romances of the weekly palladiums of freedom. How well it reads, that 'Private Muggins received a shot in the neck and *died without a groan.'* " [13]

The sense that sentimental war deaths were often created as a form of theater for an avid literary marketplace permeated Newell's humor. In one of his biting early pieces Newell described what he ironically referred to as the "dying scene" of a Zouave named Shorty, remarking, "It was enough to make the eye of a darning-needle weep." The "Southern Confederacy" had "fired six heavy balls through the head of the unfortunate Zouave, nearly fracturing his skull," and after being taken to a hospital he had asked to be wrapped in the American flag before dying. At the end of this piece, however, Kerr informed the reader, "Since writing the above, I have heard that no such occurrence took place at Alexandria. . . . Mr. Shorty, it seems, does not belong to the Zouaves, at all, and is still in New York." [14]

In Newell's view, the existing practices of commercial literary culture encouraged the production of a false and inflated war. Newspapers, publishers, and advertisers were all willing to invent a heroic war to satisfy their readerships. Newell's letter of June 25, 1862, for instance, provided an absurd sketch of a newspaper reporter, a subscription publisher, and a businessman rushing to the bedside of the Mackerel Brigade's Captain Samyule Sa-mith in order to profit from his impending death. "Our paper has the largest circulation, and is the best advertising mejum in the United States," Kerr recorded the reporter saying. " 'As soon as our brother-in-arms expires,' says the useful chap, feelingly, 'just fill up this printed form and send it to me, and I will mention you in our paper as a promising young man.' " Newell then printed a fill-in-the-blanks form that began: "BIOGRAPHICAL SKETCH OF THE LATE ————. This noble and famous officer, recently slain at the head of his ————, . . . was born at ———— on the ———— day of ————, 1776, and entered West Point in his ———— year." [15]

Immediately following the reporter in this comic sketch was a subscription publisher who "made a dash for the bedside," saying that he desired "to know if you have anything that could be issued in book-form after your lamented departure." " 'We could make a handsome 12mo book,' says the shabby chap, persuadingly, 'of your literary remains. Works of a Union Martyr—Eloquent Writings of a Hero—Should be in every American Library—Take it home to your wife—Twenty editions ordered in advance of publication—Half-calf, $1.—Send in your orders.' " [16]

Finally completing this parade of cultural profiteers was a "hairy chap" named Brown, of Brown's Patent Hair-Dye, who offered to erect a monument "to the memory of our departed hero" and said that he would "give ten thousand dollars to have my advertisement put on the panel next to the name of the lamented deceased. We can get up something neat and appropriate, thus: WE MUST ALL DIE; BUT BROWN'S DYE IS THE BEST." The sketch ended with the "dying" soldier Samyule Smith deciding, "If I can't die without some advertising cuss's making money by it, I'll defer my visit to glory until next season." [17]

Such burlesque was not necessarily so far from reality during the war. A firm selling "Radway's remedies," for instance, a product reputed to relieve "diarrhoea, cholera, giddiness, melancholy, weakness, rheumatism, tooth-ache, and sprains," among dozens of other ailments, advertised the bene-fits of this "excellent medicine" in a broadside that also reprinted patriotic poems and songs such as "Hail Columbia," "Ye Sons and Sires of Liberty," and "The Patriot's Battle Call." In New York a retailer selling blankets advertised "Rebellion! Its downfall is never so clearly seen as when we examine BLANKETS!!" Such advertising explicitly combined patriotism and commerce.[18]

Many Northern commentators during the war, however, remarked with distaste on the profiteering engaged in by manufacturers who supplied the army with uniforms or foodstuffs. What is unusual about Newell and other war humorists is that they remarked on the *cultural* profiteering that also took place during the war. They recognized that there was a deep sym-biosis between commercial culture and the war—and that the war effort was infused with commercialism, patriotic myths to the contrary. Indeed, patriotic war culture drew Newell's scorn. "Patriotism, my boy, is a very beautiful thing," Kerr said in one letter. "The surgeon of a Western regi-ment has analyzed a very nice case of it, and says that it is peculiar to this hemisphere. He says that it first breaks out in the mouth, and from thence extends to the heart causing the latter to swell. He says that it goes on raging until it reaches the pocket, when it suddenly disappears, leaving the patient very Constitutional and conservative." [19]

Newell questioned patriotic conventions such as *dulce et decorum est pro patria mori*. He made clear that despite what an extensive patriotic war literature claimed, soldiers were not eager to die heroic deaths for their country. In one of Kerr's letters, the members of the Mackerel Brigade were "inspired to emulate great examples by the biographies of great sol-diers which have been sent to the camp for their reading by the thoughtful women of America." After providing a parody of the kind of reading sent to soldiers, an inspirational biography of Garibaldi, Newell commented that "this finely-written life of the great Italian patriot had such an effect upon the Mackerels, my boy, that they all wished to *live* like Garibaldi—hence, they are in no hurry to die for their country." Newell concluded, "Lives of great men all remind us, my boy, that we may make our lives sublime; but I never read one yet, that gave instructions for making our deaths sublime—to ourselves." In another sketch, Captain Villiam Brown attempted without success to use patriotic appeals to lead the Mackerel Brigade in a bayonet charge. "The United States of America, born on the Fourth of July, 1776," he said, "calls upon you to charge bayonets, Come on, my brave flowers of manhood!" But only one soldier responded, a "fearless chap" who "stepped out of the ranks" to claim that "heavy dew" had made the roads "impassable." An offer of drink, however, did the trick: Orpheus C. Kerr reported that "in an instant [he] was blinded with a cloud of dust, through which came the wild tramp and fierce hurrahs of Company 3, Regiment 5, Mackerel Brigade." [20]

Although Newell was especially critical of the grandiose, commercialized patriotism of publishers and newspapers, he did not spare the patriotic enthusiasms of newspaper readers. Instead, he saw the newspaper reading public, including both soldiers and civilians on the home front, as complicit in the creation of an inflated patriotism. Private Samyule Sa-mith may have initially refused to die a heroic death for an "advertising cuss," but later the commercial literary culture of war proved irresistible to him. In a September 1862 sketch, now Captain Samyule Sa-mith performed a theatrical battlefield death for the illustrated newspapers. Though uninjured, he "hastily fell upon his back, and beckoned for the artist of Frank Leslie's Illustrated paper, motioned for the nearest reporter to take out his note-book, drew a lock of red hair from his bosom and kissed it, waved his left hand feebly toward his country's standard, and, says he '*Tête d'Armée!*' I die for the old fla——'" before being rudely interrupted in his heroic dying by another Mackerel and springing to his feet.[21]

Civilians on the home front were also responsible for the excesses of wartime patriotic culture. One man, Kerr reported, had "subscribed for all the papers" with "all the enthusiasm of vegetable youth." On reading "the reliable war news"—a frequent target of Newell's scorn—"he learned that all was quiet on the Potomac, and immediately went to congratulate his friends, and purchase six American flags." Learning the next morning that all continued quiet on the Potomac (Newell's way of criticizing not just McClellan's lack of action early in the war but also newspapers' reiterated use of this phraseology in reports from the front), he "wrapt himself in the banner of his country," "hoisted a flag on the lightning-rod of his domicil, purchased a national pocket-handkerchief, bought six hand-organs that played the Star-Spangled Banner, and drank nothing but gunpowder tea." Eventually this victim of patriotism "was driven to lunacy by reliable war news." [22]

In Newell's view, excessive home-front patriotism was as damaging to the war effort as the bumbling antics of the Mackerel Brigade at the battle-front. Newell was merciless, for instance, in lampooning women's contributions to the war as hopelessly impractical. In his letter of April 18, 1862, he commented, "My arm has been strengthened in this war, my boy, by the inspiration of woman's courage, and aided by her almost miraculous fore-sight. Only yesterday, a fair girl of forty-three summers, thoughtfully sent me a box, containing two gross of assorted fish-hooks, three cook-books, one dozen of Tubbses best spool-cotton, three door-plates, a package of patent geranium-roots, two yards of Brussels carpet, Rumford's illus-trated work on Perpetual Intoxication, ten bottles of furniture-polish, and some wall-paper." Accompanying these articles, "so valuable to a soldier on the march," Kerr said, was a note in which "the kind-hearted girl said that the things were intended for our sick and wounded troops, and were the voluntary tributes of a loyal and dreamy-souled woman." Furthermore, she said that "her deepest heart-throbs and dream-yearnings were for the crimson-consecrated Union, and that she had lavished her most harrowing hope-sobs for its heaven-triumph." [23]

This was a pointed parody of the language of sentimental feminized patriotism, but Newell was not alone in making fun of the ubiquitous sentimental war. The song "Mother Would Wallop Me," for instance, delib-erately parodied the popular song "Mother Would Comfort Me," whose refrain imagined a wounded soldier saying:

Gently her hand o'er my forehead she'd press,
 Trying to free me from pain and distress;
Kindly she'd say to me, "Be of good cheer,
 Mother will comfort you, mother is here."

"Mother Would Wallop Me" transformed this refrain into:

Gently her foot o'er my forehead she'd press,
 Trying to sober me, when tight in distress;
Gently she'd say: as I've got you so near:
 Mother will wallop you, Mother is here.

Another song, "Mother on the Brain," humorously noted that "As you look on the songs that you see now-a-days, / The gentle words of Mother will sure meet your gaze." [24]

Although Newell did not explicitly mock sentimental celebrations of mother, he did mock women's efforts as nurses and the pompous, reverential way in which their work was often described during the war. Describing a visit to a hospital, Kerr commented that "woman—lovely woman! was there, administering hot drinks to the fevered head, bathing with ice-water the brow of those shivering with the cruel ague, pouring rich gruel over the chin and neck of the nervous sufferer, and reading good books to the raving and delirious. It was with a species of holy awe that I beheld one of those human angels stand a hot coffee-pot upon the upturned face of one invalid, while she hastily flew to fill the right ear of a more urgent sufferer with cologne water." This pointed satire underlined Kerr's recurring argument that the overblown language of patriotism obscured those practices that actually undermined the war effort.[25]

• • •

War humor refused to treat the war efforts of soldiers and civilians with reverential solemnity. Rather than universalizing the war as heroic, it laughed at the particulars of war. Many war humorists, for instance, created comic local worlds of war, vividly imagining the absurd ways in which small-town societies interpreted or responded to the national crisis of war. Charles Farrar Browne, the creator of Artemus Ward, set many of his humorous war pieces in the imagined village of Baldinsville, Ohio. Browne first introduced Ward to a Cleveland newspaper audience in 1858, imagining him as a small-time, itinerant showman and purveyor of waxworks— a sort of failed P. T. Barnum. In May 1861, Browne became editor of *Vanity Fair* and published his first war-related pieces as Artemus Ward in that journal. His "The War Fever in Baldinsville" was especially adroit at capturing the provincial localism of American life at the outbreak of war.[26]

In that piece Browne portrayed the itinerant showman Ward returning to his hometown of Baldinsville after war had broken out only to discover that his fellow citizens did not yet know that war had begun. "They don't git news very fast in Baldinsville," Ward commented, "as nothin but a plank road runs in there twice a week, and that's very much out of repair. So my nabers wasn't much posted up in regard to the wars." One of his neighbors, Squire Baxter, "sed he'd voted the dimicratic ticket for goin on forty year, and the war was a dam black republican lie." But once newspapers "got along at last, chock full of war," a "patriotic fever fairly bust out in Baldinsville." [27]

Like Newell, Charles Farrar Browne invented a hapless group of would-be soldiers, the Baldinsville Company, with Artemus Ward as its "Captin." Mocking the early wartime creation of numerous officers in local militias, Browne said that Ward "determined to have my company composed ex-cloosively of offissers, everybody to rank as Brigadeer-Ginral." The questions he put to would-be recruits included "Do you know a masked battery from a hunk of gingerbread?," "Do you know a eppylit from a piece of chalk?," and "If I trust you with a real gun, how many men of your own company do you speck you can manage to kill durin the war?" Such humor affectionately mocked the amateurish localism of the early war effort, making a point that most overtly patriotic literature elided—that the nation was simply not prepared for war at its outset. Browne's humor was not therefore unpatriotic: it simply regarded the war effort from a critical distance not possible within earnest war literature that insisted on the heroic nobility of every aspect of the conflict.[28]

That critical distance was especially apparent in the searing humor of David Ross Locke, whose writings in the character of Petroleum V. Nasby were among the favorites of Lincoln. An ardent Republican and owner/editor of the *Hancock County (Ohio) Jeffersonian*, Locke was a strong supporter of emancipation in 1862. Feeling besieged by antiwar Butternuts and Copperheads in Ohio, Locke invented the character of the dyed-in-the-wool Democrat and extreme racist Petroleum V. Nasby in order to expose through exaggeration the absurdity and small-mindedness of local Democratic views. Thus one of the first Nasby pieces, the April 1862 "Letter of a Straight Democrat," showcased Nasby's racist alarm over the tiny number of African Americans living in the imagined town of Wingert's Corners, Ohio: "There is now fifteen niggers, men, wimin, and childern, or ruther, mail, femail, and yung, in Wingert's Corners, and yesterday another arrove. I am bekomin alarmed, for, ef they inkrese at this rate, in suthin over sixty years they'll hev a majority in the town, and may, ef they git mean enuff, tyrannize over us, even ez we air tyrannizin over them. The danger is imminent!" [29]

Nasby proposed that "the niggers be druv out uv Wingert's Corners, and that sich property ez they may hev accumulatid be confiscated," with the proceeds used to pay "the bills of the last Dimekratik Centrel Committee" and Nasby himself. This was a typical piece of Nasby humor. Throughout the war Locke's biting satires exposed the alarmism, ignorance, and greed that he felt lay behind local Democratic racism and antiwar activity. There was nothing subtle about this humor: in such pieces Locke emerged as a direct, blatant propagandist for the administration and the war, one who equated lack of support for the war effort with vicious forms of ignorance and hate-mongering at the local level.[30]

Locke's anti-Democratic humor found much to mock in the local Democratic war culture of Wingert's Corners. An early Nasby piece, for instance, presented Nasby's plans for a Fourth of July celebration that included a "perceshun" with a "wagin with a nigger a lyin down, and mi esteemd frend Punt a standin onto him—a paregorical illustrashun uv the sooperiority uv the Anglo-Sacksun over the Afrikin rases." The procession would also include the singing of the "Nashnel oad, 'We've Cuffee by de Wool,'" a reading of an address by Clement L. Vallandigham, and a "patryotick song" whose lyrics included the verse

Sambo, ketch dat hoe,
   And resine dat vane idee;
We've got de power, you kno,
   And you never kin be free.[31]

By mid-1863, Locke imagined Nasby founding the "First Dimekratik Church of Ohio," whose "exercises" included singing "O, John Brown's body hangs a danglin in the air," which worshiped the "marterd Vallandigum," and whose opening hymn was

Shed niggers black this land possess,
   And mix with us up here?
O no, my frends, we rayther guess
   We'll never stand that 'ere.[32]

In such scenes Nasby satirically captured the wartime blending of song, oratory, and racist invective that characterized local Democratic culture. Like Newell, Locke also satirized the way in which ordinary citizens were complicit with illustrated newspapers in creating a heightened and inflated war for popular consumption. In his July 27, 1863, letter, Locke imagined a meeting between Nasby and Vallandigham in which Vallandigham rushed into Nasby's arms and then asked Nasby to continue holding the embrace, as "the artist uv the Noo York Illustratid Flapdoodle is makin a sketch us." It "wuz exhaustin and tiresum" to stand "locked in2 each other's arms" while "weepin profoosely for 15 minits," Nasby commented, but "fer the cause I endoord it."[33]

Locke's humor especially captured the hypocrisy of Democrats who viewed the presence of African Americans in the North with alarm until they themselves were threatened with the draft. Although Nasby had demanded that all African Americans leave Wingert's Corners in 1862, in 1863 Locke portrayed him changing his tune under the threat of conscription. Once it became clear to Nasby that the "enrolement cood not be prevented," the "Church uv St. Vallandigum" resolved "that we consider the employment uv niggers, ez soljers, ez not only justifiable, but highly commendable" and recommended that "a committee be appinted to sekoor the settlement uv 2 hundred families uv niggers in this township, excloosively for volunteerin purposes." [34]

Other war humorists also noted the hypocrisies that marked white Americans' attitudes toward race. Robert Henry Newell, for instance, imagined the Union officer Villiam Brown making a ludicrously pompous speech to a contraband who had come into Union lines: " 'Mr. Black,' says Villiam, gravely, turning to the emancipated African, 'you have come to the right shop for freedom. You are from henceforth a freeman and a brother-in-law. You are now your own master,' says Villiam, encouragingly, 'and no man has a right to order you about. You are in the full enjoyment of Heving's best gift—Freedom! Go and black my boots.' " Likewise, Newell made fun of Northern officers' sending contrabands "out to enjoy the blessings of freedom, digging trenches." [35]

War humorists whose political sympathies made them supporters of emancipation exposed the racial hypocrisies of Northern life. But most war humor simply imagined African Americans as objects for hilarity. The "contraband joke," for instance, became a staple of the many collections of "incidents and anecdotes" of the war published during and immediately after the conflict, whether in the columns of newspapers and illustrated weeklies or in book-length volumes. "Swearing a Contraband," for instance, was an "incident" published in the pseudonymous Tim Tramp's 1862 *War Life: Illustrated Stories of the Camp and Field*. Reprinted from a Cincinnati newspaper and circulated widely, it portrayed a dialogue between a corporal and an African American:

> "See here, Dixie, before you enter the service of the United States, you must be sworn."
> "Yes, massa, I do dat," he replied. . . .
> ". . . You do solemnly swear that you will support the Constitution of the United States and see that there are no grounds floating upon

the coffee at all times . . . and you do solemnly swear that you will put milk in the coffee every morning, and see that the ham and eggs are not cooked too much or too little."

"Yes, I do dat; I'se a good cook."

"And lastly," continued the corporal, "you do solemnly swear that when this war is over you'll make tracks for Africa almighty fast."

"Yes, massa, I do dat. I allers wanted to go to Cheecargo."

Revealing for its hostility to full black participation in American life, its denial to blacks of the right to be officially "sworn in," and its wish that African Americans would leave America entirely, this incident was part of widespread white supremacist humor published during the war.[36]

Often that humor centered on tricking contrabands and stressed their ignorance, as in another much reprinted anecdote, titled "A Frightened Contraband" in one collection. This story was an "amusing incident" involving a "portly contraband" who had escaped from his rebel master at Antietam. This "sable attendant" was not aware that the Union officer to whom he was now a body servant had an artificial leg. The officer instructed the "darky servant" to help pull off his riding boots, all the while enjoying the "prospective joke" that would result. When indeed "contraband, cork leg, riding boot, and ligatures tumbled across the tent in a heap," the "one-legged officer fell back on his pallet, convulsed with spasmodic laughter." "I ain't done nuffin," the contraband yelled "lustily," before running "for the woods in his desperation." He had not been "seen or heard from" since, the anecdote concluded.[37]

Laughing at contrabands was a form of amusement that had its roots in whites' antebellum enjoyment of minstrelsy, and thus it is no surprise that minstrel-derived imagery dominated such jokes and anecdotes, with their invocation of blacks' "shining ivories" and their repetition of "Yah, yah!" Artemus Ward's "Thrilling Scenes in Dixie" included a vignette of a "nigger sittin on a fence a-playin on a banjo." "My Afrikan Brother," said Ward in this piece, "you belong to a very interesting race. Your masters is going to war excloosively on your account." "Yes, boss," he replied, "an' I wish 'em honorable graves!" and he "went on playin' the banjo, larfin all over and openin his mouth wide enuff to drive in an old-fashioned 2 wheeled chaise." Such humor underlined the persistence of minstrelsy-derived images of African Americans within Northern popular war culture, especially among Democrats.[38]

Charles Farrar Browne, the creator of Ward, had been an ardent Doug-

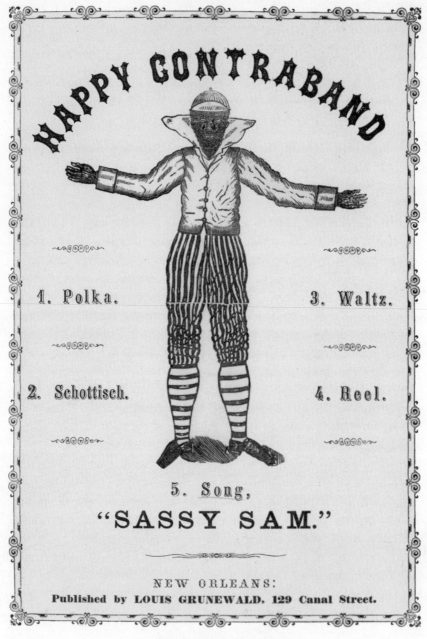

"Happy Contraband."
(Courtesy of the Rare Book, Manuscript and Special
Collections Library, Duke University)

las Democrat before the war. A believer in African colonization for free blacks, he wrote numerous explicitly racist newspaper pieces besides his columns of humor. As Ward said in January 1861, "Praps [the Negro] was created for sum wise purpuss, like the measles and New England Rum, but it's mity hard to see it. At any rate he's no good here, & as I statid to Mister What Is It, it's a pity he cooden't go orf sumwhares quietly by hisself." [39]

Given these views, it was not surprising that as editor of *Vanity Fair* in 1861 and 1862 Browne printed a number of pieces of "contraband humor." An April 1862 cartoon of a degraded-looking black, with distorted physiognomy, was ironically titled "The Highly Intelligent Contraband." The phrase "intelligent contraband" had become commonplace in newspaper correspondence, but *Vanity Fair* mocked the idea of contrabands as reliable sources of information for newspaper reporters. "Where is Beauregard, at Corinth or Richmond?" asked a reporter for the *Tribune* in one sketch.

> *Intelligent Contraband* . "Yis, Mars'r."
> *Tribune Correspondent.* "Where, at Richmond?"
> *Int. Con.* "Yis, Mars'r."
> *Trib. Cor.* "And how many men has he?"
> *Int. Con.* "Niggers, Mars'r?"
> *Trib. Cor.* "No. Soldiers."
> *Int. Con.* "'Bout sixty hundred t'ousand, I 'spec's."
> *Trib. Cor.* "What! Are you sure? Aren't you mistaken?"
> *Int. Con.* "Yis, Mars'r."

The April 1862 *Vanity Fair* said that "intelligent contrabands" had been the source of nine erroneous reports in the *New York Tribune* "within the past month or so." [40]

"Intelligent contraband" humor provides an important connection to popular humor in the South, reminding us of the many similarities between the popular literature of Union and Confederacy. Indeed, F. G. De Fontaine, the war correspondent "Personne" for the *Charleston Courier*, recycled the above "intelligent contraband" sketch in a volume of "incidents and anecdotes" of the war published in 1864, approvingly commenting that *Vanity Fair* had made an "excellent hit at the 'intelligent contrabands,' who figure so largely in the correspondence of the press from the various seats of war." Other Southern publications also made their "hits" at intelligent contrabands. The October 1863 *Southern Punch* featured a "Scene in a Yankee Barber Shop" in which an "Intelligent Contraband" asked a white barber to have his "har shampooned," with the Barber courteously replying, "Yes, sir, please sit down." Presumably this byplay, which imagined a white serving an African American in a menial capacity involving physical contact, was intended to shock a Southern audience with its inversion of a "natural" racial order. The final lines of the caption to this cartoon underlined this inversion, as the African American customer asked, "Mayby I can gat yer to go in de army as my substitute? Brudder Linkum say black is no culler an white is no culler, an derfore, ob cours, consequently you an me is equals."[41]

If there were similarities in Northern and Southern racist treatments of intelligent contrabands, there were also similarities in humorous treatments of black soldiering. One of the more striking Northern verses of the war, as we have seen, was Charles Graham Halpine's pitiless endorsement of black soldiering in his "Sambo's Right to Be Kilt":

Some tell us 'tis a burnin' shame
    To make the naygers fight;
And that the thrade of bein' kilt
    Belongs but to the white:
But as for me, upon my sowl!
    So liberal are we here,
I'll let Sambo be murthered instead of myself,
    On every day in the year.
        On every day in the year, boys,
            And in every hour of the day;
        The right to be kilt I'll divide wid him,
            And divil a word I'll say.[42]

A member of General Hunter's staff at Port Royal and a war Democrat, Charles Halpine had little use for contrabands, writing to his wife in 1862 that they "ought all to be drowned." But he did support military prosecution of the war by all possible means, including the use of African Americans as soldiers. Like David Ross Locke, Halpine recognized that humor could be a potent political weapon and argued that "truth, by arraying itself in the garb of humor, may often attract the attention which has been denied to her most serious appeals." Instead of satirizing racism, however, Halpine embraced it as a means of persuading recalcitrant Democrats to support the war. In a series of humorous sketches published in the Democratic *New York Herald*, he drew on the well-known Irish antipathy to blacks in inventing an "odd character named Miles O'Reilly," who he pretended had "frequently relieved the monotony of camp life by scribbling songs on all sorts of subjects, and writing librettos for the various 'minstrel companies,' got up in imitation of George Christy's." In 1864 Halpine published a collection of these sketches as *The Life and Adventures, Songs, Services, and Speeches of Private Miles O'Reilly (47th Regiment, New York Volunteers).*[43]

In this volume Halpine provided commentary on "Sambo's Right to Be Kilt," claiming that "the practical results of its popular diffusion redounded undoubtedly to the best interests of the service." "The white soldiers of the Department began singing it round their camp-fires at night, and humming it to themselves on their sentry-beats. It made them regard the enlistment of the despised sons of Ham as rather a good joke at first; and next, as a joke containing some advantages to themselves." General Hunter, Halpine continued, had urged the use of black troops "purely as a military measure, and without one syllable or thought of any 'humanitarian proletarianism.' Every black regiment in garrison would relieve a white regiment for service in the field. Every ball stopped by a black man would save the life of a white soldier." Under this interpretation, black soldiering did little more than shore up the racial hierarchy of the North.[44]

This racist view of black soldiering provided another connecting link between popular Northern Democratic humor and Southern popular humor. A series of pointed political cartoons and vignettes published in the *Southern Punch* during 1863 and 1864, for instance, also worked to shore up the racial order of the South by making fun of black soldiers. But this Southern humor typically had an additional agenda not shared by Northern humor: the continued justification and rationalization of slavery. In the December 1863 cartoon "Birds of a Feather," a comic-looking, scarecrow-like Yankee general told an African American, "Now Sambo, I have made you Captain of the Odoriferous Guards," exhorting him to "fight till you die." In an aside to the reader, however, Sambo expressed dissatisfaction with this plan, saying, "I's gwine to git out ob dis. Ole missus used to say dat white men dat puts demselves on 'quality with niggar, no better dan niggar demselves." Likewise, in the vignette "Mastered but Not Manned," an "Abolition Captain" commented to "Sambo," "Well, Sambo, I guess you feel a man now that you're your own master." But Sambo denied feeling like the master of himself: "Gollies, Cap, Ise de wost masser dat eber I 'longed to yet. Eberry one drives me; now here, thar, and the lor' knows whar," and "when I tell me masser ob it—dats meself—I gets noting to gi' me help or take my part; so dis har boy aint so sure its all best to be masser ob hisself, wid all de odder massers toted on me back for 'mancipation sake." Better to have one master under slavery than many masters under freedom, this vignette argued.[45]

The idea that slaves were better off under slavery than under freedom was a recurrent theme of this comic literature, just as it was of Southern popular fiction more generally (see chapter 5). Cartoons and comic vignettes often indulged in the fantasy that slaves chose to return to slavery. The *Southern Punch* cartoon "The Returned Prodigal" featured a former slave relieved to come back "home" after working for General Butler at Norfolk: "He is monstrous hard on black folks," said this character, another Sambo. "It was work, work, all de time, and so I runs away and cums home." In the July 1864 cartoon "Home Again—Back from the Yankee Camp," two African Americans danced together gleefully, relieved to be slaves again.[46]

The most famous Southern humorist of the war also laughed—or scoffed—at emancipation. Much like Charles Farrar Browne or David Ross Locke, the Georgia lawyer Charles Henry Smith wrote a series of humorous, misspelled wartime letters as the character Bill Arp, a staunchly pro-Confederate yeoman farmer. First published in a Rome, Georgia, newspaper, these sketches received wide fame through newspaper exchanges before being collected into an 1866 volume.

Bill Arp, So Called: A Side Show of the Southern Side of the War included several letters written to "Abe Lincoln" to express Arp's views on emancipation. His December 2, 1862, "Letter from Bill Arp to Mr. Lincoln," for instance, spoke of the "eventful period which you have fixed when Africa is to be unshackled, when Niggerdom is to feel the power of your proclamation," and "when all the emblems of darkness are to rush frantically forth into the arms of their deliverers, and with perfumed and scented gratitude embrace your Excellency and Madam Harriet Beecher Stowe!" Arp refuted the idea that the Emancipation Proclamation would have any impact, sarcastically commenting that though there was "only one more brief week to slide away before we must part, forever part, with all our negro heritage," yet "our stubborn people continue to buy and sell them." In another letter to Lincoln on the subject of emancipation, Arp mockingly commented, "The world, the flesh, and the devil are looking to you to extend the aegis of freedom over all creation—over things animate and inanimate—over bull bats and screech-owls, grub-worms and grindstones, niggers and alligators, and every thing that don't spill as the earth turns upside down." The bestiality of such racist invective needs little comment.[47]

In later sketches Arp upheld the Southern racial order in the face of emancipation, asking, "What does it all amount to?" and deciding that emancipation was no more than semantics. "I had just as lief by a chunk of a *free* nigger as any other sort," Arp said. "I don't care a bobee about his being free, if I can subjugate him; and if he gets above his color, I will put thirty-nine whelks right under his shirt, and make him wish that old Lincoln stood in his shoes."[48]

Arp's racist vernacular was a connecting thread to the humor of such Northern writers as Charles Farrar Browne and David Ross Locke (even if tongue in cheek in Locke's case). But there were other connecting threads as well, including the intense localism with which Smith approached the war from its beginning. Like Browne, Smith gently mocked the patriotic fever that overtook the small hamlet of Rome, Georgia, at the outbreak of war. In an April 1861 letter to Abe Lincoln, Arp talked of "the boys around here" being so "hot" for war that "they fairly siz when you pour water on them, and that's the way they make up their military companies here now—when a man applies to join the volunteers, they sprinkle him, and if he sizzles they take him, and if he don't they don't."[49]

Yet by 1863 Arp had a series of devastating criticisms to make of the Confederate war effort, revealing the same deflationary impulse that lay behind Robert Henry Newell's humor. One of Arp's targets was the Confederate cavalry, "which ever and anon migrates and varigates and perambulates through and through a bleeding country." "They are perhaps the most majestic sight that belong to the animal kingdom," Arp sarcastically commented, "and such are the profound impression which their august presence do make upon a close observer, that one week's view will satisfy his whole curiosity for the next fifty years to come." The problem with the cavalry, in Arp's view, was that they were "invincible" after a battle in "laying in wait for a train of cars, or assaulting an unguarded caravan of wagons," occasions on which "they load themselves down with dry goods and wet goods, and blankets, and hats, and boots and booty, and ticklers, and canteens with contents noticed." One "poor infantry" had commented after "hunting over the ground he fought, 'Let's go home, Jim, the cavalry have been here and licked up every d-a-m thing.'"[50]

Arp also complained of "that numerous class who are dodging conscription," sarcastically commenting of those men who claimed to be too old to be drafted, "How rapidly some folks grow old in these trying times!" "Such is the rapid progress of human events in these fighting times, that a man who was only forty last year, can be forty-six this." He was not alone among humorists in making this complaint: a broadside titled "I Am Not Sick, I'm over Forty-five" included the verse

Oh! what do I care, what my neighbors may say,
That I've jumped o'er ten years in less than a day?
Oh! what do I care for my nation and laws?
I heed not her shame, I seek not applause;
But still for the Almighty Dollar I'll drive,
I'm exempt, I'm exempt, I'm o'er forty-five![51]

Like Newell and Browne, Arp found much that was ludicrous in the culture of war. In May 1863, he wrote of an anticipated Yankee raid on Rome, Georgia, imagining that the "citizens of the Eternal City were aroused from their slumbers with the chorus of the Marseilles hymn": "To arms, to arms, ye brave; Abe Lincoln is pegging away." In preparation for this raid, "two cracked cannon, that had holes in the ends, and two or three in the sides, were propped up between the cotton bags, and pointed strait down the road to Alabama. They were first loaded with buckshot and tacks, and then a round ball rammed on top. The ball was to take the raid in the front, and the bullets and tacks to rake 'em in the flank. These latter it was supposed would go through the cracks in the side, and shoot around generally." At the same time, "sharpshooters got on top of cemetery hill with their repeaters and pocket pistols." At the local level, as Smith pointed out, amateurism dominated the war effort.[52]

Yet if Smith, like Newell, found much that was ludicrous in war, he also painted a fundamentally affectionate portrait of small-town life in wartime. In Rome, "everybody and every thing determined to die in their tracks or *do something*" in the face of Yankee invasion, Arp noted, without the sarcasm concerning false patriotism that underlay Newell's work. In the preface to the 1866 collection of his war pieces, too, Smith made clear that he continued to believe in the rightness of the Confederate cause, describing himself and his countrymen as "conquered, but not convinced," and bitterly describing the "desolation with which our conquerers have visited us," including the "rape and arson which barbarians under arms enforced and heartless officers permitted." Not for Charles H. Smith the critique of the falseness of all war that Newell provided; Newell found war itself ridiculous in a way that Smith, a believer in the Confederate cause, could not and did not.[53]

In September 1865 Smith wrote a postwar letter in the character of Arp, defiantly setting limits to his reconciliation to the Union. "I'm a good

Union man," he began, affirming, "I ain't agwine to fight no more. I shan't vote for the next war. I ain't no gurilla. I've done tuk the oath, and I'm gwine to keep it." But, he added, "As for my being subjugated, and humilyated, and amalgamated, and enervated, as Mr. Chase says, it ain't so—nary time. I ain't ashamed of nuthin neither."[54]

If Arp set personal limits to reconciliation, however, he set no literary limits to reunion between North and South. His September letter was in fact addressed to Artemus Ward, perhaps as a response to Ward's May 1865 "Artemus Ward in Richmond." In that letter, written just after the end of the war, Ward had addressed defeated Southerners in a spirit of reconciliation, saying, "You fit [fought] splendid, but we was too many for you," and commenting sadly on "the sea of good rich blud that has been spilt on both sides in this dredful war." "Let us all give in," Ward concluded, "and put the Republic on a firmer basis nor ever." Arp, however, did not "give in," instead later saying that he was "a good Union reb, and my battle cry is Dixie and the Union."[55]

Still, Arp's September 1865 letter did offer a form of literary reconciliation with the North and an implicit assertion that Arp's humor was part of a national literature of humor, not a separate Confederate literature. "The reason I write to you in perticler," Arp commented to Ward, "is because you are about the only man I know in all 'God's country' *so-called*." "See here, my friend," he concluded, "you must send me . . . a ticket to your show, and me and you will harmonize sertin." By the end of the war Confederate humor, like so many other genres of popular war literature, was not so much an independent national literature as a regional literature, highly attuned to and even dependent on the humor of the North.[56]

· · ·

Jokes can be subversive, anthropologist Mary Douglas has pointed out. They create "a temporary suspension of the social structure" and allow an "opportunity for realising that an accepted pattern has no necessity." This observation holds true for Civil War humor up to a point. Several humorists, for instance, leveled existing social hierarchies by imagining meetings between comic characters and President Lincoln. Artemus Ward met the president shortly after his election in an "Interview with President Lincoln." Bill Arp addressed letters to "Abe Linkhorn." The "Disbanded Volunteer," the creation of lesser-known humorist Joseph Barber, wrote of his experiences as "Honest Old Abe's Bosom Friend and Unofficial Adviser." Comic war literature thus democratized and personalized the war, and by extension the nation, rejecting the idea that there was a social distance between high and low among its citizens.[57]

However, war humor was also used to maintain a racial order of white supremacy at a time of great dynamism and transformation in racialized representation. With a very few exceptions, including the work of David Ross Locke and James Russell Lowell, wartime humor reinscribed crude, minstrel-based images of African Americans. And even the work of David Ross Locke is open to a reading that stresses its racism. Although Locke exposed the hypocrisies that underlay discussions of African Americans in the North, his writings drew deeply on the racist shorthand that characterized popular literary treatments of race. Even while questioning racist beliefs and practices, his work left in place the language in which such practices were framed. Thus if Northern war humor was racially subversive, it was, ironically, primarily subversive of the emerging radicalism of the war.

Still, war humor should remind us that even within mainstream patriotic culture, there was room during the war for a chorus of discontent within popular literature. "It is the nature of war," Samuel Hynes has noted, "to diminish every value except war itself and the values war requires: patriotism, discipline, obedience, endurance." But in the diversified commercial literary culture that characterized the Civil War, a democratization of the imagined war allowed for points of view at a substantial remove from these values. Instead of merely reaffirming the values of patriotism, discipline, obedience, and endurance, war humor acknowledged that sloth, laziness, cupidity, disobedience, and negligence were also among the values associated with the war. Most of all—and most transgressive of the heroic norms of patriotic literature—war humor made the simple but profoundly subversive point that war was ridiculous.[58]

The Sensational War

Along the line, with star and plume,
    And crimson waving sash,
A horseman rides, all reckless of
    The battle-lights that flash;
But why that check, that quiv'ring start?
Ah! see the tide gush from his heart
    That bears his life away!

His hands relax, he reels, he falls,
    But on a loving breast;
While o'er him bends a Young Dragoon,
    With snow-white flowing crest:
"My Harry, 'tis thy Jennie speaks!"
She cried, while o'er his brow and cheeks
    Her tears of anguish fell.

"Look up, and in the Young Dragoon,
    Long known, thy Jennie trace!"
His eyes unclose; with sweet surprise
    He gazed into her face;
He smiled—to hers his lips were press'd,
His head sank back upon her breast—
    The hero's heart was still.

One long, despairing look she cast
    Upon her love, her life,
And cried, "I will avenge thee!" rushed

Into the fiercest strife;
And many from that field now tell
That "bravest of the brave," there fell
The beautiful Dragoon!

—Mrs. B. M. Z. [*Bettie M. Zimmerman*],
 "*The Young Dragoon,*" Southern Illustrated News,
 October 17, 1863

In May 1863 a full-page *New York Times* advertisement for a new war story by the prolific author John Hovey Robinson announced "Startling News from Tennessee! Love, War, Adventure! Desperation, Devotion, Heroism!" Extolling *The Round Pack* as a "series of wonderful adventures in the very heart of the guerrilla region of Tennessee," it invited "the million to a peep" into this "grand story" soon to run in the *New-York Mercury,* which offered "such delectable 'notions' as hair-breadth escapes, heroic exploits, thrilling situations, plots and counterplots, and delightful little episodes of a tender nature." "Romance and reality" were most "wonderfully interwoven" in a story that would "stir the Northern heart." [1]

Beginning in late 1861, but especially from 1863 through the end of the war, a number of Northern story papers and publishers produced sensational literature that stressed the romance, excitement, and adventure of war. The American News Company, for instance, the most important distributor of "cheap" literature late in the war, advertised "a series of original and choice ROMANCES OF THE WAR" in 1864, promising a "stirring story of the war" in *The Border Spy;* an "exciting tale" of "the terrors of life on the border" in *The Guerrillas of the Osage;* "one of the most exciting and exhilarating romances of the war yet produced" in *Old Bill Woodworth;* "an exciting tale of scouting life in the West" in *Bob Brant, Patriot and Spy;* and a story "full of all that is novel in war, exciting in adventure and stirring in love," in *The Prisoner of the Mill,* among other war novels.[2]

Although it has often been suggested that the war acted as an impetus for the development of realism in American letters, popular wartime literature reveals that the experience of war acted just as much—if not more—as the impetus for the development and wide dissemination of adventurous romance, the domain of "cheap novels." Although such cheap literature was already popular before the war, as David S. Reynolds, among others, has pointed out, the war itself—not just as imagined experience but also, especially, as commercial opportunity—gave a tremendous push to a cheap literature of adventurous romance within American life. Indeed, adventurous romance became a keynote of American popular literary culture in the postbellum period, reminding us that the usual story of the "rise of realism" in the Gilded Age tells only a partial truth about the development of literature in that era.[3]

Sensational novels occupied a particular niche in commercial literary culture in wartime, distinguished from other popular literature by a set of conventions including price, physical appearance, subject matter, and distribution. Priced at a nickel, a dime, fifteen cents, or a quarter, sensational novels were published in pamphlets running from forty-eight to a little more than a hundred pages. Often published as a series, such as T. R. Dawley's "Dawley's Camp and Fireside Library," they had garish, crudely drawn color covers — often but not always yellow — that acted as a visual signal to their contents.

Sensational novels emphasized bold action, striking effects on the emotions, sharply drawn heroes and villains, and highly conventionalized, florid, even lurid language. War novels and stories were only a small part of a larger sensational literature that included such topics as "the old conventional Indian," with his "wampums, and third-person talking," as well as "trappers & scouts, and masculine young ladies, & pirates and baronets," as one contemporary commentator sarcastically characterized them. Strongly linked to melodrama in language, plot, and characterization, sensational literature emphasized a world of moral certainty composed of dastardly villains and spotless heroes, and of pure good and evil. Melville had commented about melodrama audiences in *The Confidence Man* that they rejected the merely ordinary, looking "not only for more entertainment, but, at bottom, for even more reality than real life itself can show." Sensational war literature, drawing on the melodrama, approached war in a similar way: rejecting a "commonplace" war, it created a heightened war that stressed the "thrilling," the "exciting" — words used over and over in the titles of sensational works.[4]

Not all sensational novels were alike, however, instead ranging along a spectrum from exciting tales of adventure to more lurid accounts of murder and attempted rape. An 1865 *Harper's Weekly* cartoon titled "What Sensation Has Come to at Last" reflected these more lurid aspects of sensationalism with its humorous portrayal of a little girl asking for a "pretty story" about a "nice 'ittle girl who has murdered her Papa and Mamma." In another cartoon, two women talked about how "perfectly delicious" the latest "sensation novel" full of "delightful Horrors" was. Such cartoons both critiqued and confirmed the popularity of sensational literature in wartime.[5]

Some publishers, mindful of what many considered the morally dubious aspect of sensational novels, denied that what they produced was "sensational." "Beadle's Dime Novels are not 'sensational,'" the publisher Beadle and Company advertised in the *New York Tribune* in 1863. Rather, they were "good, pure, and reliable," "exhilarating without being feverishly or morbidly exciting," and "adapted to all classes, readable at all times, fit for all places." Yet despite this disavowal of sensationalism, the firm's novels, including Civil War novels as well as stories of "Border Life and Character, Indian Warfare and Frontier Experience, Early Settlement Romance and Fact, Revolutionary Events and Incidents, Sea and Ship Life," were seen by many to fall within the larger category of sensationalism. As William Everett caustically remarked in an 1864 article about Beadle and Company's dime novels, "Not 'sensational.' O dear no: the publishers were determined to see if it would not be popular to offer everything of the best, and the experiment has succeeded! The best!" Everett had "faithfully read through" ten of these novels, he said, and "more uphill work we never had." To an observer such as Everett the category of sensational fiction included "dime" and other "cheap" novels of adventure. Indeed, the boundaries among these types of literature often seem arbitrary, and in this chapter "sensational literature" often includes what publishers described as "cheap" or "dime" literature.[6]

As many publishers of cheap novels recognized during the war, soldiers were an important audience and market for "light literature." Sinclair Tousey, one of the founders of the American News Company, advertised "A New Idea. Army and Navy Literature" composed of "first-class novelettes" in September 1863. "In view of the great demand for light literature among our brave boys in camp and on the ocean," Tousey wrote, who "while not fighting the battles of their country, have nothing to do but to read and write to the dear ones at home," he had "determined to get up, in cheap form," stories that included "romances of the battlefield" among other types of romance. One of the resulting series was the "American Tales," the "romances of the war" listed above.[7]

Other publishers, too, produced series aimed at least in part at soldiers: T. R. Dawley's "Dawley's Camp and Fireside Library" included such 1864 titles as *Justina, the Avenger* and *The Mad Bard;* "Dawley's War Novels" included a number of sensational war novels by "Dion Haco." So popular was such cheap literature during the war that Boston abolitionist James

Redpath was inspired to form his own short-lived publishing company in 1863, with titles intended to be a cut above those of his competitors. His "Books for the Camp Fires," a series of "ten cent" books, were advertised as "of a much higher class than the dime publications now in the market."[8]

That soldiers read "cheap literature" in quantities we know from abundant anecdotal evidence. Looking back over his wartime reading habits, John Billings remembered that "there was no novel so dull, trashy, or sensational as not to find some one so bored with nothing to do that he would wade through it. I, certainly, never read so many such before or since." "I received the Dime Novel," another soldier wrote home, "and will commence to read it as soon as I am done with this letter." A soldier who fought in Tennessee recalled that "miserable," "worthless" novels "were sold by the thousand." He added, "The minds of the men were so poisoned that they almost scorned the idea of reading a book or journal which contained matter that would benefit their minds. I can remember when the Atlantic and Continental Monthlies were considered dull reading, while the more enticing literary productions, such as Beadle's novels, novelettes and other detestable works were received with popular favor." The artist Edwin Blashfield recalled that during the war he "gloated over" war stories in papers such as the *True Flag* and the *American Union*. A story that "lingers in my memory," he said, was that of a vivandière named Miss Minnie Ball present at Bull Run. (The minie ball was the bullet used in Civil War rifles.) Confirming soldiers' interest in cheap story papers as well as novels, the *Sunday Mercury* ran a regular feature of correspondence from soldiers; the *Mercury* had "been the entire round of the camp," one soldier in New York's Forty-seventh Regiment reported from South Carolina.[9]

Sensational novels were distributed widely to a home-front audience, as well, and were particularly noticeable at newsdealers' stalls, railway stations, and even saloons. In an article about Beadle's dime novels, William Everett noted in 1864 that the fact that these books "circulate to the extent of many hundred thousands need hardly be stated to any one who is in the way of casting his eye at the counter of any railway bookstall or newsdealer's shop." In addition, he commented, "our readers have probably seen" volumes of Beadle's "Tales" of Daniel Boone and Bob Brant, a sensational war novel, "bound up in bulky volumes alternately with illustrated advertisements, and lying on the tables in refreshment saloons in Boston." The American News Company, the major distributor of cheap literature during the war, reported selling "about 225,000 'dime' and other ten-cent publications" monthly in 1865.[10]

Though distributed in unprecedented quantities during the Civil War, sensational literature was not new to the conflict. Several publishers drew on their antebellum experiences of producing sensational novels in their response to the Civil War. The Civil War sensational publisher Erastus Barclay of Philadelphia, for instance, began his career in the 1840s with "true" crime accounts and sensational novels, including the story of Amanda Bannorris, a female land pirate, and the 1843 *The Female Warrior*, an account of Leonora Siddons, "who, led on by patriotism, joined the Texas army under General Houston" and "fought in the ever memorable battle of San Antonio." With the start of the Civil War Barclay began to publish a new series of sensational fictions, many of them war-related. A number of other publishers also produced what they called "cheap novels" in wartime, including Beadle and Company, Dick and Fitzgerald, Robert M. DeWitt, T. R. Dawley, Frederic A. Brady, and George Munro and Company, all of New York; T. B. Peterson and Company, Barclay and Company, and C. W. Alexander, all of Philadelphia; and U. P. James of Cincinnati.[11]

Antebellum sensationalist novels had frequently featured female heroines, including female warriors and female "land pirates." Portraying girls who ran away from home, disguised themselves as men, and even served as soldiers, sensational novels were often energized by plots of transgression against prevailing norms of behavior for women. At the start of the war, such novels provided a means of imagining women's active participation in the conflict. Indeed, one author later admitted that she had been inspired to disguise herself as a man both before and during the war by an antebellum sensational novel titled *Fanny Campbell, the Female Pirate Captain: A Tale of the Revolution.* Drawing on this and other sensational literature, Sarah Emma Edmonds published a highly embroidered account of her wartime adventures in 1864 titled *Unsexed: or, the Female Soldier. The Thrilling Adventures, Experiences and Escapes of a Woman, As Nurse, Spy and Scout, in Hospitals, Camps and Battle-fields.*[12]

Christine Bold has commented that "dime novels were a male-dominated genre" in terms of "publishers, writers, and fictional formulas," but a study of Civil War cheap literature reveals instead that sensational war stories often gendered the war as a set of "exciting," "thrilling," and "stirring" adventures for both women and men. "How I wish I could go and fight for my country!" exclaimed the heroine of *Miriam Rivers, the Lady Soldier; or, General Grant's Spy,* one of a number of northern sensational novels featuring female soldiers and spies published during the war. Louisa

May Alcott had expressed much the same desire in April 1861: "I've often longed to see a war," she confided to her journal, "and now I have my wish." Alcott, however, had reluctantly resigned herself to the fact that she could not fight: "I long to be a man," she said, "but as I can't fight, I will content myself with working for those who can." In contrast, in the pages of sensational war literature women characters acted on such longings, not only refusing to content themselves with "working for those who can" fight but often fighting alongside men or even disguising themselves as soldiers.[13]

Although domestic war stories tightly constrained women's roles in the war, a sensational literature of women spies, scouts, and cross-dressing soldiers revealed that there was significant imaginative space within popular print culture, if not within domestic ideology, for portraying a more active—and transgressive—women's role in the war. To some extent such martial portrayals of women during the war arose out of social realities; by some historians' count, well over four hundred women disguised themselves as soldiers during the war, and there were numerous mentions of such female soldiers in popular literature throughout the war. But even "factual" portrayals of female soldiers were usually rooted in the breathless conventions of sensational literature. The *New York Illustrated News*, for instance, in 1863 published an anecdote of one Annie Lillybridge, whose lover was a lieutenant in the Twenty-first Michigan Infantry. Because "the thought of parting from the gay lieutenant nearly drove her mad," Annie "resolved to share his dangers and be near him." After "purchasing male attire," she "behaved with marked gallantry" in the battle of Pea Ridge and "by her own hand shot a Rebel captain who was in the act of firing upon Lieutenant W——." Throughout, "she managed to keep her secret from all—not even the object of her attachment, who met her every day, was aware of her presence so near him." Both the details of this plot summary and its language were familiar from the pages of sensational fiction. Indeed, the *News* itself acknowledged the blurred line between fact and fiction during the war by publishing this war anecdote under the heading "The Romance of a Poor Young Girl" and commending this "history" to "Miss Braddon [a popular romantic novelist] for elaboration in her next new novel."[14]

In sensational stories women directly expressed a longing for danger and excitement: "She did *so* long to be mounted on her gallant Spitfire," commented the narrator of the 1865 *Kate Sharp; or, The Two Conscripts*, "galloping when and where she chose, with enough danger to heighten [*sic*] the excitement." Acting on this longing, the heroine, Kate Sharp, engaged in a military expedition, leading fifty men "who greeted our heroine with a hearty cheer," against guerrillas and bushwhackers in Tennessee. "I wouldn't miss such an adventure for a great deal," she commented. She even rebutted criticisms of her transgressive role. A dandyish "bandbox hero" told Kate that her "present occupation" was "extremely unladylike, and not such as I should recommend to a sister or friend of mine." Instead, he advised her to "go home, and settle down as the wife of some good, honest fellow, and leave this work of war to bearded men." Kate's scathing put-down of this "pusillanimous puppy," a "martial Adonis" with a "silky mustache," was followed by a meeting with General Sherman in which he absentmindedly handed her a cigar, to her amusement, before authorizing her expedition and telling her that he would promote her if she succeeded.[15]

If sensational war stories approvingly allowed women to transgress norms of gender that prevented them from fighting in the war, they also celebrated the physicality and fighting spirit of men in muscular, swaggering language. In the 1861 *Scotto, the Scout,* for instance, the main character, Scotto, was "tall and athletic," with a "strongly-defined and sun-browned face." "I want to fight!" he announced. "If I don't eat my bigness into rebellion, if I don't cut and hack, hash, slash, and gash, right and left, it'll be because my hand forgets its cunnin', and my arm loses its patriotism, and my brain its sense!" His "Union Rangers" "rallied around Scotto" as their leader because they knew "he would not flinch, and was the man to lead them to victory, if it were within human attainment. His hardy frame, well-seasoned muscles, and universally accredited courage, gave promise of great effectivenes." An exaggerated physicality and braggadocio marked the portrayal of Scotto throughout the novel, as it marked the portrayal of numerous sensational heroes during the war.[16]

Sensational war stories strongly marked the gender of both men and women, but in ways strikingly different from the gendered norms of feminized, sentimental, or early wartime patriotic literature. Sensational stories not only inflated the masculinity of white soldiers, scouts, or spies but also allowed white women a heightened sexuality. Indeed, such stories often created a sexually charged war in which sexual threat and sexual possibility alternated in a deliberately exciting dynamic. In doing so, such stories emphasized the personal daring, defiance, and risk occasioned by war for both men and women.

• • •

Sensational war stories often drew on the actual events of war, especially in the border states of Tennessee, Missouri, and Kentucky, where internecine warfare and guerrilla fighting characterized the conflict in late 1861 and early 1862. Such war stories did not just reflect the already dramatic events of war in these states, however; they superimposed a particular fictional order on the chaos of conflict. Story after story created a narrative arc of disruption and eventual restoration, settling key issues of the war in a tidy narrative form that rarely corresponded to the actual events of war. From early 1862 through the summer of that year *Harper's Weekly*, for instance, published a series of stories exploring the highly charged question of whether Unionism would obtain in those states or be defeated by pro-Confederate forces. These stories often centered around families split in their loyalties by the war, energized by plots in which pro-Confederate bands of men marauded indiscriminately, and with denouements featuring the conversion of erstwhile Confederate sympathizers to staunch Unionists. They also often featured heroines with an intensified sexuality, as well as male characters who embodied a rough but compelling masculinity.[17]

Harper's Weekly's February 1862 "On the Kentucky Border," for instance, featured a Confederate sympathizer converted to staunch Unionism by the end of the story. Described as "about six foot three," Dan spoke in dialect and was a "rough-looking fellow," who made a "homely-attired but manly figure." A "crack shot at turkeys, deer, or 'possum," he counted it "a disgrace not to bring down a squirrel as dead as a hammer with the wind of my bullet." In contrast, his half brother, Maurice, who had lived in the North, was pro-Union, and eventually became a captain in the army, spoke apparently accentless English, with his politics signaling greater education and refinement. The lesson was clear in this as well as in other border stories: those who were pro-Union were superior in culture and education to those who supported the Confederacy.[18]

Still, it was Dan's rough, manly courage that became the centerpiece of the story. After his disillusionment with "seceshers" and his conversion to Unionism, Dan attempted to fight off a band of Confederate sympathizers attacking his home. Described "with the light of battle illuminating his rough features," Dan vowed defiance against these attackers, suddenly speaking in the accentless English that signaled Unionism: "Come on, all of you, cowards that you are, and see if I can't use this bowie to some effect!" Outnumbered by his attackers and beaten to his knees, Dan "still defended himself desperately, having already slain one and wounded two men." [19]

This defiant courage also characterized the heroine of the story, Harry, whose name, "notwithstanding its masculinity, designated a girl of eigh-teen," in "accordance with a practice" of naming "not yet extinct among the rougher denizens of Kentucky and Tennessee." As her masculine name suggested, Harry possessed great physical courage, refusing to leave her father when their house was threatened with attack. Instead, she "folded her arms with a look of resolution," telling her father that she could "load your rifle for you, if I can do nothing else." "You're true grit, gal," her father replied.[20]

Harry embodied a glowing physicality and sexuality rarely to be seen in domestic fiction. She was "a brilliant brunette, with magnificent black hair and eyes, ripe scarlet lips, and a face whose bold, symmetrical beauty of feature and ruddy health seemed in part to justify her masculine appel-lation." She was also "tall in stature like her race," "not too neatly dressed," and with "bare, brown, handsome arms" and feet—a detail the author re-turned to twice in the story. Indeed, the beauty of her bare feet and ankles "made their nudity a matter of congratulations to the masculine spectator," the narrator commented, inviting a form of Victorian voyeurism typical of sensationalist stories.[21]

As such a description suggested, women in the border states were often imagined to embody a heightened sexuality, one whose racialized basis was suggested by recurrent references to these heroines' "brown" skin and black hair. One such heroine was even named "brown Meg." This focus on sexuality was also played out in the plots of several sensational novels, in which the disruptions of war were mirrored by disruptions in the sexual order, as women came under direct sexual threat for their adherence to the Union.[22]

Several sensational novels took their inspiration for plots that com-bined physical daring and sexual threat from the highly publicized, though quite possibly apocryphal, actions of Susan Brownlow, the daughter of the famous Parson Brownlow. The "fighting parson" William G. Brownlow of Tennessee toured the North to often tumultuous acclaim during the spring and summer of 1862 before publishing one of the few best-sellers of the war, his 1862 *Sketches of the Rise, Progress, and Decline of Secession; with a Narrative of Personal Adventure among the Rebels.* The Unionist editor of the *Knoxville Whig*, Brownlow had spent months holding forth against the Confederacy from the pages of his newspaper in highly vituperative language before being escorted across Union lines by exasperated Con-federate officials in March 1862. What became known simply as *Parson Brownlow's Book* presented dramatic evidence of Unionist sentiment in

Tennessee—a subject of intense concern to Northerners. But the success of *Parson Brownlow's Book*, which sold more than seventy-five thousand copies in thirty days that summer, and eventually more than two hundred copies, revealed far more, as well: the appeal for Northerners of a war framed as sensationalized melodrama. As one Chicago dignitary commented during Brownlow's triumphant lecture tour of the Midwest and East, "Our children need no romance to stir their young hearts." Instead, "the truthful picture of your sufferings and heroism will fill the place of high-wrought fiction."[23]

This comment revealed a central source of Brownlow's appeal for Northerners. His story was popular not because it was so different from "high-wrought" fiction but precisely because it was so similar—because he told the tale of his devotion to the Union in the "thrilling" language of popular sensationalism. Indeed, Northern audiences met him more than halfway in imagining and celebrating a sensationalist war, especially in response to his daughter Susan. Early in the war Brownlow had defiantly flown the American flag over his house, and an early *Rebellion Record* also reprinted a report that Brownlow's daughter Susan had used a revolver to defend the flag against two marauders—a story that was "later embellished by saying that two men came back with ninety reinforcements." Whatever the truth of Susan Brownlow's actions may have been (and she may well have defended the flag), she was celebrated throughout the North in the guise of a sensationalist heroine. Accompanying her father on part of his lecture tour, in Hartford she was ceremonially presented with a Colt's revolver; in Philadelphia she was presented with a silk flag. Her picture appeared on "Card Photographs" available for twenty-five cents. When she appeared with her father in New York, the *New York Times* wrote, "No one can forget her heroic conduct, when, revolver in hand, she kept at bay a crowd of 'chivalry' who threatened and attempted to pull down the Stars and Stripes from her father's house, and no one will forget to yield her all the praise and honor which such patriotism and unflinching bravery deserve."[24]

For Brownlow's Northern audiences, his daughter Susan already existed in an imaginary relation to social reality—a relation mediated by the conventions of sensationalist fiction, with its emphasis on norms of womanhood differing from the often passive suffering to be found in the pages of domestic stories. Not surprisingly, her story also inspired sensational novels that emphasized both her daring and sexual threat. The 1864 *Miss Martha Brownlow, or the Heroine of Tennessee* drew directly on the story of Parson Brownlow and his daughter (whose name unaccountably changed here) in order to produce "A Truthful and Graphic Account of the Many Perils and Privations Endured by Miss Martha Brownlow, the Lovely and Accomplished Daughter of the Celebrated Parson Brownlow, During Her Residence with Her Father in Knoxville." Close in style to a stage melodrama, it began with "Scene First—Game of the Traitors," in which a Confederate lieutenant and captain wagered "which of us shall lower the 'stars and stripes' at Parson Brownlow's, and kiss his handsome daughter." After suggesting the sexual threat that Martha faced ("D——n me, I'll have her yet," announced one of the traitors), the novel immediately made clear that Martha would be more than a match for her would-be attackers: she was "a handsome bouncing lass," "a noble girl," who could, "after attending to her domestic duties, cross a sword, handle a musket," and "follow in the chase with success, equal to any man of equal years in Tennessee." Indeed, one character said, "I would forewarn the man who is so fortunate to win the honor of kissing even the hand of that brave girl, to beware; she will not be trifled with." [25]

One of the central ironies that the story exposed was the fact that in wartime the nation could no longer protect its individual members, including women; instead, individuals were often needed to protect the nation. When her father had to leave on a "short journey," Martha told him that she would "feel perfectly safe, even in your absence, father. For 'our flag is still there.' Surely, I am safe beneath its protecting folds." But of course she was not safe—indeed, far from the flag being able to protect her, she had to protect the flag, a task she was willing to take on as an heir to Revolutionary womanhood: "Women there were in the American Revolution, who, with their husbands, fathers, brothers, sisters, lovers, braved every danger, faced the foe, and defended that flag against the assaults of our country's invaders. I emulate their daring example, and I'll protect it now." Thus, when the two traitors arrived to demand that she take the flag down just after she had sung the "Star-Spangled Banner" to herself, her response was to level "a musket at her foes": "Back, you cowardly dogs! Leave me, ere I make you bite the dust! Touch not the sacred folds of that good old flag!" Here, once again threats to the Union were linked to a specific sexual threat against a white woman, a threat that, because of the disruptions of war, took on political overtones. [26]

Such sexual threat also energized the 1862 novel *Six Months among the Secessionists: A Reliable and Thrilling Narrative of the Sufferings and Trials of Miss Sarah L. Palmer, a Native of Pennsylvania who, at the opening of the Great Southern Rebellion, was teaching School in Knoxville, the home of Parson Brownlow.* The heroine of this novel was even reported to have had a brief conversation with Parson Brownlow, who told her that the outbreak of war was "bad, bad news for the whole country; but still worse for the South itself. It is suicide!"[27]

In this novel the linkage between political loyalties and sexual danger became immediately clear after the outbreak of war. Sarah Palmer, the heroine, had previously rejected the advances of the villain, the Southern planter's son Alfred Poindexter. Now mockingly calling her "my Yankee maid of love and valor," Poindexter locked her in a room and told her, "I have taken care that we shall be undisturbed, and it is my full intention to revenge myself upon you for all the injury your stubbornness has caused me." Although Sarah managed to flee from this threat of rape, she later was caught by a mob, "stripped of my apparel from the waist upward," tied to the tail of a cart, and dragged twice around a field. This scene made clear the voyeuristic tendencies of much sensationalist fiction.[28]

If sexual threats to women structured the narratives of several sensational novels, these often alternated with celebrations of the possibilities opened by the war for women. Metta V. Victor's June 1862 *The Unionist's Daughter: A Tale of the Rebellion in Tennessee,* for instance, was an account of the wartime travails of Eleanor Beaufort, another Susan Brownlow–inspired heroine, whose Unionist father was jailed in Nashville for his beliefs and then—unlike the real Parson Brownlow—died. The usefulness of his death as a plot device was clear: as in many sensational novels, such wartime disruption of a family paved the way for adventures outside the home without entirely overturning prevailing ideals of domesticity. After Beaufort's death, Eleanor told her would-be lover, a young Unionist hero named Beverly Bell, that her heart was now "as cold as ice" and that "I am devoted now to my country—it is all that gives me any interest in life." Asking him to "give me work to do," she wanted to know "what are your secret commissions? Can not you trust some of them to a woman's wit?" In return, Bell asked her, "Do you think you could be my courier, Eleanor?— that you could ride on horseback, unmolested, through an army-cursed, secessionist country for sixty miles?—that you could even play the part of a saucy secessionist lady, if such a ruse should become necessary?" Such questions, with their titillating language ("unmolested") and suggestions of melodrama ("the part of a saucy secessionist lady"), could have acted as thumbnail sketches of the plots of a number of sensationalist novels. Eleanor's answer was simple: "Try me" was all she said, but "her eyes lighted with more fire than he had seen in them, of late days." [29]

Throughout, the novel played with ideas of what constituted female courage. One character, for instance, commented that "women have a heroism of their own." "Theirs is as much in endurance as ours in action. I think they shame us men—even girls." At another point, a former suitor of Eleanor's told her, "You have too much courage, Eleanor; you are not womanly enough." She simply replied, "Our standards of womanly excellence differ." After Eleanor and Beverly Bell's wedding at the end of the novel, Bell asked her, "How can I take care of such a frail, fair flower?" She responded by asking, "Have I not proven, in the last few months, that I could take care of myself, and others, too, Beverly?" [30]

In focusing on women's courageous deeds during the war, Victor, an established author of Beadle's dime novels as well as other cheap fictions, claimed that she was basing her story on "bare facts." Indeed, at the back of her volume she reproduced a number of "original statements and documents" to buttress the authenticity of her narrative, much as Harriet Beecher Stowe had done in her *Key to Uncle Tom's Cabin*. One of the documents Victor cited, for instance, was "a letter written from the camp of the 1st Tenn. regiment, in the fall of 1861." "One of the features of the 1st Tenn. regiment," this letter said, "is the person of a brave and accomplished young lady of but eighteen summers, and prepossessing appearance, named Sarah Taylor, of East Tenn.," who had "formed the determination to share with her late companions the dangers and fatigues of a military campaign." Wearing a "neat blue *chapeau*, beneath which her long hair is fantastically arranged," and with "a highly-finished regulation sword, and silver-mounted pistols in her belt," she was "quite the idol of the Tennessee boys." Not only did they "look upon her as a second Joan of Arc," but they believed that "victory and glory will perch upon the standard borne in the ranks favored by her loved presence." Significantly, "Miss Captain Taylor" was "all courage and skill. Having become an adept in the sword exercise, and a sure shot with the pistol, she is determined to lead in the van of the march, bearing her exiled and oppressed countrymen back to their homes, or, if failing, to offer up her own life's blood in the sacrifice." The language in which Sarah Taylor was described bore the marks not of the "bare facts" Victor aspired to but of sensational fiction, and it pointed to a circular dynamic within the commercial literary culture of war. Sensational fiction often provided a language for representations of the war's events—and the resulting representations were often then used as the "factual" basis for sensational fiction.[31]

Like *The Unionist's Daughter*, several sensational wartime novels imagined disruptions in women's home life that allowed—or even forced—them to step out of their domestic roles and become spies or even soldiers. E. E. Barclay's 1862 *The Lady Lieutenant*, for instance, a slim, forty-page pamphlet, was described as "a wonderful, startling and thrilling narrative of the adventures of Miss Madeline Moore, who, in order to be near her lover, joined the Army, was elected lieutenant, and fought in western Virginia under the renowned General McClellan and afterwards at the great Battle of Bull's Run." *The Lady Lieutenant* promised that "Her Own and Her Lover's Perilous Adventures and Hair-Breadth Escapes" would be "Graphically Delineated." [32]

Like many heroines of sensationalist fiction, Madeline Moore was an orphan—a status that helped to justify her departure from home. Although she lived with an aunt, this relative was "cross, crabbed and tyrannical," and "toward me she behaved with a vindictive boldness," all of which Madeline mentioned "to show how unpleasant was my *home*, and what strong inducements I therefore had for leaving it." As in much domestic fiction of the antebellum era, home was not so much celebrated as scrutinized and found wanting here.[33]

Romance was the keynote of Madeline's character; she described herself as "young, ardent, and rather romantic" and promised to give the reader "an account of the wonderful adventures through which it has been my fortune to pass." When her lover, Frank, decided to join a regiment after the fall of Sumter, initially Madeline "felt lonely and almost heartbroken" but soon grew excited when "suddenly a new idea flashed across my mind"—to disguise herself as a soldier in order to join Frank. Now she was no longer heartbroken over Frank's departure, a change he immediately noticed. As he plaintively remarked, "I think I could go better satisfied could I see you weep." Madeline "tried to weep to pacify him; but, for my life, I could not start a tear, owing to the rapturous delight I felt in anticipating the result of my new scheme. But I covered my eyes, and forced a few sobs, and in broken sentences and faint tones asked him when he was to go." Here Madeline was disguising her disguise—and in portraying her as doing so the author of *The Lady Lieutenant* drew on literary conventions stretching back to Shakespeare and beyond.[34]

Sensational literature often emphasized the need for concealment of true or genuine identity—an emphasis that had everything to do with the perceived limitations imposed by class, gender, and race in structuring individual identity. It thus implicitly offered a commentary on society's limitations; far from being a simple celebration of the possibilities for fluid social identities, sensational literature instead arose from a recognition that such fluid identities were unusual. The motif of disguise in *The Lady Lieutenant* had everything to do with a recognition of the limitations imposed on female identity and the shock or titillation value that adhered to overturning gendered norms. *The Lady Lieutenant* also played with a central irony: the only way for a woman to be a genuine soldier was to be an imposter. It presented an implicit theory of female identity outside the home as inherently theatrical, involving simulation.

It also played with the confused erotic charge that resulted from female disguise. Once Madeline had put on "a complete suit of male attire, with a small pair of whiskers," she found herself attractive in new ways. "I looked in the glass," she confessed, "and must say I fell in love with myself—that is, I should have been apt to take a fancy to just such a youth as I appeared to be." This erotic confusion was shared by Frank, once she joined his regiment under the assumed name Albert Harville. After "Albert" mentioned that Madeline was "a relation" of hers, Frank confessed that he saw "a resemblance between you—enough at all events to cause me to feel a deep interest in your welfare." Frank and "Albert" became inseparable companions; and after her mustache had fallen off, Frank marveled, "Oh, more than ever, Albert, do you resemble my dear, dear Madeline!" Madeline's adoption of male disguise allowed for expressions of autoeroticism and homoeroticism not socially acceptable within the confines of heterosexual society.[35]

It also allowed for nonfeminine experiences proving her bravery. In battle, Madeline had no fear, even though "while giving orders to my men a ball whizzed close past my face and lodged in the brain of the sergeant, who stood a little behind me." When she found herself "almost ridden over by a rebel trooper," she not only "drew my revolver and shot my assailant dead" but found it "the work of a moment to seize the fiery animal by the bit and vault upon his back." Twice wounded—once in the "right temple" and once, at "Bull's Run," with "a deep gash in the back of my head"— she nevertheless continued without complaint. In the pages of *The Lady Lieutenant*, war provided a glorious opportunity for physical heroism and personal adventure.[36]

Sensational literature such as *The Lady Lieutenant* deliberately crossed not only boundaries of gender but also those of class: it invented a war in which persons of "low" status could easily meet those of "high" status as equals. A recurrent motif in such literature was the meeting between the protagonist and an important general: in *The Lady Lieutenant,* not only did Frank and "Albert" meet General McClellan, but they also carried his "despatches" to Washington. Thus sensational literature, much like war humor, "democratized" the war, in fantasy obliterating the distinctions that existed between ranks, between classes, and between men and women.[37]

The fantasy that female heroines had ready access to high-ranking generals merged with the fantasy that the wartime nation could offer individuals a new version of family in the 1862 *Pauline of the Potomac,* which marked the literary debut of "Wesley Bradshaw," pseudonym for author and publisher Charles Wesley Alexander of Philadelphia. Born in 1837, Alexander was in his mid-twenties when the war began and, as Philadelphia city directories show, had not yet found a permanent occupation. Listed in 1861 as clerk, in 1862 he appeared as advertising agent, in 1863 as reporter, in 1864 as author, and—finally—in 1865 as publisher, a position into which he settled.[38]

Alexander seized the sensational publishing opportunities offered by the war. After publishing *Pauline of the Potomac* with Barclay and Company, Alexander began his own imprint under which he printed a sequel, *Maud of the Mississippi.* During the war he wrote or published a list composed entirely of war-related titles, including *The Volunteer's Roll of Honor* (the only other title he published with Barclay and Company); *The Picket Slayer; Washington's Vision; General Sherman's Indian Spy;* and *Angel of the Battlefield* (published by the American News Company). In 1865 he published a short-lived periodical, the *Soldier's Casket.* In addition, as Wesley Bradshaw he published several pieces of wartime ephemera, including two broadsides, "General McClellan's Dream" and "Jeff Davis' Confession! A Singular Document Found on the Dead Body of a Rebel!"[39]

Barclay and Company made the titillating theme of *Pauline of the Potomac* clear with a cover that pictured its heroine, dressed in Union army uniform, leaning nonchalantly on a cannon. As with several other sensational stories featuring female heroines, what initially energized the plot was family disruption, in this case the death of Pauline's father, "a distinguished French exile" devoted to his adopted country. On his deathbed M. D'Estraye made the connection between patriotism and patriarchal authority clear when he told Pauline that he wished to "dedicate" her to a "glorious cause" and then draped the American flag over her head and

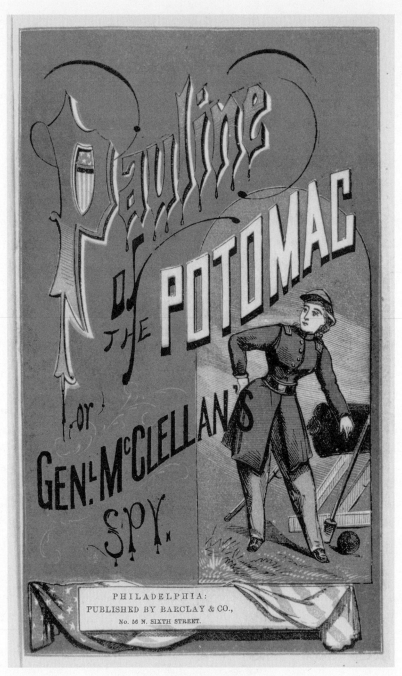

Pauline of the Potomac.
(Courtesy of the Brown University Library)

GEN'L GRANT'S DARING SPY
PASSING THE VICKSBURG BATTERIES DURING A TERRIBLE STORM

C. W. ALEXANDER & CO.,
PUBLISHERS,
123 SOUTH THIRD STREET, PHILADELPHIA.

Maud of the Mississippi.
(Courtesy of the American Antiquarian Society)

shoulders "like a bridal veil." "On the battlefield heroes will be wounded beneath its folds," he said; "you will be there to smile upon them, and to give drink to their parching lips. They will die; you will be there to pray for them, to weep for their mothers and sisters, who may be far away." "America," he concluded, "I give you my child, the offering of my heart." [40]

With this dedication of Pauline to country, Alexander carefully authorized her adventures as the last and therefore sacred wish of a dying father. He also addressed any potential criticism of Pauline's role as unfeminine by explaining that though "many might consider the course of Miss D'Estraye as rather masculine or at least out of the established line of conduct for a female and a refined lady," his readers should remember "that Miss D'Estraye was French, and that what would seem indecorous to American women, is by no means so regarded by the gentler sex in France." Both sacred and foreign (and not only foreign but French), Pauline was doubly "other." [41]

After her father's death, Pauline initially followed his wishes by "attaching herself to a regiment of volunteers in the capacity of nurse." Present at Bull Run, she afterward commented, "Oh, what a terrible, what a fearful day was yesterday; and yet its horrors were strangely blended with romance," with "touching and thrilling incidents." As this sensationalist language revealed, within wartime popular culture the meaning of Bull Run was malleable; widely interpreted in the Northern press as both a disaster and a goad to strengthen Northern resolve, within sensationalist literature it was also a source of romance and adventure. [42]

After Bull Run Pauline "thirsted, however, for a more important part in the great drama than she had hitherto occupied" and decided to go to the "newly appointed Commander in Chief of the Union Army, General M'Clellan [sic], and offer him her services as a scout or spy." This theatrical language—the fact that she wanted a more important "part" in the "great drama" of war—was telling, a reminder that sensationalist literature and the popular drama of the day tended to inform each other. In a scene that, significantly, transferred the authority for Pauline's actions from father to nation, McClellan decided to accept her "patriotic proposition." Though he cautioned her that the "office of a Scout or a Spy is one of the most responsible ones in the army" and that it was "attended by innumerable and oftentimes insurmountable difficulties and dangers," he was won over by her "knowledge of the geography of the Southern states" as well as her "loyalty to the sacred cause in which we are all engaged." [43]

In the adventures that followed, Pauline was often obligated, "in the performance of this duty, to assume different costumes and even names." Initially deeply veiled, she later procured "the uniform and equipment of a zouave" and later still disguised herself as a "Colonel of the Confederate Army." Like Madeline Moore, Pauline easily performed physical feats of derring-do and was consistently as "cool as she was courageous," often outwitting the enemy. After each of her adventures she returned to McClellan to receive his praise as well as further assignments; at one typical meeting "the General's face was covered with glad and gracious smiles as he cordially greeted Pauline."[44]

By the end, she had found a new soldier lover, and "our heroine and her betrothed had confided" to McClellan, "as children to a father, their intentions for the future, and obtained from him his ready assent to honor their nuptials, at the conclusion of the war, with his presence." This ending indicated that there were limits to the transgressive or subversive nature of gendered sensationalism. Sensational novels featuring female "scouts" often made a point of reestablishing their heroines' dependence on a husband or father figure by the end of the narrative, thereby lessening the perceived threat to society of an adventurous single female "on the loose." But their narratives also established a new relationship between women and the nation. The explicit substitution of a national family for the private, nuclear family was an aspect of imagining gendered nationalism in wartime. In the pages of *Pauline of the Potomac* not only did the nation provide a reconstituted family for Pauline, but it also provided a theatrical backdrop against which she could embark on exciting adventures.[45]

A different but related narrative strategy characterized wartime sensational novels featuring male scouts as heroes. Many of these novels began by stressing the solitary character of their protagonists, drawing on a long-standing antebellum tradition of popular frontier stories in the tradition of James Fenimore Cooper, whose Natty Bumpo lived in harmony with nature but apart from society. The comparison with Cooper was often explicit: "There is nothing finer in the whole range of Cooper's stories," the *New-York Mercury* said about the sensational novel *The Round Pack*. Wartime novels of heroic scouts also began by emphasizing scouts' solitary nature but typically shifted the contours of the frontier story by integrating their protagonists into a new national economy produced by war. If female scouts eventually became part of a new national "family" by becoming dependent on male authority, male scouts became a functional part of the new nation by working and fighting with other men in an egalitarian "brotherhood."[46]

We can see this process at work in John Hovey Robinson's 1863 *Mountain Max; or, Nick Whiffles on the Border: A Tale of the Bushwhackers in Missouri*. The prolific Robinson, who published numerous cheap novels before the war, attempted to graft the frontier novel tradition onto a Civil War story in this novel and in the process created a new hybrid narrative. In 1858 Robinson had introduced a frontier hero in his *Nick Whiffles: A Drama in Three Acts;* now he self-consciously reintroduced Nick Whiffles in a sensationalist Civil War story. Bursting into a scene in which "villainous" Confederates threatened to hang an aged Missouri Unionist, Whiffles was "dressed like a pilgrim from the far trapping-grounds of the West," in "buckskin frock," "moccasined foot," "leggined calf, and cap of skin," and with a "weather-beaten" face and beard that "presented a flourishing growth of several years." He immediately drew two guns on a "rebel outlaw" so that "each of his brown hands now held six shots." But his intended victim protested against this sudden entrance of the frontier literary tradition into a Civil War setting. "I've heard of you," the well-read Confederate villain announced. "Much has been said and written about you; but I don't believe half on't. You've been published in the newspapers, put on the stage, served up in books, translated into French, and hashed up in every style to suit the modern appetite." Despite his admission of Nick Whiffles's literary fame, however, he questioned Nick's ability to handle the new crisis of war: "This is a bad place for you to come to, Nick Whiffles. There's a different pastime going on here from trapping beaver, shooting bears, and picking off a naked Indian, now and then."[47]

Yet Nick Whiffles's frontier skills were just what the war needed, the novel made clear. "Major-General Fremont had sent for him to come down from the mountains, with a few chosen woodsmen and sharpshooters, to take a hand in playing out the game of Rebellion," the narrator commented. In the course of the story, Whiffles gathered a group of mountain men who "proved a scourge and a terror" to the Missouri bushwhackers. "These brave fellows are doing good service for the Union," the story concluded. "Nick has distinguished himself in many battles." He "occasionally turns a longing eye to the mountains; but no wandering thought can attract his honest heart from its devotion to Liberty and the Old Flag. The star that now directs his steps by day and by night, is not the North star of the old trapping grounds, but the pole-star of Freedom."[48]

One lesson of sensational war novels was that the nation gathered even the staunchest individualists to it in wartime. But as the plot of *Mountain Max* also revealed, as it careened from one adventure to another, sensationalist war novels taught a complementary lesson: that adherence to the nation furthered the possibility of exciting individual adventures.

Such individual adventures had a highly racialized cast. A number of sensational novels featured white characters who disguised themselves as "contrabands" in order to act as spies or escape from tight situations. In *Kate Sharp*, both Kate and her admirer, Jim Allen, disguised themselves as two old "contrabands." In *Six Months among the Secessionists*, the heroine, Sarah, escaped from sexual slavery to the villainous Alfred Poindexter only by being disguised as a slave. These disguises were part of the changeability of identity that generally characterized sensational literature, but they also had specific pleasurable and transgressive connotations within a white Northern culture that celebrated and enjoyed putting on "blackface" in minstrelsy.[49]

A recurrent motif in these stories was the desire on the part of African Americans to aid whites. In *Six Months among the Secessionists*, it was slaves who helped Sarah escape. Thrust into a "miserable hut occupied only by a negro and his wife," Sarah attracted the sympathy of the "poor old creature" Chloe, who told her, "Dar now, Missus, don't cry no more! Sampson nor Chloe won't let nobody hurt ye!" To help her to escape, they "completely metamorphosed" her "into a young negress, the skin of my face, neck, arms, and hands being ingeniously colored, my own hair after being trimmed, concealed by woolly locks, and my own dress being replaced by the regular attire of a slave girl." The fantasy that blacks would devote themselves to the freedom of whites dominated the remainder of the novel, as Sarah made her way Northward *"assisted invariably by negroes!"* [50]

To be sure, many sensational stories and novels also acknowledged African Americans' own desires for freedom, as well as their awareness that the war might result in emancipation. In *Harper's Weekly*'s March 1862 "In Western Missouri," for instance, the female slave Dinah "demanded with great earnestness" whether one character was going to fight for the Union: "You gwine to fight for de Stars and Stripes and Massa Lincoln, ben't you, Cap'n Elliot?" When he told her he was, she blessed him: "De good Lord in hebben bress both you and him! dat's all. Nebber doubt you're in de right and dat He *will* bress you." In other sensational stories, too, black characters emerged briefly from their usual location in the background of the story to state their interest in freedom.[51]

Yet by and large sensational stories and novels depicted African Americans as loyal appendages of whites, interested in freedom only if they could stay with their white masters and mistresses. In *Scotto, the Scout*, the slave

Dagon, who "spoke often of the North Star," nevertheless "declared a firm determination not to leave his young mistress." When he thought his mistress had been killed, he exclaimed, "Who car's for liberty now? I doesn't! I doesn't car' a hill o' corn for't. I's a miser'ble contraban', I is!" Likewise, though the slave Black Jack allowed that "we should all like to hev the freedom" in *The Round Pack*, he also said that "t'won't make so much dif'rence to me as it does to some others," since "I stays kase I likes to." In *Harper's Weekly's* March 1862 "The Tennessee Blacksmith," the white hero asked the "stalwart negro" Joe whether he would like his freedom. "Well, Massa John," Joe replied, "I wouldn't like much to leabe you, but den I'se like to be a free man." Joe's master then explained a theory of freedom based on masculine whiteness: "Joe, the white race have maintained their liberty by their valor. Are you willing to fight for yours? Ay! fight to the death?" Joe's response, while embracing freedom, also revealed to what extent white authors maintained a fantasy of black love of and subservience to whites. "I'se fight for yous any time, Massa John," Joe said.[52]

The idea that black men deserved freedom only through fighting for (and like) white men was a gendered theory of freedom that also had a feminized counterpart: although black female slaves, in contrast to white women, were never represented as fighting, they were sometimes represented as sacrificing themselves for their white mistresses and obtaining freedom as a result. C. W. Alexander's 1865 *Angel of the Battle-Field*, for instance, created a Southern heroine, Eleanor Poindexter, who emancipated her mulatto slave Rosa as a reward for total devotion. After Rosa had risked her life for the sake of her mistress, saying, "I'd sooner be killed twenty times over than have any hurt come to you, Miss Eleanor, God bless you," Eleanor exclaimed, "Slave, then, you shall be no longer!" in "accents that showed she had forever swept from her mind prejudices and opinions which had been inculcated there by lifelong education and custom."[53]

Nevertheless, the severe limitations of this emancipation fantasy were immediately clear. Rosa's emancipation involved paid servitude for her former mistress: "Hereafter," Eleanor told her, "I will pay you four dollars a week." What's more, before Rosa had a chance to exercise her new freedom, the plot demanded that she make the ultimate sacrifice for her former mistress: she died protecting Eleanor from a lascivious villain. As a would-be rapist threatened Eleanor, Rosa "sprang upon him with the fury of a tigress, and, clutching him by the throat, almost bore him to the floor." "Alas! however, the next moment a bowie-knife glittered above her, and flashed down into her bosom like the lightning bolt falls from heaven to earth." Even at the moment of death, this sensational novel imagined that Rosa's last thoughts were of her mistress, emphasizing this point by repeating the word "faithful" twice in one sentence: "The faithful mulatto sank back with a wild shriek of despair; but, faithful to the last, stretched out her arms toward Eleanor, as though to reach and enfold her cherished mistress to her stricken heart." Thus Rosa's convenient death followed in a long line of "tragic mulatto" stories, vividly revealing the imaginary limits that Northern racism imposed on conceptions of black life after emancipation.[54]

• • •

By 1864 and 1865, cheap publishers were producing sensational war literature in an increasing crescendo, with both publication and distribution aided by the merger of several wholesale news agencies into the American News Company in February 1864. This new company had "facilities for the dissemination of current literature throughout the distant and remote portions of our vast country," the *Round Table* commented in 1866. "Along the line of every car, stage, or steamboat route, and in every large city and town, it has its agents and correspondents, from whom every paper, book, or pamphlet can be obtained as soon as published."[55]

Although Southerners were necessarily outside this distribution network, even they took note of this cheap literature, which occasionally fell into their hands. In a December 1864 article titled "Yankee War Literature," the *Southern Field and Fireside* complained of the "unhealthy, mendacious, yellow covered style of creative literature" published in the North, which emphasized the "wild, the monstrous," and "the terrific" and had a "morbid and diseased tone." It particularly scorned border stories set in east Tennessee, in which Southern "Union loving" heroines were represented as fleeing from "rebel violence." The *Southern Illustrated News* was also caustic at the expense of John Hovey Robinson's east Tennessee tale *The Round Pack*, which it said should instead be titled "The Round Pack of Lies." For "audacity of statement and a pleasant humor of lying it may challenge a comparison even with the dispatches of Major General John Pope," the *News* sarcastically concluded. The *Field and Fireside* congratulated itself on the fact that "nothing comes before us from Southern pens that could bring a blush to the cheek of innocence, or spot with a single stain the purity of youth." Whereas Yankee literature took "passion and pride, lust, fury and sin for its subjects," Southern literature dealt with "patriotism and honour, household affection, and a stainless love," as well as "virtue, honesty and truth." [56]

Such self-congratulation was premature, however. Several Southern publishers produced a cheap war literature of their own, sometimes equally as sensational as that of their Northern counterparts. A few weeks before publishing its scathing editorial on "Yankee war literature," for instance, the *Southern Field and Fireside* itself had run the sensational serial "The Scout of Albado; or, Vengeance Is Mine: A Tale of Retribution" (discussed in chapter 5). Both the *Southern Field and Fireside* and the *Southern Illustrated News* also began cheap novel–publishing ventures that highlighted war novels late in the war. The *Southern Field and Fireside* advertised five "novelettes" either in print or in press during late 1864 and early 1865, four of which were war novels. W. D. Herrington's *The Captain's Bride* was a "thrilling tale of the war," followed by Edward Edgeville's *Castine*, a "charming romance" featuring a cross-dressing Confederate soldier. A third novel was W. D. Herrington's *The Deserter's Daughter*, an "exciting tale." The last war novel in this series was a reprinting of "The Scout of Albado," announced as "in press" in early 1865.[57]

This crescendo of cheap war novels in late 1864 and early 1865 mirrored the increased publication rate of Northern sensational war novels during the same period, though the volume of publication was necessarily different. Still, the fact that the *Southern Field and Fireside* began to publish its cheap novels in a numbered series of "Southern Field and Fireside" novelettes suggests that Southern publishers paid close attention to the conventions of Northern cheap novels, which were often published in numbered series. There were few similarities in their respective markets, however. Advertisements even for successful Southern war novels underlined not only the much smaller audience for such novels but also the difficulties Southern publishers faced in getting their books to market. In early 1865 the *Southern Field and Fireside* proudly advertised that *The Captain's Bride* had sold five thousand copies in three months, claiming that "the great demand for it not only continues but increases from day to day." But it also acknowledged difficulties in meeting this "great" demand: "We regret that unavoidable circumstances, in the supply of paper, will limit the number of the second edition." Likewise, though the *Field and Fireside* advertised "The Scout of Albado" as "in press" in January 1865, this title was not printed as a book during the war. Similar difficulties may have cut short the entrepreneurial career of one Simon Spicewood of Thomasville,

North Carolina, who advertised "Junaluskie, the Cherokee: A Tale of the War" in the *Southern Field and Fireside* in February 1865. "Please forward orders immediately," Spicewood requested, as "there will be but a limited edition published at present." Perhaps Spicewood received no orders for his "neat little pamphlet without covers." At any rate, there is no record of the publication of this title.[58]

Because of such publishing difficulties, there were relatively few sensational stories and novels published in the South during the war. Those published, however, revealed interesting differences from, as well as similarities to, their Northern counterparts. Early in the war, Northern sensational war literature had attached itself to the topic of threats to Unionists in the border states, a subject that never lost its interest during the war. The Southern trajectory was necessarily somewhat different. At first Southern fiction turned not to the border states but to the memory of John Brown's 1859 raid at Harpers Ferry and invoked the imagined figure of the black rapist in sensationalized terms. In "Ned Arlington; or, Harper's Ferry Scenes," a serial that ran in the *Southern Illustrated News* during the fall of 1862, the white hero saved the white heroine in the nick of time: after hearing "a faint cry" from his beloved and "leaping through an open window, he rushed to the apartment of Alice, from whence the cries seemed to come, and reach [*sic*] it just in time to fell to the floor a large negro, who was about to lay hold of Alice to bear her off." [59]

After the rescue of Alice, Arlington was elected captain of a company of men to fight the Yankees and made a speech to them emphasizing the sexualized threat posed by Yankees in collusion with slaves: not only had the "Yankee abolitionists" "invaded our state," but they had "enticed our negroes from their homes, and, urged them to insurrection." Indeed, "these white devils have already sent forth the negroes to bring to their clutches our fair, unprotected females." The figure of the black rapist loomed large in this story, a trope that would be more highly developed after the war.[60]

Perhaps because this sensationalized fantasy of slave betrayal was too threatening within a slaveholding culture that stressed benign paternalism and the contentment of slaves, however, most sensational Southern literature, like racialized war poetry and other forms of popular literature, clung to the myth of slaves' intense loyalty to whites. Even in "Ned Arlington," it was only those slaves who had been enticed by Yankees who metamorphosed into rapists or otherwise posed a threat of violence. Ned's loyal "body-servant" Joe instead provided evidence against the leader of the insurrectionary slaves, who was summarily hanged. "Joe continued ever afterwards to be the body-servant of Ned," the story concluded, "and would tell any that requested, 'How Mars Ned saved him from being hung, and how de Yankee scoundrels wanted him to kill his Mars Ned, but he warnt gwine do it no how, for he was too good a gintleman, dat he was." As the November 1862 *Southern Illustrated News* "The Little Incendiary" put it, "In no one thing have the Abolitionists been so completely disappointed as in the conduct of our slaves during the war. The theory of the Northern people was, that we of the South stood on a volcano, which would burst forth into the wild excesses of a servile insurrection the moment the Union was dissolved." But instead "our slaves have remained quiescent," and "very large plantations, crowded with negroes, have been left for weeks in charge of females alone." [61]

Later in the war, the 1864 "The Scout of Albado" reflected ongoing wartime reality more closely by admitting that slaves had left the idyllic plantation of River Rest, but it nevertheless pictured this desertion as the result of coercion and blandishment rather than choice on the part of African Americans. The slaves at River Rest "had all been enticed or forced away," and at the end of the story former black soldiers were "crazy to exchange the musket for the hoe and the camp for the cotton field." "The Scout of Albado" pictured the war brutally disrupting what had been a pastoral idyll in which slaves were a central part of a harmonious landscape. "Before the devastations of war swept over this happy valley," the narrator commented, "the whole country bloomed and blossomed like the rose." Now, however, "the long rows of cabins in the quarters" at the plantation River Rest were "tenantless and bare, with falling rafters and broken doors, a prey to the elements." [62]

If Yankees had disrupted a harmonious racial order in the South, they also threatened the sexual order of the South. Indeed, imagining threats to Southern women's honor was an important way in which sensational stories responded to the larger political threat of Yankee invasion. In "The Scout of Albado," such sexual threat was embodied in the figure of Colonel Peleg Weaver, who was in love with the virtuous and loyal Southern heroine Lucy Pleasants. The exaggerated gendering that often accompanied the fictionalizing of the war was nowhere more obvious than in this story, in which Weaver was represented as "the epitome of all that is base in man," just as Lucy was "the embodiment of all that is good in woman." The "impudent villain" proposed to Lucy by promising to restore the pastoral perfection of her plantation, which he promised "shall once more blossom like the rose." But he revealed his true, base, unmanly nature by comparing himself to a slave, telling her, "Among all your slaves there will not be found one so obedient to the death as the unhappy soldier who now kneels at your feet." When Lucy indignantly refused him, she embodied Southern resistance to the North: " 'How dare you,' cried the high spirited girl, kindling with indignation, 'how dare you to make me the subject of your ruffianly solicitation. You are the enemy of my country.' " Lucy concluded by "impetuously pointing to the door, with the air of an offended queen." The larger story of Southern resistance to Norther invasion was here encapsulated in her story and gestures.[63]

While indignant Southern heroines were a staple of sensational as well as feminized literature, the cross-dressing adventurers found in Northern sensational fiction were only occasionally present in Southern fiction. Edward Edgeville's 1865 *Castine* was one of the rare fictions or poems that featured "a youth of about nineteen summers, delicate in frame and effeminate in features," who "was brave as well as handsome, gallant as well as neat and tidy in his dress." Although the reader early on realized that Sergeant Walter Larksly was actually a woman (indeed, the title character Castine), other characters did not manage to penetrate her disguise. " 'Who, Walter, who are you,' asked Captain Waterfield, trembling with emotion and greatly agitated, nervously grasping Walter's arm and jerking him suddenly around so that he could look square into his boyish face." As in such Northern stories as *The Lady Lieutenant*, "Walter" fought bravely in battle. At a crucial moment, when "the brigade wavered" because "its gallant commander had fallen wounded," Walter even led the action: "With a soul full of fearless heroism and daring patriotism, Sergeant Walter rushed forward with a forlorn hope—his company, then his regiment and then his brigade followed."[64]

Yet even Walter/Castine was represented as fighting not because she desired excitement and adventure—the motivation of many Northern heroines—but because she was intent on revenging the seduction of her sister by a Yankee officer. The particular constraints on gendered behavior in the South, with its strong emphasis on a womanhood associated with and confined to the domestic realm, acted to restrict the imaginations of popular writers, as well. Certainly few sensational writers explored the idea that women left their homes to fight alongside men, instead continuing to imagine the threat to Southern homes literally embodied in women's bodies. In W. D. Herrington's 1864 *The Captain's Bride: A Tale of the War,* for instance, the Confederate heroine's evil Yankee brother wanted to force her into marriage with a despised Yankee officer. Desiring to pro-

Castine.
(Courtesy of the North Carolina Collection, University
of North Carolina Library, Chapel Hill)

tect her from this fate at the hands of "fiends! incarnate," Estelle's lover, Captain Horton, told her, "You had better go with me now, and continue with my mother or some of your friends." But Estelle, "the beautiful fairy formed, the terrestrial angel," demurred: "No, I will not be driven from my home." [65]

While Northern heroines of feminized fiction were also strongly associated with the ideology of home, they often were able to use their domestic identification to carry home into the public sphere of the hospital or battlefield. Unionist Southern heroines of Northern sensational border stories were likewise able to transgress the strictures of domesticity, largely because their glowing, physicalized sexuality and their "brown" skin marked them as only tenuously domestic. But Southern heroines in Southern fiction were only rarely pictured entering the public sphere of the hospital or battlefield, much less transgressing gender boundaries by actually engaging in battle. If Northern sensational stories embraced the transformative possibilities to be found in the disruptions of war, most Southern stories insisted on the reverse: that even in the crucible of war, an immutable and intertwined Southern racial and sexual order survived unscathed.

A Boys' and Girls' War

"O would I were a soldier,"
  Cried little Bertie Lee;
"If I were only older,
  How very brave I'd be:
I'd fear not any danger,
  I'd flee not from the foe,
But where the strife was fiercest
  There I'd be sure to go.

"I'd be the boldest picket,
  Nor fear the darkest night;
Could I but see a rebel,
  How bravely I would fight.
I'd nobly do my duty,
  And soon promoted be,—
O, would I were a soldier,"
  Sighed little Bertie Lee.

— "The Little Soldier,"
  Youth's Companion, *June 4, 1863*

Late in the war children became a significant part of the audience for adventurous war literature in the North. As one reader remembered of John Townsend Trowbridge's war novel *Cudjo's Cave* (discussed in chapter 5), it was "half a 'juvenile' and half for grown ups" and was "prodigiously popular with young and old." Cheap literature of all kinds, including war novels, also became popular with children, as William Everett attested in 1864 in the *North American Review*. "A young friend of ours," he said, was "recently suffering from that most harassing of complaints, *convalescence*, of which the remedy consists in copious drafts of amusement prescribed by the patient. Literature was imperatively called for, and administered in the shape of Sir Walter Scott's novels. These did very well for one day — when the convalescence running into satiety of the most malignant type, a new remedy was demanded, and the 'clamor de profundis arose.' 'I wish I had *a dime novel.*' The coveted medicine was obtained," Everett reported, "and at once took vigorous hold of the system." [1]

Grenville Norcross, an eleven-year-old Massachusetts boy in 1865, recorded his interest in dime novels in a remarkable wartime journal providing a rare glimpse of a child's war-related fantasy life. Norcross was an avid reader of a wide range of children's books and cheap literature during the war, including a number of war-related dime novels late in the war. Luckily for historians, he kept careful records of what he read. On March 2, 1865, for instance, Norcross recorded beginning and finishing the war novel *Kate Sharp* (discussed in chapter 7) before lending it to a friend a few days later. Since *Kate Sharp* had been published for less than two weeks when Norcross read it, his reading was a sign of both his avidity for such fiction and the extensive Northern distribution system for cheap literature late in the war. During 1864 and 1865 Norcross also read the cheap war novels *Old Bill Woodworth*, *Vicksburg Spy*, *Crazy Dan*, and *Old Hal Williams*, all part of Beadle's series of "American Tales," in addition to numerous other dime novels. [2]

The war played a central role in Norcross's fantasy life. He formed a company called the "Garibaldi Guards" in 1862 and recorded drilling with them in his diary. He kept a collection of "Union and Secession" envelopes and began playing elaborate games with paper soldiers in 1863, recording skirmishes, battles, and a "grand battle" that included tin soldiers. He "made a Monitor" and played a manufactured war game called "the game of rebellion." He formed a second military company called the Suffolk Club and was elected major. And especially from 1863 to 1865, he read and exchanged with friends an extensive array of war literature produced by a variety of publishers. [3]

The adults in Norcross's life encouraged his interest in the war. A family friend gave him a "common minie ball," and his father gave him a toy brass cannon, a piece of an old battle flag that had been through Antietam and Fredericksburg and that Norcross noted had "stains of blood" on it, and a "piece of shell from the battle of Gettysburg." Adults also gave

Norcross several popular war books for children produced by mainstream publishers beginning in 1863. For Christmas in 1863, for instance, Grenville received the war correspondent Charles Carleton Coffin's *My Days and Nights on the Battlefield*. For Christmas in 1864, he received Oliver Optic's novel *The Sailor Boy* from his father as well as its companion volume, *The Soldier Boy*, from his aunt. Both of these latter titles incorporated children themselves into an imagined war by stressing boy soldiers' and sailors' adventures in battle.[4]

These three titles were an important part of a burgeoning juvenile war literature that from 1863 to the end of the war marked an emerging wartime shift in the imagined relationship between child, family, and nation. Dime novels allowed children to experience vicariously an imagined war through the adventures of scouts, spies, and "lady Zouaves." But children's war novels and war histories invited children to imagine *themselves* as protagonists in the war. "You take your place in the ranks, nervous, excited, and trembling at you know not what," began an account of a call to arms in the middle of the night in Charles Carleton Coffin's *My Days and Nights on the Battlefield*, a book that invited boys to imagine themselves in camp, on the march, and in battle. Children's war novels by Horatio Alger Jr., Oliver Optic (William Taylor Adams), and Harry Castlemon (Charles Austin Fosdick) also created an exciting imagined war that stressed juvenile war adventures both on the home front and at the battlefront. These adventurous juvenile war novels not only launched the careers of the prolific Alger and Castlemon—the latter only a teenage soldier when he wrote his first war juvenile—but also provided an important link to a postwar juvenile culture that stressed adventure and excitement for boys. Indeed, not only were Alger, Optic, and Castlemon all extremely popular authors of adventurous boys' novels in the postwar period, but Optic and Castlemon reinterpreted the war in new Civil War series for boys late in the century.

• • •

At the beginning of the war, however, children figured primarily in sentimental and religious war literature, including tales of dying drummer boys that remained a popular genre throughout the conflict. In such early wartime stories boys were imagined more as victims of war than as actors in the conflict. Emphasizing the potentially redemptive experience of witnessing children's suffering, the 1861 *The Little Drummer Boy*, a religious publication, lingered over one of the most "heart-stirring incidents" of the war, the accidental killing of twelve-year-old Clarence McKenzie in camp by a member of his own brigade in the summer of 1861. Here the drummer boy was posed as a "triumph of grace" for the Brooklyn Sunday school that had presented him with a Bible before he went off to war; he was described as a pious child who had daily read his Bible even among the distractions of camp before his death.[5]

Because of his "pure and innocent character," Clarence not only "won the affection of his commanders," but by his "simple faith and correct deportment, was exerting an influence for good among them." His last moments, too, were recorded as exemplary: "Not one fear did he express of dying—not the least uneasiness." "Very many will not soon forget to sorrow for him, nor will the influence of his short life ever die," another publication instructed. With its appeal to observers' sympathy and a lengthy depiction of the drummer boy's death, such writing positioned itself as part of the larger project of sentimentalism, which insisted on shared emotion between observers of suffering and their audiences.[6]

The story of Clarence McKenzie circulated widely throughout Northern popular literary culture in the summer of 1861. The *Youth's Companion*, a popular children's magazine that Grenville Norcross, among others, recorded reading during the war, quoted "the New York papers" in describing Clarence's death as "one of the mournful events of the present war." The magazine presented Clarence as an exemplum for its young readers: "When the sorrowing soldiers took up the dying boy, after he was shot, they found in his pocket the Bible which had been to him so constant and loved a companion."[7]

This Christian sentimentalization of dead or dying drummer boys remained a potent mode of representing drummer boys throughout the war. The popular song "The Drummer Boy of Shiloh," for instance, emphasized both a dying drummer boy's last prayer and its transformative impact on the soldiers who witnessed his death:

"Oh, mother," said the dying boy,
    "Look down from heaven on me,
Receive me to thy fond embrace—
    Oh, take me home to thee.
I've loved my country as my God;
    To serve them both I've tried,"
He smiled, shook hands—death seized the boy
    Who prayed before he died.

Each soldier wept, then, like a child —
　　Stout hearts were they, and brave;
The flag his winding-sheet — God's Book
　　The key unto his grave.
They wrote upon a simple board
　　These words: "This is a guide
To those who'd mourn the drummer boy
　　Who prayed before he died."

In witnessing the death of a faithful child, these "stout hearts" became like children themselves — an indication that the sentimental figure of the child could be used as reassurance that soldiers had not lost their hearts to war.[8]

Although sentimental depictions of pious drummer boys remained a powerful mode of representation throughout the war, after the early months of conflict they were increasingly supplemented by depictions that recognized children's desire to be active participants in, rather than pious victims of, the war. "The Boy Soldier," a story that ran in the July 1862 children's magazine *Merry's Museum*, began by acknowledging boys' active desire to participate in the war. "Oh! if I was only a man!" said "little Charlie Bruce as he was listening to his father's stories about the war." When his father asked what he would then do, Charlie answered, "I'd have a sword and a gun and a hat with a feather in it, and I'd go to the war, and be a general." At least he could "drum, if I am only a boy," he asserted. After his father gave him a drum and a toy gun, he paraded with it and "ordered arms and shouldered arms" — much like the real-life Grenville Norcross — and even attempted to "make a soldier" of his dog, Bounce. Other stories, too, acknowledged children's keen interest in the war. "The Little Soldiers," an 1863 story in the *Youth's Companion*, was one of many wartime fictions in Northern children's magazines that portrayed children playing at being soldiers with "umbrellas, pokers, and whatever other species of domestic fire-arms they could lay their hands upon."[9]

While children's magazines acknowledged children's interest in a "pretend" or "play" war, they also increasingly acknowledged children's interest in the "real" war. *Merry's Museum* noted that "a few descriptions of modern warlike implements will no doubt be interesting to our young friends" in a fact-laden article on guns, gunpowder, cannons, shells, and other "modern implements of war" in November 1861. In a similar vein, the *Youth's Companion* explained "How a Man Feels When He Is Shot," one of a number of such factual pieces it published for children. "You read in the

"The Drummer Boy of Shiloh," by Will S. Hays.
(Courtesy of the Rare Book, Manuscript and Special
Collections Library, Duke University)

papers about 'picket firing,' about capturing pickets, 'driving in' pickets, and so on," the *Companion* said in another 1863 piece. "Perhaps you would like to know what the pickets of an army are." The apotheosis of this "you are there" style of children's war literature was war correspondent Charles Carleton Coffin's 1863 *My Days and Nights on the Battle-field*, which invited children to use their imaginations to accompany him to the seat of war. "You followed the soldiers to the railroad depot and hurrahed till the train which bore them away was out of sight," Coffin commented about the early days of war. "Let us follow them to Washington, and see the gathering of a great army" there. Coffin provided eyewitness-style accounts of Bull Run, Shiloh, and Fort Donelson, among other engagements.[10]

Marking a shift from early wartime representations of children, in 1862 children's magazines began to run stories about the heroic exploits of drummer boys—no longer viewed merely as passive, pious victims of war but as active and courageous agents in the conflict. *Merry's Museum*, for instance, told the story of "The Drummer-Boy of Marblehead" in July 1862, noting that in the heat of battle Albert Mansur had "slung his drum over his shoulder, and seizing a rifle from a wounded man near, dealt true shots for his country" before himself being shot. His death scene marked a significant contrast to the death scenes of exemplary soldiers. Instead of offering a last prayer, Albert said "only this, boy-like, 'Which beat? quick, tell me!'" Although his death scene remained within sentimental parameters—"tears ran like rain down the blackened faces" of the soldiers gathered around him—the point of the story nevertheless was to acknowledge Albert's heroism, not his piety. The 1862 illustrated volume *The Drummer Boy: A Story of the War. (In Verse). For the Young Folks at Home* also portrayed a young boy who became a drummer boy and fought in battle:

> In all the fight
> Bill stood upright;
> A noble boy was he,
> Who knew no fear,
> Though very near
> The rebels he could see.[11]

By the middle of the war, depictions of heroic drummer boys were widespread in Northern culture. Many stories of heroic drummer boys published in children's magazines were first published in newspapers. The

Youth's Companion, for instance, picked up an account of "the Michigan Drummer Boy," Robert Henry Hendershot, from the *Detroit Free Press.* At Fredericksburg Hendershot had not only captured a rebel soldier but had had his drum "blown to atoms" by a shell, the *Free Press* said. General Burnside had reportedly said to him, "Boy, I glory in your spunk. If you keep on in that way, you will be in my place before many years." Once at home again in Michigan, Hendershot had "created much enthusiasm by his appearance on the platform at a public meeting held in the market to encourage enlistments." [12]

As such an account suggested, a variety of adults, including parents, publishers, and military personnel, purposefully integrated children—particularly boys—into the war. In doing so they responded in part to children's own interest in the war but even more to the demands of a home-front war perceived to require the support of the entire population, including children.

Some commentators, however, recognized the dangers in an enthusiastic embrace of the war by children. In July 1863 the *Youth's Companion* issued a warning to children considering running away to become soldiers. "The Boy Soldier" described a little boy who "ought to have been satisfied with his nice home, but he was not. He saw the troops going through with their gay uniforms, their flags and music, and he wanted to be a soldier." A runaway to a nearby army camp, he was found and "brought back to his mother, whose heart was made glad by the return of her darling boy." "Now what I want you to learn from this," the author moralized, is "that you should not do like this little boy. Don't fall in love with the gay clothes of the soldier, for you little know how hard it is to be out during the rainy days and the long, stormy nights, and to go into battle where you may lose an arm, or limb, or perhaps your life. This is not your place. You are too young for that." But some boys did not consider themselves "too young for that." Certainly a major event in Grenville Norcross's wartime diary was his July 1864 notation that his close friend Bill Tryon, with whom he had played many games of paper soldiers, had "run away" to the war. [13]

From mid-1863 to the end of the war, a variety of illustrations and popular books pictured drummer boys and boy soldiers as active participants in the war. Colorful paper fans produced by T. W. Strong of New York included the verse "The Soldier Boy":

Young Willie was a soldier boy,
 I'll tell you how he came

To put aside each idle toy,
    And mount the hills of fame;
That you may be
    As wise as he,
And win yourself a name.[14]

Anecdotes and stories of drummer boys became highly conventionalized within Northern popular literary culture, a fact reflected in Thomas Nast's full-page December 1863 illustration of "The Drummer Boy of Our Regiment—Eight War Scenes" for *Harper's Weekly*. Here a generic drummer boy was pictured in a tearful parting from his mother; sitting on the knee of a soldier as "the favorite in camp" in a group of soldiers telling stories; busily "writing home"; joining his older comrades as they charged forward "in action"; and striking a manly pose as he arrived "home again." More and more, popular portrayals of drummer boys and boy soldiers moved away from emotive portrayals of juvenile death to stress instead the adventure of war.[15]

Publishers and writers began to produce war juveniles that seized a combined patriotic and commercial opportunity. In June 1863 Boston's J. E. Tilton and Company announced John Townsend Trowbridge's *The Drummer Boy*, written, the author later explained, because he was "eager to bear [his] own humble part in the momentous conflict" with a "patriotic story." In its advertising the publisher stressed the appeal of the war for children, as well as the perceived duty of parents, by commenting, "The newspapers teem with anecdotes of brave little warriors, and the boys hear and burn with enthusiasm, counting the months or years before they can be old enough to go. This book is just the one to put into their eager hands."[16]

A far cry from sentimentalized literature of dead or dying drummer boys, *The Drummer Boy* provided a compelling fictional fantasy of boyish participation in the war. Advertised as a "correct historical account of the Burnside Expedition in North Carolina" that was "full of war-scenes," *The Drummer Boy* featured a boy hero, Frank Manly (the name was part of the exaggerated gendering that accompanied the war), who engaged in a number of exciting escapades once he had joined the army.[17]

The Drummer Boy did not eschew sentimental Christianity. On the contrary, its adventures were structured within a Christian fable of temptation, sin, remorse, and ultimate redemption. Before joining the army, Frank promised his mother on his Bible that he would not drink, swear,

THE LITTLE VOLUNTEER.

The Little Volunteer.
(Courtesy of the Library Company of Philadelphia)

or gamble in camp. But these were all promises he was destined to break in the interests of forwarding the plot. Indeed, Trowbridge's use of the structure of a Christian fable allowed him to include lengthy passages devoted to the sins Frank Manly committed: an entire chapter, for instance, detailed a carefully planned exploit in which Frank and some companions tricked a rebel, stealing a turkey from him. The remorse Frank felt about stealing, tacked on after the event, did not take away from either the gleeful high spirits of the incident itself or the brio with which it was described. Here conventional moralism forwarded an ethic of adventure—a combination that would prove to be important in later wartime juvenile literature as well.

Trowbridge's *The Drummer Boy* marked the beginning of what would become a flood of wartime "boy" books. But in its imagination of the war as an adventure featuring an ordinary boy hero, *The Drummer Boy* was initially the exception, not the rule: in 1863 and early 1864 most "boy" books were instead inspirational biographies of public figures such as Lincoln, Grant, Horace Greeley, or Salmon Chase. Such biographies—a form of exemplum literature providing children with inspiring examples of individual moral victories and worldly success—had been a mainstay of antebellum juvenile literary culture, a widely accepted mode of educating young boys to become responsible citizens.[18]

In wartime such books offered a form of literary nationalism that sought to bind boys to the nation's war aims by reaffirming a common set of national symbols and myths. In the introduction to his 1864 *The Farmer Boy*, a biography of Washington, William M. Thayer explained why the "appearance of this volume is timely": "In this period of mighty struggles and issues, when our nation is groaning and travailing in pain to bring forth a future of surpassing renown and grandeur, it is important to inspire the hearts of American youth by the noblest examples of patriotism and virtue. And such is WASHINGTON, the 'Father of his Country.' It is best that the young of this battling age should study his character and emulate his deeds." This was a familiar form of antebellum nationalism, to be learned through emulation and careful study of exemplary individuals. The politics of loyalty expressed here—individual love of country, individual loyalty to country—were also widespread in 1863, as such organizations as the Loyal Publication Society were formed to promote loyalty to country through the dissemination of political pamphlets. In December 1863, too, Edward Everett Hale published his widely admired "The Man without a

Country" in the *Atlantic Monthly*—a story that hammered home the need for devotion to country as a central aspect of individual identity.[19]

Shortly after the publication of *The Drummer Boy*, other inspirational war-related biographies for children began to appear in the literary marketplace. A second biography published during the summer of 1863 was William M. Thayer's *The Pioneer Boy, and How He Became President*, a life of Lincoln that proved highly profitable for its publisher. James Perkins Walker of Walker, Wise and Company called it, along with other similar war juveniles, his "pecuniary salvation"—a statement that has the ring of truth when one considers that Walker struggled throughout the war to sell his primarily Unitarian booklist to a reading public uninterested in anything but war. By December 1863 the firm had sold eleven thousand copies, with another fifteen thousand copies sold during the election year of 1864. This was an exceptionally strong sale: a good comparison is with Ticknor and Fields, which in the 1850s reprinted on the average about one thousand copies annually of Mayne Reid's popular adventure books for boys.[20]

Just as J. E. Tilton had promoted the "Bobbin-Boy series," Walker, Wise and Company attempted to capitalize on its success by creating and promoting sequels in "The Pioneer Boy Series." And after the initial successes of *The Drummer Boy* and *The Pioneer Boy* in late 1863, numerous publishers scrambled to enter this potentially lucrative field. Their titles revealed how imitative they were: Roberts Brothers announced *The U.S. Boy, and How He Became Lt. General* in March 1864; Carleton announced *The Editor Boy*; and Walker, Wise and Company announced *The Ferry Boy and the Financier* in that same month. The coming 1864 election spurred a number of publications: James G. Gregory announced a "Boys' Life of General McClellan" in May 1864; in that same month Walker, Wise and Company announced *The Tailor Boy—Hon. Andy Johnson, the Candidate for Vice-President*. In June 1864 William H. Appleton weighed in with its "Young American's Library of Modern Heroes," to include *The Hero Boy*, a life of Grant, and *The Errand Boy*, a life of General O. M. Mitchell. In September 1864 Ashmead and Evans announced *Winfield, the Lawyer's Son, and How He Became a Major-General*, a biography of Winfield Scott Hancock; and William H. Appleton announced *The Miner Boy*, a biography of John Ericsson, the engineer famous for the ironclad ship the *Monitor*.[21]

Boy biographies represented clear attempts on the part of authors, publishers, and parents to inculcate children with a set of shared national beliefs—to create an imagined nationhood that included the antebellum values of duty, thrift, and moderation. They sought to mold the individual to conform to a homogeneous national culture. But during late 1863 and 1864 a new group of juvenile war fictions also followed in the footsteps of *The Drummer Boy* by instead imagining the adventures of ordinary boys, using the war as backdrop and occasion for individual adventure. These novels drew less on the antebellum literary tradition of exemplum literature than on the 1850s rise of a new fashion in juvenile fiction: adventure novels featuring boy heroes. Primarily British imports, these were novels such as R. M. Ballantyne's *The Young Fur Traders* and Mayne Reid's *The Boy Hunters*, the latter reprinted many times during the 1850s. Reid's and Ballantyne's work signaled the beginnings of a fashion in boys' fiction that eventually reached its apotheosis in the vast outpouring of dime adventure novels late in the century.[22]

Like these British precursors, Oliver Optic's *The Soldier Boy*, Horatio Alger's *Frank's Campaign*, and Harry Castlemon's *Frank on a Gunboat* each narrated the adventures of an ordinary boy, and each was successful enough to be followed by sequels in series for boys. Significantly, both Alger and Castlemon launched their prolific careers as writers for boys with titles published during the war. Clearly the war gave a new, younger generation of juvenile writers a chance to enter the literary marketplace.[23]

Horatio Alger's *Frank's Campaign*, written and published in 1864, was his first novel; in an election year its title was a double entendre with both military and political overtones. Alger had written other war literature; starting in early 1862, Alger had published propagandistic poems and short stories in *Harper's Weekly* and *Harper's Monthly*, receiving "five dollars per column or magazine page, and ten dollars per poem." These writings led directly to an idea for a war novel. "One day," he later remembered, "I selected a plot for a two-column sketch for the Harpers. Thinking the matter over, it occurred to me that it would be a good plot for a juvenile book. I sat down at once and wrote to A. K. Loring of Boston, at that time a publisher in only a small way, detailing the plot and asking if he would encourage me to write a juvenile book. He answered, 'Go ahead, and if I don't publish it, some other publisher will.' In three months I put in his hands the manuscript of 'Frank's Campaign.' "[24]

Frank's Campaign was unusual among adventurous war juveniles for imagining war-related adventures at home rather than in camp or on the battlefield. In the style of patriotic pieces in the *Youth's Companion*, Alger wrote about what boys could do for the war, arguing, "Now that so large a number of our citizens have been withdrawn from their families and their ordinary business to engage in putting down this Rebellion, it becomes the duty of the boys to take their places as far as they are able to do so. A boy cannot wholly support the place of a man, but he can do so in part. . . . If he does this voluntarily, and in the right spirit, he is just as patriotic as if he were a soldier in the field."[25]

The hero of *Frank's Campaign* was fifteen-year-old Frank Frost, who took over running the family farm so that his father could go to war. The novel's adventures were structured not around war but around Frank's class-based rivalry with John Haynes, the son of the wealthy (and melo-dramatically evil) Squire Haynes, who threatened to foreclose on the Frost family's farm. The younger Haynes was a villain who took after his father: his manner was "full of pretension," and "he never forgets that his father is the richest man in town." Though he attempted to sabotage Frank's efforts at farming, he did not succeed; and Frank, not John, was eventually voted captain of a newly formed local company for boys. Published in November 1864, *Frank's Campaign* sold well, with a second printing advertised in December. For A. K. Loring the publication of *Frank's Campaign* was part of a new venture into juvenile fiction inspired by the dynamics of war.[26]

The author Harry Castlemon also made the connection between war and adventurous juvenile fiction. Castlemon's first novel was not a war novel but an adventure novel about a boy hunter that was directly influenced by the example of the British adventure writer Mayne Reid. Reid had called one of the main characters of his *The Boy Hunters* a "Hunter Naturalist," and Castlemon now titled his first novel *Frank the Young Naturalist.*[27]

Castlemon, born in 1842, completed writing the manuscript of *Frank the Young Naturalist* by 1861; as he remembered, "About this time war broke out, and after that I didn't do much work." Instead, "I was in a fever of suspense, and I wanted to take a hand with the defenders of my country; so at last I enlisted in the navy." After going "down to Cairo as landsman," Castlemon "served on several boats, getting my promotion as fast as I learned my duties." At last, ensconced in what seemed likely to be a permanent position as assistant to the fleet paymaster, Castlemon decided to try finding a publisher for his book. R. W. Carroll of Cincinnati not only paid him $150 for his manuscript but also suggested that he write several more books in a series that would exploit his wartime experiences. Advertising Castlemon as "The Gunboat Boy," R. W. Carroll in swift succession published *Frank on a Gun-boat*, *Frank before Vicksburg*, and *Frank on the Lower Mississippi.* These, along with *Frank the Young Naturalist,* were marketed as the "Gun-boat Series."[28]

Directly influenced by antebellum juvenile adventure literature, Castlemon in turn conceptualized the war as a boys' adventure. His publishing history makes clear the transactional nature of the wartime production of juvenile literature. Existing literary conventions shaped Castlemon's wartime representations, but the perceived new opportunities within popular literary culture also played an important role in shaping his work. The imagined war, envisioned through the lens of commercial nationalism, animated and energized a new culture of adventure.

The adventurous boys' war created by Trowbridge, Optic, and Castlemon articulated a new wartime "family romance" of the state. Like sentimental soldier literature, these novels initially stressed a soldier's relationship to his mother. Trowbridge's *The Drummer Boy,* for instance, opened with a scene in which Frank's mother tearfully consented to his going to war. *The Soldier Boy,* too, began with the hero shouting, "Fort Sumter has surrendered, mother!" as he "rushed into the room where his mother was quietly reading her Bible"—an emblematic scene that simultaneously stressed the enthusiasm of youth, the "invasion" of the home by war, and the mother's role as spiritual and moral guardian of her family. There were concrete social realities behind this reiterated drama: the War Department would not accept enlistees under the age of eighteen without parental consent.[29]

As in sentimental soldier literature, the nation's demand that her "sons" leave the domestic culture of mothers at home for the sake of "mother" country was portrayed as a national family drama. Significantly, popular juvenile war literature did not explore relationships between sons and fathers, who were usually portrayed as peripheral to the action of the story. *The Drummer Boy* presented Frank's father as a feeble figure: "His wife had become more the head of the family than he was, and every important question of the kind, as Frank well knew, was referred to her for decision." In Optic's *The Soldier Boy* the father was conveniently absent when war broke out. In *Frank on a Gunboat* the father was dead. As was true of sentimental literature, juvenile adventure novels presented the question of enlistment as a mother-son drama.[30]

However, here the similarities with sentimental soldier literature ended, for whereas sentimental soldier literature explored dying soldiers' yearnings for mothers and home, juvenile adventure novels instead enacted cheerful—even gleeful—separations from home. By separating sons from their mothers, these stories provided the former with adventures under the auspices of country. What's more, these adventures were highly individualized: in *The Drummer Boy, The Soldier Boy,* and *Frank on a Gun-boat,* the heroes' most exciting adventures took place when they were accidentally cut off from their fellow soldiers and had to fend for themselves, living by their wits alone. In Optic's *The Soldier Boy,* for instance, Tom Somers was taken prisoner after fighting at Bull Run but managed to escape by deceiving his rebel guards into thinking he was a superior officer. After his escape, Tom hid in a farmer's house and singlehandedly captured a rebel soldier in a feat of physical derring-do in which he threw a rock to disable the rebel, "leaped out of the chimney upon the roof of the house, descended to the eaves, and then jumped upon the ground" before disarming him. Later Tom, disguised as a rebel soldier, floated down the Shenandoah past a number of rebel troops. Having successfully passed one picket guard, Tom "could not resist the temptation to celebrate the signal strategic victory he had obtained." His "triumphal demonstration was not very dignified, nor, under the circumstances, very prudent or sensible," Optic wrote. "It consisted in placing the thumb of his right hand upon the end of his nose, while he wiggled the four remaining digital appendages of the same member in the most aggravating manner, whistling Yankee Doodle as an accompaniement to the movement." [31]

The delight taken by the author in these antics was clear; that they were individualized exploits was especially telling. In the pages of *The Soldier Boy* the army was not just a new source of group identity and loyalty; it also provided occasions for individual heroics and boyish escapades. The war created here was a celebration of adventurous individualism as well as fraternity: the form of nationalism created in the pages of *The Soldier Boy* was congruent with an ideology of self-interest as well as with an adherence to a new collectivity. As Optic wrote in the preface to *The Soldier Boy,* his novel was a "narrative of personal adventure," although he also mentioned "the perils and privations, the battles and marches" that Tom Somers "shared with thousands of brave men in the army of the Potomac." The idea that patriotism and personal adventure underlay each other was a major legacy of the war in children's fiction.[32]

The Soldier Boy appealed widely: inscriptions within individual copies of the book reveal that teachers sometimes gave it as a prize to outstanding pupils; and a small but suggestive group of book orders within Lee and Shepard's archives shows that parents bought the book for their children. Grenville Norcross, as noted earlier, received *The Soldier Boy* from his aunt for Christmas in 1864 and its companion volume—about Tom Somers's twin brother in the navy—as a Christmas present from his father. Lee and Shepard's book orders also reveal that soldiers themselves took an interest in the book. Writing from Fort Warren, Massachusetts, Benjamin Tarr of Company C 1st Battalion responded to an advertisement for the book that had appeared in a Boston story paper: "Reading the Boston true [*sic*] Flag today my eye lit on a paragraph about a book titled the Soldier boy now I want to read just such a book as that to pass away dull care inclosed is $1.25." Other soldier orders, too, offered suggestive, if fragmentary, evidence of soldiers' desire to transform their own experiences into entertainment. Orders from soldiers in Tennessee, Virginia, and Georgia were testimony, however partial, to the wide communications network of the wartime literary marketplace.[33]

Two intriguing soldier orders in the Lee and Shepard archives asked that *The Soldier Boy* be sent to girls. For the most part, war juveniles created a strikingly male universe of war. Not only was most juvenile war fiction written by male authors, featuring male heroes, but it was marketed explicitly to boys as well. *The Drummer Boy* was advertised as "A Capital Book for Boys" and as "A Splendid Story for Boys of Camp Life and War Scenes." William H. Appleton's "Young American's Library of Modern Heroes," which included *The Hero Boy* and *The Errand Boy*, was described as "Written expressly for the use of Boys." Charles Carleton Coffin's *My Days and Nights on the Battle-field* was subtitled "A Book for Boys."[34]

Yet girls were not entirely absent from Northern juvenile war literature or literary culture. As the fragmentary evidence of *The Soldier Boy* orders suggests, they may well have been part of the audience for war juveniles. Grenville Norcross, for instance, primarily exchanged dime novels with male friends, but he also occasionally noted exchanges with "W. Thompson's servant girl." At the same time, girls were sometimes imagined as participants in stories of playing soldier. The *Youth's Companion*'s 1863 "Little Soldiers" pictured a mixed group of children playing at war, with "Janet, who was quite a large girl," holding "the parlor broom defiantly pointed at an imaginary rebel," while "Tiny Nell carried papa's best ivory-headed cane, which was about as large as the brave soldier herself." The magazine also ran several brief anecdotes, reprinted from other sources, of girls' and women's bravery in the border states: "A Brave Kentucky Girl," for instance, told of a girl who "levelled her gun" at the head of marauding guerrillas.[35]

Certainly both boys and girls were urged to help the war effort: "Every boy and girl can do something to cheer and benefit our soldiers," announced a piece entitled "Give to the Soldiers" in February 1863. "Money can be given for their benefit, letters can be sent to cheer them in the tent and by the camp fire; appropriate and useful articles can be forwarded to protect them from exposure, and to lessen somewhat the hardships of a soldier's life." [36]

Still, most juvenile literature created an imagined war sharply differentiated by gender. A number of articles and stories urged girls to knit, sew, or pick lint for the soldiers, creating an echo of the feminized literature directed at their mothers. "Nelly sat beside her mother picking lint," began Louisa May Alcott's 1865 "Nelly's Hospital," making the mother-daughter connection explicit. The December 1861 "Mittens for the Soldiers" asked "patriotic girls" "how many pairs of mittens they are going to knit, for the noble fellows" in the army.[37]

The August 1863 "What the Boys and Girls Can Do," a prescriptive patriotic article, explicitly addressed the gendering of children's war work. Acknowledging that "the boys and girls all want to *help* save the country," the author advised boys to use "that very hand of yours" to "pick and dry a few blackberries that will do as much toward saving some sick soldier's life as the best doctor in the State can do." When the soldier "gets your nice berries he will say, 'God bless that dear little boy!'" But the physical discomfort involved in picking berries might be too much for girls, the author suggested. "And now, my little girl, what can *you* do for the soldiers?" the author asked. "You may be afraid the briars would scratch your dear little hands. Well, what if they do? You can have it to say that you '*bled for your country*,' and that is saying a good deal. You can do this much, anyhow: You can pick and dry a quart of cherries or plums for the soldiers, can't you? Certainly you can, and will, too, I feel confident." [38]

In the pages of juvenile war fiction, too, girls' and boys' roles were sharply defined by gender. *The Soldier Boy,* for instance, included a romantic subplot—an echo of numerous adult war romances published during the war—that centered around a pair of socks a young girl had knitted for the soldiers. "My Dear Soldier," began the letter that Tom Somers discovered from Lilian Ashford in his socks, "this is the first pair of socks I ever knit; and I send them to you with my blessing upon the brave defenders of my country." Describing herself as a "silly girl," Lilian sent Tom her photograph and expressed curiosity to see him. At the end of the novel Tom called on Lilian to thank her personally, making a short speech in which he told her, "The socks inspired me with courage and fortitude."

Less adept at portraying girls than boys, Optic wrote that she responded "in a kind of silvery scream." [39]

Most juvenile war fiction, directed explicitly to boys, relegated girls to a peripheral role in the war effort, portraying them as minor characters in stories whose main protagonists were boys. But a few war stories in periodicals featured girls as their main characters, stressing their influence on those around them in a way consonant with domestic ideology. The *Youth's Companion*'s 1863 "In an Ambulance" portrayed a little girl who visited wounded soldiers in a Washington hospital. Reminding a convalescing soldier of his daughter in Ohio, she did "more good" by her mere presence, an inspirational reminder of home, than did the adult visitor she accompanied. *Harper's Weekly*'s 1864 "Lula's Letter: A Child's Story" featured a little girl whose letters to a soldier "saved him" at a time he felt "forsaken" and "desperate." [40]

Louisa May Alcott's 1865 "Nelly's Hospital" also portrayed a little girl who acted as an inspiration and even education to those around her. Setting up a play hospital on the model of the Sanitary Commission, Nelly worked as a "nurse" to save various wounded animals and insects in an allegory of war. A fly caught in a spider's web she imagined as a "contraband" named Pompey; a gray snake was a rebel named Forked-tongue; a turtle was Commodore Waddle. [41]

At first this seemed "a childish pastime," the narrator remarked, "and people laughed." But the story revealed that a little girl's home-front actions could have an important positive influence on people around her, particularly in converting men and boys to become more "cheerful" and less "rough." Her older brother Will, home from the war and convalescing with a lame foot, had lost the "cheerful courage which had led him safely through many dangers." He was "often gloomy, sad, or fretful, because he longed to be at his post again." But Nelly's hospital plans "interested and amused him," and he "laughed out more heartily than he had done for many a day" as he chatted with her. He eventually was "ashamed to complain after watching the patience of these lesser sufferers, and merrily said he would try to bear his own wound as quietly and bravely as they." [42]

Nelly's actions also worked as a "charm" to convince "rough lads" in the neighborhood to stop hurting "harmless creatures," and they vowed that they would not "stone birds, chase butterflies, and drown the girls' little cats any more." Imagining both men and boys in need of girls' influence in wartime, the story created a "girls' war" that in many respects matched the feminized war of popular magazines for adults. [43]

Although a few children's magazines published war stories featuring girl heroines, book publishers apparently saw little commercial potential in marketing a girls' war to match the many "boy" series published in 1864 and 1865. But one publisher proved an exception late in the war. In December 1864 J. E. Tilton, publisher of *The Drummer Boy*, announced Jane Goodwin Austin's *Dora Darling, the Daughter of the Regiment*. Austin, born in 1831, had previously published *Fairy Dreams* in 1859; but it was during the war that she really launched her prolific literary career, with three titles published in 1865 alone.[44]

Dora Darling attempted the difficult project of combining the politics of domesticity with the new wartime ethos of adventure. Set in Virginia, the novel told the story of twelve-year-old Dora, whose slaveholding family was split between rebel and Unionist sympathies. Dora and her invalid mother were both staunchly Unionist: "Father doesn't feel as we do about the war," Mrs. Darley told her daughter. "Well, mother," Dora responded, "I feel the way you do about everything, and the way you feel, is the right way." In contrast, Mr. Darley, a "selfish and depraved man" who mistreated his wife, was also a cruel master: "Mrs. Darley had steadfastly stood between the slave and many a threatened injustice or cruelty on his master's part." Completing the family circle, Dora's older brother Tom, a "young advocate of male supremacy," aligned with his father.[45]

Though on her deathbed Mrs. Darley told Tom that she would rather "that you died fighting for freedom, than lived and rose to the highest rank in the rebel army," after her death both he and his father enlisted. "Tom had not forgotten his mother's last wishes," the narrator commented, "but although he was extremely fond of her," he "still secretly held the idea common to the class of men with whom he had been bred, that a woman's opinions upon matters of public interest were hardly worth the attention of the sterner sex, and were necessarily feeble and one-sided." This assertion of women's right to opinions on public matters was unusual in popular war literature.[46]

Escaping from the tyranny of an aunt, with whom she had been placed when her father enlisted, Dora joined forces with the slave Pic, the "sole retainer of the house of Darley," who, like the loyal slaves of dozens of race stories published during the war, "clung to its decaying fortunes with the tenacity of his race and temperament." Together they stumbled across a battle; Pic climbed a tree to get a better view of the conflict, describing it to Dora, who "sat with flushed face and gleaming eyes, drinking in the somewhat fragmentary description of the skirmish." "O, Picter," said she, breathlessly, when he was again beside her, "will there be more fighting? will there be a real battle? O Pic, can't you take me somewhere to see it?"[47]

Surprised at her excitement, Pic commented, "Lors, honey, who'd tink of a pooty leetly gal wantin' ter see a big fight wif lots o' men bleedin' an' a dyin' all 'bout her." He suggested that she'd "be right for a sojer's wife," to help "take care ob de pore wounded fellers in de hospital." "And so I will," cried Dora with enthusiasm. "I am not old enough to be a soldier's wife, but I will be the sister or daughter of every soldier that I can help. There will be men wounded in this very battle—won't there, Pic?" Shortly after this expression of sentimentalized bloodthirstiness, Pic and Dora joined forces with the "Twenty—Ohio regiment," whose colonel renamed her "Dora Darling" and gave her the nursing opportunity for which she had been looking.[48]

Up to this point in the story, Austin portrayed Dora as eager, decisive, impulsive, and independent in her actions; but once she had joined the regiment, Austin's portrait changed radically to accommodate the sexual tension inherent in a story of a young girl, without family, living with the army. Now Dora was described variably as ignorant, submissive, and dependent; she was "a child of nature" to be put "under the care and instruction of the chaplain," her "spiritual father." Her language occasionally became ungrammatical; she was given lessons that helped her correct "her little inaccuracies of language and deportment," and for the first time the reader learned that Mrs. Darley "had been unable to give her daughter the education she had never herself received." She was christened "the daughter of the regiment," and all the men were instructed to call her "*Miss Dora*."[49]

All these devices revealed the tension inherent in melding sentimental norms of womanhood with a plot of wartime adventure. This task could only be accomplished by transforming the regiment into Dora's substitute family and by making her dependent on it—exactly the opposite dynamic from that to be found in masculine war juveniles. In that literature, the army not only offered a life separate from family but even posed a threat to family ideals of virtue. In *Dora Darling* the opposite was the case: her own family (with the exception of her mother) posed the threat of moral disorder, while the army allowed a more virtuous life and provided her with tender care.

Boy heroes learned to trust their wits during individual exploits, but Dora had a more complicated lesson to learn: to be her own mistress and yet at the same time to be dependent on the judgment of older and wiser men. Going against the advice of the chaplain, for instance, Dora rashly rode out of camp for "a little excursion into the country" with a young soldier friend, Captain Karl. Though Mr. Brown, the chaplain, told her that "it seems hardly proper for you to go off in this manner, with no protector but so young a man," Dora, feeling rebellious, went anyway. She then regretted her action, making "a firm resolution to confess to Mr. Brown, on her return, the weakness and folly of her course, as she now viewed it." [50]

Yet it was precisely her disobedience that resulted in an "adventure" in which Dora's horse was shot dead beneath her by rebels, while Captain Karl heroically protected her from a "ruffian" who demanded that he "give up the girl." This incident revealed the paradox inherent in a sentimental novel of female adventure: it was inappropriate for a girl to be in an adventurous situation, and yet it was exactly such situations that fueled the plot. A strained interplay between disobedience and obedience, dependence and independence, became the structuring principle of the novel, as it veered between sensationalist adventure and sentimental domesticity. [51]

The centerpiece of *Dora Darling* was a long adventure in which Dora was tricked by a forged letter, purportedly from her brother Tom, into slipping out of camp to meet him. Taking Pic with her (another authorial device for providing Dora with chaperoned respectability), she found that "Tom" was actually her rebel cousin Dick, who put "an arm around her waist" and told her he was going to "carry [her] home" to his mother—her tyrannical aunt. "[I will] let her keep you till the war's over, and you're a little older; and then I reckon I shall take you for my old woman." [52]

In this desperate situation Dora used "quick wits" to make a "precise plan of action" for escape: she used her pocket knife to fashion a rope out of strips of blanket, cut herself free from captivity, and then stealthily let herself down from a second-story window. Once on the ground, Dora had to contend with a wolf, which "made a savage leap at her throat, and would have seized it," "had not the *vivandière*, with a sudden and decided movement, enveloped the head and neck of the beast in the folds of the cloak held ready upon her arms for this very purpose." [53]

This sensationalist adventure highlighting Dora's resourcefulness soon dissolved, however, when the chaplain and Captain Karl caught up with her. Once again, Dora was transformed from sensationalist to sentimental heroine, and "when she found herself once more in safety," she cried "as if her heart would break. Even her elastic courage and endurance were exhausted by the scenes of the night and morning, and the heroine gave place to the little girl, who longed for nothing so much as her mother's arms." Whereas boys' juvenile adventures made them more manly, Dora's adventures simply reduced her to girlhood again.[54]

The sexually charged instability of her identity as girl heroine was explicitly acknowledged in the text, as the two characters most responsible for her—Captain Karl and the chaplain—argued over with whom she would live after they were mustered out. Captain Karl wanted to take her to New York with him; the chaplain asked her, "What do you think of going to Ohio to live with me, Dora, when that time comes?" At Dora's response—"I'd like best to live with the aunt I'm going to look for"—Captain Karl exclaimed, "You little coquette! You want to secure us both, do you, and keep your own liberty? There's the feminine element cropping out with a vengeance!" And the chaplain remarked, "We're apt to forget what a little girl you are, after all, Dora . . . you are so womanly in many things." [55]

When they were alone, the chaplain made his case: though he had "no mother to take you to, no sister to offer you as a companion," he himself would be "brother, father, guardian, all that a man may be to the most precious charge God could give him." He would place her in the charge of "an excellent woman," but he himself would "watch over and educate you." "I will develop the strong, pure nature that God has given you," he told her. "I will train you to such womanhood as the world has seldom witnessed. Dora, I startle you with my vehemence, but you cannot yet understand how this plan has become a part of my whole future." [56]

In this seemingly intractable situation, the author opted for an easy out: Dora went home with Captain Karl to help in his convalescence from wounds, but once there she discovered that his mother was actually her aunt. At one fell swoop Austin provided an aura of unimpeachable respectability for a situation teetering precariously on the edge of the scandalous. *Dora Darling* had clearly revealed the instability of a girl's identity in war—perhaps a central reason why so few authors chose to create a girls' war.

Still, the adventurous girls' war presented in *Dora Darling* apparently sold well: the publisher advertised in December 1864 that "this most interesting volume has had a rapid sale thus far," with the first printing "already sold." The fact that Austin wrote a sequel certainly suggests that the publisher was satisfied with the sales of *Dora Darling*. Thus at the end of the war girls were provisionally included in the new juvenile adventure literature of war. But their inclusion was hedged with the uncertainty and contradictions inherent in an attempt to meld an ethos of adventure with the antebellum ideology of domesticity.[57]

• • •

By the end of the war adventure was the keynote in juvenile war-related novels—just as it was the keynote of juvenile fiction in general published during the war. Authors who did not understand this new market reality were often swimming upstream. On July 10, 1864, for instance, a would-be author named Eliza Davis from North Andover, Massachusetts, sent James Perkins Walker a juvenile manuscript that she described as "a plain, unvarnished tale of English domestic life—nothing *sensational* or senti-mental, much of it has truth for its bases." Two weeks later she had already been rejected, but in such a sensitive manner that she wrote once again to thank the publisher for the refinement of his rejection. Apologizing for putting herself "before the public as a writer," she told him, "I ought to say the idea was suggested to me by some literary people in Boston and Salem—who told me, 'these sensation stories, are vitiating the taste of the young people of the present day. Something ought to be done to remedy this growing evil.'" Significantly, she singled out *Cudjo's Cave* as an ex-ample of such literature, commenting, "I can only regret that the love of excitement depresses effort for the rising generation" and "they will prob-ably go on in the pursuit of such *literary* information as is to be gained from 'Cudjo's Cave' and works of a similar character." [58]

Eliza Davis was right about the new love of excitement in children's literature, a trend that Thomas Wentworth Higginson also remarked in a review of children's literature published in the *North American Review* a few months after the end of the war. "In speaking of contemporary chil-dren's books," Higginson said in January 1866, "the first place must of course be given to narratives of adventure. Whatever else fails, these are always palatable, and secure of their market." The "twin stars" of this field were British authors Mayne Reid and W. H. G. Kingston, with Kingston's books "a sort of pemmican of adventure, bear and Indian boiled down to the utmost concentration." [59]

"To these tales, of chiefly foreign adventure," Higginson continued, "the war has of course added its full share of the domestic product." "Mr. Trow-bridge, who never writes very ill and rarely very well, has given us quite a graphic picture of camp-life in his 'Drummer-Boy'; while 'Dora Dar-ling,' by an anonymous author, gives a companion-sketch of a little *vivan-*

dière, with a good many charming touches of nature, and quite enough improbability to add spice. Moreover, Mr. Adams ('Oliver Optic') has written two army and two navy books, which are all spirited and correct enough, though seeming rather hasty in point of execution." Alger's *Frank's Campaign*, which "comes naturally in at the end of the war-books," was "a good story of home life." [60]

Higginson then turned to the subject of race. By "keeping his heroes at home," Higginson commented about Horatio Alger, "this author escapes one formidable responsibility which waits on all these writers of war-stories—namely, that they must bring their heroes in contact with the inevitable 'contraband,' first or last, and then must report the conversation." "Then ensues a Babel of dialect, a chaos of misspelling, a travesty of a travesty of good English. Is it designed as a piece of retribution on the negro race, that we should distort their talk even more than they distort ours?" [61]

As Higginson rightly noted, African American characters routinely spoke in the virtually unintelligible dialect common to antebellum fiction and minstrelsy. In *Dora Darling*, Pic began the novel by saying, "Hi! Dat good un! Bully for de 'federates, dis chile say." Moreover, he was a "faithful retainer," utterly loyal to Dora and without any other discernible interest in life, as well as being childishly ignorant in a way that the reader was invited to laugh at. In Optic's *The Soldier Boy*, the only appearance by a black was an abject, whining "darkey." Alger's *Frank's Campaign*, despite Higginson's comments, did include the "inevitable 'contraband'": however, though overtly sympathetic to emancipation, Alger described Pomp, the child of a runaway slave, as "a bright little fellow, as black as the ace of spades, and possessing to the full the mercurial temperament of the Southern negro. Full of fun and drollery, he attracted plenty of attention when he came to the village, and earned many a penny from the boys by his plantation songs and dances." [62]

Although Northern children's magazines published numerous "scathing critiques of slavery," as James Marten has pointed out, and, like adult periodicals, brief articles on contrabands, they did not explore African Americans' new role in American life to the extent that the major illustrated weeklies did. African American soldiers, for instance, a major feature of *Harper's Weekly* and *Frank Leslie's Illustrated Newspaper* from 1862 to the close of the war, rarely appeared in juvenile literature. Instead, children's literature clung to older stereotypes. [63]

It is hardly news that even "right-thinking" Northerners were often deeply prejudiced against blacks, many times unconsciously so. But what is important to remember in a consideration of children's war books is that this literature was a conduit for the replication of adult racial attitudes in the young. Such attitudes were an important part of wartime nationalism, providing crucial boundaries to the concept of nationhood as blacks became the "others" who would define a nation for whites. Only one book that was "half a juvenile"— *Cudjo's Cave*—attempted to imagine an African American as a military hero. Most juvenile literature of war, which portrayed a conflict in which whites condescended to give freedom to blacks, underlined the shallow support available within popular culture for any radical vision of a biracial society.

• • •

By the end of the war Northern publishers had expanded their juvenile publishing programs exponentially. In 1864 the *American Annual Cyclopaedia* commented that the "number of new books issued" in 1863 surpassed that "of any previous year," with the "most numerous class of publications" being "those for juvenile readers." Underlining the flourishing state of juvenile publishing in the North, in early 1865 the publisher Ticknor and Fields printed the first issue of a major new children's magazine, *Our Young Folks*, which included John Townsend Trowbridge, Harriet Beecher Stowe, James Roberts Gilmore, and Louisa May Alcott among its editors and contributors and which also printed a number of poems, stories, and articles about the war. Grenville Norcross received a subscription to this magazine for Christmas in 1864 and faithfully recorded reading the first few monthly issues, which he also lent to friends. The magazine was an immediate success.[64]

The situation could not have been more different—or dire—in the South, where late in the war many Southern popular publications were struggling for their very existence. But even in 1862 and 1863, when Confederate literary ambition ran high and numerous popular magazines were established, almost no juvenile literature was published outside of a few religious publications. Confederate publishers instead put their energies into creating Confederate schoolbooks and textbooks for children, a task that seemed of more importance in a new nation than the establishment of a literature of entertainment for young readers.

Not that Confederate readers did not miss popular juvenile literature during the war. In 1863 *Uncle Buddy's Gift Book for the Holidays*, one of the rare children's books published during the war, commented that because of the blockading of Southern ports "we are unable to obtain a great many things to which we were once accustomed." Among these were "juvenile books, with which our bookstores were wont to be largely supplied during the holidays." Now, however, we must "either do without, or procure the best substitutes that we can." Addressing his "young friends," the author of this new volume commented that he hoped that it would "supply the deficiency in the respect mentioned."[65]

Uncle Buddy's Gift Book for the Holidays could not by itself supply the Confederate deficiency in children's literature. But it, together with another rare Confederate juvenile, *The Boys and Girls Stories of the War*, can give us some indication of points of similarity and difference between Northern and Southern children's literature. Included among Uncle Buddy's "Tales, Translations, Poetry, Chronology, Games, Anecdotes, Conundrums, etc., etc.," for instance, was a brief tale titled "The Young Confederate Soldier" that bore remarkable similarities to Northern soldier boy stories. In it "little Johnny Williams," a "brave little hero" who had resolved to "have some share in the fight," was in the process of securing a Federal banner as a trophy of battle when a group of Federal soldiers approached him. To his surprise, after he "drew out a revolver from his belt" and presented "the muzzle towards the approaching foe," the entire group surrendered to him, with one officer handing his sword to Johnny. "The party then started off for the head quarters of Johnny's General," the story reported, "Johnny proudly leading the way, with the flag and the sword in his hand." After praising him for his actions, his general presented him with the sword to keep for himself. Such fantasy was quite close to a story such as *Harper Weekly*'s 1864 "The Little Hero," which portrayed a daring boy who warned Union troops of a Confederate ambush and became "the hero of the hour."[66]

After having "given the boys a story—and a war story, at that," Uncle Buddy then proposed "to give one for the girls," which he said "must be a peace story." In keeping with the gendering of a girls' war in Northern literature, "Helen Norcross, or the Two Friends" portrayed a young girl who was dedicated to "sewing up garments for the soldiers, knitting socks for them, and doing various other good acts for the comfort of the Confederate army." But the story ultimately focused more on a friend who was selfish and disobedient and needed to learn to obey her mother. Although there was some sense in Northern juvenile literature of the development of a "girls'" war to complement a boys' war toward the end of the conflict, there was little such sense in the scant volumes of Confederate juvenile literature.[67]

The few volumes of Confederate popular war literature for children did, however, rehearse racial attitudes and fantasies for a young audience. *The Boys and Girls Stories of the War*, like Confederate popular literature more generally, fantasized slave loyalty to masters and hatred of the Yankees. In the story "The Mountain Guide," the slave Uncle Ned "was very much scared" when he "thought the Yankees had come," for he "hated the Yankees. They had once been in his cabin, stole his milk and bread, robbed his potato patch, and carried off his young master as a prisoner." When he discovered instead that the soldiers requesting his services as a guide were Confederate, he cried, "'Hurray! I goes wid you all ober de Blue Ridge! hurray' and he swung his old hat in the air." After serving as a guide, Uncle Ned was "taken prisoner" by the Yankees and "forced away with them." But by the end of the story, the tables had turned: Uncle Ned "rode into town in great glee" with a captured Yankee sitting behind him on "a little pony." "Hold on, Yank!," said Uncle Ned, "hold on, for if you don't I'll blow your head off with dis here pistol. You is de chap dat took my milk and potatoes, and now I'se goin' to carry you to de prison where all de rogues lib." The text invited children to find this scene amusing: "A crowd of soldiers and people were gathered on the street, laughing fit to kill themselves," it concluded. On the surface, this text included slaves in the imagined adventure of war, as Uncle Ned inverted the racial order by holding sway over a Yankee. But the text was careful to diminutize him as well, picturing him riding on a "little pony" rather than on a more dignified horse. A loyal slave's war adventures were, ultimately, cause for "great amusement."[68]

• • •

"All wars are boyish, and are fought by boys," wrote Herman Melville in his 1866 *Battle Pieces*. It was an observation that had particular applicability to the brutal war he lived through, for the Civil War was truly a "boyish" war—and not only because it was often fought by teenagers or children. It was also a war imagined for a boyish audience: during the conflict Northern authors and publishers produced an outpouring of popular juvenile war literature that purposefully integrated children—especially boys—into the body politic.[69]

Popular war literature for children might well be expected to empha-

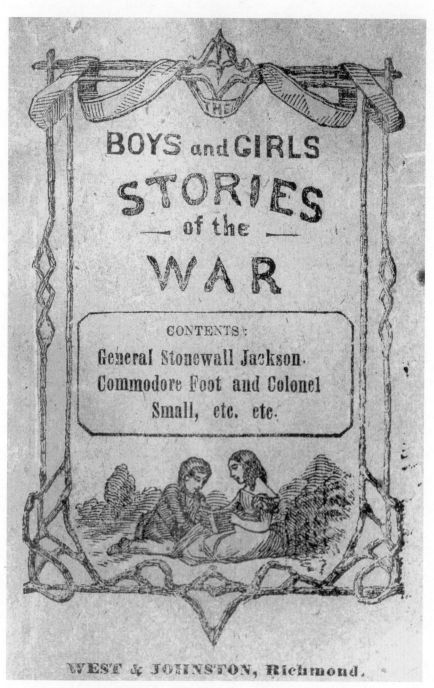

Boys and Girls Stories of the War (Richmond: West and Johnston).
(Courtesy of the Rare Book, Manuscript and Special
Collections Library, Duke University)

size only conservative or traditional values: loyalty to country, loyalty to family, obedience to both. Certainly most boys' biographies stressed virtues of self-restraint and civic duty consonant with such antebellum norms. Yet war-related novels written for and marketed to children were subversive of antebellum familial ideals in several respects. They were attuned to patriotism *and* entertainment, nationalism *and* individualism, obedience *and* adventure.[70]

The very act of imagining a child "war hero" was potentially subversive, in that it provided a means of envisioning the child as a powerful actor outside the embrace of family. Antebellum adventure novels had begun this process, but war juveniles energized and extended it; they loosened, even if only metaphorically, the imagined ties between child and family. It was the figure of the child adventurer, separate from family or even the family surrogate of the army, that was the legacy of juvenile war fiction in the postwar period—not the idea of a national family. Indeed, it is telling that this later fiction—including novels by Horatio Alger Jr. and Mark Twain—emphasized the figure of the orphan and in so doing offered a reminder of both the literal and metaphorical effects of war on the American family.[71]

In their celebration of the war as an individualized adventure, juvenile war novels also provided a connecting link to the definition of war by the end of the century as a splendid white supremacist adventure—an adventure to be undertaken by men who had been merely children during the Civil War itself. Theodore Roosevelt, just two and one-half when the war began and seven when it ended, remembered in his *Autobiography* "reveling in such tales of adventure as Ballantyne's stories," as well as "Mayne Reid's books and other boys' books of adventure" when he was a small boy. "[I] was too young to understand much of Mayne Reid," he confessed, "except the adventure part and the natural history part—these enthralled me."[72]

Although he looked back at his childhood reading with a great deal of nostalgia—"I enjoy going over *Our Young Folks* now nearly as much as ever," he said—Roosevelt also found fault with the literature of his youth. "Take my beloved *Our Young Folks*," he said. "Everything in this magazine instilled the individual virtues, and the necessity of character as the chief factor in any man's success." Roosevelt agreed that individual virtues were important: no man could be "a worthy citizen unless he has within himself the right stuff, unless he has self-reliance, energy, courage, the power of insisting on his own rights and the sympathy that makes him regardful of the rights of others." But Roosevelt saw a crucial flaw in this teaching of "individual morality": there was "almost no teaching of the need for collective action, and of the fact that in addition to, not as a substitute for, individual responsibility, there is a collective responsibility." Although the teaching he received "was genuinely democratic in one way," it "was not so democratic in another." "I grew into manhood thoroughly imbued with the feeling that a man must be respected for what he made of himself," he said. "But I had also, consciously or unconsciously, been taught" that "the whole duty of man lay in thus making the best of himself." Such teaching, Roosevelt concluded, "if not corrected by other teaching, means acquiescence in a riot of lawless business individualism." [73]

The Civil War has often been described as a force for consolidation, organization, and centralization, but it is clear from a study of popular literature that in the lived experience of many juvenile readers it was not experienced in that way: the war instead was portrayed and perceived as part of a new adventurous individualism, with war itself a splendid adventure facilitated by the embryonic national state.

The Market Value of Memory

HISTORIES OF THE WAR

Come, children, leave your playing; a tale I have to tell—
A tale of woe and sorrow, which long ago befell;
'Twas in the great rebellion, in eighteen sixty-one;
Within the streets of Baltimore the bloody deed was done.

Of gallant Major Anderson I told you yesternight,
Of Moultrie's shattered battlements, and Sumter's bloodless fight;
And how the cannon's echo shook the North and East and West,
And woke a flame in loyal hearts which would not be repressed.

—Edward Sprague Rand Jr., "A Tale of 1861,"
Rebellion Record *1*

In December 1864 the popular historian John S. C. Abbott, hard at work on the second volume of his *History of the Civil War in America*, defended writing a history of the war even as it was still being fought. As he explained to his editor and publisher, Ledyard Bill, "It is frequently supposed that a really reliable history of this war can not be written *now*. I think, on the contrary, that *now* is the very best time to write it. For instance, the causes of the war are more closely discussed now than they will be when all the present living actors have passed away. The time will never come in future years when one can write of the capture of New Orleans, of the campaign of the Chickahominy, of the battle of Gettysburg, better than now."[1]

In making this argument for wartime history on the grounds of immediacy, Abbott offered a striking contrast to writers who thought histories of the war should at least wait until the end of the conflict. In early 1862, for instance, John Lothrop Motley, one of the preeminent historians of antebellum America, turned down an invitation from Philadelphia publisher George W. Childs to write a history of the war. Motley was "much inclined to doubt whether the time to write such a history" would "soon arrive," he said in his letter of refusal. It was "impossible—while no man is yet wise enough to know when, how & where this momentous episode in our national history is to end—for any man to describe it thoroughly."[2]

Even though Abbott certainly disagreed with this assessment—indeed, he hoped that his own history would be "so full and reliable that no one shall hereafter be able to write a better"—he was not therefore immune to a host of practical, even absurd problems that arose out of trying to write the history of a war still in progress. When he started work on his manuscript in 1862, for instance, a major concern was that the war might end so quickly as to disrupt his publishing plans: "Present appearances do not indicate a sudden closing of the war," he wrote to his publisher with a measure of relief in May of that year. "We shall have time enough to read carefully our proof sheets." By 1864, however, Abbott was worried about the opposite possibility—that the continuation of the war might pose a serious publishing problem: "I still hope," he wrote in December, "that the war will close so that we can get the whole History in two volumes." Far from being merely a frivolous concern, the question of whether to publish in two or three volumes went to the heart of mid-nineteenth-century publishing convention, involving a critical calculation of what the market would bear.[3]

It is precisely this connection between the war and the perceived demands of the literary marketplace that makes Abbott, one of a group of Northern popular war historians who published histories during the war, so important to analyze for an understanding of how meanings of the war were shaped in wartime for a broad reading public. Explicitly concerned with constructing a lasting print memory of the war, war histories occupied a special place within the commercial literary culture of war. Though their authors often drew directly from the columns of newspapers for their content, popular histories were situated quite differently than newspapers within wartime print culture: whereas newspapers were presented as immediate, urgent, disposable, war histories were conceived and advertised using a language of futurity and permanence. Marketed as keepsakes that provided a "permanent" history of the war, they were offered to subscribers in a variety of cloth and leather bindings embossed with gilt and were meant to join other important works on the Victorian parlor table as items for display as well as edification, collectibles as well as sources of information.[4]

Yet their insistent claim to permanence was ironic: like Abbott's work, most histories of the war published in the midst of the fighting provided distended narratives of 1861 or 1862—and sometimes provided no closure to the war. We can use this central irony, however, to fuel an examination of why popular histories constructed meanings of the Civil War as they did, for it reminds us of the central importance of the practices of commercial literary culture in structuring and defining these histories.

Some writers objected to the commercialization of wartime history, arguing that memories of the Civil War were sacralized and therefore should be entirely beyond commerce. When popular biographer James Parton decided against writing a history of the war in 1864, for instance, he drew on an already well established set of tropes when he wrote that "a theme so vast & glorious, so sacred & sublime, ought not to be slighted or regarded as a means of making a little money. The man who writes it should dedicate his life to the noble task, & do it as an act of religion." But many other authors seized the opportunities afforded by the commercial culture of war.[5]

John S. C. Abbott's *History of the Civil War in America,* for instance, was a major publishing success during and immediately after the war. Although sales figures are hard to prove, there are several indications that his work sold in the hundreds of thousands of copies. In late 1864, for instance, at a time when Abbott and his publisher were considering whether to embark on a third volume, Abbott wrote to Ledyard Bill, "With the subscription list you now have, it can I think be hardly doubted that you will be able to sell 100,000 copies of a third volume." By 1867, Bill advertised that "more than 300,000 volumes have been subscribed for," the "largest sale of any book on the war." With Abbott's original contract stating that he would receive "20 cents copy-right for the first 10,000 sold, and 15 cents for all over that," he stood to earn tens of thousands of dollars from his work. Several other war histories sold more than 100,000 copies as well, but Abbott's work does indeed seem to have had the "largest sale" among them.[6]

Part of Abbott's success must be attributed to his own established popularity as a historian on the eve of the war. In the 1850s Abbott, a Congregational clergyman, had published numerous volumes of European history, including works on the French Revolution, Marie Antoinette, the Austrian empire, Italy, and Russia—not to mention such works as his *Kings and Queens; or Life in the Palace.* His most famous—and infamous—work had been a celebratory history of Napoleon that drew attacks from Horace Greeley and Charles A. Dana, with Emerson acidly commenting that it seemed "to teach that the great object of Napoleon in all his wars was to establish in benighted Europe our New England system of Sunday-schools." Despite such criticisms, however, Abbott's books sold well to a broad public.[7]

Abbott's established popularity on the eve of the war partially explains his success, but equally important was the way in which both he and his publishers used the subscription publishing business to exploit his popularity. Indeed, it is no accident that most of the histories of the war published in wartime were issued by subscription publishing houses, many of them located in New York or in Hartford, Connecticut, an eastern center of subscription book publishing at this time. As one historian of the book has commented, it was the war that marked "the beginning of the real growth and expansion of the subscription book business in the United States." Among the titles sold by subscription were Horace Greeley's *The American Conflict,* Benson J. Lossing's *Pictorial History of the Civil War in the United States of America,* Joel Tyler Headley's *The Great Rebellion; a History of the Civil War in the United States;* Evert A. Duyckinck's *National History of the War for the Union, Civil, Military and Naval;* Orville Victor's *The History, Civil, Political & Military, of the Southern Rebellion;* Ann S. Stephens's *Pictorial History of the War for the Union;* Elliot Gray Storke's *The Great American Rebellion;* Robert Tomes's *The War with the South; A History of the Great Rebellion;* E. G. Squier's *Pictorial History of the War of 1861;* and Thomas B. Kettell's *History of the Great Rebellion.* Abbott himself contracted with the subscription publisher Henry Bill, who became partners with his brothers Ledyard and Gurdon in order to finance and produce this venture. All three had experience in selling subscription books.[8]

Subscription houses were well equipped to gauge the market for the memory of the war. Their books were presold by canvassing agents who signed up subscribers on the basis of a salesman's dummy or prospectus, unlike books published by the "regular trade" and sold in bookstores or by "book agents" supplied with copies of finished books. The subscription sales approach reduced the risk to the publisher: not only could he tailor his history to a given market, but he could predict his market share. Subscription publishers could manufacture books on the basis of orders received from canvassing agents in the field; in contrast, the trade publisher had difficulty predicting the potential audience for books. Trade publishers, who depended primarily on retail booksellers, were also in a much more precarious position because such booksellers had often been hard hit by the war.[9]

The Bill brothers and Abbott shared a shrewd commercial sense of the war, and Abbott's letters to Henry and especially to Ledyard Bill, who acted as his editor, provide a number of insights into the process by which a subscription publisher and author jointly shaped a wartime history. Both publisher and author understood, for instance, that representations of the war had to be shaped with marketability in mind. When Henry Bill suggested "an increase of pages in Vol. I," Abbott readily obliged, expanding his version of the war so that the book would be more than five hundred pages—a sales plus for canvassing agents. With his eye on potential readership, Abbott also wrote to his publisher, "As Ellsworth was the first Officer killed, and one who had inspired such enthusiasm, perhaps it might be well to have his face to adorn our pages." Abbott's comment represented a clear understanding of what might appeal to a popular audience.[10]

"After much deliberation," Abbott also "decided to write the History according to Campaigns and not Cronologically [sic]," explaining, "I am satisfied that this decision was a wise one, and that it enables me to create much more interest in the mind of the reader. Donelson & Fort Henry were connected with Paducah & Cairo. The heroic battle of Mill Springs is naturally connected with the Campaign in East Kentucky & Tennessee, and will come in the second volume." Although there were "some advantages in the Cronological order of narrative, giving an account of whatever occurred all over the wide field *each month*," by "pursuing this course one loses the power of a vivid, continuous glowing narrative." Abbott concluded, "The Campaigns in the West are certainly among the most glorious in the war. I think that the second volume will be even more rich in scenes of exciting interest than the first." Such comments underlined Abbott's acute understanding of his market role: to respond to the public's perceived desires by creating an enthralling war.[11]

Though Abbott and his publishers shared a savvy sense of the popular literary marketplace, they did not always see eye to eye in their own relationship, however. As the war lengthened indefinitely, for instance, it forced a change in the Bills' publishing plans: though "according to our contract I was to write a book of over 700 pages," Abbott reminded his publisher in November 1862, "we have now decided upon 2 Vols. embracing over a thousand pages." While the Bill brothers, citing an "unexpected rise in paper, binding, printing, etc.," hoped to reduce Abbott's copyright (royalty), Abbott, not unreasonably, wanted an increase. Reflecting on his hard-won status as a popular historian, Abbott pointed out to the Bill brothers, "It has taken the unintermitted toil of a life time to put me in a position to write this book, and I do not feel that I shall receive too large a reward." [12]

The war clearly exacerbated author-publisher tensions; it also encouraged Abbott to work extremely fast, as he and his publishers wanted to issue their history while the public's interest in the war remained high and before numerous other historians joined the field. By June 1862 Abbott reported that he had "*five* chapters ready for the printer"; in September 1862 he announced that "over 300 pages" of his first volume were stereotyped, and he added, "I have all the chapters written but the last, upon which I am now at work & shall send it on in a few days." [13]

What enabled Abbott to work so rapidly was his reliance on already published reports; like other popular war historians, he drew extensively from newspapers. Although his research also involved "writing and collecting facts from a wide correspondence, and from many of our leading generals with utmost care," Abbott primarily depended on newspaper reports, a number of which his publishers sent him. "Your parcel of 'clippings,' I have just received, & for them please accept my thanks," Abbott wrote Bill in May 1862. "I find many valuable items among these, as in those sent me by your brother." A short time later he thanked Bill for "the Boston journal" and mentioned that "the Louisville Journal I shall be glad to receive." [14]

Like many other war historians, Abbott also found the newspapers more reliable than other sources. In his finished history he offered a "tribute of commendation and gratitude to the reporters of the leading journals" and was "constrained to say, that not unfrequently the newspaper report has been more correct, more truthful, than the official bulletin." Newspapers might well have been more "correct" than official bulletins, but it should also be remembered that newspapers themselves often offered highly fictionalized accounts of the war to attract their own readership. Accepting newspaper accounts as "truthful" thus often gave the authority of "fact" to fiction. As one newspaper reporter wrote to his editor in 1863, "Your suggestions about more of the Romance & picturesqueness of the war, & less of the common place will be of great service to me." [15]

While Abbott was apparently unconcerned about the interpretive implications of his reliance on newspapers as sources, other popular historians explicitly reflected on the problems inherent in interpreting a modern print war in which masses of print information were available. In the preface to his 1861 *History Civil, Political & Military of the Southern Rebellion,* for instance, the popular author Orville Victor mused about the difficulties of writing the history of the war. "From the outset," he said, "I have had to contend *against* the quantity of data offered as material for my work." The historian "generally seeks for multiplicity in his authorities," Victor said, "thus to be the more able to secure a correct version of his story; but in the present instance at least, there has been only too much 'authority' offered." He had been "fairly oppressed with the weight and multitude of [his] witnesses," what with "interminable versions of the same affair in almost countless papers — with news dispatches from responsible and irresponsible sources — with letters written in a partisan spirit, in ignorance or in malice — with endless Convention reports, speeches, ordinances, resolutions, etc. — with Legislative proceedings of many States — with the proceedings of two Congresses, and the documents of two cotemporary [*sic*] Executives" and "with the great ebb and flow of popular feeling in all sections, as represented by two thousand newspapers." [16]

Abbott's history revealed no such interpretive uncertainties about the war, perhaps because a dramatic narrative, rather than meticulous detail, was his main concern in writing. Then, again, his own partisan politics as an antislavery advocate and Fremont Republican provided a strong interpretive framework for his text. The great contest of the war, he said in his first chapter, was between slavery and freedom — "between the claims of aristocratic privilege on the one hand, and the demand for equal rights on the other, which for countless ages has made our globe one vast battlefield." In the florid, sometimes bombastic style characteristic of his writing, he commented, "This fierce fight, which has arrayed more than a million of men in arms, and which made our ship of state reel and stagger, as if smitten by thunderbolts and dashing upon rocks, was but one, though a sublime act, in the drama of that great conflict, between patrician arrogance and plebeian resistance." [17]

In finding the main cause of the war to be the "antagonism between the system of aristocratic privilege and democratic equality," Abbott repeated a theme voiced by numerous Northern writers about the war, whether Democrats or Republicans. But his own antislavery politics also led him to make far more radical statements as well. "One takes a very narrow view of this question," Abbott said, "in regarding it as one which affects a particular race, the African alone. It is as broad as humanity." Calling into question any attempts to distinguish races from one another, Abbott asserted that such divisions were "quite arbitrary" and that "these divisions run into and blend with each other inextricably." He denied any biological basis for racial distinction: "There are black men, and red men, and yellow men, and tawny men, and white men—men of every shade of color between whiteness as of snow and jet black," Abbott declared. "The declaration of Scripture seems abundantly sustained by science, that God made of one blood all nations, that Eve is our common mother—that all the varieties of mankind now existing are the result of climate, food, habits, and what we call accidental occurrences." [18]

In denying any biological basis for racial distinction, Abbott was at the radical end of mid-nineteenth-century racial thought. Such radicalism did not permeate his text; he made few statements on racial theory per se. But laced throughout his military narratives were personal anecdotes that, in a style reminiscent of Harriet Beecher Stowe, repeatedly stressed the horrors of slavery in dividing families or the joy of contrabands at being reunited with their loved ones in Union camps. Abbott told the story, for instance, of a church deacon from Hilton Head who was reunited in Beaufort, South Carolina, with the wife "who had been sold from him fourteen years ago, and of whom he had heard nothing all that time": "In the streets of that deserted village, which war had swept of the barbarism of slavery, they clasped each other again, in their free arms." These were reunions, Abbott commented in his emotive, novelistic style, "which opened the deepest fountains of feeling in the human heart." Yet, Abbott reminded his readers, "notwithstanding all these facts, there were those in the North who were bitterly opposed to any measures which tended towards emancipation." Only emancipation, Abbott stated in the final chapter of his history, could purify "our land from that great crime which, in God's retributive justice, had imperilled our National life." [19]

Although Abbott clearly stated that emancipation was the most important result of the conflict and that in addition "the introduction of colored men into the army was one of the most momentous events in the history of the war," neither topic received sustained discussion until the end of the text. In this case we can clearly see that market imperatives shaped a narrative in ways that took away from the force of Abbott's own beliefs. For instance, Abbott's decision to tell the story of the war by military campaign rather than chronologically made it difficult to integrate the politics of antislavery during the war, a story Abbott eventually chose to tell more fully in the last chapter of his final volume. Then again, the fact that Abbott had finished the first volume of his history by September 1862 ironically meant that Lincoln's preliminary Emancipation Proclamation, issued that same month, was excluded from his first volume. Yet even though market imperatives affected the presentation of Abbott's political beliefs, it is also important to note that the popular and the political were by no means opposed concepts within his text. He instead created a hybrid mixture of entertainment and ideology.[20]

Who actually bought Abbott's subscription history? Readership, of course, is notoriously difficult to establish, but there are tantalizing clues available in a few surviving prospectuses for the *History of the Civil War in America*. Prospectuses, the salesmen's dummies that canvassers used to sell these wartime histories, were leather-bound samples, often copiously stamped with gilt. They were meant to provide an enticing, even irresistible preview of the coming book; they included some text, a number of engravings, and, most important, an interleaved section of blank pages on which potential subscribers would write their names, addresses, and often their occupations. Several "confidential" guides for canvassers published soon after the war, including the *Agent's Companion* and Henry Bill's own *Practical Instructions*, gave an indication of the received wisdom about how best to canvas with these samples.

The difference between canvassing in Europe and America, the *Agents' Companion* noted, was that in Europe the "books circulated are generally expensive and elegant works," with the subscribers "the nobility and gentry, who alone can afford such," whereas "here, publishers of subscription books look for their customers almost entirely among farmers and mechanics;—the great body of the people." Subscription books were thus circulated "among that class who seldom or never enter a book-store" and "who live remote from cities." Emphasizing the "*power of the subscription list*," the *Agents' Companion* advised that "if the Agent understands the business, he first makes the acquaintance of a few of the leading influential men, and induces them to subscribe." This was such an important step that "if unsuccessful in obtaining the influence of such in any other way, he can at any rate get them to subscribe on condition of leaving it optional with them, when he delivers, to take or not take the book." "Having thus got started," the *Companion* continued, "the thing goes like an epidemic. Men subscribe because their neighbors have." "The showing of the book will in each individual case have little effect compared with the next operation, that is the unfolding of the subscription list, when the *array of signatures* strikes the person with a sort of mesmeric influence." *The Henry Bill Publishing Company's Private Instructions to Their Agents for Selling Their Sub-*

scription Books agreed and also warned the canvasser to "be careful not to start the list with inferior names; it is better to reject them entirely than to receive them at the head of the list, as it prevents influential men from subscribing." Although the list was vital, it was important, too, the *Companion* said, to "create a desire" by painting *"vividly upon the imagination an impression that the book is of a deeply interesting character, and filled with useful information."* [21]

Surviving prospectuses for Abbott's *History of the Civil War in America* suggest not only that the *Agents' Companion* might have been largely correct in its assessment of audience but also that Civil War canvassers followed precepts such as those the *Companion* outlined. One prospectus, with a listing of 148 subscribers from small towns in upstate New York, led off with one A. L. Bennett, who identified himself as "Merchant." There were no other merchants listed; instead, the largest self-identified occupations listed were farmer (47); housekeeper (18, all women); housework (11, all women); teacher (8); mechanic (5); soldier's wife (4); carpenter (4); and then in descending order lady and cooper (3 each); clergyman, cabinetmaker, harness maker, boatman, hotel keeper, and painter (2 each); and blacksmith, wagon maker, artist, clothier, bookkeeper, paper dealer, glazier, lumberman, picture painter, produce dealer, grocer, woodworker, furnace worker, shoemaker, dressmaker, tailoress, banker, dentist, editor, tailor, miller, and mason (1 each). This was a listing that painted a portrait of small-town America.[22]

A second prospectus, containing hundreds of names, began with an extensive list of pillars of the community of Norwich, Massachusetts, including clergymen, manufacturers, newspaper editors, bank presidents, postmasters, attorneys at law, physicians, and merchants. But when the list moved to small towns such as Lunenberg, Fitchburg, South Royalston, and Winchendon, its listed occupations changed, too, with farming by far the most common occupation. This evidence suggests that a book such as Abbott's appealed to a wide-ranging audience in small-town and rural America.[23]

• • •

The first volume of Abbott's history was distributed to subscribers during April 1863, in a postemancipation world that Abbott had hoped for but had been able only to imagine in his own text. Between the writing of his text and the distribution of his finished books, a dramatic shift in public opinion had occurred: in mid-1863 the politics of antislavery were popular as they had never been before—indeed, a number of abolitionists were astonished to be lionized for the first time in their careers.

It was in this newly radicalized atmosphere, and only three months after the distribution of Abbott's highly successful first volume, that Horace Greeley contracted to write a subscription history of the conflict. As he recounted in his memoirs, it was shortly after "the national triumph at Gettysburg" and the "(so-called) 'Riots'" that he "was visited by two strangers, who introduced themselves as Messrs. Newton and O. D. Case, publishers, from Hartford, and solicited [him] to write the History of the Rebellion." Greeley, the editor of the *New York Tribune* for the duration of the war and an icon of Northern Republicanism, "hesitated": "My labors and responsibilities were already most arduous and exacting." But the combination of the right political moment and Greeley's own pressing financial need (he was perpetually in debt) proved irresistible: "The compensation offered would be liberal, in case the work should attain a very large scale," Greeley acknowledged, although it would otherwise be "quite moderate." [24]

Greeley had previously entertained "no thought of ever becoming the historian" of the conflict. "In fact," he said, "not till that War was placed on its true basis of a struggle for liberation, and not conquest, by President Lincoln's successive Proclamations of Freedom, would I have consented to write its history." Although the Emancipation Proclamation was a necessary precondition to writing a wartime history, the July 1863 Draft Riots were a galvanizing factor: "Not till I had confronted the Rebellion as a positive, desolating force, right here in New York, at the doors of earnest Republicans, in the hunting down and killing of defenceless, fleeing Blacks, in the burning of the Colored Orphan Asylum, and in the mobbing and firing of the Tribune office," Greeley wrote, "could I have been moved to delineate its aims, progress, and impending catastrophe." [25]

For Greeley politics and marketplace dynamics proved a compelling fit, and his resulting two-volume history, *The American Conflict*, did indeed provide an unequivocal emphasis on slavery, as illustrated by its subtitle: *A History of the Great Rebellion in the United States of America, 1860–1864: Its Causes, Incidents, and Results; intended to Exhibit especially its Moral and Political Phases, with the Drift and Progress of American Opinion respecting Human Slavery from 1776 to the Close of the War for the Union.* Greeley characterized his own work as "one of the clearest statements yet made of the long train of causes that led irresistably to the war for the Union, showing why that war was the natural and righteous consequence of the American

people's general and guilty complicity in the crime of upholding and dif-
fusing Human Slavery." Slavery was at the heart of his history, even in its
chapter titles. Chapter 2, for example, was "Slavery in America prior to
1776"; chapter 16 was "The Era of Slave-Hunting." [26]

Though Greeley provided a substantial discussion of the politics of
slavery as the cause of the war, his first volume discussed little of the war
itself and indeed ended in late 1861. Competitors in the field of popular war
history were savvy enough to attempt to use this fact against him: as one
subscription publisher pointed out in a prospectus for his own 1865 volume, "The first volume of Greeley's is almost wholly devoted to political
history as it closes with the description of the battle of Ball's Bluff, just at
the opening of the war." [27]

However, as Greeley explained in the opening of his second volume, he
regarded even the military aspects of the war "under a moral rather than
a purely material aspect." While others had "doubtless surpassed" him in
"the vividness, the graphic power of their delineations of 'the noise of the
captains, and the shouting,'" he had sought to portray the influences involved in "molding and refining Public Opinion to accept, and ultimately
demand, the overthrow and extinction of Human Slavery, as the one vital,
implacable enemy of our Nationality and our Peace." [28]

Shortly after publication in April 1864, Greeley's *The American Conflict* reportedly produced some ten thousand dollars in royalties; by spring
1867 the first volume had reportedly sold 125,000 copies. Such success
showed that a strong market existed in the postemancipation North for
a politicized history of the war that engaged slavery as its central issue.
Subscribers to *The American Conflict* clearly expected a strong statement
from the famous Republican editor of the *Tribune*.[29]

At the same time, the fate of Greeley's second volume showed that if an
author's politics were perceived to stray too far from an approved set of
beliefs, the reactions of subscription book buyers might put subscription
booksellers—including author, publisher, and especially the door-to-door
subscription agent—at serious risk. Immediately after Lee's surrender in
April 1865, Greeley began to editorialize for what he called "magnanimity
in triumph": "What we ask is that the President say, in effect, 'Slavery
having, through rebellion, committed suicide, let the North and the South
unite to bury its carcass and then clasp hands across the grave.'" [30]

Many Northerners disagreed with any policy that advocated friend-
ship with the South, but no real outcry arose against Greeley until 1867
when he agreed to act as one of the bondsmen for Jefferson Davis, who had

been imprisoned without a trial since the end of the war. Unfortunately for Greeley, his publisher, and the canvassing agents for *The American Conflict*, this public outcry coincided with the distribution of the second volume of his history. As Greeley remembered, "The sale of my history was very large and steady down to the date of the clamor raised touching the bailing of Jefferson Davis, when it almost ceased for a season; thousands who had subscribed for it refusing to take their copies, to the sore disappointment and loss of the agents, who had supplied themselves with fifty to a hundred copies each, in accordance with their orders; and who thus found themselves suddenly and most unexpectedly involved in serious embarrassments." Agents, who typically bought copies of subscription books at a reduced rate from the publisher and then charged full price to the customer, stood to lose not only their profits but their own capital outlay.[31]

Though Greeley's second volume eventually sold some fifty thousand copies in 1867, this was a significant drop from the sales of his first volume. Furthermore, his sales never entirely recovered. In 1870 Greeley's publisher O. D. Case wrote to him, "It has taken a great deal longer for the storm to blow over, caused by the Davis Bail Bond, than I anticipated, and the fruitless efforts we made the first year to overcome it cost us a good deal of money." Case thought "there must be 30,000 to 40,000 who have Vol. I but not Vol. II."[32]

Ultimately, Greeley's visibility as a public figure and his strong political stance made him both highly marketable and highly vulnerable to shifts in public opinion. Perhaps it is not surprising, then, that a number of wartime histories sought a wide audience by attempting to avoid partisan political discussion as much as possible, stressing instead the "heroic" or "thrilling" aspects of the war. In featuring sensationalized accounts of individual adventures, such histories closely aligned themselves with the rhetoric of sensational war fiction.

One such historian had in fact been a popular novelist before the war. Ann S. Stephens, the author of the 1863 subscription history *Pictorial History of the War for the Union* and an editor of *Peterson's Magazine* during the war, had already achieved substantial popularity in the antebellum period with such novels as *Fashion and Famine* (1854), *High Life in New York* (1843), and *Malaeska, the Indian Wife of the White Hunter*, the first dime novel published by Beadle and Company in 1860. When she turned to writing a history of the war, Stephens drew on her extensive experience as a novelist to create a tale of suspense that avoided politics as much as possible in favor of the "events" of war themselves: her account, she explained, would deal "not with causes, but with the terrible events that spring out of them; avoiding so far as possible the threatening clouds of political dissension that preceded and still follow the tempest." "In this book," she asserted, "there is a positive rejection of those partizan dissensions which have burst asunder the sacred ties of the greatest nation on earth, and deluged the soil trodden by millions of happy men with the blood of as brave a soldiery as ever drew breath." [33]

Instead, Stephens's account stressed the "spectacular" and "adventurous" aspects of war, promising "a graphic picture of its encounters, thrilling incidents, frightful scenes, hair-breadth escapes, individual daring, desperate charges, personal anecdotes, etc., gleaned from eye-witnesses of, and participants in, the terrible scenes described." [34] Such rhetoric aligned Stephens with the melodramatic world of sensational war novels, with their promise that life was "truly inhabited by primal, intense, polarized forces." [35]

In Stephens's hands, the florid, high-wrought language employed by Abbott achieved a new hyperbolic, anguished intensity. As she commented in her opening pages, "That the revolt of these Southern States would in less than a year fill the whole length and breadth of the land with widows and orphans — that American brothers could ever be brought to stand face to face in mortal strife as they have done — that women, so lately looked on with love and reverence, should grow coarse and fiendish from a scent of kindred blood, mocking at the dead and sending victims into a death-snare by their smiles, alas! alas! who could have foreseen it? The very angels of Heaven must have turned away from the suggestion in unbelief." Such melodramatic style extended to battles and military leaders as well: the "capture of New Orleans" was a scene of "thrilling grandeur," for instance, in which the "flashes of fire" and "the clouds of smoke" presented "a spectacle awfully sublime"; the early wartime "martyr" Colonel Ellsworth was "an eagle struck in its high soaring," "a spirit of fire." [36]

It is easy to dismiss this melodramatic style as merely excessive, vacuous in its bombast, but it should also be remembered that the melodramatic mode created a particular version of imagined nationhood, in which the chief meanings of the war adhered not to the politics of slavery, as Horace Greeley would have it, but to the deeds and sufferings of individuals. Stephens's history thus contributed to a larger popular literature that stressed the personal adventure of war. And although Stephens's work did not achieve the major success of Abbott's, it nevertheless did well: in 1870 the *Nation* reported her history had sold sixty-two thousand copies.[37]

By 1864 and 1865, subscription histories of the war flooded the literary marketplace, making the task of clearly distinguishing one from another a challenge for publishers. To overcome this marketing obstacle, some subscription publishers treated their histories as products to be weighed and measured rather than read. The most absurd example of this style of commodification was Thomas P. Kettell's 1865 subscription volume *History of the Great Rebellion,* published by L. Stebbins of Hartford. Published after wartime subscription histories by Abbott, Joel T. Headley (whom Poe had once called "The Autocrat of All the Quacks"),[38] and Greeley were already in the field, it contrasted itself with the competition in the following terms:

In announcing a complete history of the War in one volume, the first impression will be that it will be an abridged work. This is an error, as we will show by comparison: A full page of Kettell's history, taking the average of type, contains 600 words per page; we will furnish at least 750 pages of reading. Headley's history contains, full page, 320 words; 750 pages of Kettell's will be equal to 1400 pages of Headley; his first volume has only 476 pages of reading matter, therefore Kettell's is nearly equal to three volumes of Headley, which is now selling at $4.00 per volume.

Abbott's has more reading per volume than Headley's but nearly one half is devoted to political topics; in the first 106 pages there is equal to 28 pages of quotations from newspapers, speeches of politicians, etc., on the Slavery question.

The first volume of Greeley's is almost wholly devoted to political history as it closes with the description of the battle of Ball's Bluff, just at the opening of the war. Allowing the second volume of the three works named to contain the same amount of reading as the first, Kettell's will contain one-third more reading than Headley's and deducting political matter, will contain as much as Abbott's, and nearly or quite as much as Greeley's. Headley is now selling at $8.00 the two volumes, Greeley's $10.00, we think, Abbott $8.00.[39]

Given the crudity of this history-by-the-pound approach, perhaps it was not surprising that Kettell and his publisher did not plan to garner prepublication "testimonials" for their history. "We cannot afford time," the publisher announced, "to send the work to the leading literary men of the country." But, the publisher reassured would-be subscribers, "the reputation of Mr. Kettell" would "satisfy the most incredulous as to his literary ability." Despite the apparent absurdity of this sales approach, Kettell's work sold extremely well: by 1870 the *Nation* reported that "Kettell's 'Rebellion,' a work we hear of for the first time," had sold 120,000 copies. It is quite possible that the publisher's emphasis on price was a savvy selling point for an audience unwilling to spend more money for Abbott's or Greeley's work.[40]

No Southern publisher was equipped to produce and market subscription histories similar to those that saturated Northern popular literary culture during the war. But the Richmond firm West and Johnston did publish two wartime volumes—the only histories of their kind in the Confederacy—by the journalist Edward A. Pollard, a member of the editorial staff of the *Richmond Examiner*. His 1862 *The First Year of the War*, followed in 1863 by *The Second Year of the War*, revealed some similarities in style and sensibility with Northern subscription histories. Published at a time of literary ambition and relative prosperity in the Confederacy, his volumes clearly attempted to follow the style of Northern histories by including a few interleaved engraved portraits of Confederate leaders and generals. At the same time, Pollard, like John S. C. Abbott before him, offered a spirited defense of writing a history of the war in wartime. Although he admitted the "futility of attempting high order of historical composition in the treatment of recent and incomplete events," he nevertheless argued that "it does not follow that the contemporary annal, the popular narrative, and other inferior degrees of history, can have no value and interest. The vulgar notion of history," Pollard said, is "that it is a record intended for posterity." But Pollard's rationale for writing history in wartime ultimately differed from that of Abbott, who had argued primarily for the greater accuracy of contemporary depictions of war. Pollard instead argued for the nationalistic aims of such literature, contending that "history has an office to perform in the present, and that one of the greatest values of contempoary annals is to vindicate in good time to the world the fame and reputation of nations."[41]

Pollard was a controversial figure, for while he claimed the importance of wartime history as a way of "vindicating the principles of a great contest to the contemporary world," he did not offer a politics of loyalty to the Confederate government in his account. Instead, following the lead of *Richmond Examiner* editor John Moncure Daniel, he harshly criticized the administration of Jefferson Davis. In a revised edition of his *The First Year of the War*, Pollard took on critics of this approach, attacking those "persons so childish and contemptibly ignorant as to have decried his work on the ground that it has exposed abuses in our administration and faults in our people." There are "ignoramuses in the Southern Confederacy who think it necessary in this war that all the books and newspapers in the country should publish everything in the South in *couleur de rose;* drunken patriots, cowards in epaulets, crippled toadies, and men living on the charity of Jefferson Davis." These people "damn all newspapers and publications in the South for pointing out abuses in places of authority, for the sage reason that knowledge of these abuses will comfort the enemy and tickle the ears of the Yankees." Such critics "would make a virtue of falsehood; they would destroy the independence of all published thought in the country," Pollard charged. He concluded that he "spits upon the criticisms of such creatures." [42]

Yet Pollard's critics may have been right that his criticisms would "tickle the ears of the Yankees." Republished in the North and advertised as a curiosity, Pollard's "Rebel History of the War" attracted attention as "the only formal attempt yet made to narrate the history of the war from a Southern point of view." But *Harper's Monthly* concentrated entirely on Pollard's criticisms of Davis's government in its brief notice of the book, including Pollard's colorful assertion that Davis's cabinet members were "intellectual pygmies." [43]

Pollard's *The Second Year of the War,* published in 1863, closed with a defiant reassertion of Southern independence that characterized "mobocratic Yankees" as "savages who have taken upon their souls the curse of fratricidal blood." "Any contact, friendly or indifferent, with the Yankee, since the display of his vices, would be painful to a free and enlightened people," he claimed. Yet such proud assertion of independence could not overcome the wartime difficulties of Southern publishers. Ironically enough, rather than publishing his *The Third Year of the War* in the South, Pollard published it, along with a final volume titled *The Last Year of the War,* in New York after the close of the conflict in 1865. In the uncertain world of Southern publishing late in the war, no other Southern history emerged as a competitor, or even companion, to Pollard's work, although numerous local publishers produced accounts of individual campaigns and battles. In 1866 Pollard himself turned to subscription publishing with *The Lost Cause: A New Southern History of the War of the Confederates,* a volume published by E. B. Treat of New York. [44]

If Northern subscription histories held the field during the war, they did not all achieve success. One popular historian in particular, wedded to painstaking practices of writing history that had stood him well in the antebellum period, failed to meet the new wartime demands of a speeded-up commercial culture. Yet when Philadelphia publisher G. W. Childs turned to Benson J. Lossing in early 1862 to write a pictorial history of the war, he turned to a proven and popular writer whose combined skills as artist, engraver, and author seemed to promise success—particularly because of the public's intense interest in illustrations of the war. In contracting with Lossing, Childs clearly hoped to repeat the earlier success of Lossing's *The Pictorial Field-Book of the Revolution* (1850–52), a narrative "sketchbook" originally published with Harper and Brothers. For that work Lossing had visited historic sites of the Revolution in order to sketch the "relics" of that war and "snatch their lineaments from the grasp of Decay before it should be too late." Lossing had hoped that a record of his "pilgrimage" would attract an audience "who could not be otherwise decoyed into the apparently arid and flowerless domains of mere history." He succeeded so well in that endeavor that by the eve of the Civil War he was widely called a "popular historian"; not only did he self-consciously write for "our whole population," including the "humble ones," but he was read widely as well in the pages of *Harper's Monthly*.[45]

Childs had good reason, then, to hope that he had achieved a publishing coup by contracting with Lossing. He trumpeted "Lossing's Pictorial History of the Great Rebellion" in April 1862 as "the very thing required by the popular taste of the present day" and included in his announcement one of many "testimonials" he had obtained from leading men in support of the work—a standard mid-nineteenth-century publishing practice to establish the importance and salability of a book. Edward Everett, for instance, said he had "examined with interest and pleasure, the prospectus of the 'PICTORIAL HISTORY OF THE GREAT REBELLION'" and affirmed that "Mr. Lossing's diligence in exploring the localities which he describes, his fidelity and accuracy as a historian, and the spirit of his illustrations, are too well known, from his volumes which are already before the public, to need any recommendation."[46]

However, there were two major obstacles in the way of Lossing's success: the war itself, and Lossing's own plan "to go to every place of interest" and to "make sketches" and "confer with civil and military officers and people." An antiquarian who created a romantic, Walter Scott–like sense of history in his works, Lossing's approach to history was to transform sites of battle into sacred sites of memory; his engravings aestheticized and gave visual texture to the landscape of war. But the war made Lossing's approach unpredictable, at best: a week after Gettysburg, for instance, he wrote to his wife that "we found it impossible to get to the battle-field from Harrisburgh without submitting to the most outrageous extortion, and even by such submission the *time* in which we might accomplish it" was at best "uncertain"; ultimately he was forced to leave his sketching of Gettysburg for a later day, after friends and relatives had cleared the wounded and dying from the battlefield. Clearly, producing a ruminative "sketchbook" in wartime was a far different experience from sketching at his leisure as he wandered over the ruins and battlefields of the Revolution.[47]

Lossing's desire to "sketch" and "confer" also meant that he would require a large amount of time for his work. At first the issue of time did not concern his publisher particularly. Though other publishers began to announce war histories, in March 1862 Childs reassured his author: "The announcement of Duyckinck [a popular historian] seems tame along side of yours. Virtue [a publisher] has canvassers already in the field & Johnson & Fry [Duyckinck's publisher] are getting ready to run them. We must be willing to bide our time. I shall leave no stone unturned as far as I am concerned."[48]

Soon, however, some nervousness about the competition edged into Childs's letters: "I regret that the Harpers intend getting up a rehash of their paper," he wrote to Lossing in April 1862. "I am working away like a beaver on it, and if we were ready I could put on 500 agents."[49]

By July 1862 Childs had a new plan for beating the burgeoning competition: "Let us get up a strong pamphlet, a stunner, and I will print thousands of them and we will keep actively and efficiently circulating them, so that the good people will be on the constant look out for the great work, and consequently will not be likely to purchase the crude and imperfect works rushed out," Childs said. "It will be our policy to be very indefinite as to *when* our work is to be published, for it may injure us if they think it will be a very long time. I will keep on agitating it constantly and keep the market open for it."[50]

In December 1862 he continued his nervous encouragement of his author: "What a field you will have for your book. You were right in deferring its publication. Others are crowding the market but it will remain for yours to become the universal and popular work. I am glad I am your publisher as I feel I can appreciate your labors." But by April 1863 it was becoming clear that Lossing's work might not be the "universal and popular work." "War literature is all the rage now," Childs wrote. "The meanest of the 'Histories of the Rebellion' are having large sales. It is really astonishing how little our people know, & it is singular that they should purchase these trashy works." Another correspondent, the Reverend Thomas B. Fairchild, warned Lossing, "I fear you are delaying your work on the rebellion to a late day. Abbott's book has been distributed in this region & I suppose elsewhere & as it is a large work I fear you will find it in your way." [51]

By July 1863 Childs had decided on a new strategy, announcing that Lossing had never intended to publish his war history during the war itself: "Mr. Lossing resolved at the beginning (and we think wisely) not to attempt to write the History of the Great Rebellion until the war should cease, and men and events should take their proper places in relation to each other." Still, despite this public face, a few months later Childs plaintively commented to his author, "Oh if we only had your great work; I am daily importuned for it from all quarters." [52]

Lossing's approach, however, could not allow a quick treatment of the war; if anything, he became more and more deeply immersed in its unfolding events, more and more determined to be a witness not just to battlefields but to battles themselves. In December 1864 he went to Fortress Monroe, where General Benjamin Butler received him "most cordially" and then made what seemed to Lossing an extraordinary offer. As Lossing reported to his wife, Butler asked, " 'Did you ever see a naval fight?' I answered no. 'You ought to,' " he said, " 'for you cannot fitly describe what you never saw. No man can. If you will go with me I promise a view of a bombardment to which that of Copenhagen will afford no parallel.' " [53]

Lossing could not refuse; he wrote to his wife with excitement that it would delay his return home but that "if this shall end in seeing one of the most sublime sights that man can produce—namely an attack, by a navy bearing 470 heavy guns! how well I shall be repaid!" Five days later his wish was granted: "I have seen a spectacle, my beloved, vouchsafed to few men," he wrote solemnly to his wife. "That spectacle was the bombardment of Fort Fisher," which had lasted for seven hours on Christmas Day. "Our vessel (Gen. Butler's head quarters) was so near that we saw several shots fall in the water not far from us." He reflected, "My experience since I left home, has been of the most varied, wonderful and instructive kind. I have been employed, *every hour*, in the business on which I have come." [54]

Such experience no doubt deepened Lossing's sense of his "great work" —a history clearly to be framed by a vision of war as "sublime," as a glorious aesthetic "spectacle"—but it did not produce a publishable history in wartime. As an old-fashioned empiricist who collected relics and keepsakes, as an artist bent on absorbing the "atmosphere" of war firsthand,

Lossing was overwhelmed by war's details, immersed in its documents; he could not possibly rapidly produce a history of the war.

Lossing's approach to the Emancipation Proclamation is indicative of his antiquarian style. In his finished work he, like Abbott and Greeley, celebrated the proclamation: it "was one of the most important public documents ever issued by the hand of man." But rather than dwelling verbally on its political or social impact, as Abbott and Greeley had done in lesser or greater detail, Lossing carefully reproduced a facsimile of the written proclamation, as well as a facsimile of the pen with which it was written. Below the engraving of the pen Lossing informed his readers, "It is a steel pen, known as the 'Washington,' with a common cedar handle—all as plain and unostentatious as the President himself." [55]

Given Lossing's intent to provide both a written and visual record of the war, and given this level of attention to the "artifacts" of war, it is not surprising that his first volume did not appear until 1866. By 1868, the year his second volume appeared, G. W. Childs had bowed out of the project, and the subscription publisher T. Belknap of Hartford had taken over. By then Lossing had "made a journey of several thousand miles in visiting the historical localities within the bounds of the Confederacy, observing the topography of battle-fields and the region of the movements of the great armies, making sketches, conversing with actors in the scenes, procuring documents, and in every possible way gathering valuable material for the work." In "this and kindred labor," Lossing confessed, "months were consumed, and the delay in the appearance of the second volume was the consequence." [56]

Lossing's approach reminds us that there were a number of different methodologies employed by popular historians, in addition to differing styles of expression or political beliefs. In the case of Lossing, his unwillingess to recycle newspaper accounts of the war, as many of his competitors did, meant that he was out of sync with the dynamics of a wartime marketplace that stressed immediacy and speed of production.

• • •

By 1865 the dominance of the popular historians within the wartime marketplace began to draw critical notice, some of it scathing. In January 1865, for instance, E. L. Godkin launched a series of attacks on John S. C. Abbott in letters to friends and in the pages of the *Nation*. Writing to Charles Eliot Norton, editor of the *North American Review*, Godkin explained, "I single out Abbott for special hostility not because I think he himself or his books worth half a page, but because his 'histories' are fair specimens of a kind of literature of which there is an immense quantity issued every year, and which the half-educated look on as 'solid reading.'" An "enormous number of respectable people," Godkin complained, thought "his history of the rebellion" a "solid" work; it was "sickening to see him treated in the newspapers with great deference as 'Abbott the historian.'" Continuing his attack in a November 1865 *Nation* article titled "History by the Yard," Godkin called Abbott an example of "misemployed incapacity" and said he was determined to "exhibit the viciousness of that disposition which tosses off a book as lightly as a child a soap-bubble, with equal amusement to itself and equal indifference to the consequences." Among the "contractors for this kind of shoddy," Godkin said, "it is not surprising to find Mr. John S. C. Abbott busy and prominent." [57]

Godkin, like a number of authors during the Civil War, thought that the "real" history of the war could not be written in wartime. "We do not, and shall not for long years, know all the facts," Godkin said. "We cannot yet distinguish the pretended from the real." John Lothrop Motley agreed that "it should be left to another generation to *write* the history. It is for our generation to *make* the history, & to make it so thoroughly, that our successors will be proud to write it." Such authors shared a view of history writing that had originated in the 1830s and 1840s, a time when the discipline of history had achieved both unparalleled prestige and popularity through the writings of Motley, Prescott, and especially Bancroft, the preeminent historian of epic romanticism. For Bancroft in particular, educated in Germany and strongly influenced by German traditions of romantic nationalism, history was a literary art whose tools included inspiration and intuition. Historians possessed, according to Bancroft, "not merely the senses opening to us the eternal" but also "an eternal sense, which places us in connection with the world of intelligence and the decrees of God." Bancroft's romantic view of the importance of the individual historian was complemented by his epic view of the nature of history, which he saw as composed of eternal, providential truths and heroic individual action.[58]

Such a view contrasted strongly with the approach of popular historians, who also achieved widespread recognition within the burgeoning literary marketplace of the 1840s. Lossing, for instance, who published a number of books in the late 1840s and 1850s, created synopses in which "we freely appropriated to our use the fruits of the labors of others." His aim was both democratic and pragmatic: indeed, he explicitly connected the democratization of culture with price, as he hoped to "condense facts into the space of a volume so small, that the price of it would make it accessible to our whole population. It is the mission of true patriotism to scatter the seeds of knowledge amid those in the humbler walks of society," he concluded.[59]

A critic such as Godkin strongly objected to the pragmatic approach of popular historians and their subscription publishers, who tended to submerge the individual identity of the artist in the identity of the product they offered. Thus it is not surprising that Godkin compared subscription publishers negatively to the "regular trade." The "requirements of the subscription business are such," he commented in the *Nation*, "that it is generally impossible" for an author "to do his best or anything like his best." Godkin found five "elements of success" for an original subscription work: first, "it must be timely—the subject of a biography, for instance, is hardly cold underground before the biographer has contracted to deliver twenty or thirty pages of copy per diem until the life is written." Second, Godkin said, such a work "must be 'popular,' and that is a sufficient reason, besides haste, why it cannot be first-rate." Third, "it must be bulky"; fourth, "it must be flashily bound"; and fifth, "it must be high-priced, or else it will never give support to canvassers, whose commissions amount to 50 or 60 per cent." Finally, Godkin concluded that the subscription publishing business "depends for its prosperity on the want of literary discrimination and practical knowledge of books of the people of the rural districts, and on American good-nature, which cannot withstand the appeal *ad misericordiam* of a subscription agent in the guise of a one-legged soldier, a widow, a young lady supporting her only mother, or a superannuated clergyman."[60]

As Godkin's comments suggested, the immediate postwar period saw a continued boom in the business of selling subscription histories of the war. Indeed, as Godkin had sarcastically indicated, the war provided not only the subject for subscription histories but also salesmen for these works. It was true that a number of veterans became book agents immediately after the war, with some subscription firms advertising directly for this group even before the war ended. A February 1865 ad in the *Cincinnati Commercial Gazette*, for instance, called for "book agents" to "sell by subscription with sample, excellent popular illustrated family works, just adapted to the times." Among these, the ad said, "is a low price History of the Rebellion, of which 50,000 of vol. 1 have already been sold. It is a good business for ex-soldiers and others out of employment."[61]

Godkin was right, too, that a number of women became book agents after the war. Annie Nelles, who in 1868 published a memoir (by subscription, of course) of her life as a book agent in the Midwest, remembered that in Indianapolis she had very little luck selling subscription books, the "citizens of Indianapolis" already being "too well supplied with literature of the class I was selling." Instead, "it was necessary for me to have something else—something which had not been already sold there; and at the same time I was sufficiently aware of the state of the public mind, to know that something connected with the late rebellion would sell better than anything else." Nelles chose to canvass with " 'The Lost Cause,' a Southern history of the war, by Mr. Pollard, late editor of the 'Richmond Examiner.' " In "about two weeks," she boasted, she and a fellow agent sold "no less than fifty copies," and "my profits from that source alone were about fifty dollars."[62]

• • •

The meanings popular war histories held for their audiences are tantalizingly unrecoverable. If we imagine ourselves, for instance, as witnesses to the moment when the subscription canvasser pulled out his "mesmerizing" list for a rural customer, or if we imagine the rural book buyer on the evening after a heavy volume had finally been delivered and paid for, we enter a realm of speculation. Did such rural customers actually read these volumes? Or did these histories instead reside on parlor tables for display only? Did book buyers buy these volumes as an impulse of patriotism, or did they agree to subscribe only because their neighbors did, as subscription publishers privately indicated to their canvassing agents?

The fact of the tremendous success of the wartime histories remains the most telling evidence we have in attempting to answer these questions. Numerous trade book publishers could attest to the public's enormous interest in literature pertaining to the war; thus, though it may be true that rural customers bought these books because their neighbors did, the larger point is that they and their neighbors shared an intense interest in the war that could be expressed through possessing a history of it. Books acted as emblems of patriotism as well as sources of knowledge. As items that depicted national affairs and yet were sold in intimate, face-to-face encounters at the local level, they provided a compelling link between the local and the national. They also provided a connection between an uncertain present and an imagined future, creating a gilded and engraved object of memory out of the chaos of conflict.

EPILOGUE

So we may, in a certain sense, call this whole war of freedom an acted poem, and find a melody of some divine ode in each of its unnumbered deeds of heroism and self-sacrifice.
—*Oliver Wendell Holmes, "The Poetry of the War," 1865*

Just as the Civil War was what Lincoln called "a People's contest" involving an entire society, so too it was a people's literary war. Not only did ordinary citizens create a popular literary war in countless poems during the conflict, but numerous writers and publishers, established and fledgling, produced a wide variety of literature for a diverse and widespread reading public. This popular literary war was not just a war of soldiers or politicians: it was a war that also reached out to women, children, city dwellers, farm inhabitants, people traveling on the railway "cars," those who waited for war news at home. It not only invited a diverse spectrum of ordinary people to imagine themselves as part of the conflict but often portrayed ordinary people as active participants in the war. In doing so, it democratized the conflict, but only within a set of constraints related to the conventions of commercial literary culture, including constraints regarding representations of race and gender.[1]

The sense that war had created an inexhaustible supply of stories, that there were innumerable "incidents and anecdotes" of the war to be collected and told, energized popular literature both during and after the conflict. This understanding of the storied abundance of the war was one of the chief legacies of popular Civil War literature. No other war in American history has had this profound sense of narrativity associated with it, centered around the abiding faith that every individual experience of the war was not only worthy of but demanded representation. Today that narrativity continues to find outlet not just in popular literature, film, and television but also in the nationwide movement of reenactors, who imagine themselves as individual participants in the war, both part of the war's myriad stories and the creators of new war stories of their own.[2]

Some forms of war-related popular literature had lasting impact in the postwar period. Material testimony to the long-lived impact of subscription histories of the war can be found, for instance, in an inscribed copy of E. A. Duyckinck's *History of the War for the Union*, first published in 1862. In 1885, some twenty-three years later, Harry Bailey Otis received a copy of this history "from his affectionate Parents on his Sixteenth birthday," with the additional motto and piece of advice "Be true to your country." Given that few histories of the war were published between the end of the war and 1885, it is fair to assume that within the parlors of hundreds of thousands of homes in small-town America, the print memory of the war remained that provided by the wartime subscription historians.[3]

The adventurous, individualized war celebrated in both sensational and juvenile literature also had lasting impact in the late nineteenth century. Several publishers republished dime war novels after the war, creating new audiences for this literature. Wartime juveniles were also republished in the postwar period, creating a profound link between an ethos of adventure and the history of the war. The reminiscences of one admirer of Harry Castlemon's works, for instance, provide us with a strong sense of the continuing popularity of his war novels in the 1880s. Franklin P. Adams recalled, "One Christmas morning in the late Eighties I found, under the tree, three brown-covered, gold-lettered volumes. I finished reading 'Frank on a Gunboat' before dark. You whose grandfathers may have told you about the Civil War," Adams recounted, "don't realize that we who were children in the Eighties got first-hand information about battles from participants; and 'Frank Before Vicksburg' and 'Frank on the Lower Mississippi' were wonderful. They were Adventure and they were History."[4]

Not all forms of Civil War literature, however, had lasting impact in the postwar period. Ideas of *whose* war it was changed dramatically over the late nineteenth century. The conditioned inclusivity that had characterized the Civil War years gave way to a more narrow sense of ownership in the war, one firmly bounded by both race and gender.

At first, in the immediate postwar period, remembering and celebrating the war continued to be an important project for a diverse group of publishers and writers. Beadle and Company, for instance, published a continued outpouring of sensational war novels in the months after the war ended. Benson J. Lossing published the first volume of his three-volume

Pictorial History of the Civil War in the United States of America in 1866. In 1867 two omnibus volumes, Linus P. Brockett and Mary C. Vaughan's *Woman's Work in the Civil War: A Record of Heroism, Patriotism, and Patience* and Frank Moore's *Women of the War: Their Heroism and Self-Sacrifice*, celebrated women's contributions to the war effort. And Southern writers turned to Northern publishers again: E. A. Pollard published his *The Third Year of the War* in 1865, and William Gilmore Simms published his *War Poetry of the South* in 1866. This was just a sampling of the diversity of war literature published in the postwar period, augmented in the North by numerous volumes of tribute to Lincoln in the wake of his assassination.[5]

During the late 1860s and early 1870s, then, a continuing stream of war-related publications appeared within commercial literary culture, but in the mid- to late 1870s interest in all aspects of the war waned dramatically. There had been signs of this war weariness as early as 1866: a Cincinnati ad for canvassers of nonwar subscription books, for instance, claimed that people were "tired of being importuned to buy various Histories of the War, Life of Lincoln, Grant and Sherman." But it was in the 1870s that this diminished interest in the war became obvious. *Harper's Weekly*, which had published well over one hundred Civil War stories during and immediately after the war and which continued to advertise a readership of more than one hundred thousand, published only two Civil War stories during the entire decade of the 1870s. As Sanitary Commission leader Mary Livermore remembered, in the postwar period people "turned with relief to the employments of peaceful life, eager to forget the fearful years of battle and carnage." James Henry Harper of Harper and Brothers noted that "the public was tired of reading about the war, which had been the all-absorbing subject for four years, and other important topics now demanded their attention." The pages of *Harper's Weekly* were filled with articles about war in Europe, Tammany Hall scandals, and the reconstruction of black life in the South. But the Civil War itself as a topic rarely intruded in its pages.[6]

In the 1880s and 1890s, however, there was a resurgence of interest in the war, as shown by the stunning growth of the Grand Army of the Republic (GAR). Membership in this Civil War veterans' organization rose dramatically in this period: from 30,000 in 1878 to 146,000 in 1883; to 233,000 in 1884; and to 320,000 in 1887. It reached a high-water mark at 428,000 members in 1890. Increasingly the GAR dominated memorialization of the war throughout the North, especially in public parades of veterans in annual Decoration Day (later Memorial Day) ceremonies. Local "posts" of the GAR also sponsored the publication of numerous regimental histories. Organizing itself on a military model with camping, drilling, and parading in uniforms as major activities, the GAR signaled a military revival that also addressed the generational concerns of veterans: it "licensed veterans to employ their positive memories of the war in compensation for the insufficiencies of their civilian lives." [7]

In the 1880s and 1890s, too, new popular magazines emerged that not only responded to revived interest in the war but helped to increase that interest. Foremost among these was the *Century* magazine, begun in 1881, which published its famous "Battles and Leaders of the Civil War" series from November 1884 until November 1887. This extensive series, envisioned as articles "by the men who directed the battles of the Civil War" and which included contributions from Generals Grant, McClellan, Beauregard, Longstreet, and Hill, among many others, was an immediate hit with readers, and by the second year of the series, monthly circulation of the magazine "had increased from 127,000 to 225,000," almost double the circulation of *Harper's Weekly*. The series soon expanded to cover a wide range of topics related to the war. [8]

Both the growth of the GAR and the popularity of the "Battles and Leaders" series signaled important shifts in representations of the war. First and foremost was a new reconceptualization of the war as primarily a military event rather than a larger social event involving entire societies both north and south. By the late 1880s and 1890s, a new veteran-oriented war literature asserted that the central meaning of the war was the shared bravery of white Union and Confederate veterans, thereby contributing to the political and cultural project of national reconciliation and reunion. As the *Century* magazine commented in an 1889 article titled "Soldiers' Memorial Services," "Upon the common ground of honoring the brave, the Union and Confederate veterans unite to offer tribute to departed valor." Likewise, *Harper's Weekly*'s 1888 "Decoration Day" illustration portrayed a wounded Yankee and Confederate, both ordinary soldiers, embracing on a monument inscribed "To the Nation's Dead Heroes," and the *Weekly*'s 1896 Decoration Day illustration showed "The Blue and the Gray" chatting amicably "at Appomattox after General Lee's Surrender." The culmination of this Memorial Day emphasis on reunion among white veterans came in the *Weekly*'s poem "Memorial Day: May 30, 1899," which linked the Civil War and Spanish-American War by claiming: "On Santiago summits we unite / The grizzled foes of Chickamauga's day; / The hatreds of a Shiloh sink from sight / Beneath the waters of Manila Bay." [9]

Theodore Roosevelt elaborated on this theme in a 1901 address titled

"Brotherhood and the Heroic Virtues" delivered before a Vermont veterans' reunion. "At the opening of this new century," Roosevelt said, "all of us, the children of a reunited country, have a right to glory in the countless deeds of valor done alike by the men of the North and the men of the South." Such tribute was hardly racially innocent, as David Blight and Kirk Savage, among others, have pointed out. Rather, the memory of the Civil War as the shared bravery of white soldiers was used to underwrite ideas of the nation as a whites-only brotherhood, ideas that received stunning fictional expression first in Thomas Dixon's 1905 novel *The Clansman* and then in D. W. Griffith's 1915 film based on that novel, *Birth of a Nation*.[10]

The idea of the war as a whites-only brotherhood served to masculinize and racialize the memory of the war in the pages of popular literature in more sharply drawn ways than had been true during the 1860s. At the time of the war, as well as in the immediate postwar period, the idea of sacrifice for the nation as a central meaning of the war had been available to both white men and women—and, after 1862, to black soldiers as well. In the 1880s and 1890s, however, commentators and writers increasingly attached the idea of Civil War sacrifice for the nation to white men only, thus gendering and racializing the memory of the war in a new way.[11]

A new boys' war fiction also began to contribute to this emphasis on white reconciliation in popular war literature. In 1888 the prolific Oliver Optic (William Taylor Adams), responding to the renewed interest in the war, decided to publish a new series of war stories. Although he commented with pride that his previous war stories, including *Soldier Boy* and *Sailor Boy*, remained "as much in demand to-day as any of his other stories," he also noted that recently the "call upon him to use the topics of the war" had been "so urgent" that he "could not resist." Optic hoped that his new series of Civil War books for boys, "The Blue and the Gray Series," would "do more ample justice than perhaps was done before to those 'who fought on the other side.'" Optic included scenes in his new novels in which white Union and Confederate officers offered each other tributes of admiration. He acknowledged that there were both ideological and market-driven reasons for this shift in the meaning of the war. "From their nature," Optic commented about his Union-centered Civil War–era books, "the field of their circulation" had been "more limited."[12]

While much Civil War literature focused on the shared bravery of Confederate and Union soldiers, some fiction also began to express nostalgia for slaveholding society and the institution of slavery itself. During the 1880s and 1890s, "plantation stories" by Thomas Nelson Page, Joel

Chandler Harris, Maurice Thompson, and others became a staple of popular magazines, inventing a world in which the relations between slave and master, or between former slave and planter, were affectionate and untroubled. New war fictions by Constance Fenimore Woolson, Maurice Thompson, Thomas Nelson Page, Constance Cary Harrison, and Virginia Boyle Frazer, among others, featured white Southern heroines—an imaginative process that would ultimately culminate in Margaret Mitchell's creation of Scarlett O'Hara, still seen by many as the consummate Civil War heroine. Far from this nostalgia being confined to the South, it was expressed in the most popular national magazines of the 1880s and 1890s, including *Century* and *McClure's*, both published in New York. Ironically, then, it was Northern magazines and books that eventually became the mouthpieces for the Southern literary nationality that Southerners during the war had so desperately wanted to create.[13]

As these shifts in popular literary culture remind us, memories of wars are far from static or permanent. During the 1880s and 1890s a significant reinvention of the war took shape, as various writers "reclaimed a past of their own creation," to use Tony Horwitz's phrase. Numerous articles and illustrations in popular magazines discussed the military aspects of the war, but only rarely did popular literature discuss the active roles of African Americans in obtaining and fighting for their freedom or the wartime roles of Northern women. With the exception of Louisa May Alcott's 1868 girls' novel *Little Women*, popular literature rarely explored Northern women's or girls' experiences on the home front. Nor did new novels emerge to explore wartime black male heroism—making the tentative steps in that direction taken by John Townsend Trowbridge's *Cudjo's Cave* and Epes Sargent's *Peculiar* during the war seem more radical than they might have otherwise. Frances Ellen Watkins Harper's *Iola Leroy*, with its exploration of a black woman's experiences during the war, was a substantial exception to the general rule. For the most part, however, the "people's contest" was more and more narrowly defined to include only white men and Southern white women.[14]

Ideas of what constituted the "experience of war" also narrowed. A new emphasis on the "real" or "actual" experience of battle marked the evolving Civil War literature of the 1890s, part of a new "cult of experience" that permeated American culture in this decade and that was clearly marked as a white masculinist ethos excluding both women and African Americans. As Gerald Linderman has written, "Participation in war became an important mark of merit. Honor attached itself less to courageous or cowardly conduct, battles won or lost, causes preserved or destroyed than to one's simple presence in the war." Whereas during the war Northern women's experiences on the home front or African American soldiers' exploits had been imagined as a form of participation in the war, increasingly only men's experiences in battle counted as the "real" war. Thus it is no accident that Stephen Crane's 1895 best-selling novel *The Red Badge of Courage*, which traced the horrific and confusing battle experiences of Henry Fleming at Chancellorsville, was widely embraced as a realistic accounting of the war. Ironically, Crane himself, born in 1871, not only had not experienced the war firsthand but drew on the *Century's* "Battles and Leaders" series for the historical underpinnings of his work.[15]

Significantly, Crane's novel ended with the assertion that his protagonist had achieved, as a result of his battle experiences, "a quiet manhood, non-assertive but of sturdy and strong blood." Henry Fleming "was a man," the novel repeated within the same paragraph. The imaginative association of the Civil War with a new manhood was stressed by numerous writers in the 1890s, as they returned to the war to find within it the underpinnings of a robust new masculine identity, one that often abandoned earlier attributes of manhood such as self-restraint and "civilized cultivation" in favor of "unrestrained nature" and "athletic virility." At the end of the decade, writers appealed to these new interpretations of the Civil War in order to justify and glorify participation in the Spanish-American War. In his 1899 essay "The Strenuous Life," for instance, Theodore Roosevelt defended American imperialism by invoking an imagined Civil War past, including the "iron in the blood of our fathers, the men who upheld the wisdom of Lincoln, and bore the sword or rifle in the armies of Grant!" He would later extol the "virile virtues" of war in his autobiography.[16]

The new masculinization of the memory of the war dovetailed with the rise of literary realism in this period, both reflecting and reinforcing a newly masculinized literary marketplace. The cult of experience and of a "strenuous life" permeated the pages of a wide range of realist literature at the turn of the century, from the stories of Stephen Crane to the writings of Jack London and Frank Norris. Such writings often deliberately repudiated Victorian "feminized" writing in favor of a new masculinist ethos. Many writers and editors, including some "New Women" writers, affirmed the new masculinist ethos of realism, sometimes explicitly disavowing earlier sentimental and domestic norms. Willa Cather, for instance, expressed disgust with women who had "scorn for the healthy commonplace." "I have not much faith in women in fiction," she wrote in

1895. "When a woman writes a story of adventure, a stout sea tale, a manly battle yarn, then I will begin to hope for something great from them, not before." [17]

Ironically, our popular memories of the Civil War in many respects still match the contours of this late-nineteenth-century masculinized culture. While it was in the 1880s and 1890s that the masculinization of the war's memory was filtered through the new precepts of realism, it was in the twentieth century that such masculinization achieved not just ascendancy but also an astonishing longevity when realism itself became a canonical part of American literary culture. "There was no real literature of our Civil War," Ernest Hemingway said in 1942, "until Stephen Crane wrote 'The Red Badge of Courage.'" Today, as James McPherson has commented, "the huge Civil War constituency that exists outside the ranks of professional historians and the halls of academe" remains interested "mainly if not exclusively in campaigns and battles." Crane's *Red Badge of Courage* is still often celebrated as the first "realistic" depiction of the war because it portrayed the horrific confusions of the battlefield. Yet it can equally be argued that Crane's novel was a new invention of an all-masculine world of war that said far more about the changing social, cultural, and literary climate of the 1890s than about the "real" war of the 1860s.[18]

That "other" real war included not only soldiers but also the men, women, and children who constituted a "People's contest." It occurred on the home front as well as on the battlefield. And it included a complex, variegated popular literature that was itself a part of the war experience, not separate from it. In that literature, with its sometimes heartfelt, sometimes calculating reactions to the war, we find all the contradictions of a war that occurred within a burgeoning commercial democracy.

NOTES

INTRODUCTION

1. Whitman, *Specimen Days*, as quoted in Masur, *"Real War Will Never Get in the Books,"* 281. Aaron, *Unwritten War*. As Louis P. Masur has pointed out, as early as 1867 William Dean Howells commented that the war "has laid upon our literature a charge under which it has hitherto staggered very lamely." Masur, *"Real War Will Never Get in the Books,"* vii. Wilson, *Patriotic Gore*, ix.

2. For the use of the term "imagined community," see Anderson, *Imagined Communities*. Scholars have only recently turned to the popular culture of the war. See Diffley, *Where My Heart Is Turning Ever*; Sweet, *Traces of War*; and Cullen, *Civil War in Popular Culture*. See also Joyce Appleby's pioneering essay on popular Civil War literature, "Reconciliation and the Northern Novelist." For studies on popular culture more generally, see especially Lott, *Love and Theft*; Lipsitz, *Time Passages*; and Mukerji and Schudson, *Rethinking Popular Culture*.

3. Aaron, *Unwritten War*, xviii.

4. The foremost among studies of elite literature is Fredrickson, *Inner Civil War*. The best literary histories of the war remain Aaron, *Unwritten War*, and Wilson, *Patriotic Gore*. A compelling recent anthology of Civil War literature is Masur, *"Real War Will Never Get in the Books."* On the development of the high-low dichotomy, see especially Levine, *Highbrow/Lowbrow*. For the twentieth century, see Rubin, *Making of Middlebrow Culture*.

5. On Alcott's publication of "thrillers," see Stern, *Behind a Mask*. George William Curtis to Charles Eliot Norton, April 26, 1865, Charles Eliot Norton Papers, Houghton Library, Harvard University (hereafter cited as Houghton Library). *Magnolia Weekly*, April 11, 1863, 129.

6. *Magnolia Weekly*, April 11, 1863, 129. The weekly African American newspaper the *New York Anglo-African* included both poetry and fiction during the war, including a reprinting of Martin Delany's antebellum novel *Blake: Or the Huts of America*. Unfortunately, as James M. McPherson first pointed out in *The Negro's Civil War*, most issues after April 1862 are not extant, depriving scholars of a potentially rich resource of African American literature during the war. For more on the *Anglo-African* and on black publications during the war more generally, see McPherson, *Negro's Civil War*, esp. 345–49. See also the San Francisco

African American weekly newspaper the *Pacific Appeal*, begun in 1862, which published a number of poems in response to the war and the politics of emancipation. Of particular interest is poetry by James Madison Bell from the *Appeal* included in the *Black Abolitionist Papers, 1830–1865* (Sanford, N.C.: Microfilming Corp. of America, 1981).

7. Smith, *Urban Disorder and the Shape of Belief*, 1. Cmiel, *Democratic Eloquence*. On Southern white women's participation in this culture during the war, see Faust, *Mothers of Invention*.

8. In its conception of commercial literary culture this study is dependent on the work of a large group scholars working within the history of American print culture, including Brodhead, *Cultures of Letters*; Davidson, *Revolution and the Word*; Davidson, *Reading in America*; Gilmore, *Reading Becomes a Necessity of Life*; Greenspan, *Walt Whitman and the American Reader*; Gross, *Printing, Politics, and the People*; Hall, *Worlds of Wonder, Days of Judgment*; Kelley, *Private Woman, Public Stage*; Kelley, "Reading Women/Women Reading"; Coultrap-McQuin, *Doing Literary Business*; Nord, *Evangelical Origins of Mass Media in America*; Radway, *Feeling for Books*; Radway, *Reading the Romance*; Reynolds, *Beneath the American Renaissance*; Reynolds, *Walt Whitman's America*; Sedgwick, *Atlantic Monthly, 1857–1909*; Warner, *Letters of the Republic*; Wilson, *Labor of Words*; Zboray, *Fictive People*.

Ten-year-old Grenville Norcross of Massachusetts, for instance, recorded buying a "ten-cent novel" in 1864 "to read in the cars"; Grenville H. Norcross, July 28, 1864, Grenville H. Norcross Journals, American Antiquarian Society, Worcester, Mass. (hereafter cited as American Antiquarian Society). Selling literature on the railroad was not uncommon. Flora Simmons of Rochester, New York, sold her twelve-cent *The Spirit of Washington: Or, McClellan's Vision: A Wonderful Revelation of the Present Rebellion* "on the cars" to support her "aged, infirm mother" in 1863. Simmons, *Spirit of Washington*, "Introductory," n.p. Holmes, "Poetry of the War." William Everett, "Beadle's Dime Books," manuscript, Charles Eliot Norton Papers, Houghton Library.

9. On Southern publishing during the war, see especially Crandall, *Confederate Imprints*; Detlefsen, "Printing in the Confederacy"; Harwell, *Confederate Belles-Lettres*, 13–27; Harwell, *More Confederate Imprints*; Hubbell, *South in American Literature*, esp. 447–61; Moss, *Confederate Broadside Poems*, 1–49; Parrish and Willingham, *Confederate Imprints*, 9–26. "Are We a Literary People," *Southern Punch*, February 27, 1864, 2.

10. See the October 17, 1863, "The Blue Flowers," a reprinting of *Harper's Weekly*'s September 5, 1863, "The Blue Flowers"; the November 7, 1863, "Sybil Miller, or the Wounded Soldier," first published in *Harper's Weekly* as "A Gift by the Wayside"; the July 30, 1864, "The Heart of Miriam Clyde," published under that same title in the February 27, 1864, *Harper's Weekly*; and the November 5, 1864, "Worth a Leg," published under that title in *Harper's Weekly* on October 22, 1864.

11. Virginia F. Townsend, "After the Battle," *Youth's Companion*, January 8, 1863, 5. Agnes Leonard, "After the Battle," in Raymond, *Southland Writers*, 115, 121–24. For contemporary comments on the dispute over "All Quiet on the Poto-

mac," see *Southern Illustrated News,* July 11, 1863, 18. *Magnolia Weekly,* November 7, 1863, 44.

12. Reynolds, *Beneath the American Renaissance,* 7. On the popular literature of the Mexican War, see Johannsen, *To the Halls of the Montezumas,* esp. 175–269.

13. Southern periodicals also used such headings. See "Poems of the War," *Southern Illustrated News,* December 6, 1862, 7. Royster, *Destructive War,* 252.

14. Kirkland, *Pictorial Book of Anecdotes and Incidents,* 7, 8.

15. For Bagby's comments, see "Editor's Table," *Southern Literary Messenger* 33 (September 1861): 237.

16. For reported sales of *Incidents of American Camp Life,* see *Harper's Weekly,* March 12, 1864, 176. This figure must be used with caution, however, as it was announced in an ad by the publisher. For Redpath's publishing career, see Stern, *Imprints on History,* 76–83.

17. On reading, see especially Davidson, *Reading in America,* and Kelley, "Reading Women/Women Reading."

18. As Benedict Anderson has argued, the nation is an "imagined political community" that is "always conceived as a deep, horizontal comradeship." National consciousness—a simultaneous consciousness of shared interests with complete strangers, often at great distances—is made possible, Anderson argues, through the facilitating medium of print culture. It is precisely this imagined "fraternity that makes it possible," he notes, "for so many millions of people, not so much to kill, as willingly to die for such limited imaginings." Anderson, *Imagined Communities,* 6, 7. Faust, *Creation of Confederate Nationalism,* 6.

19. "Notes on Books and Booksellers," *American Literary Gazette and Publishers' Circular,* April 15, 1864, 406.

20. Allan Nevins as quoted in McPherson, introduction to Nevins, *Ordeal of the Union,* 4, vi–vii. Both Nevins's and Fredrickson's works were published during an era in which federal power was tested as it had not been since the Civil War by states' resistance to the civil rights movement. Thus the themes of national organization and national concentration of power were very much a product of a particular moment of American history. More recently, political historians have provided an important corrective to Nevins's emphasis on organization instead of the actions of individuals. James M. McPherson and Eric Foner have separately foregrounded the wartime importance of abolitionists, radical Republicans, and the actions of freedmen themselves. McPherson has pointed out that Nevins not only "depreciated the abolitionists" but also disparaged the "radical Republicans who demanded justice for the freedmen and tried to overcome the very neglect of them" that Nevins condemned. See Nevins, *Ordeal of the Union,* 4, viii. See also Foner, *Reconstruction,* for an emphasis on the importance of the individual actions of freedmen and freedwomen.

21. McConnell, "Reading the Flag," 111.

22. But it was closely related to the literary politics of Mexican War literature. See Johannsen, *To the Halls of the Montezumas.* Popular novels during the Revolutionary period often dealt with the theme of the seduction of virtue. See Davidson, *Revolution and the Word.*

23. Carleton, *My Days and Nights on the Battle-field*, 154.

24. Brooks, *Melodramatic Imagination*. For one example among many of this melodramatic mode, see Rouse, *Bugle Blast*, whose subtitle promised "*Dashing Raids, Heroic Deeds, Thrilling Incidents, Sketches, Anecdotes*," and so on.

25. "A Word of Greeting," *United States Service Magazine* 1 (January 1864): 3. *Round Table*, January 9, 1864, 59.

26. *Round Table*, January 9, 1864, 59; January 23, 1864, 91. One of the authors the *Round Table* complained about vociferously was Henry Morford, who published several long-winded popular novels in wartime including his *Days of Shoddy*. See "Shoddy Literature," *Round Table*, January 23, 1864, 90–91. *Southern Punch*, February 27, 1864, 2; August 22, 1864, 2.

27. Masur, *"Real War Will Never Get in the Books,"* vii–viii. Wilson, *Patriotic Gore*, 474, 487–88. Aaron, *Unwritten War*, xviii.

28. On the Victorian culture of the Civil War era, see especially Rose, *Victorian America and the Civil War*.

CHAPTER ONE

1. Oliver Wendell Holmes, "Bread and the Newspaper," *Atlantic Monthly* 8 (September 1861): 347; Chesnut, *Mary Chesnut's Civil War*, 72.

2. Dannett, *Noble Women of the North*, 45–46.

3. Stone, *Brokenburn*, 14. George William Curtis, "Editor's Easy Chair," *Harper's New Monthly Magazine* 23 (July 1861): 266; (August 1861): 411.

4. Holmes, "Bread and the Newspaper," 347, 348. Chesnut, *Mary Chesnut's Civil War*, 354. Curtis, "Editor's Easy Chair," *Harper's New Monthly Magazine* 23 (August 1861): 411.

5. Holmes, "Bread and the Newspaper," 346, 348; *Southern Monthly* 1 (April 1862): 632. Holmes, "Bread and the Newspaper," 348.

6. *Southern Literary Messenger* 33 (November 1861): 395; *Southern Monthly* 1 (November 1861): 231–32; *American Publishers' Circular and Literary Gazette*, July 20, 1861, 229; Ticknor and Fields, Rough Cost Book, 1860 and 1861, Ticknor and Fields Archives, Houghton Library; Henry Wadsworth Longfellow as quoted in Tryon, *Parnassus Corner*, 252, 253.

7. Tryon, *Parnassus Corner*, 253–54; James Perkins Walker to "Friends," 1866, James Perkins Walker Papers, Firestone Library, Princeton University; *Harper's New Monthly Magazine* 23 (August 1861): 414; Simms, *Letters of William Gilmore Simms*, 4:326.

8. Henry Timrod to Rachel Lyons, September 6, 1861, as quoted in Timrod, *Last Years of Henry Timrod*, 9–10; Alcott, *Selected Letters*, 72.

9. *Manufactures of the United States in 1860*, cxxxii–cxlv; *Richmond Whig*, April 19, 1861. See also the *Southern Literary Messenger* 32 (June 1861): 481, which announced, "We take pleasure in informing our Southern friends that Messrs. Henry L. Pelouze & Co., have established a Type Foundry in Richmond, and are prepared to supply those in want, with printing material generally. Should the

Southern printers give them proper encouragement, we have no doubt that they will, in time, establish a foundry here equal to any in the Northern cities." Parrish and Willingham, *Confederate Imprints*, 12. On printing in wartime, see Detlefson, "Printing in the Confederacy." *Daily Richmond Enquirer*, January 9, 1862; *Southern Literary Companion*, June 15, 1864; advertisement of Burke, Boykin & Co., Macon, Ga., in *Confederate States Almanac* (Macon, 1864), 24, as reprinted in Harwell, *Confederate Belles-Lettres*, 26.

10. At the same time, a smaller reading audience existed in the South than in the North. Approximately 70 percent of the free male population in the South was literate, in contrast to some 90 percent in the more populous North. See Kaser, *Books and Libraries in Camp and Battle*, 3–4.

11. Henry Timrod to Rachel Lyons, December 10, 1861, in Timrod, *Last Years of Henry Timrod*, 10; Stone, *Brokenburn*, 14; Thomas, *Secret Eye*, 188–89.

12. "Editor's Table," *Southern Literary Messenger* 33 (August 1861): 160; *Charleston Courier* as quoted in the *Southern Field and Fireside*, May 18, 1861, 2; *Southern Monthly* 1 (November 1861): 231–32.

13. *New Orleans Delta* as quoted in the *Southern Literary Messenger* 33 (October 1861): 317; *Charleston Courier* as quoted in *Southern Field and Fireside*, May 18, 1861, 2. For more calls for a new Southern literature, see "To the Literati," *Mercury*, April 30, 1864, 4, and "Literature of the South," *Mercury*, June 11, 1864, 6.

14. On antebellum calls for a Southern literature, see Hubbell, *South in American Literature*, 363–66. *New Orleans Delta* as quoted in "Editor's Table," *Southern Literary Messenger* 33 (October 1861): 317–18. Paul Hamilton Hayne reflected on the market realities of Southern popular literary culture in 1864, commenting, "The curse of the South has been, that we have had *no* organized Literary fraternity,—no persons constituting a class, whose labors were worth as much *in the Market*, as those of the Lawyer, Doctor, Merchant, or any other *practical* workmen! Our Periodicals, have all failed, chiefly because they started with no *capital*." See Paul Hamilton Hayne to Clara Dargan, March 27, 1864, Clara Victoria Dargan Maclean Papers, Special Collections Library, Duke University, Durham, N.C.

15. *Southern Monthly* 1 (September 1861): 3; Thomas, *Secret Eye*, 188–89.

16. *Southern Literary Messenger* 33 (August 1861): 160; *Southern Field and Fireside*, May 18, 1861, 2; *Southern Illustrated News*, October 4, 1862, 5; *Charleston Courier* as quoted in *Southern Field and Fireside*, May 18, 1861, 2.

17. *Southern Illustrated News*, September 13, 1862, 5.

18. *Magnolia Weekly*, April 11, 1863, 129; *Southern Monthly* 1 (September 1861): 2; "Editor's Table," *Southern Literary Messenger* 33 (September 1861): 237.

19. "Editor's Table," *Southern Literary Messenger* 33 (September 1861): 237.

20. "The Magnolia Stories," *Magnolia Weekly*, April 11, 1863, 129; "Popular Literature," *Magnolia Weekly*, May 30, 1863, 184.

21. *Southern Monthly* 1 (September 1861): 4.

22. For another example of commentary on Northern depictions of slavery, see *Southern Field and Fireside*, December 15, 1860, 236. In such accounts Southerners rarely acknowledged Northern diversity of opinion concerning slavery or the

stridently antiblack party culture of Northern Democrats. On that party culture, see especially Baker, *Affairs of Party*. William H. Holcombe, "Characteristics and Capabilities of the Negro Race," *Southern Literary Messenger* 33 (December 1861): 401. On polygenesis and antebellum justifications of slavery, see especially Gould, *Mismeasure of Man*, and Faust, *Sacred Circle*.

23. *Southern Literary Messenger* 33 (November 1861): 395.

24. Ibid.

25. *Southern Literary Messenger* 34 (April 1862): 266; "Editor's Table," *Southern Literary Messenger* 34 (September–October 1862): 581; *De Bow's Review* 33 (May–August 1862): 96.

26. *Southern Monthly* 1 (September 1861): 6; *Southern Literary Messenger* 34 (January 1862): 70. For the publication date of *War Songs of the South*, see the *Richmond Daily Dispatch* of July 5, 1862, which commented, "This book of patriotic lyrics, although issued but a few days since, has met with general favor with the public."

27. Shepperson, *War Songs of the South*, 3–4.

28. Chesnut, *Mary Chesnut's Civil War*, 282. Interestingly enough, C. Vann Woodward chose throughout Mary Chesnut's diary to excise the poetry she copied into her text—one of his few excisions of the text. Kate D. Foster Diary, Manuscript Department, Special Collections Library, Duke University. Willliam Galt Notebook, Ms. 0362, Virginia Military Institute Archives, available online at www.vmi.edu. M. J. Solomons Scrapbook, Manuscript Department, Special Collections Library, Duke University. See additional examples of scrapbooks kept by Southern women during the war in the collection of the Eleanor S. Brockenbrough Library, the Museum of the Confederacy, Richmond, Va.

29. "The Poet's Corner" was a term used by many writers to describe the spot where poems were published in the newspaper. Indeed, they were often published in the corner of a page, though not always. For the use of the term, see, for instance, Edmondston, *"Journal of a Secesh Lady,"* 282, and John Henry Boner to Clara Dargan, April 14, 1864, Clara Victoria Dargan Maclean Papers, Manuscript Department, Special Collections Library, Duke University.

30. *Southern Literary Messenger* 33 (December 1861): 468. The publications mentioned were *Chisholm's Manual of Military Surgery; Gilham's Manual for Volunteers and Militia; Ordnance Manual, 1861; Confederate States Army Regulations; Handbook of Artillery;* and *The Volunteer's Hand Book*.

31. Harris, *On the Plantation*, 21–22. On the *Countryman*, see also Turner, *Autobiography of "The Countryman."*

32. Coulter, *Confederate States of America*, 509. A good comparison to the *Southern Illustrated News* is the *Southern Field and Fireside*, which advertised in 1864 that it had "some 13,000 subscribers." *Southern Field and Fireside*, March 6, 1864, 5. Breckinridge, *Lucy Breckinridge of Grove Hill*, 50, 130, 133.

33. "Editor's Table," *Southern Literary Messenger* 34 (September–October 1862): 581; *Southern Illustrated News*, September 13, 1862, 4.

34. *Southern Illustrated News*, November 1, 1862, 3.

35. *Southern Illustrated News*, January 3, 1863, 8; *Southern Literary Messenger* 37

(July 1863): 447; "Uncle John on Poetry," *Magnolia Weekly*, September 19, 1863, 316. In 1864 Paul Hamilton Hayne expressed a similar weariness with war poetry. Pronouncing himself "thoroughly disgusted" with "contemporary themes," he said, "I shall not, probably, compose *another* line upon battles, sieges, or Generals, however distinguished." See Paul Hamilton Hayne to Clara Dargan, March 27, 1864, Clara Victoria Dargan Maclean Papers, Manuscript Department, Special Collections Library, Duke University.

36. "We take pleasure in enrolling this morning among our list of regular contributors the name of Paul H. Hayne, Esq., one of the sweetest poets of our own sunny land," the *Southern Illustrated News* announced in its December 6, 1862, issue. *Frank Leslie's Illustrated Newspaper*, February 2, 1861, 168, 170. Moore, *Paul Hamilton Hayne*, 53.

37. *Southern Monthly* 1 (September 1861): 5; *Southern Literary Messenger* to Clara Dargan, July 24, 1862, Clara Victoria Dargan Maclean Papers, Manuscript Department, Special Collections Library, Duke University; Paul Hamilton Hayne to John R. Thompson, May 1, 1864, Paul Hamilton Hayne Papers, Special Collections Library, Duke University; Paul Hamilton Hayne to Clara Dargan, February 26, 1864, Clara Victoria Dargan Maclean Papers, Special Collections Library, Duke University.

38. On John Reuben Thompson's career, see especially Garmon, *John Reuben Thompson*, and Moss, *Confederate Broadside Poems*, 1–49. For McCabe, see *Southern Illustrated News*, March 19, 1864, 84; *Mercury*, May 21, 1864, 4. For Bagby, see *Southern Illustrated News*, February 14, 1863, 2. For Simms and Hayne, see *Southern Field and Fireside*, November 5, 1864, 4; *Southern Illustrated News*, February 14, 1863, 2; *Magnolia Weekly*, June 13, 1863, 200; and *Mercury*, June 18, 1864, 4.

39. *Southern Illustrated News*, September 13, 1862, 4.

40. Ibid., 5. For another ad for engravers, see *Mercury*, June 11, 1864, 1.

41. *Southern Monthly* 1 (March 1862): 557–58. On attempts to obtain boxwood for engraving, sometimes from blockade runners, see *Southern Illustrated News*, May 9, 1863, 2, 8; *Southern Monthly* 1 (March 1862): 580.

42. *Southern Illustrated News*, October 4, 1862, 8; "Our Illustrations," *Mercury*, April 30, 1864, 4.

43. *Southern Illustrated News*, October 4, 1862, 8; *Daily Richmond Examiner*, July 26, 1862.

44. See, for instance, "Christmas in Camp," *Richmond Whig*, January 1, 1863: "A large file of papers from Nashville was handed us this morning. New York Pictorials, Cincinnati and Louisville papers were among them."

45. *Richmond Whig*, December 10, 1862; Refugitta, "A Confederate Christmas," *Magnolia Weekly*, October 3, 1863, 6. For the advertisement of "Yankee literature" and the reaction of the *Southern Illustrated News*, see *Southern Illustrated News*, August 8, 1863, 36–37. For republished stories, see the October 17, 1863, "The Blue Flowers," a reprinting of *Harper's Weekly*'s September 5, 1863, "The Blue Flowers"; the November 7, 1863, "Sybil Miller, or the Wounded Soldier," first published in *Harper's Weekly* as "A Gift by the Wayside"; the July 30, 1864, "The Heart of Miriam Clyde," published under that same title in the February 27, 1864, *Harper's Weekly;*

and the November 5, 1864, "Worth a Leg," published under that title in *Harper's Weekly* on October 22, 1864.

46. *Frank Leslie's Illustrated Newspaper,* September 27, 1862, 3.

47. *Southern Illustrated News,* October 11, 1862, 5; November 8, 1862, 2.

48. *Southern Illustrated News,* September 27, 1862, 4.

49. For announcements of *The Bugle Horn of Liberty* and the *Confederate Spirit and Knapsack of Fun,* see *Magnolia Weekly,* August 8, 1863, 264, and *Magnolia Weekly,* October 31, 1863, 36. On the *Mercury's* hiatus, see "A Card," *Mercury,* April 30, 1864, 4. *Southern Punch,* August 15, 1863, 2.

50. "Southern Literature," *Magnolia Weekly,* January 23, 1864, 132; *Southern Monthly* 1 (April 1862): 626; *Southern Illustrated News,* November 8, 1862, 2; London, "Confederate Literature and Its Publishers," 84.

51. On Thompson's attempts to publish a volume of war poetry, see Moss, *Confederate Broadside Poems,* 12, and Garmon, *John Reuben Thompson,* 111. William Gilmore Simms to John Reuben Thompson, January 16, 1862, in Simms, *Letters of William Gilmore Simms,* 6:223. See also Simms to William Porcher Miles, January 31, 1862, in *Letters of William Gilmore Simms,* 4:396–98. John Henry Boner to Clara Dargan, February 5, 1865, Clara Victoria Dargan Maclean Papers, Manuscript Department, Special Collections Library, Duke University.

52. Moss, *Confederate Broadside Poems,* 10; Paul Hamilton Hayne to Clara Dargan, March 27, 1864, James Wood Davidson to Clara Dargan, April 4, 1862, Clara Victoria Dargan Maclean Papers, Manuscript Department, Special Collections Library, Duke University.

53. "Our Paper," *Southern Illustrated News,* January 3, 1863, 2.

54. "Editor's Table," *Southern Literary Messenger* 34 (September–October 1862): 581. *Magnolia Weekly,* August 6, 1864, 292. Likewise, in January 1863 the *Southern Field and Fireside* commented on the "suspension of this paper, during a part of November and all of December." *Southern Field and Fireside,* January 10, 1863, 12.

55. "Southern Literature," *Southern Field and Fireside,* April 4, 1863, 110. *Southern Illustrated News,* August 8, 1863, 37. "Literary Convention," *Southern Punch,* February 6, 1864, 6.

56. *Harper's Weekly,* June 15, 1861, 369. For circulation figures, see Mott, *History of American Magazines, 1850–1865,* 10, 11, 359, 505, 371, 372.

57. *Manufactures of the United States in 1860,* cxxxiii–cxxxiv.

58. *Independent,* April 18, 1861, 7; *New York Tribune,* May 2, 3, 4, 1861, and June 11, 1861.

59. Dannett, *Noble Women of the North,* 33; Strong, *Diary of George Templeton Strong,* 3:127;. Dannett, *Noble Women of the North,* 45. Hanaford and Webber, *Chimes of Freedom and Union,* 13.

60. Richards, *Village Life in America,* 131. In February 1862 Richards again noted, "I have some new patriotic stationery. There is a picture of the flag on the envelope and underneath, 'If any one attempts to haul down the American flag shoot him on the spot.—John A. Dix.'" Ibid., 139.

61. *New York Daily Tribune,* May 3, 1861; Grant, *Handbook of Civil War Patri-*

otic Envelopes and Postal History, 1–6; *Union and Patriotic Album Illustrated Envelope Holder.*

62. *Post-Office Assistant* of April 1862, as quoted in Grant, *Handbook of Civil War Patriotic Envelopes and Postal History*, 1–12. Northern printers even produced "Secesh" designs for collectors so that their collections would include representative Confederate envelopes.

63. *Harper's Weekly*, January 12, 1861, 17; March 30, 1861, 195.

64. *Frank Leslie's Illustrated Newspaper*, February 23, 1861, 207; April 27, 1861, 353.

65. On partisan and nonpartisan culture, see Altschuler and Blumin, "Limits of Political Engagement in Antebellum America," and Altschuler and Blumin, " 'Where Is the Real America?' " Undated newspaper clipping of interview with Robert Bonner after his 1887 retirement, Robert Bonner Papers, New York Public Library.

66. *Flag of Our Union*, May 18, 1861, 4.

67. *Frank Leslie's Illustrated Newspaper*, May 4, 1861, 387; Strong, *Diary of George Templeton Strong*, 3:123.

68. *Harper's Weekly*, May 4, 1861, 274.

69. Ibid., May 25, 1861, 322.

70. Ibid., April 20, 1861, 241. *Frank Leslie's Illustrated Newspaper*, June 1, 1861.

71. See, for example, *Harper's Weekly*, June 15, 1861, 369. *American Publishers' Circular and Literary Gazette*, October 14, 1861, 257; February 1862, 19. Putnam, *George Palmer Putnam*, 289; Derby, *Fifty Years among Authors, Books, and Publishers*, 34.

72. *Frank Leslie's Illustrated Newspaper*, May 25, 1861, 31.

73. *American Publishers' Circular and Literary Gazette*, April 27, 1861, 153; June 29, 1861, 222.

74. Ibid., May 25, 1861, 183. On Victorian culture, see especially Rose, *Victorian America and the Civil War*; Howe, *Victorian America*; Stevenson, *Victorian Homefront*; and Halttunen, *Confidence Men and Painted Women.*

75. Putnam, *George Palmer Putnam*, 334. Quoted in an advertisement for the *Rebellion Record* in the *American Publishers' Circular and Literary Gazette*, August 17, 1861, 243.

76. *American Publishers' Circular and Literary Gazette*, May 25, 1861, 183; *Frank Leslie's Illustrated Newspaper*, June 8, 1861, 62; August 17, 1861.

77. White, *National Hymns*, 62; *Harper's New Monthly Magazine* 23 (July 1861): 347; *Boston Daily Transcript*, May 21, 1861. The details of Fields's takeover of the *Atlantic Monthly* are to be found in Austin, *Fields of the Atlantic Monthly*, 50–52.

78. Hanaford and Webber, *Chimes of Freedom and Union*. For a description of the publication of this volume, see Mary J. Webber to Caroline A. Mason, July 15, 1861, Briggs Family Papers, Series III, Schlesinger Library, Radcliffe College. *American Publishers' Circular and Literary Gazette*, July 20, 1861, 234; October 14, 1861, 264. James G. Gregory, Catalog, October 1, 1861, Houghton Library. Duganne, *Ballads of the War*. Following the publication of the first ballad, "March to the Capital," Duganne and his publisher proposed to publish ballads titled the

"Fall of Sumter," "Death of Colonel Ellsworth," "Death of Gen. Lyon," "Battle of Bull Run," and so on. However, this first volume of the *Ballads* was also the last. By 1862, the early wartime interest in a highly decorative war had waned, which may explain why there were no more volumes published of this proposed serial.

79. Shea, *Fallen Brave*, unpaginated preface. Other memorial volumes early in the war included Lyon, *Last Political Writings of Gen. Nathaniel Lyon*, and Burns, *Patriot's Offering*.

80. Tryon, *Parnassus Corner*, 143. On the decoration of the Victorian parlor, see Stevenson, *Victorian Homefront*, and Grier, *Culture and Comfort*.

81. Moss, *Confederate Broadside Poems*, 31. Early wartime songsters included *The Union Song-Book* (Philadelphia: Lee & Walker, 1861); *The Stars and Stripes Songster* (New York: R. M. DeWitt, 1861); *The Flag of Our Union Songster* (New York: T. W. Strong, 1861); *The Yankee Doodle Songster* (Philadelphia: A. Winch, 1861); *The Camp-Fire Companion* (Philadelphia: King and Baird, 1861); *Songs for the Union* (Philadelphia: A. Winch, 1861); *War Songs of the American Union* (Boston: William V. Spencer, 1861); and *Beadle's Dime Knapsack Songster* (New York: Beadle & Co., 1861). Charles Godfrey Leland, "War-Songs and Their Influence in History," *United States Service Magazine* 1 (January 1864): 48. On Northern and Southern songs, see Heaps and Heaps, *Singing Sixties*. See also Faust, *Creation of Confederate Nationalism*, 18–19.

82. During 1863, the *Weekly* published forty-one war stories, while in 1864 the *Weekly* published fifty-nine war fictions.

83. *Frank Leslie's Illustrated Newspaper*, May 10, 1862, 34. Other illustrated newspapers also published such spin-offs. The *New York Illustrated News* published the *Portrait Monthly* in 1863 and 1864; the first volume included engravings of Lincoln, Hooker, and Halleck. "It will form a handy book for reference after the war is over," the *Portrait Monthly* commented, "especially when it may be a matter of interest for our readers to know who such a prominent person was, and what he may have done during these exciting times of war and rebellion." *Portrait Monthly* 1 (July 1863): 2.

84. George William Curtis to Charles Eliot Norton, March 25, 1862, Charles Eliot Norton Papers, Houghton Library.

85. George W. Childs to Benson J. Lossing, March 24, 1862, Benson J. Lossing Papers, Huntington Library, San Marino, Calif. (hereafter cited as Huntington Library). John S. C. Abbott to Ledyard Bill, May 27, 1862, June 9, 1862, John S. C. Abbott Papers, American Antiquarian Society. Abbott, *History of the Civil War in America*, vol. 2, interleaved advertisement in copy held by the American Antiquarian Society.

86. "Literature and Literary Progress in 1862," *American Annual Cyclopaedia*, 544; "Literature and Literary Progress in 1863," *American Annual Cyclopaedia*, 573. Other publications also noticed the increase in the price of paper; see *Youth's Companion*, February 26, 1863, 34.

87. "Notes on Books and Booksellers," *American Literary Gazette and Publishers' Circular*, April 15, 1864, 406.

88. For a checklist of Currier and Ives prints, see Conningham, *Currier and Ives*

Prints. See advertisement for John Gibson's Publications, New York, in McCallister Civil War Scrapbooks, vol. 2 of Civil War Miscellanies, Library Company, Philadelphia, Pa. (hereafter cited as Library Company). See Goodrich, *Graphic Art of Winslow Homer.* A collection of these cards are in the holdings of the American Antiquarian Society. See, for instance, humorous sets of war cards published in 1863 by Wm. A. Stephens and by A. A. Burner, McCallister Civil War Scrapbooks, Civil War Caricatures, Photos, etc., Library Company.

89. See "United States' Volunteers Paper Soldiers" in "Full Uniform" offered by McLoughlin Bros., New York; paper soldiers with directions for cutting them out by G. Heerbrandt, New York; and an advertisement for "The Game of the Rebellion," all in McCallister Civil War Scrapbooks, vol. 2 of Civil War Miscellanies, Library Company. "Game of Visit to Camp" (New York: McLaughlin Brothers, n.d.), collection of the American Antiquarian Society. "The Game of Secession or Sketches of the Rebellion," Print Department, Library Company. Fans can be found in McCallister Civil War Scrapbooks, vol. 2 of Civil War Miscellanies, Library Company. See also Civil War Paper Fan Collection, Print Department, Library Company. Advertisement for "Ladies' Patent Electro 'Union' Collars and Cuffs," and Union Playing Cards, McCallister Civil War Scrapbooks, vol. 2 of Civil War Miscellanies, Library Company.

CHAPTER TWO

1. Shepperson, *War Songs of the South,* 3–4; White, *National Hymns,* 62; Shepperson, *War Songs of the South,* 3.

2. For flag presentation poetry, see, for example, "To a Company of Volunteers Receiving Their Banner at the Hands of the Ladies," *Southern Literary Messenger* 33 (July 1861): 17–18. In January 1862 the *Messenger* printed a poem that had been written by Augusta Foster for "an evening entertainment for the benefit of our soldiers." *Southern Literary Messenger* 34 (January 1862): 77. For an excellent description of the ceremonial formality of such occasions, see Harrison, *Recollections Grave and Gay,* 61–64. Shepperson, *War Songs of the South,* 3–4, 5.

3. John Savage, "The Muster of the North: A Ballad of '61," in "Poetry and Incidents," Moore, *Rebellion Record,* 3:1. For another poem on this theme, see J. C. Hagen, "The Uprising of the North," Moore, *Rebellion Record,* 1:121.

4. Savage, "Muster of the North"; Lucy Larcom, "The Nineteenth of April, 1861," Moore, *Rebellion Record,* 1:32.

5. Tyrtaeus, "The Voice of the South," *Charleston Mercury,* as reprinted in Simms, *War Poetry of the South,* 33.

6. G. H. M., "Uprise Ye Braves," *Richmond Daily Dispatch,* June 27, 1861.

7. Susan Archer Talley, "Rallying Song of the Virginians," *Southern Literary Messenger* 32 (June 1861): 480. For more on Talley, see Raymond, *Southland Writers,* 2:750–74.

8. Annie Chambers Ketchum, "Battle-Call," in Raymond, *Southand Writers,* 707.

9. Holmes, "The Poetry of the War," lecture, 1865, Huntington Library; Tyrtaeus, "The Voice of the South," *Charleston Mercury*, as reprinted in Simms, *War Poetry of the South*, 33. See also Faust, *Mothers of Invention*.

10. Timrod, "A Cry to Arms," in Moore, *Songs and Ballads of the Southern People*, 73.

11. Higonnet et al., *Behind the Lines*, 4.

12. John W. Overall, "Seventy-six and Sixty-one," in Moore, *Songs and Ballads of the Southern People*, 260.

13. On the Southern "cavalier," see Taylor, *Cavalier and Yankee*. *Southern Monthly* 1 (September 1861): 7, 9.

14. Annie Chambers Ketchum, "Battle-Call," in Moore, *Songs and Ballads of the Southern People*, 131.

15. Walt Whitman, "Beat! Beat! Drums!," *Harper's Weekly*, September 28, 1861. Walt Whitman, "Eighteen Sixty-one," in Whitman, *Walt Whitman: Leaves of Grass: Comprehensive Reader's Edition*, 282–83. Whitman received a rejection from the *Atlantic Monthly*, then edited by James T. Fields, which said that the magazine could not possibly use the poem before its "interest—which is of the present,—would have passed" (Traubel, *With Walt Whitman in Camden*, 2:213).

16. Sarah Warner Brooks, "On! Brothers, On!," Moore, *Rebellion Record*, 1:45; John Clancy, "A Northern Rally," Moore, *Rebellion Record*, 1:15.

17. Charles Godfrey Leland, "Northmen, Come Out!," Moore, *Rebellion Record*, 1:5.

18. "Cora," "To a Company of Volunteers Receiving Their Banner at the Hands of the Ladies," *Southern Literary Messenger* 33 (July 1861): 17.

19. Caroline A. Mason, "The Will for the Deed," Moore, *Rebellion Record*, 1:87.

20. Augusta Cooper Kimball, "My Country," Moore, *Rebellion Record*, 1:3.

21. Ibid.

22. White, *National Hymns*, 63; Greenwood, *Records of Five Years*, 111.

23. Hiram Barney to Salmon P. Chase, April 23, 1861, Chase Papers, microfilm ed. by John Niven, Huntington Library. My thanks to Mark Neely for this quotation. Strong, *Diary of George Templeton Strong*, 3:125–26; Hiram Barney to Salmon P. Chase, April 23, 1861, Chase Papers, microfilm ed. by John Niven, Huntington Library. See also Grace Greenwood's comments on the raising of the flag "from the dome of our new Catholic Cathedral." Greenwood, *Records of Five Years*, 107.

24. "Our Flag," Moore, *Rebellion Record*, 1:75; H. E. T., "Our Star-Gemmed Banner," *Rebellion Record*, 1:5.

25. H. E. T., "Our Star-Gemmed Banner," Moore, *Rebellion Record*, 1:5; William Oland Bourne, "Oh! Let the Starry Banner Wave," Moore, *Rebellion Record*, 1:62–63.

26. Edna Dean Proctor, "The Stripes and the Stars," Moore, *Rebellion Record*, 1:3.

27. On the flag in wartime, see Bob Bonner, "Wartime Nationalism in the First Confederate Flag Controversies," unpublished paper in the author's possession. "Our Flag," *Richmond Daily Dispatch*, May 21, 1861; Cora Livingston, "The Con-

federate Flag," *Richmond Daily Dispatch*, January 11, 1862; J. D. P., "Stand By That Flag," *Richmond Daily Dispatch*, December 7, 1861. J. R. Barrick's invocation to "The Confederate Flag" imagined that

> Thy stars shall cheer each eye,
> Thy folds a sacred banner be,
> To all beneath our sky;
> From where the blue Ohio flows,
> Far to the sea-gulf's stream,
> Borne by each gentle breath that blows,
> Thy hues shall flush and gleam.

J. R. Barrick, "The Confederate Flag," in Moore, *Songs and Ballads of the Southern People*, 192.

28. "Kentucky," "Away with the Stripes," in Ellinger, "Southern War Poetry of the Civil War," 64; Barrick, "Confederate Flag," 193; Mrs. E. D. Hundley, "Farewell, Forever, the Star Spangled Banner," in Ellinger, "Southern War Poetry of the Civil War," 92. Text of this poem, under the title "Farewell to the Star-Spangled Banner," is from Wharton, *War Songs and Poems of the Confederacy*, 378.

29. Tucker, "The Southern Cross," in Shepperson, *War Songs of the South*, 35; "The Flag of Secession," *Richmond Daily Dispatch*, October 24, 1861.

30. M. B. Wharton, "The Starry-Barred Banner," *Richmond Daily Dispatch*, May 14, 1861.

31. "Editor's Table," *Southern Literary Messenger* 34 (January 1862): 67.

32. "A Volunteer Song," *Independent*, April 25, 1861; C. B., "Song for Battle," *New York Evening Post*, May 30, 1861, in Moore, *Rebellion Record*, 1:105–6. "The Gathering of the Southern Volunteers," *Southern Literary Messenger* 32 (June 1861): 449–50. For other examples of songs to the tune of "La Marseillaise," see E. F. Porter, "The Marseilles Hymn—Translated and Adapted as an Ode," in Ellinger, "Southern War Poetry of the Civil War," 121, and "The Southern Marseillaise," in Ellinger, "Southern War Poetry of the Civil War," 45.

33. *New York Times*, May 20, 1861, 3. White, *National Hymns*, 18.

34. White, *National Hymns*, 63, 81.

35. Ibid., 75.

36. Ibid., 90, 114, 87, 67–68.

37. George William Curtis, "Editor's Easy Chair," *Harper's New Monthly Magazine* 23 (October 1861): 706. See also Curtis's response to criticism of the National Hymn Committee in "National Hymn," *Harper's Weekly*, June 1, 1861, 338. For a collection of parodies of national hymns, see Kerr, *Orpheus C. Kerr Papers* (1862), 54–62.

38. Kerr, *Orpheus C. Kerr Papers* (1862), 54, 55.

39. Ibid., 54–58. For another parody of national hymns, see "A Nashinal Him, by a Nashinal Her," in *Frank Leslie's Budget of Fun* (April 1862): 14.

40. "Rejected National Hymns," *Vanity Fair*, June 29, 1861, 302.

41. "A Hint to Poets: Showing How to Make a War Song," *Vanity Fair*, March 8, 1862, 123.

42. Henry Timrod as quoted in Moss, *Confederate Broadside Poems*, 13–14.

43. "A National Hymn," *Southern Illustrated News*, September 27, 1862, 4; "National Ballads," *Magnolia Weekly*, October 3, 1863, 4.

44. "Song Writing," *Southern Punch*, March 19, 1864, 7. Timrod, *Essays of Henry Timrod*, 163.

45. Timrod, *Essays of Henry Timrod*, 163.

46. Holmes, "Poetry of the War." Second verse as reprinted from the *New York Tribune*, July 28, 1861, in Moore, *Rebellion Record*, 2:105.

47. Holmes, "Poetry of the War"; Hall, *Story of the Battle Hymn of the Republic*, 51–52; Howe, *Reminiscences, 1819–1899*, 274–75.

48. Wilson, *Patriotic Gore*, 92–93.

49. Rev. Dr. Bethune, "God for Our Native Land!," Moore, *Rebellion Record*, 1:45; Elizabeth D. Wright, "Song of Columbia's Daughters," Moore, *Rebellion Record*, 1:51; David J. Dickson, "God and the Right," Moore, *Rebellion Record*, 1:73; H. A. Moore, "To Arms!," Moore, *Rebellion Record*, 1:88; Harriet Beecher Stowe, "The Holy War," Moore, *Rebellion Record*, 1:89–90. See also Oliver Wendell Holmes, "Army Hymn," *Atlantic Monthly* 7 (June 1861): 757; "The Soldier's Hymn," Moore, *Rebellion Record*, 1:140–41; and John Neal, "Battle Anthem," Moore, *Rebellion Record*, 1:119. W. F. L., "Redemption," Moore, *Rebellion Record*, 1:104–5.

50. E. K. Blunt, "The Southern Cross," in Simms, *War Poetry of the South*, 16; George H. Miles, "God Save the South," in ibid., 12; Wilson, *Patriotic Gore*, 59.

51. "Song Writing," *Southern Punch*, March 19, 1864, 7. Brander Matthews, *Pen and Ink*, 172–73.

52. Holmes, "Poetry of the War." James R. Randall, "My Maryland," in Shepperson, *War Songs of the South*, 138. Original publication date in Ellinger, "Southern War Poetry of the Civil War," 127. Simms, *War Poetry of the South*, 65–68.

53. Matthews, *Pen and Ink*, 145–49.

54. On the stereotyping of Yankees, see Taylor, *Cavalier and Yankee*. "The Cotton States' Farewell to Yankee Doodle," *Richmond Daily Dispatch*, June 25, 1861, "copied from a Georgia paper."

55. "Scum" in "My Maryland," Simms, *War Poetry of the South*, 68; "vampires" in ibid., 37.

56. John Killum, "Old Betsy," in Shepperson, *War Songs of the South*, 56.

57. S. Teakle Wallis, "The Guerrillas," *Southern Literary Messenger* 34 (July–August 1862): 444–45.

58. For an insightful explanation of the relationship between private and public obligation in wartime, see Westbrook, " 'I Want a Girl.' " "The South in Arms," dated September 18, 1861, M. J. Solomons Scrapbook, Special Collections, Special Collections Library, Duke University.

59. Wallis, "Guerrillas."

60. Catherine Warfield, "Southern Chant of Defiance," in Moore, *Songs and Ballads of the Southern People*, 156–57 (titled "Southrons" in that volume, "Southern Chant of Defiance" in Ellinger, "Southern War Poetry of the Civil War," and "You Can Never Win Them Back" in De Leon, *South Songs*).

61. On Victorian attitudes to death and rituals of mourning, see Halttunen, *Confidence Men and Painted Women*, and Laderman, *Sacred Remains*.

62. As quoted in Ingraham, *Elmer E. Ellsworth and the Zouaves of '61*, 32–3.

63. Alcott, *Selected Letters*, 67. Currier and Ives, for instance, produced a commemorative print of Ellsworth after his death. See Conningham, *Currier and Ives Prints*, 60.

64. J. W. F., "To Ellsworth," Moore, *Rebellion Record*, 1:89. A. A. A., "Elmer E. Ellsworth," Moore, *Rebellion Record*, 1:102; Charles William Butler, "Weep o'er the Heroes As They Fall," Moore, *Rebellion Record*, 2:97.

65. Shea, *Fallen Brave*, unpaginated preface. See also Greenwood, *Records of Five Years*, 109: "Not in vain fell Ellsworth, the second Warren of the Republic. The cry of his blood, in the hearts of his followers, will be more effectual than the shout of command, or the wild cheer of the Zouave." Burns, *Patriot's Offering*. See also the list of fallen heroes on the cover of Duganne, *Ballads of the War*.

66. Shea, *Fallen Brave*, unpaginated preface.; advertisement for *The Victims of the Rebellion*, in McCallister Civil War Scrapbooks, vol. 1 of Civil War Miscellanies, Library Company.

67. Theodore Winthrop, "Our March to Washington," reprinted in his *Life in the Open Air*, 220, 245, 247, 243. Winthrop offered his "tableau" in a letter to James Russell Lowell, May 10, 1861, James Russell Lowell Papers, Houghton Library. Theodore Winthrop, "Washington as a Camp," reprinted in Winthrop, *Life in the Open Air*, 276.

68. George William Curtis, "Theodore Winthrop," *Atlantic Monthly* 8 (August 1861): 242–51.

69. Ibid. Advertisement in *American Publishers' Circular and Literary Gazette*, October 14, 1861, 263. *Cecil Dreeme* was a substantial success, running through ten editions (printings) by February 1862, for a total of 6,500 in print, and continuing to be printed in small increments throughout the war, with an eighteenth printing in February 1865 that brought the total in print to 10,500. Winthrop's second novel, *John Brent*, published in January 1862, also performed well; by May 1864, there had been twelve editions, for a total of 9,000 in print. Three other works by Winthrop were also published during the war: *Edwin Brothertoft*, on July 19, 1862; *Canoe and Saddle*, on November 22, 1862; and *Life in the Open Air*, on May 23, 1863. Though these did not sell so many copies as Winthrop's first two novels, they each made respectable sales of several thousand copies. For the printing history of Winthrop's novels, see the Cost Books of Ticknor and Fields, 1861–65, Ticknor and Fields Archives, Houghton Library.

70. An advertisement for this volume appeared in the *American Publishers' Circular and Literary Gazette* on November 15, 1861, 274; Lyon, *Last Political Writings*, 244, 245.

71. Lyon, *Last Political Writings*, 246; H. P., "Lyon," Moore, *Rebellion Record*, 3:20–21; F. G. C., "Half-Mast," Moore, *Rebellion Record*, 3:3–4.

72. "Our Sanctum," *Southern Monthly* 1 (October 1861): 149. See also "Necrology," in the same issue, 160. "Jackson, Our First Martyr," M. J. Solomons Scrapbook, Special Collections Library, Duke University.

73. Wm. H. Holcombe, "Jackson, the Alexandria Martyr," in Simms, *War Poetry of the South*, 51; James W. Simmons, "The Martyr of Alexandria," in ibid., 52; *Richmond Whig*, April 22, 1862. Every Southern popular publication produced numerous poems to commemorate Jackson's death. On the commemoration of Stonewall Jackson, see Royster, *Destructive War*, 193–231.

74. "Hurrah for Jeff. Davis" and "Bull Run," Confederate Broadside Poetry Collection, Wake Forest University; Susan Archer Talley, "Battle of Manassas," in Shepperson, *War Songs of the South*, 126; Mrs. Clark [*sic*] (Mary Bayard Clarke), "The Battle of Manassas," in Shepperson, *War Songs of the South*, 123.

75. Alice B. Haven, "Bull Run, Sunday, July 21st," *New York Evening Post*, July 27, 1861, as reprinted in Moore, *Rebellion Record*, 2:1; Sarah Helen Whitman, "After the Fight at Manassas," *Providence Daily Journal*, August 6, 1861, as reprinted in Moore, *Rebellion Record*, 2:2.

76. M. J. H., "Christmas Day, A.D. 1861," *Richmond Daily Dispatch*, December 25, 1861. See also "Our Last Festival," which talked of "the darkness and desolation of our present hallowed anniversary," *Southern Literary Messenger* 33 (December 1861): 469. "Libertina," "Can the Glory of War Atone for Its Misery?" *Richmond Daily Dispatch*, November 28, 1861.

77. Gertrude Grant, "One Year Ago," M. J. Solomons Scrapbook, Special Collections Library, Duke University.

78. Mary Bayard Clarke to Messrs. McFarlane and Ferguson, September 21, 1861, McFarlane and Ferguson Papers, Virginia Historical Society.

79. Charles T. Congdon, "The Sword and the Pen," *Harper's New Monthly Magazine* 23 (August 1861): 351.

80. "Editor's Easy Chair," *Harper's New Monthly Magazine* 25 (September 1862): 565; Congdon, "Sword and the Pen," 351–52.

81. Mrs. Furness, "Our Soldiers," *Atlantic Monthly* 13 (March 1864): 364.

CHAPTER THREE

1. James G. Percivial, "It Is Great for Our Country to Die," Moore, *Rebellion Record*, 1:105; *Southern Monthly* 1 (December 1861): 249; Richards, *Village Life in America*, 131.

2. Fredrickson, *Inner Civil War*, 90.

3. On the social nature of sentimentalism, see Halttunen, *Confidence Men and Painted Women*. On sentimentalism as a mode of thought and language, see especially St. Armand, *Emily Dickinson and Her Culture;* Tompkins, *Sensational Designs;* and Bold, "Popular Forms I."

4. St. Armand uses the term "Sentimental Love Religion" in *Emily Dickinson and Her Culture*. See Tompkins, "Sentimental Power: *Uncle Tom's Cabin* and the Politics of Literary History," in *Sentimental Designs* for a discussion of Little Eva's death and Victorian sentimentalism.

5. Walt Whitman, "A Sight in Camp in the Day-Break Grey and Dim," in Whitman, *Walt Whitman's Drum-Taps*, 46.

6. George William Curtis, "Editor's Easy Chair," *Harper's New Monthly Magazine* 25 (June 1862): 123. See also Curtis's comments on the "unrecorded heroism of the private soldier, who, in this war at least, so often sacrifices as much as many an officer whose name is blazoned in our current history." *Harper's New Monthly Magazine* 25 (October 1862): 709. In an 1864 lecture Grace Greenwood asked, "But who shall number and name the great host of fiery young leaders, and the glorious thousands of the rank and file,—the mighty, melancholic multitude of brave men slain in battle, buried from hospitals, martyred in prisons!" Greenwood, *Records of Five Years*, 135. Guy, "Unlaureled Heroes," *Southern Monthly* 1 (March 1862): 559. See also "An Unclaimed Body," *Harper's Weekly*, July 12, 1862, 442.

7. Walt Whitman to Louisa Van Velsor Whitman, March 29, 1864, in *Collected Writings of Walt Whitman*, 1:205.

8. Alcott, *Hospital Sketches*, 36–37; See also "Lines by a Private Soldier," *Spirit of the Fair*, April 12, 1864, 77. In this poem, the narrator acknowledged the problem of mass, anonymous death:

> To be buried alone, alone—
> Even that is an honor rarely shown;
> In a common grave
> Lie many brave
>   We have no means of knowing;
> Their hopes and fears are forever hid
> In the cold ground—some ill-carved box lid
>   Their regiment only showing.

But this narrator accepted this anonymity as the price of war, acknowledging that soldiers could not stop "for every comrade gone / To raise a fitting funeral stone," since "Were we to stop for memory's tears / The work, the grief, would last for years." Instead, monuments and "funereal dirges" would have to wait until after the war ended. Still, even this poem assumed that the "tale" of the war should be told "from sire to son" as a record of the war. It simply put off the process of remembering the individual heroism of war.

9. "Somebody's Darling," in De Leon, *South Songs*, 67.

10. John Reuben Thompson, "The Burial of Latané," in De Leon, *South Songs*, 20–21. For a discussion of popular painting inspired by this poem later in the war, see Faust, *Mothers of Invention*, 188–89.

11. "Somebody's Darling," in *South Songs*, 67.

12. "Beautiful Lines," Moore, *Rebellion Record*, 3:30.

13. "The Dying Soldier," in Shepperson, *War Songs of the South*, 158.

14. "Missing," in Simms, *War Poetry of the South*, 225–27.

15. Johannsen, *To the Halls of the Montezumas*, 212; ad by Sawyer & Thompson, Music Publishers, in *Harper's Weekly*, October 8, 1864, 655.

16. Oliver Wendell Holmes, "The Poetry of the War," lecture, 1865, Huntington Library.

17. On the literature of World War I, see Hynes, *War Imagined*.

18. "You'll Tell Her, Won't You?," *Daily Richmond Dispatch*, October 4, 1862.

19. Ibid.

20. See also Cuba, "The Dying Soldier," *Southern Illustrated News*, May 7, 1864, 137.

21. On readers' enjoyment of "The Charge of the Light Brigade," see Royster, *Destructive War*, 257–58. Alfred, Lord Tennyson, "The Charge of the Light Brigade," in Abrams et al., *Norton Anthology of English Literature*, 2:898–99. One of many poems that imitated Tennyson's poem during the war was George H. Boker's "The Second Louisiana," Moore, *Rebellion Record*, 7:3.

22. Holmes, "Poetry of the War."

23. Charles Carroll Sawyer, "Mother Would Comfort Me" (Brooklyn, N.Y.: Sawyer & Thompson, 1863), Sheet Music Collection, Special Collections Library, Duke University.

24. Ibid.

25. Walt Whitman, unpublished Hospital Note Book, Huntington Library.

26. For Civil War manliness, see Mitchell, *Vacant Chair*. For the end of the century, see Bederman, *Manliness and Civilization*. Viola, "By the Camp Fire," *Southern Illustrated News*, April 11, 1863, 7.

27. Caroline A. Mason, "The Soldier's Dream of Home," in Moore, *Lyrics of Loyalty*, 139–41. Mason was an established poet on the eve of the war who had published a volume of poems, *Utterance*, in 1852.

28. H. B. Howe to Caroline A. Mason, March 22, 1863, Briggs Family Papers, Series III, Schlesinger Library, Radcliffe College. Howe reported reading Mason's poem in the *Anti-Slavery Standard*.

29. "A Soldier's Letter," *Frank Leslie's Illustrated Newspaper*, February 7, 1863, 309; *Magnolia Weekly*, December 3, 1864, 30.

30. On the portrayal of patriarchal authority during the Revolutionary era, see Fliegelman, *Prodigals and Pilgrims*. For a psychohistory claiming that Lincoln had "powerful patricidal desires" against the revolutionary fathers, see Forgie, *Patricide in the House Divided*, 284. "Ana of the War," *United States Service Magazine* 3 (January 1865): 20.

31. Horatio Alger Jr., "Mother, Can I Go?," *Harper's Weekly*, March 22, 1862, 187. Holmes, "Poetry of the War."

32. George F. Root, "Just before the Battle, Mother" (Chicago: Root & Cady, 1863), Sheet Music Collection, Special Collections Library, Duke University.

33. Charles Carroll Sawyer, "Who Will Care for Mother Now?" (Brooklyn: Sawyer & Thompson, 1863); "The Dying Volunteer" (New Orleans: Louis Grunewald, 1865); Edward Clark, "The Dying Soldier or Kiss Me Good Night Mother" (Boston: Oliver Ditson, 1861); J. C. Johnson, "Is That Mother Bending o'er Me?" (Boston: Oliver Ditson, 1863); Henry C. Work, "Our Captain's Last Words" (Chicago: Root & Cady, 1861). See also A. B. Chandler, "I've Fallen in the Battle" (New Orleans: Louis Grunewald, 1864); Ednor Rossiter, "I Loved That Dear Old Flag the Best" (Philadelphia: Lee & Walker, 1863); and Thomas Manahan, "Bear This Gently to My Mother" (New York: Horace Waters, 1864). Sheet Music Collection, Special Collections Library, Duke University.

34. Holmes, "Poetry of the War"; Wiley, *Life of Billy Yank*, 299, 303; McPherson, *Ordeal by Fire*, 355. "Nearly two-fifths of the soldiers were 21 or younger at the

time of enlistment," according to McPherson. But of course this also means that a majority of soldiers were not "boys." On the usage of "boys" to mean soldiers, see *A Dictionary of American English On Historical Principles* (Chicago: University of Chicago Press, 1936), 300.

35. Eben Hannaford, "In Hospital after Stone River," *Harper's New Monthly Magazine* 28 (January 1864): 264–65.

36. Walt Whitman to Ralph Waldo Emerson, January 17, 1863, in Whitman, *Collected Writings of Walt Whitman*, 1:69.

37. Erkkila, *Whitman the Political Poet*, 206, 199; Reed, *Hospital Life in the Army of the Potomac*, 141, 153. Reed noted this common belief but in the wake of war also asserted that "still, the men who lie there are only average men" (141–42).

38. *Notes of Hospital Life*, xiii; Mary E. Nealy, "Dying in the Hospital," *Continental Monthly* 4 (August 1863): 229.

39. Whitman, "Hospital Visits," *New York Times*, December 11, 1864, reprinted in Whitman, *Complete Writings of Walt Whitman*, 7:126.

40. Reed, *Hospital Life in the Army of the Potomac*, 140.

41. *Notes of Hospital Life*, 39.

42. Alcott, *Journals of Louisa May Alcott*, 118; Whitman, "Hospital Visits" 7:101.

43. Alcott, *Hospital Sketches*, 49.

44. Ibid., 49–51.

45. Ibid, 52, 49; *American Publishers' Circular and Literary Gazette*, September 1, 1863, 346.

46. Alcott, *Hospital Sketches*, 54–58.

47. Whitman, *Collected Writings of Walt Whitman*, 1:162.

48. Ropes, *Civil War Nurse*, 108. Her journal was not published. Charles Edward Lester to George W. Childs, November 6, 1862, Ferdinand J. Dreer Autograph Collection, Historical Society of Pennsylvania (hereafter cited as Dreer Collection).

49. Charles Edward Lester to George W. Childs, November 6, 1862, Dreer Collection.

50. Walt Whitman to James Redpath, October 21, 1863, in Whitman, *Collected Writings of Walt Whitman*, 1:171–72.

51. Ropes died in January 1863, as the result of an illness caught while she nursed soldiers. See Ropes, *Civil War Nurse*, 122–26. Redpath wrote to "Friend Whitman" that there was "a lion in the way" of his project—money. Traubel, *With Walt Whitman in Camden*, 415. *American Publishers' Circular and Literary Gazette*, September 1, 1863, 346.

52. Stearns, *Lady Nurse of Ward E*, 102.

53. A. S. Hooker, "Hospital Heroes," *Frank Leslie's Illustrated Newspaper*, October 3, 1863, 21; Mrs. H., *Three Years in Field Hospitals of the Army of the Potomac*, 47; Reed, *Hospital Life in the Army of the Potomac*, 148.

54. Alcott, *Hospital Sketches*, 36–37.

55. *Notes of Hospital Life*, xii, dedication page; Ropes, *Civil War Nurse*, 58. See also p. 74 for Ropes's claim that privates "were really the heroes of the war."

56. "Private in the Ranks," *Southern Punch*, August 22, 1863, 7; "Common Sol-

diers," *Southern Punch*, October 24, 1863, 2; Evans, *Macaria*, 390. The account of Willie's death offers an interesting comparison with Alcott's description of John's death. See *Macaria*, chap. 34, 382–93.

57. Col. W. S. Hawkins, "The Hero without a Name," in De Leon, *South Songs*, 33–37.

58. *Notes of Hospital Life*, 25; Alcott, *Hospital Sketches*, 31, 47; Reed, *Hospital Life in the Army of the Potomac*, 146–47.

59. Whitman, "Hospital Visits," 7:127; Whitman, *Collected Writings of Walt Whitman*, 1:115.

60. Alcott, *Hospital Sketches*, 50–51.

61. "The Picket-Guard," in White, *Poetry Lyrical, Narrative, and Satirical*, 120.

62. Carrie Bell Sinclair, "All Quiet along the Savannah To-Night," Laura Waldron Papers, Special Collections Library, Duke University.

63. "Picket Guard," in White, *Poetry Lyrical, Narrative, and Satirical*, 120; "The Picket Guard," *Richmond Dispatch*, March 20, 1862, in the M. J. Solomons Scrapbook, Special Collections Library, Duke University. Royster, *Destructive War*. See also Rosa Wild, "On Guard," *Southern Illustrated News*, February 7, 1863, 3, whose opening line is "I'm watching now at my lonely post."

64. Alice B. Haven, "One Day," *Harper's New Monthly Magazine* 25 (October 1862): 669.

CHAPTER FOUR

1. "Stockings and Mittens," *Harper's Weekly*, January 11, 1862, 30; "The Army of Knitters," *Arthur's Home Magazine* 19 (January 1862): 61; *Arthur's Home Magazine* 18 (December 1861): 326. On Northern women's roles in the war, see Young, "Wound of One's Own"; Attie, *Patriotic Toil*; Clinton and Silber, *Divided Houses*; Silber, *Romance of Reunion*; Sizer, " 'Revolution in Woman Herself' "; Wood, "War within a War"; and Leonard, *Yankee Women*. Older volumes that focus on Northern women's war experiences include Dannett, *Noble Women of the North*; Greenbie, *Lincoln's Daughters of Mercy*; Massey, *Bonnet Brigades*; and Young, *Women and the Crisis*.

2. Mary J. Upshur, "Knitting for the Soldiers" and "A Southern Woman's Song," in Shepperson, *War Songs of the South*, 177, 176. On this theme, see also Augusta Foster, "Our Mothers Did So before Us," *Southern Literary Messenger* 34 (January 1862): 77. Carrie Bell Sinclair, "The Homespun Dress; or, The Southern Girl," as reprinted in Heaps and Heaps, *Singing Sixties*, 348–49. See also Carrie Bell Sinclair, *The Southern Girl with the Home-spun Dress*, broadside, n.p., 186–. On the patriotic use of homespun, see also Faust, *Mothers of Invention*, 46–52. "Izilda," "A True and Simple Tale of 1861," *Southern Monthly* 1 (December 1861): 282. On Southern women's roles in the war more generally, see especially Faust, *Mothers of Invention*; Rable, *Civil Wars*; and Whites, *Civil War as a Crisis in Gender*. For an older work on Southern women during the war, see Simkins and Patton, *Women of the Confederacy*.

3. For a discussion of antebellum women writers' views of the Revolution, see Baym, *American Women Writers and the Work of History;* "The Mothers of To-Day," *Arthur's Home Magazine* 18 (November 1861): 263; "Rumors and Incidents," Moore, *Rebellion Record*, 1:55.

4. On republican motherhood, see Kerber, *Women of the Republic*. On the antebellum culture of domesticity that supported the ideology of republican motherhood, see especially Cott, *Bonds of Womanhood;* Douglas, *Feminization of American Culture;* Kelley, *Private Woman, Public Stage;* and Halttunen, *Confidence Men and Painted Women*. Ernest Linn, "The Southern Mother," *Magnolia Weekly,* March 28, 1863, 111; "The Patriot Mother," *Southern Illustrated News,* December 26, 1863, 200; Foster, "Our Mothers Did So before Us," 77. "Go, My Boy, Where Duty Calls You," *Harper's Weekly,* June 21, 1862, 395; "Mother, Can I Go," *Harper's Weekly,* March 22, 1862. See also "A Mother's Answer," in Moore, *Lyrics of Loyalty,* 107–8.

5. Poovey, *Uneven Developments*, 16.

6. "The Southern Matron to Her Son," Confederate Broadside Poetry Collection, Wake Forest University.

7. Virginia F. Townsend, "Home Pictures of the Times," *Arthur's Magazine* 18 (November 1861): 235, 237. The idea that women were at the emotive center of the nation had been widely established in antebellum literature, with Harriet Beecher Stowe's *Uncle Tom's Cabin* (1851) only the most prominent example of sentimental literary nationhood. Historian Elizabeth Ellet, for instance, also emphasized the vital role of patriotic mothers and "home-sentiment" in her 1848 *The Women of the American Revolution;* according to Ellet, the power of the "leading spirits" of the Revolution derived from public sentiment that "depended, in great part, upon the women." See Ellet, *Women of the American Revolution*, 13–14. For more on Ellet's work, see Baym, *American Women Writers and the Work of History*, and Kerber, " 'History Can Do It No Justice.' " On nineteenth-century sentimental culture, see especially Douglas, *Feminization of American Culture;* Halttunen, *Confidence Men and Painted Women;* St. Armand, *Emily Dickinson and Her Culture;* and Tompkins, *Sensational Designs*. Townsend, "Home Pictures of the Times," 235, 237. See also such popular songs as Mrs. Cornelia D. Rogers, "Ah! He Kissed Me When He Left Me" (Chicago: Root & Cady, 1863), Sheet Music Collection, Special Collections Library, Duke University. As J. Matthew Gallman has shown, soldiers' own accounts of partings often matched these literary versions in stressing the tears of women. See, for instance, Will Colton's account of his departure in Gallman, *Mastering Wartime*, 63.

8. Samuel Osgood, "The Home and the Flag," *Harper's New Monthly Magazine* 26 (April 1863): 665.

9. Ibid.

10. "Cora," "To a Company of Volunteers Receiving Their Banner at the Hands of the Ladies," *Southern Literary Messenger* 33 (July 1861): 17; "God Bless Our Southern Women!," *Countryman,* December 1, 1862, 75. See Constance Cary Harrison's account of an elaborate flag presentation in Harrison, *Recollections Grave and Gay,* 61–63. See also Evans, *Macaria,* 310.

11. Whittier initially steadfastly asserted the veracity of the story on which his ballad was based, which had been sent to him by the popular writer E. D. E. N. Southworth, but after the war he backpedaled in his claims for its "truth." See Pickard, *Life and Letters of John Greenleaf Whittier*, 2:454–59. John Greenleaf Whittier, "Barbara Frietchie," *Atlantic Monthly* 12 (October 1863): 495–97.

12. T. S. Arthur, "Blue Yarn Stockings," *Harper's New Monthly Magazine* 24 (December 1861): 112; Kate Sutherland, "The Laggard Recruit," *Arthur's Home Magazine* 19 (January 1862): 11.

13. Alexander B. Meek, "War Song," *Richmond Daily Dispatch*, July 24, 1861.

14. M. F. Q., "Address," May 3, 1861, Confederate Broadside Poetry Collection, Wake Forest University.

15. Westbrook, "'I Want a Girl,'" 588–89.

16. Melodramas and sentimental literature often involved different styles of plot, with sentimental literature more interiorized, often set within domestic spaces, whereas melodramas involved more dramatic exteriorized action and settings. However, as *Uncle Tom's Cabin* shows, melodrama and sentimental literature were not always distinct categories but instead blended into each other, especially drawing on similar structures of feeling. Brooks, *Melodramatic Imagination*, 13, 205.

17. Faust, *Mothers of Invention*, 18; Rogers, "Ah! He Kissed Me When He Left Me." "I Have Kissed Him, and Let Him Go" was widely popular north and south: see Moore, *Lyrics of Loyalty*, 107–8, and Faust, *Mothers of Invention*, 18. Moore, *Lyrics of Loyalty*, 108.

18. "Izilda," "A True and Simple Tale of 1861," *Southern Monthly* 1 (December 1861); "Red, White, and Blue," *Harper's Weekly*, October 19, 1861, 666–67. Similarly, the heroine in Mary C. Vaughan's "Wounded at Donelson," published in the *New York Ledger* on November 29, 1862, initially told her enlisting lover with "angry excitement" that she no longer loved him: "Why should I, when you care so little for me? You, who have now my promise to marry you, and then deliberately leave me." But when the news came that her lover had been badly wounded at Donelson, she had a change of heart: "I have loved him all the time, but it was my wicked pride, my selfishness." "I know I am all unworthy," she told her lover's mother, before being married to him at his bedside, a "bed of pain" that her "care and presence had made a couch of roses for the wounded soldier." Mary C. Vaughan, "Wounded at Donelson," *New York Ledger*, November 29, 1862, 2.

19. "Jessie Underhill's Thanksgiving," *Harper's Weekly*, December 6, 1862, 775.

20. "A Leaf from a Summer," *Harper's Weekly*, November 8, 1862, 718.

21. Henry James, "The Story of a Year," *Atlantic Monthly* 15 (March 1865): 257–81; "Romances of the War," *Round Table*, January 9, 1864, 59. In April 1863 *Harper's New Monthly Magazine* also commented that "nobody reads anything but war stories, all about a gallant and gay soldier (with variations), who goes to the wars and comes gloriously home in six weeks and marries the girl he left behind him." *Harper's New Monthly Magazine* 26 (April 1863): 696.

22. See the October 17, 1863, "The Blue Flowers," a reprinting of *Harper's Weekly's* September 5, 1863, "The Blue Flowers"; the November 7, 1863, "Sybil

Miller, or the Wounded Soldier," first published in *Harper's Weekly* as "A Gift by the Wayside"; the July 30, 1864, "The Heart of Miriam Clyde," published under that same title in the February 27, 1864, *Harper's Weekly;* and the November 5, 1864, "Worth a Leg," published under that title in *Harper's Weekly* on October 22, 1864. "The Heart of Miriam Clyde," *Harper's Weekly*, February 27, 1864, 135; Margaret Stilling, "Love versus Pride," *Southern Illustrated News*, July 11, 1863, 11.

23. As Megan McClintock has pointed out, early in the war public aid "went only to families whose breadwinners were in the military; payments stopped with a soldier's discharge or death." See McClintock, "Civil War Pensions and the Reconstruction of Families," 461. *Frank Leslie's Illustrated Newspaper*, September 7, 1861, 262.

24. Carry Stanley, "The Volunteer's Wife," *Peterson's Magazine* 40 (October 1861): 256.

25. Ibid., 258–59.

26. "The Tuberose: A Story of the War," *Harper's Weekly*, November 16, 1861, 731.

27. Fanny Fern, "Soldiers' Wives," *New York Ledger*, November 8, 1862, 4. Literature sympathetic to the economic plight of soldiers' families drew on a long literary tradition in which the only working-class women imagined positively were pale, genteel, passive victims; they were sharply distinguished from their "disorderly" sisters. See Stansell, *City of Women*.

28. Fanny Fern, "Soldiers' Wives," *New York Ledger*, November 8, 1862, 4.

29. Margaret Stilling, "Love versus Pride," *Southern Illustrated News*, July 11, 1863, 10. "Refugitta" [Constance Cary], "A Blockade Correspondence," *Southern Illustrated News*, August 15, 1863, 45. There was a striking congruence on this point between feminized war literature and some women's letters, which shared a similar sensibility and even style of language. As Elizabeth Boynton of Crawfordsville, Indiana, wrote to her soldier lover in August 1862, "I sometimes think it must seem almost like mockery to you when we talk of *appreciating* the sacrifices you make—We, who are sitting quietly at home. True, dear Will, we may not know of, no, not even *dream* of the *horrors* of war, but—oh, we do *know* what *weary waiting* is we *do know* what it is to say to our *loved* ones, 'go,' and with calm brow & cheerful voice, cheer them on to victory, then return to *our lonely, desolate* homes to *wait*—and when I see the pale faces around me I think that perhaps Columbia's sons know not what gifts we lay at the altar of freedom." Elizabeth Boynton to Will Harbert, August 11, 1862, Elizabeth Boynton Harbert Papers, Huntington Library.

30. On the "sacrifice" laid at the "altar of freedom," see Evans, *Macaria*, and Elizabeth Stuart Phelps, "A Sacrifice Consumed," *Harper's New Monthly Magazine* 28 (January 1864): 240. "The Brave at Home," in De Leon, *South Songs*, 108. "The Brave at Home" was also printed in newspapers as "The Heros at Home" during the war. See M. J. Solomons Scrapbook, Special Collections Library, Duke University.

31. Browning, "Parting Lovers," in *Poems by Elizabeth Barrett Browning*, 4:181. First printed in the *Independent*, March 21, 1861. For a sampling of quotations of

this poem within wartime fiction, see "One of Our Heroes," *Harper's Weekly,* July 5, 1862, 427; Catherine Earnshaw, "Loyal," *Flag of Our Union,* January 28, 1865, 58; and Phelps, "Sacrifice Consumed," 240.

32. Louise Chandler Moulton, "One of Many," *Atlantic Monthly* 27 (July 1863): 120. For stories concentrating on women's equal or greater suffering and sacrifice, see "Milly Graham's Rose Bush," *Harper's Weekly,* May 14, 1864, 311; "May Flowers," *Harper's Weekly,* May 28, 1864, 343; and "My Contribution," *Harper's Weekly,* June 14, 1862, 374.

33. This trope was repeated in the postwar period, as well. In 1866, for example, Longfellow published his popular "Killed at the Ford," which reiterated the wartime theme that war killed on the home front as well as at the battlefront. "Killed at the Ford" told of the killing of a "beautiful youth," with "the heart of honor, the tongue of truth, / He, the life and light of us all, / Whose voice was blithe as a bugle-call." After he was shot — "Sudden and swift a whistling ball / Came out of a wood, and the voice was still" — the bullet had a second impact:

> And I saw in a vision how far and fleet
> That fatal bullet went speeding forth,
> Till it reached a town in the distant North,
> Till it reached a house in a sunny street,
> Till it reached a heart that ceased to beat
> Without a murmur, without a cry;
> And a bell was tolled, in that far-off town,
> For one who had passed from cross to crown,
> And the neighbors wondered that she should die.

Henry Wadsworth Longfellow, "Killed at the Ford," *Atlantic Monthly* 17 (April 1866): 479. It is not known when Longfellow wrote this poem, but a September 1, 1862, journal entry reveals that its themes were then much on his mind: "Yesterday we had report of a great battle at Manassas, ending in defeat of the Rebels. The moon set red and lowering; and I thought in the night of the pale, upturned faces of young men on the battle-field, and the agonies of the wounded; and my wretchedness was very great. Every shell from the cannon's mouth bursts not only on the battle-field, but in far away homes, North or South, carrying dismay and death." From Longfellow, *Life of Henry Wadsworth Longfellow,* 2:387.

34. Moulton, "One of Many," 120, 121. For a variation on this theme, see "Women and War," *Flag of Our Union,* January 28, 1865, 59. "My Absent Soldier," *Harper's Weekly,* May 31, 1862, 343. Julia Eugenia Mott, "Within a Year," *Peterson's Magazine* 41 (July 1862): 29. See also Almena C. S. Allard, "The Soldier's Dying Wife," *Arthur's Home Magazine* 20 (September 1862): 174; "The Soldier's Mother," *Frank Leslie's Illustrated Newspaper,* April 26, 1862, 414; and F. H. G., "The Soldier's Mother," *Sunday Mercury,* April 6, 1862, n.p.

35. "Waiting," *Magnolia Weekly,* September 26, 1863, 317. "A Picture," *Magnolia Weekly,* April 25, 1863, 147; Evans, *Macaria,* 345.

36. Scarry, *Body in Pain;* "Our Wounded," *Continental Monthly* 2 (October 1862): 465. On the popular embrace of violence, see Royster, *Destructive War,* 232–95.

37. See Young, "Wound of One's Own." "Wounded," *Harper's Weekly*, July 12, 1862, 442.

38. "Wounded," *Harper's Weekly*, July 12, 1862, 442.

39. Ibid.

40. "Refugitta" [Constance Cary], "Implora Pace," *Southern Illustrated News*, May 30, 1863, 3.

41. Moulton, "One of Many," 121.

42. Rose Terry, "A Woman," *Atlantic Monthly* 10 (December 1862): 696, 706, 707. On this theme, see also Louisa May Alcott, "Love and Loyalty," *United States Service Magazine* 2 (July, August, September, November, December 1864), 58–64, 166–72, 273–80, 469–75, 543–551; and "Love's Sacrifice and Its Recompense," *Harper's Weekly*, March 5, 1864, 155.

43. On nursing during the Civil War, see especially Schultz, "Inhospitable Hospital"; Kristie Ross, "Arranging a Doll's House," in Clinton and Silber, *Divided Houses*; Leonard, *Yankee Women*; Sizer, " 'Revolution in Woman Herself' "; and Wood, "War within a War." "Our Women and the War," *Harper's Weekly*, September 6, 1862, 570. For a sample of the rhetoric reflecting disapproval of women's nursing, see "The Women in the Hospitals," *Sunday Mercury*, January 26, 1862. "Many of the men," this piece stated, "would much prefer to be changed" by "their own sex."

44. See Young, "Wound of One's Own." Virginia F. Townsend, "Hospital Nurse," *Arthur's Home Magazine* 20 (August 1862): 122. Bella Z. Spencer, "One of the Noble," *Harper's New Monthly Magazine* 29 (July 1864): 205, 206. See also "Missing," *Harper's Weekly*, October 18, 1862, 662–63.

45. Harriet Beecher Stowe to Annie Adams Fields, November 29, 1864, as quoted in Austin, *Fields of the Atlantic Monthly*, 281.

46. Mrs. H. B. Stowe, "The Chimney-Corner," *Atlantic Monthly* 15 (January 1865): 109–10, 112. St. Armand, *Emily Dickinson and Her Culture*, 111. For a powerful story in which an anguished mother denied the power of Christian consolation offered by the narrator, see Rose Terry, "A Tragedy of To-Day," *Spirit of the Fair*, April 16, 1864, 126–27.

47. Stowe, "Chimney-Corner," 113, 114.

48. "Lora," "Deo Vindice," *Southern Field and Fireside*, November 19, 1864, 3.

49. Ibid.

50. Faust, *Mothers of Invention*. "The Women and the Revolution," undated newspaper clipping, M. J. Solomons Scrapbook, Special Collections Library, Duke University.

51. "God Bless Our Southern Women!," *Countryman*, December 1, 1862, 75.

52. "Mrs. Poynter's Reflections," *Southern Illustrated News*, November 29, 1862, 5.

53. On the sales figures of *Macaria*, see *Magnolia Weekly*, December 3, 1864, 28; Evans, *Macaria*, 376, 412–13.

54. See Faust, *Mothers of Invention*, 175–78; A. V. S., "What Can Woman Do?" *Southern Illustrated News*, March 7, 1863, 3.

55. M. Louise Rogers, "Our Country," in M. J. Solomons Scrapbook, Special Collections Library, Duke University. "A Prayer for Peace," in De Leon, *South Songs*, 139. Edmondston, *"Journal of a Secesh Lady,"* 512. The entry is for December 29, 1863.

56. "The Old Year's Dirge," *Southern Field and Fireside*, January 1, 1865, 7; Preston, *Life and Lettters*, 202–3; Coulling, *Margaret Junkin Preston*, 152–53.

57. Preston, *Life and Letters*, 202; Preston, *Beechenbrook*, 71–74.

58. Preston, *Life and Letters*, 207–8.

59. Phelps, "Sacrifice Consumed," 236, 237.

60. Ibid., 238, 240.

61. *Ruth: A Song in the Desert*, 18, 35–6, 41–42, 58.

62. Phelps, *Chapters from a Life*, 96–98. Similarly, Emily Dickinson wrote in an 1864 letter that "sorrow seems more general than it did, and not the estate of a few persons, since the war began; and if the anguish of others helped one with one's own, now would be many medicines." See Dickinson, *Letters of Emily Dickinson*, 2:436.

63. Phelps, *Chapters from a Life*, 98.

64. Ibid., 97; Phelps, *Gates Ajar*, 130, 134–35, 38, 155, 161.

65. Fleta, "Woman and War," *The Flag of Our Union*, January 28, 1865, 59.

66. Phelps, "Sacrifice Consumed," 240.

CHAPTER FIVE

1. Mrs. Howard, "Plantation Scenes and Sounds," *Southern Field and Fireside*, January 1, 1865, 5.

2. Aaron, *Unwritten War*, xviii; *Harper's Weekly*, June 8, 1861, 354; *Frank Leslie's Illustrated Newspaper*, June 8, 1861, 55.

3. Weiss, *Catalog of Union Civil War Patriotic Covers*, 391, 389; "Advertisements," *Weekly Anglo-African*, August 24, 1861. Unfortunately, few wartime issues of this important journal survive.

4. Edward L. Pierce, "The Contrabands at Fortress Monroe," *Atlantic Monthly* 8 (November 1861): 627. Weiss, *Catalog of Union Civil War Patriotic Covers*, 389.

5. Except among abolitionists who had argued before the war for black freedom and equality, this had also been the tendency of most popular antebellum discussions advocating the end of slavery. But war intensified this mode of discussing the place of blacks in American life.

6. Lott, *Love and Theft*, 185.

7. Kirke, *Among the Pines*, 16; Heaps and Heaps, *Singing Sixties*, 272–3.

8. *Harper's Weekly*, June 29, 1861, 416.

9. *Frank Leslie's Illustrated Newspaper*, December 21, 1861, 70.

10. *Harper's Weekly*, January 18, 1862.

11. *Frank Leslie's Illustrated Newspaper*, January 18, 1862, 144.

12. Henry C. Work, "Kingdom Coming" (Chicago: Root & Cady, 1862), Sheet Music Collection, Special Collections Library, Duke University.

13. Leland, *Memoirs*, 242. Its first issue was ten thousand copies, and its editorial viewpoint circulated widely through the medium of newspaper exchanges.

14. "Editor's Table," *Continental Monthly* 1 (January 1862): 97, 98. This was a fairly common argument in early 1862: as Ralph Waldo Emerson wrote in the *Atlantic Monthly*, "Emancipation at one stroke elevates the poor white of the South, and identifies his interest with that of the Northern laborer." Ralph Waldo Emerson, "American Civilization," *Atlantic Monthly* 9 (April 1862): 510.

15. Austin, *Fields of the Atlantic Monthly*, 248.

16. For more on Gilmore's career, see Gilmore, *Personal Recollections*, and Leland, *Memoirs. American Publishers' Circular and Literary Gazette* 8 (June 1862): 67; October 1, 1862, 97; December 1, 1862, 142; July, 1862, 74.

17. "Conversations recorded in these papers," Gilmore informed the reader, were "taken down" within "twenty-four hours after [their] occurrence." Edmund Kirke [James Roberts Gilmore], "Among the Pines," *Continental Monthly* 1 (January 1862): 44. The *Sunday Mercury* remarked in reviewing Gilmore's book that though *Among the Pines* "purports to be a veracious account of a veritable visit to North Carolina, [it] is evidently pure fiction from beginning to end." *Sunday Mercury*, January 26, 1862, n.p.

18. Kirke, *Among the Pines*, 36, 37, 38.

19. Ibid., 44, 36.

20. Ibid., 45.

21. Ibid., 57–58.

22. *Frank Leslie's Illustrated Newspaper*, June 7, 1862, 147, illustration on 145.

23. *Frank Leslie's Illustrated Newspaper*, June 21, 1862, 180; *Harper's Weekly*, June 14, 1862, 372.

24. On nineteenth-century celebrations of the heroic individual, see Levine, *Highbrow/Lowbrow*.

25. *Frank Leslie's Illustrated Newspaper*, June 21, 1862, 181; *Harper's Weekly*, June 14, 1862, 372, 373.

26. *Frank Leslie's Illustrated Newspaper*, September 20, 1862, 403; [Halpine], *Life and Adventures*, 55.

27. *Frank Leslie's Illustrated Newspaper*, August 30, 1862, 364; *Harper's Weekly*, March 14, 1863, 174, 168–69; March 28, 1863, 196.

28. Fredrickson, *Black Image in the White Mind*, 168–69.

29. *Harper's Weekly*, March 14, 1863, 161.

30. *Frank Leslie's Illustrated Newspaper*, January 24, 1863, 275.

31. On these artists, see Starr, *Bohemian Brigade*.

32. Brown's 1853 *Clotel* was published in London. After the war, Brown published *Clotelle* again under the title *Clotelle; or, the Colored Heroine. A Tale of the Southern States* (Boston: Lee & Shepard, 1867). In this version Brown added four chapters in which he imagined Clotelle taking part in the war as a nurse, titling one of his chapters "The Angel of Mercy." *The Black Man* also included discussions of three African American women writers: Phillis Wheatley, Frances Ellen Watkins, and Charlotte Forten. Thomas Hamilton, James Redpath, and R. F. Wallcut of Boston all published versions of Brown's *The Black Man* in 1863. Hamilton's

firm, run by his sons Robert and William, published the periodical the *Weekly Anglo-African*. Interestingly, a version of *The Black Man* was also published for James M. Symms & Co. of Savannah, Georgia, in 1863. According to records at the Library Company of Philadelphia, Symms was probably James Meriles Simms, a prominent free black man of Savannah. Brown continued to argue for black heroism after the war in his *The Negro in the American Rebellion: His Heroism and His Fidelity* (Boston: Lee & Shepard, 1867). While detailing the "Gallantry, Loyalty, and Kindness of the Negro" (309), this work also used familiar popular literary categories such as "Wit and Humor of the War" (273) as an organizing principle. See Bullock, *Afro-American Periodical Press;* Joyce, *Black Book Publishers;* and Penn, *Afro-American Press.*

33. Louisa May Alcott, "The Brothers," *Atlantic Monthly* 12 (November 1863): 593; Du Bois, *Black Reconstruction in America*, 110.

34. Savage, *Standing Soldiers, Kneeling Slaves.* On the "double consciousness" of African Americans themselves, see Du Bois, *Souls of Black Folk.*

35. "A Typical Negro," *Harper's Weekly*, July 4, 1863, 429.

36. *Liberator*, January 15, 1864, 11.

37. On the "tragic mulatto" in antebellum literature, see especially Susan Gillman, "The Mulatto, Tragic or Triumphant?," and Sollors, "'Never Was Born.'" Phoebe Cary, "An Incident at Fort Wagner," Madeira Scrapbook, vol. B, Library Company.

38. "The Brothers," *Atlantic Monthly* 12 (November 1863): 586.

39. Ibid., 586, 595.

40. Ibid, 595.

41. "Tippoo Saib," *Harper's Weekly*, April 2, 1864, 215.

42. Ibid., 214.

43. Ibid., 215.

44. Ibid.

45. Ibid.

46. For another story in which black freedom quickly was converted into death as a soldier, see "Little Starlight," *Harper's Weekly*, October 29, 1864, 702.

47. "The Escaped Slave and the Union Soldier," *Harper's Weekly*, July 2, 1864, 422 (illustration on 428).

48. Ibid.

49. "Little Starlight," *Harper's Weekly*, October 29, 1864, 702.

50. Ibid.

51. Ibid.

52. Trowbridge, *My Own Story*, 261.

53. Ibid., 260, 262.

54. Ibid., 262.

55. Ibid.; Trowbridge, *Cudjo's Cave*, 113.

56. Trowbridge, *Cudjo's Cave*, 118.

57. Ibid., 132–33.

58. Ibid., 120.

59. Ibid., 444, 445, 228, 501.

60. Trowbridge, *My Own Story*, 263–64. Trowbridge also commented, "A private letter to the author from Secretary Chase, then at the zenith of his fame as a national financier, was made to do service in ways he could hardly have anticipated any more than I did when the publishers obtained permission of him to use it. It was printed, and extensively copied by the press, and the interior of every street-car in Boston was placarded with a signed extract from it, outstaring the patient public week after week in a manner that would have made the great Secretary wince, could he have seen it, as it did me" (263–64). Elizabeth Boynton to Will Harbert, February 20, 1864, Elizabeth Boynton Harbert Papers, Huntington Library.

61. "A Man Knows a Man," *Harper's Weekly*, April 22, 1865, 256.

62. "One Good Turn Deserves Another," *Southern Illustrated News*, March 14, 1863, 8. This cartoon was copied from the *Punch* (London) of August 9, 1862. "Nights on the Rapidan," *Southern Illustrated News*, March 5, 1864, 68.

63. "Nights on the Rapidan," *Southern Illustrated News*, March 5, 1864, 68.

64. "Fidelis," "The Scout of Albado; or, Vengeance Is Mine: A Tale of Retribution," *Southern Field and Fireside*, November 12, 1864, 2.

65. Ibid.

66. Ibid.

67. Ibid., November 26, 1864, 2.

68. Ibid.

69. Ibid., December 3, 1864, 2.

70. "Hermine," "The Contraband's Return," *Richmond Whig*, May 26, 1864.

71. "A Southern Scene from Life," M. J. Solomons Scrapbook, Special Collections Library, Duke University.

72. "Philanthropy Rebuked: A True Story," M. J. Solomons Scrapbook, Special Collections Library, Duke University.

73. "Hermine" [Susan Blanchard Elder], "The Old Mammy's Lament for Her Young Master," *Southern Literary Messenger* 34 (November–December 1863): 732–33. For the identification of "Hermine," see *Southland Writers*, 1:334–45.

74. Carby, introduction to Harper, *Iola Leroy or Shadows Uplifted*, xxi–xxii.

75. "Why It Could Not Be," *Harper's Weekly*, June 25, 1864, 406–7.

76. Lousia May Alcott, "M. L.," *Journal of Negro History* 14 (October 1929): 496. "M. L" appeared in the Boston *Commonwealth* between January 24 and February 21, 1863. For information on the *Commonwealth*, see Mott, *History of American Magazines, 1850–1865*, 536.

77. Alcott, "M. L.," 522.

78. *American Publishers' Circular and Literary Gazette*, October 15, 1863, 439.

79. Sargent, *Peculiar*, 116, 122.

80. Ibid., 21, 149, 349–58, 490.

81. *American Publishers' Circular and Literary Gazette*, November 16, 1863, 66; December 1, 1863, 108. Elizabeth Boynton to William Harbert, Elizabeth Boynton Harbert Papers, Huntington Library.

82. "The Negro in the War," *Frank Leslie's Illustrated Newspaper*, January 16, 1864, 267. The two-page illustration is on 264–65 of the same issue.

83. Ibid.

CHAPTER SIX

1. Seitz, *Artemus Ward*, 113–14.

2. See Locke, *Struggles (Social, Financial and Political) of Petroleum V. Nasby*, 15; interleaved advertisement from the *Springfield (Massachusetts) Republican*, in Kerr, *Orpheus C. Kerr Papers* (1871).

3. For an announcement of a new humor magazine, *Hard Tack*, see *Southern Illustrated News*, May 7, 1864, 144. For the announcement of a "new comic weekly," the *Bugle Horn of Liberty*, see *Magnolia Weekly*, August 8, 1863. *Southern Illustrated News*, April 11, 1863, 3. See the column "Humors of the War" in *Frank Leslie's Illustrated Newspaper*, April 5, 1862, 331.

4. Caricature Soldier Valentines, 1861–65, Nicholson Collection, Huntington Library.

5. "I Am Sick, Don't Draft Me, 'I have got a Doctor's certificate,'" Broadside, Confederate Broadside Poetry Collection, Wake Forest University.

6. Winner, *He's Gone to the Arms of Abraham*.

7. Kerr, *Orpheus C. Kerr Papers* (1871), xv.

8. There were lesser-known humorists publishing war humor during the war as well. See, for instance, Hills, *Macpherson, the Confederate Philosopher*; Burnett, *Incidents of the War*; and *Letters of Major Jack Downing, of the Downingville Militia*, a work that purported to be a continuation of Seba Smith's famous antebellum *Letters of J. Downing, Major, Downingville Militia*. In addition, James Russell Lowell began to publish a second series of his "Biglow Papers" in the January 1862 *Atlantic Monthly*. Lowell had achieved substantial success with his first series of "Biglow Papers," antiwar humorous verse published from 1846 to 1848. Lowell had invented the character Hosea Biglow, who spoke in a homespun, commonsensical Yankee vernacular against the Mexican War and against slavery. A foil for Biglow was the character Birdofredum Sawin, who had eagerly enlisted in the war only to suffer a series of misadventures. A third character was the cautious Parson Wilbur, who epitomized New England conservativism. Lowell reintroduced these characters during the Civil War in a second series of the Biglow Papers. But this series, which began with a meditation on the Mason and Slidell affair, did not achieve the same level of popularity as his first series. On Lowell's career, see Thomas Wortham, "James Russell Lowell," in *Dictionary of Literary Biography*, 11:291–303; McGlinchee, *James Russell Lowell*; and Lowell, *Biglow Papers. Second Series*.

9. Mark Twain not only met and was entertained by Artemus Ward, but his own use of an American vernacular was shaped by the literary tradition represented by the Civil War humorists. It is interesting to note that Joel Chandler Harris, too, got his start as a humorist during the war while working as a teenager

on the *Countryman*. For that periodical, Harris wrote humorous letters to Lincoln, in dialect, as the character Obadiah Skinflint. On Harris's wartime writings see Harris, *Life and Letters*, 44–49; and Harris, *On the Plantation*.

10. Kerr, *Orpheus C. Kerr Papers* (1871), xv; Bremner, "Orpheus C. Kerr," 122; "Editor's Table," *Southern Literary Messenger* 34 (January 1862): 73; *Southern Illustrated News*, May 14, 1864, 145. For another reprinting of an Orpheus C. Kerr column, see "Humors of the War" in the *Richmond Daily Dispatch*, September 29, 1862.

11. For a discussion of Kerr's criticisms of the 1861 National Hymn Committee, see chapter 2; Kerr, *Orpheus C. Kerr Papers* (1862), 50.

12. One of the hallmarks of Victorian culture, as Karen Halttunen has pointed out, was its status-oriented performative aspect, whether expressed in elaborate rituals of courtesy or parlor theatricals. See Halttunen, *Confidence Men and Painted Women*. Kerr, *Orpheus C. Kerr Papers* (1862), 89–90.

13. Kerr, *Orpheus C. Kerr Papers* (1862), 139–40.

14. Ibid., 47–49.

15. Ibid., 379–80. For a discussion of the Victorian fascination with war, see Royster, *Destructive War*, chap. 6.

16. Kerr, *Orpheus C. Kerr Papers* (1862), 380.

17. Ibid., 381–82.

18. "Radway's Remedies, the Soldier's Friend," Broadside Collection, n.d., American Antiquarian Society. Advertisement, McCallister Civil War Scrapbooks, vol. 2 of Civil War Miscellanies, Library Company. See also advertisements in McCallister Civil War Scrapbooks, Civil War Era Posters, vol. 5, Library Company.

19. Kerr, *Orpheus C. Kerr Papers* (1862), 239.

20. Ibid., 297, 304–5, 348–49.

21. Kerr, *Orpheus C. Kerr Papers. Second Series*, 232–33. In another of the Mackerel Brigade's comic battles, Captain Villiam Brown was described as having "just assumed the attitude in which he desired Frank Leslie's Illustrated Artist to draw him." See Kerr, *Orpheus C. Kerr Papers* (1862), 311.

22. Kerr, *Orpheus C. Kerr Papers* (1862), 219.

23. Ibid., 278–79. For another parody of women's home-front patriotism, see W. C. Eaton, "The Female War Club," *Sunday Mercury*, January 19, 1862.

24. "Mother Would Comfort Me," "Mother Would Wallop Me," Song Sheet Collection, Library Company. In this vein, see also "Mother, I've Come Home to Eat," a parody on "Mother, I've Come Home to Die," Song Sheet Collection, Library Company. "Mother on the Brain," Song Sheet Collection, Library Company.

25. Kerr, *Orpheus C. Kerr Papers. Second Series*, 91.

26. For information on Charles Farrar Browne's career as a writer, see Austin, *Artemus Ward*, and Seitz, *Artemus Ward*.

27. Ward, *Artemus Ward: His Book*, 217, 218.

28. Ibid., 219.

29. First publishd in the *Findlay (Ohio) Jeffersonian* on April 25, 1862; reprinted

as "Negro Emigration" in subsequent collections of Locke's work. See Nasby, *Struggles (Social, Financial, and Political) of Petroleum V. Nasby*, 41.

30. Ibid., 42.

31. Nasby, *Nasby*, 40–43.

32. Ibid., 84–89.

33. Ibid., 102.

34. Ibid., 96–97.

35. Kerr, *Orpheus C. Kerr Papers* (1862), 320–21, 148.

36. Tramp, *War Life*, 37–38. This incident was also reprinted under the heading "Humors of the War" in *Frank Leslie's Illustrated Newspaper*, April 5, 1862, 331. For another piece of contraband humor, see "A Contraband Story," *Frank Leslie's Illustrated Newspaper*, May 2, 1863, 94.

37. Moore, *Anecdotes, Poetry, and Incidents of the War*, 141–2.

38. Ward, *Artemus Ward: His Book*, 199. On the connection between Democratic politics and minstrelsy, see Baker, *Affairs of Party*, and Lott, *Love and Theft*. See also Roediger, *Wages of Whiteness*.

39. Austin, *Artemus Ward*, 44–47; *Vanity Fair*, January 26, 1861. Ward moved from Ohio to New York in the fall of 1860.

40. As reprinted in De Fontaine, *Marginalia*, 55; *Vanity Fair*, April 19, 1862, 188. In 1869, Mark Twain made fun of the journalistic use of the "reliable contraband" in a humorous toast before the New York Press Club. See Starr, *Bohemian Brigade*, 246–47.

41. De Fontaine, *Marginalia*, 55; "Scene in a Yankee Barber Shop," *Southern Punch*, October 10, 1863, 4.

42. [Halpine], *Life and Adventures*, 55. On Halpine's career see Hanchett, *Irish*.

43. Charles Graham Halpine to Margaret Halpine, April 3, 1862, Charles Graham Halpine Papers, Huntington Library. On the antipathy of the Irish to blacks, see Ignatiev, *How the Irish Became White*; David Roediger, *The Wages of Whiteness*; and Iver Bernstein, *The New York City Draft Riots*. [Halpine], *Life and Adventures*, viii, 26.

44. [Halpine], *Life and Adventures*, 56–57. Halpine even imagined President Lincoln's approval of Miles O'Reilly's song, reporting that Lincoln had said that "that song of his is both good and will do good."

45. "Birds of a Feather," *Southern Punch*, December 5, 1863, 5; "Mastered but Not Manned," *Southern Punch*, December 26, 1863, 4.

46. "The Returned Prodigal," *Southern Punch*, January 2, 1864, 4; "Home Again —Back from the Yankee Camp," *Southern Punch*, July 2, 1864, 4.

47. Arp, *Bill Arp, So Called*, 24–25, 28. In his wartime letters Arp referred to Lincoln as "Abe Linkhorn," with the "horn" suggesting Lincoln's devilish qualities. When Arp gathered his pieces together in a book after the war, however, he "translated" the peculiar spellings of his wartime letters in order to reach a wider national audience.

48. Ibid., 115.

49. Ibid., 19.

50. Ibid, 75, 77.

51. Ibid., 78; "I Am Not Sick, I'm over Forty-Five," Broadside, Confederate Broadside Collection, Wake Forest University.

52. Arp, *Bill Arp, So Called*, 36, 37.

53. Ibid., 37.

54. Ibid., 134.

55. Ward, *Artemus Ward (His Travels) among the Mormons*, 92; Arp, *Bill Arp, So Called*, 139.

56. Arp, *Bill Arp, So Called*, 132, 137

57. Mary Douglas, "Jokes," in Mukerji and Schudson, *Rethinking Popular Culture*, 295, 296, 305; Ward, *Artemus Ward: His Book*, 176, 185–86; Barber, *War Letters of a Disbanded Volunteer*.

58. Hynes, *War Imagined*, 57.

CHAPTER SEVEN

1. *New York Times*, May 25, 1863, 5.

2. Advertisement on back cover of Willett, *Vicksburg Spy*.

3. On cheap novels, see an 1862 ad by a consortium of cheap publishers referring to their "Cheap Novels" in Sutton, *Western Book Trade*, 245. Reynolds, *Beneath the American Renaissance*.

4. William Everett, "Beadle's Dime Books," manuscript, Charles Eliot Norton Papers, Houghton Library; Melville, *Confidence Man*, as quoted in Grimsted, *Melodrama Unveiled*, 234. On the conventions of sensationalist literature, see especially Noel, *Villains Galore*; Reynolds, *Beneath the American Renaissance*; Grimsted, *Melodrama Unveiled*; Denning, *Mechanic Accents*; and Bold, "Popular Forms I."

5. *Harper's Weekly*, September 3, 1864, 576; July 22, 1865, 464.

6. *New York Tribune*, November 12, 1863, as quoted in Johannsen, *House of Beadle and Adams*, 1:45–46; Everett, "Beadle's Dime Books."

7. Advertisement in *Phunny Phellow* 4 (September 1863): 16.

8. Not all such novels were about the war. Advertisement for Redpath's "Books for Camp and Home," *Frank Leslie's Illustrated Newspaper*, February 27, 1864, 366. On Redpath's career as a publisher, see Stern, *Imprints on History*, 76–83.

9. Billings, *Hardtack and Coffee*, 57–58; Wiley, *Life of Billy Yank*, 154, 155. Edwin Howland Blashfield, undated memoir, Blashfield Papers, New-York Historical Society. I am indebted to Marc Aronson for this reference. *Sunday Mercury*, March 2, 1862.

10. Everett, "Beadle's Dime Books"; "Sketches of the Publishers: The American News Company," *Round Table*, April 21, 1866, 250.

11. On Barclay's career, see McDade, "Lurid Literature of the Last Century." Several of these publishers banded together during the war in an attempt to regulate prices; see Sutton, *Western Book Trade*, 245.

12. On female heroines in sensational novels, see Grimstead, *Melodrama Unveiled*; Noel, *Villains Galore*; Bold, "Popular Forms I"; and McDade, "Lurid Literature of the Last Century." On Edmonds, see Frank Schneider, *Post and Tribune*,

Detroit, October, 1883, in Clarke Historical Library, Central Michigan University, as quoted in Wheelwright, *Amazons and Military Maids*, 22.

13. Bold, "Popular Forms I," 297; *Miriam Rivers, the Lady Soldier*, 42; Alcott, *Journals of Louisa May Alcott*, 105.

14. On women soldiers, see Leonard, *All the Daring of a Soldier;* "The Romance of a Poor Young Girl," *New York Illustrated News*, June 14, 1863, 99.

15. Willett, *Kate Sharp*, 23, 29–30. *Kate Sharp* was first published in the "American Tales" series in February 1865. See Johannsen, *House of Beadle and Adams*, 1:127–28.

16. Robinson, *Scotto, the Scout*, 4, 6.

17. On warfare in the border states, see McPherson, *Battle Cry of Freedom*. On the violence of warfare in Missouri in particular, see Fellman, *Inside War*. The March 1862 "In Western Missouri," for instance, featured the conversion of Squire Jennifer, whose initial diatribe against the "white-livered, blue-bellied Abolitionists" changed dramatically once he learned the "bitter lesson involved in finding himself flying, a fugitive and homeless wanderer, from those whose treason he had virtually abetted." "In Western Missouri," *Harper's Weekly*, March 1, 1862, 138, 139.

18. "On the Kentucky Border," *Harper's Weekly*, February 1, 1862, 70.

19. Ibid.

20. Ibid.

21. Ibid.

22. "Brown Meg" appears in Robinson, *Round Pack*, 4.

23. On Brownlow, see particularly Coulter, *William G. Brownlow*. For a contemporary description of Brownlow as the "fighting parson," see *Frank Leslie's Illustrated Newspaper*, June 14, 1862, 176. *New York Tribune*, July 12, 1862. On Brownlow's royalties, see *American Publishers' Circular and Literary Gazette*, October 1, 1862, 97. *New York Tribune*, July 21, 1862. Coulter, *William G. Brownlow*, 214, 217.

24. Moore, *Rebellion Record*, 1:109; Coulter, *William G. Brownlow*, 159, 231; advertisement under "New Publications," *New York Tribune*, July 4, 1862; *New York Times*, May 14, 1862.

25. Reynolds, *Miss Martha Brownlow*, 21, 22. Like a few other sensational novels, this volume was published in German as well as English.

26. Ibid., 24, 25. For an unusual sensational novel in which the threat to the Union heroine, the wife of a common soldier, came from a depraved Union officer, see Long, *Harry Todd, the Deserter*. This novel suggested some of the same class concerns that animated feminized fiction decrying the wartime living conditions of soldiers' wives. (See chapter 4.)

27. Palmer, *Six Months among the Secessionists*, 17.

28. Ibid., 17, 18, 25.

29. On Metta Victor's career, see Johannsen, *House of Beadle and Adams*, 2:278–85. Victor, *Unionist's Daughter*, 173. In 1861 Victor published *Maum Guinea; or Christmas among the Slaves*, a novel reminiscent of Harriet Beecher Stowe's *Uncle Tom's Cabin*.

30. Victor, *Unionist's Daughter*, 103, 186, 212.

31. Ibid., "Preliminary Note by the Author" and "Addenda," 217, 222.

32. For the copyright date, see Thomas McDade, comp., "List of Imprints of the E. E. Barclay Co." (1957), American Antiquarian Society. Reynolds, *Lady Lieutenant*, title page.

33. Reynolds, *Lady Lieutenant*, 13, 14. On domesticity as critique rather than celebration, see Baym, *Woman's Fiction*, and Romero, "Domesticity and Fiction."

34. Reynolds, *Lady Lieutenant*, 13, 16.

35. Ibid., 17, 19, 33.

36. Ibid., 22, 36, 25, 37.

37. Ibid., 34.

38. See *McElroy's Philadelphia City Directory* from 1861 to 1865.

39. These broadsides can be found in the collection of the American Antiquarian Society.

40. Bradshaw, *Pauline of the Potomac*, 31, 33.

41. Ibid., 49.

42. Ibid., 34.

43. Ibid., 45. On melodrama, see Grimsted, *Melodrama Unveiled*, and Brooks, *Melodramatic Imagination*. Bradshaw, *Pauline of the Potomac*, 47.

44. Bradshaw, *Pauline of the Potomac*, 63, 68, 69.

45. Ibid., 100. For other examples of sensationalist novels featuring cross-dressing women soldiers, see Buntline, *Sadia; Dora, the Heroine of the Cumberland; Modern Niobe;* and *Miriam Rivers, the Lady Soldier.*

46. Advertisement in the *New York Times*, May 25, 1863, 5.

47. Robinson, *Mountain Max*, 15.

48. Ibid., 20, 77.

49. Willett, *Kate Sharp*, 14, 19; Palmer, *Six Months among the Secessionists*, 18, 25. On minstrelsy, see Lott, *Love and Theft;* Baker, *Affairs of Party;* Roediger, *Wages of Whiteness.*

50. Palmer, *Six Months among the Secessionists*, 34, 35, 36, 37.

51. "In Western Missouri," *Harper's Weekly*, March 1, 1862, 138–39.

52. Robinson, *Scotto, the Scout*, 68, 46; Robinson, *Round Pack*, 71; "The Tennessee Blacksmith," *Harper's Weekly*, March 29, 1862, 202.

53. Bradshaw, *Angel of the Battle-Field*, 12.

54. Ibid., 12, 90–91. See an intriguing exception to this general rule for sensational literature, however. The 1862 *Rebel Pirate's Fatal Prize* was the fictionalized "Life History" of the "brave and daring negro" William Tillman, who early in the war had killed the master of a Confederate privateer after its capture of the schooner on which Tillman served as steward. This rare sensational novel provided a portrait of Tillman's individual heroism and daring, not his subservience to or love for whites. His was "a stirring history," the novel concluded, and "the next we hear of him, faithful still to his love of country, and desire to serve in some capacity in the good work of crushing out this rebellion,—he accompanied an officer of the Seventh New York Cavalry as an assistant." In response to a Confederate threat to arrest him as a slave, Tillman's "blood is up, and in his course of

vengeance through their land, we believe he will make not a few dastardly traitors bite the dust at his feet before this war is closed." Circular for *The Rebel Pirate's Fatal Prize; the Bloody Tragedy of the Prize Schooner Waring*, McCallister Civil War Scrapbooks, Library Company; *Rebel Pirate's Fatal Prize*, 46.

55. "Sketches of the Publishers: The American News Company," *Round Table*, April 7, 1866, 218. For a sample of the advertising of late wartime "thrilling" war stories, see the *Frank Leslie's Illustrated Newspaper* ad for "My Love Story; or the thrilling adventures of a Southern Soldier impressed into the rebel army, whose sympathies were with the North." "It Sells Like Hot Cakes! We pay Agents $100 per month," this ad announced. *Frank Leslie's Illlustrated Newspaper*, August 20, 1864, 350.

56. "Yankee War Literature," *Southern Field and Fireside*, December 3, 1864, 4; "A New Light in Letters," *Southern Illustrated News*, June 13, 1863, 4; "Yankee War Literature," 4.

57. *Southern Field and Fireside*, November 5, 1864, 7. *The Captain's Bride* was called "Illustrated Mercury Novelette No. 1," as it was published by the *Raleigh Mercury*. But the *Mercury* and the *Field and Fireside* merged late in 1864. Thus the other novels in the same series were called the "Southern Field and Fireside Novelette" No. 2 and No. 3. Advertisements for these novels are in *Southern Field and Fireside*, November 5, 1864; January 14, 1865; February 18, 1865; and February 25, 1865. *The Scout of Albado* was not published.

58. *Southern Field and Fireside*, Februrary 18, 1865; February 11, 1865; see also February 4, 1865.

59. Mountaineer, "Ned Arlington; or, Harper's Ferry Scenes," *Southern Illustrated News*, October 4, 1862, 2. For other stories reflecting the continuing interest in John Brown's raid, see "The Little Incendiary," *Southern Illustrated News*, October 18, 1862, 4, and "The First Campaign of a Fat Volunteer: A Sketch of the John Brown War," *Southern Illustrated News*, January 10, 1863, 4, and January 17, 1863, 4.

60. Mountaineer, "Ned Arlington," 2.

61. Ibid., 2; "The Little Incendiary," *Southern Illustrated News*, October 18, 1862, 4.

62. "The Scout of Albado; or, Vengeance Is Mine," *Southern Field and Fireside*, November 9, 1864, 2; December 3, 1864, 2; November 12, 1864, 1; November 19, 1864, 2.

63. "The Scout of Albado," November 19, 1864, 2.

64. Edgeville, *Castine*, 4, 5, 7, 8. See the epigraph to this chapter for a rare Confederate poem featuring a female soldier.

65. Herrington, *Captain's Bride*, 9, 10.

CHAPTER EIGHT

1. Edwin Howland Blashfield, undated memoir, Blashfield Papers, New-York Historical Society. William Everett, "Beadle's Dime Novels," manuscript, Charles

Eliot Norton Papers, Houghton Library. Everett's comment supports the contention of scholars of reading that nineteenth-century readers read a wide variety of material, with different works filling different needs at different times—whether in a sickbed, in the parlor, in the railroad car, or in camp. On such diverse reading, see especially Sicherman, "Sense and Sensibility."

2. Journal of Grenville Holland Norcross, March 2, 1865, American Antiquarian Society. For his lending of the book, see his March 8, 1865, entry. On Norcross, see also Marten, *Children's Civil War*, 31–32. On the publication date of *Kate Sharp*, see Johannsen, *House of Beadle and Adams*, 1:128. Johannsen surmises that these cheap war novels were published for Beadle and Company, although they bear the imprint of the American News Company. See Johannsen, *House of Beadle and Adams*, 1:127–28. Willett, *Old Bill Woodworth*; Willett, *Vicksburg Spy*; Willett, *Crazy Dan*; and Warren, *Old Hal Williams*. For Norcross's journal entries on these novels, see June 5, 1864; November 13, 1864; January 11, 1865; and February 23, 1865.

3. Journal of Grenville Holland Norcross, June 11, 1862; October 19, 1862; January 11, 1863; January 21, 1863; February 4, 1863; February 24, 1863; April 2, 1863; May 2, 1863; May 9, 1863; January 3, 1864; May 7, 1864; July 27, 1864; December 24, 1864; January 2, 1865; February 14, 1865, American Antiquarian Society.

4. Ibid., August 7, 1863; December 28, 1861; April 21, 1863; and December 25, 1863.

5. *Little Drummer Boy*, 15.

6. *Youth's Companion*, August 15, 1861, 130; *Little Drummer Boy*, 119.

7. The *Youth's Companion* commented that "the New York papers make the following record, of one of the mournful events of the present war," before introducing a description of McKenzie. *Youth's Companion*, August 15, 1861, 130. For Grenville Norcross's mention of the *Youth's Companion*, see his diary entry for June 21, 1863, Grenville H. Norcross Journals, American Antiquarian Society. For information on the *Youth's Companion*, see Mott, *History of American Magazines, 1850–1865*, 262–74.

8. Will S. Hays, "The Drummer Boy of Shiloh" (Chicago: D. P. Faulds, 186[?]). For additional sentimental drummer boy songs, see "The Drummer Boy's Farewell," "The Drummer Boy of Nashville," "The Drummer Boy of Vicksburg," and "The Drummer of Antietam," in Song Sheet Collection, Library Company.

9. For a later wartime depiction of a pious drummer boy, see Charles Carleton Coffin's account of the fifteen-year-old Frankie Bragg's death after Fort Donelson in Carleton, *My Days and Nights on the Battle-field*, 277–80. "The Boy Soldier," *Merry's Museum* 44 (July 1862): 6. "Little Soldiers," *Youth's Companion*, February 26, 1863, 35. For more examples of "playing at war" from children's magazines during the war, see Marten, *Lessons of War*, 73–86.

10. "Modern Implements of War," *Merry's Museum* 42 (November 1861): 138–41; "How a Man Feels When He Is Shot," *Youth's Companion*, October 3, 1861, 158; "Picket Guards," *Youth's Companion*, January 15, 1863, 12; Coffin, *My Days and Nights on the Battle-field*, 23.

11. "The Boy Soldier," *Merry's Museum* 44 (July 1862): 8, 9; Cousin John, *Drummer Boy*, 31.

12. "The Michigan Drummer Boy," *Youth's Companion*, February 26, 1863, 34–35.

13. "The Boy Soldier," *Youth's Companion*, July 9, 1863, 111; Grenville H. Norcross, July 20, 1864, Grenville H. Norcross Journals, American Antiquarian Society.

14. "The Soldier Boy" paper fan, McCallister Civil War Scrapbooks, vol. 2 of Civil War Miscellanies, Library Company.

15. Thomas Nast, "The Drummer Boy of Our Regiment," *Harper's Weekly*, December 19, 1862, 805.

16. For the publishing date, see *American Publishers' Circular and Literary Gazette*, June 1, 1863, 142. Trowbridge, *My Own Story*, 260. Trowbridge no doubt drew on newspaper accounts of drummer boys in writing his novel. But as Bell Irvin Wiley has warned, "martial exploits of drummer boys must be considered with caution, owing to the appeal which the subject has had for balladists and romancers." See Wiley, *Life of Billy Yank*, 297. *Youth's Companion*, July 30, 1863, 123.

17. *American Publishers' Circular and Literary Gazette*, June 1, 1863, 142.

18. On juvenile biography, see Casper, *Constructing American Lives*, and Meigs, *Critical History of Children's Literature*.

19. Uncle Juvinell, *Farmer Boy*, 4. Edward Everett Hale, "The Man without a Country," *Atlantic Monthly* 12 (December 1863): 665–79.

20. James Perkins Walker to "Friends," 1866, James Perkins Walker Papers, Firestone Library, Princeton University. By October 1, 1863, Walker, Wise and Co. advertised the "10th thousand" of *The Pioneer Boy* in the *American Publishers' Circular and Literary Gazette*; on December 15 the company said, "We are selling the Eleventh Thousand"; on February 1, 1864, the "Thirteenth Thousand"; on May 2, 1864, 21,000; and on September 15, 1864, 26,000. Figures for the sales of Mayne Reid's books during the 1850s are taken from Tryon and Charvat, *Cost Books of Ticknor and Fields and Their Predecessors*.

21. *American Literary Gazette and Publishers' Circular*, March 15, 1864, 344, 355; May 16, 1864, 54; June 1, 1864, 103; September 15, 1864, 299, 358. Though announced, *The Tailor Boy* was never published. The close competition among publishers of "boy" books resulted in some confusion and occasional acrimony. Titles were repeated: there were two books titled *The Sailor Boy*, for instance; and in May 1864 Roberts Brothers announced a life of Grant called *The Farmer Boy*, only to have to retract its announcement a few weeks later, saying that "it was an error" to announce that "they were to publish 'The Farmer Boy,' as that work is published by Walker, Wise & Co" (May 16, 1864, 66; June 1, 1864, 80). Having chosen a new title, *The Tanner Boy*, for its Grant biography, Roberts Brothers then engaged in an advertising battle with W. H. Appleton, which also published a life of Grant (*The Hero Boy*, by Phineas Camp Headley). "As we are abundantly able to supply the demand for a Boy's Life of General Grant," Roberts Brothers complained, "we do not see the necessity which calls for *another* life, and we trust 'The Trade' will also

see it in this light." *American Literary Gazette and Publishers' Circular,* October 1, 1864, 370.

22. On Mayne Reid, see Steele, *Captain Mayne Reid.* On the beginnings of adventure literature for children, see Meigs, *Critical History of Children's Literature,* 214–24.

23. Optic's series was called the "Army and Navy Stories"; Castlemon's was the "Gunboat Series"; Alger's was the "Campaign" series. Alger followed *Frank's Campaign* with the martial-sounding *Paul Prescott's Charge,* but this second volume was not about the war.

24. Scharnhorst, *Lost Life of Horatio Alger, Jr.,* 57, 62.

25. Ibid., 54.

26. Alger, *Frank's Campaign,* 20; Scharnhorst, *Lost Life of Horatio Alger, Jr.,* 63. Loring took advantage of the literary marketplace to publish an increasing number of juveniles, including works by Louisa May Alcott.

27. For Castlemon's life, see especially Blanck, *Harry Castlemon.* Reid, *Boy Hunters,* 12.

28. Blanck, *Harry Castlemon,* 4. *American Literary Gazette and Publishers' Circular,* December 15, 1864. The title page of the first volume of the series, *Frank, the Young Naturalist,* bore the phrase "By H. C. Castlemon, 'The Gun-Boat Boy.' "

29. Hunt, *Family Romance of the French Revolution.* For the American context, see especially Fliegelman, *Prodigals and Pilgrims.* Trowbridge, *Drummer Boy,* 5; Optic, *Soldier Boy,* 11. Wiley, *Life of Billy Yank,* 296–300. No word for "teenager" existed during the Civil War; boys were considered "children" until eighteen (in some cases sixteen). The ages of drummer boys and boy soldiers were variable, in part because of changes in government policy during the war. As Wiley points out, "apparently no minimum age was specified" for drummer boys "until March 3, 1864, when an act of Congress prohibited the enlistment of any person under sixteen." However, the War Department did forbid, as early as August 1861, the acceptance of soldiers under the age of eighteen without parental consent; in 1862 it forebade minors entirely. The reality, however, was that possibly as many as 1 percent of Union soldiers were underage and that a sprinkling of soldiers were as young as twelve. Some drummer boys may have been even younger (Wiley, *Life of Billy Yank,* 296–300).

30. Trowbridge, *Drummer Boy,* 9; in *The Soldier Boy,* the father was a naval captain trapped in the South when war broke out.

31. Optic, *Soldier Boy,* 159, 184, 223, 224–25.

32. Ibid., 5.

33. Benjamin Tarr to Lee and Shepard, May 10, 1864, Lee and Shepard Archives, American Antiquarian Society. See also orders from C. W. Deetrick, stationed in Tennessee; Charles C. H. Webb in Salem Church, Virginia; George L. Wright in Savannah, Georgia.

34. *Youth's Companion,* August 6, 1863, 127; *American Publishers' Circular and Literary Gazette,* October 15, 1863, 446; *American Literary Gazette and Publishers' Circular,* June 1, 1864, 103.

35. Grenville Howland Norcross Diary, January 31, 1865, Grenville Howland

Norcross Journals, American Antiquarian Society. "Little Soldiers," *Youth's Companion*, February 26, 1863, 35; "A Brave Kentucky Girl," *Youth's Companion*, January 1, 1863, 3. See also "A Brave Woman" on page 4 of the same issue.

36. *Youth's Companion*, February 5, 1863, 22.

37. Louisa M. Alcott, "Nelly's Hospital," *Our Young Folks* 1 (April 1865): 267; "Mittens for the Soldiers," *Youth's Companion*, December 12, 1861, 198.

38. "What the Boys and Girls Can Do," *Youth's Companion*, August 27, 1863, 138.

39. Optic, *Soldier Boy*, 262–63, 332.

40. "In an Ambulance," *Youth's Companion*, June 4, 1863, 89; "Lula's Letter: A Child's Story," *Harper's Weekly*, July 23, 1864, 478.

41. Alcott, "Nelly's Hospital," 272–74.

42. Ibid., 267–76.

43. Ibid.

44. For the announcement of *Dora Darling*, see *Youth's Companion*, December 15, 1864, 199.

45. Austin, *Dora Darling*, 14, 30, 13, 36.

46. Ibid., 44, 52.

47. Ibid., 52.

48. Ibid.

49. Ibid., 152, 150, 151, 217, 162, 164, 156–57, 161.

50. Ibid., 217, 225.

51. Ibid., 230.

52. Ibid., 261, 265, 263.

53. Ibid., 272, 273, 282.

54. Ibid., 294.

55. Ibid., 296, 297.

56. Ibid., 338.

57. *Youth's Companion*, December 15, 1864, 199.

58. Eliza B. Davis to James Perkins Walker, July 10, 1864, July 24, 1864, James Perkins Walker Papers, Firestone Library.

59. Thomas Wentworth Higginson, "Children's Books of the Year," *North American Review* 102 (January 1866): 240, 241.

60. Ibid., 242.

61. Ibid.

62. Austin, *Dora Darling*, 5; Optic, *Soldier Boy*, 201; Alger, *Frank's Campaign*, 78.

63. Marten, *Lessons of War*, xiv.

64. "Literature and Literary Progress in 1863," *American Annual Cyclopaedia*, 573. On *Our Young Folks*, see Mott, *A History of American Magazines, 1865–1885*, 175.

65. *Uncle Buddy's Gift Book for the Holidays*, iii.

66. Uncle Buddy, "The Young Confederate Soldier," in *Uncle Buddy's Gift Book for the Holidays*, 14–16; "The Little Hero," *Harper's Weekly*, August 27, 1864, 558.

67. *Uncle Buddy's Gift Book for the Holidays*, 17–19.

68. [Boykin], *Boys and Girls Stories of the War,* 10–12, 13–14.

69. Herman Melville, "The March into Virginia, Ending in the First Manassus (July, 1861)," in *Battle Pieces* (1866), as reprinted in Allen et al., *American Poetry,* 483. My thanks to Marc Aronson for reminding me of these lines.

70. The subversive nature of novel reading is one of the themes of Davidson, *Revolution and the Word.*

71. A comment by Jay Fliegelman at the June 1994 Budapest Conference titled "Constructing the Middle Class" suggested the importance of this orphan literature.

72. Roosevelt, *Theodore Roosevelt,* 16, 14, 15.

73. Ibid., 16, 25–26.

CHAPTER NINE

1. John S. C. Abbott to Ledyard Bill, December 21, 1864, John S. C. Abbott Papers, American Antiquarian Society.

2. Motley's *The Rise of the Dutch Republic* (1856) had established him as America's foremost historian of Europe. At the time of Childs's query, Motley was serving with the American legation in Vienna. John Lothrop Motley to George W. Childs, March 24, 1862, Dreer Collection. On the state of historiography at the time of the Civil War, see especially Pressly, *Americans Interpret Their Civil War;* Callcott, *History in the United States;* and Van Tassel, *Recording America's Past.*

3. John S. C. Abbott to Ledyard Bill, December 21, 1864, May 27, 1862, December 21, 1864, John S. C. Abbott Papers, American Antiquarian Society. As Abbott acknowledged, two-volume histories were a mid-nineteenth-century publishing convention. "[If] the history you are now publishing is going to stand the test of time," he wrote, "it will sell in all future years in two volumes better than in three." John S. C. Abbott to Ledyard Bill, December 21, 1864, John S. C. Abbott Papers, American Antiquarian Society.

4. On Victorian parlor culture and its relationship to consumption, see especially Blumin, *Emergence of the Middle Class;* Grier, *Culture and Comfort;* Halttunen, *Confidence Men and Painted Women;* Rose, *Victorian America and the Civil War;* and Stevenson, *Victorian Homefront.*

5. James Parton, undated draft of "Answer" to Wm. S. Washburn, James Parton Papers, Houghton Library.

6. John S. C. Abbott to Ledyard Bill, December 21, 1864, John S. C. Abbott Papers, American Antiquarian Society. Abbott, *History of the Civil War in America,* vol. 2, interleaved advertisement in copy held by the American Antiquarian Society. John S. C. Abbott to Henry Bill, November 6, 1862, John S. C. Abbott Papers, American Antiquarian Society.

7. See, for instance, his *Kings and Queens; or, Life in the Palace* (1848); *The History of Napoleon Bonaparte* (1855); *The History of Maria Antoinette* (1854); *The History of Josephine* (1851); *The French Revolution of 1789, as viewed in the light of republi-*

can institutions (1859); *The Empire of Austria: Its Rise and Present Power* (1859); *The Empire of Russia* (1860); *Italy, from the earliest period to the present day* (1860); *The History of Hernando Cortez* (1855); *Kings and Queens; or, Life in the Palace* (1848); and *South and North; or, Impressions Received during a Trip to Cuba and the South* (1860). *Dictionary of American Biography*, 1:23; Whipple, *Recollections of Eminent Men*, 150; as quoted in Pressly, *Americans Interpret Their Civil War*, 12.

8. On subscription publishing, see Michael Hackenberg, "The Subscription Publishing Network in Nineteenth-Century America," in Hackenberg, *Getting the Books Out*, 45–75, and Stafford, "Subscription Book Publishing." Stafford, "Subscription Book Publishing," 34. On the publishing ventures of the little-known Bills, see Bill, *History of the Bill Family*, 301–2, 304–5, and 295.

9. See Hackenberg, "Subscription Publishing Network in Nineteenth-Century America."

10. John S. C. Abbott to Ledyard Bill, May 31, 1862, John S. C. Abbott Papers, American Antiquarian Society.

11. John S. C. Abbott to Ledyard Bill, October 10, 1863, John S. C. Abbott Papers, American Antiquarian Society.

12. John S. C. Abbott to Henry Bill, November 6, 1862, John S. C. Abbott Papers, American Antiquarian Society.

13. John S. C. Abbott to Ledyard Bill, June 9, 1862, September 27, 1862, John S. C. Abbott Papers, American Antiquarian Society.

14. John S. C. Abbott to Ledyard Bill, December 21, 1864, May 27, 1862, June 6, 1862, John S. C. Abbott Papers, American Antiquarian Society. Abbott was particularly proud to be in correspondence with General Ormsby Mitchel; see Abbott, *History of the Civil War in America*, 2:489.

15. Abbott, *History of the Civil War in America*, 1:iii; Royster, *Destructive War*, 272.

16. Victor, *History, Civil, Political & Military*, 1:iii.

17. Abbott, *History of the Civil War in America*, 1:15.

18. Ibid., 1:22–23.

19. On mid-nineteenth-century theories of racial difference, see especially Gould, *Mismeasure of Man*, 19–72; Abbott, *History of the Civil War in America*, 2:612.

20. Abbott, *History of the Civil War in America*, 2:612.

21. *Agents' Companion*, 2, 3, 5. Henry Bill Publishing Company's *Private Instructions*. These works repeated much of the same information word for word. *Agent's Companion*, 9.

22. Prospectus for John S. C. Abbott's *History of the Civil War in America* (New York: Henry Bill, 1862), Prospectus Collection, American Antiquarian Society.

23. Prospectus for John S. C. Abbott's *History of the Civil War in America* (Springfield, Mass.: Gurdon Bill, 1862), Prospectus Collection, American Antiquarian Society. For another prospectus with listings of subsribers' names from Auburn, New York, for Elliot Gray Storke's *The Great American Rebellion*, see *The Order Book of the Great American Rebellion; Containing Samples of the Portraits, Diagrams, Maps and Other Illustrations, the Prospectus, and Conditions of Subscription,*

and Full Plan of the Work (Auburn, N.Y.: Auburn Publishing Co., n.d.). Prospectus Collection, American Antiquarian Society.

24. Greeley, *Recollections of a Busy Life*, 421.

25. Ibid., 420–21.

26. Ibid., 424.

27. From the prospectus for Kettell, *History of the Great Rebellion*, Prospectus Collection, American Antiquarian Society.

28. Greeley, *American Conflict*. 2:8.

29. VanDeusen, *Horace Greeley*, 355.

30. As quoted in Stoddard, *Horace Greeley*, 230.

31. Greeley, *Recollections of a Busy Life*, 355. For a postwar subscription agent's own account of her finances, see Nelles, *Annie Nelles*, 260–63. See also Likins, *Six Years Experience as a Book Agent*.

32. VanDeusen, *Horace Greeley*, 355. Greeley's work reportedly sold another 50,000 copies by 1870, for a total of 225,000. See the *Nation*, May 19, 1870, 320. O. D. Case to Horace Greeley, February 11, 1870, Horace Greeley Papers, New York Public Library.

33. The 1860 edition of *Malaeska* was in fact a reprinting of a serial that had appeared in *The Ladies Companion* in 1839. See Johannsen, *House of Beadle and Adams*, 2:262. Stephens, *Pictorial History of the War for the Union*, 7.

34. Stephens, *Pictorial History of the War for the Union*, title page.

35. Brooks, *Melodramatic Imagination*, 13, 205.

36. Stephens, *Pictorial History of the War for the Union*, 19, 434, 87.

37. *Nation*, May 19, 1870, 320.

38. Frank Monaghan, "Joel Tyler Headley," *The Dictionary of American Biography*, 8:479–80.

39. Prospectus for Kettell, *History of the Great Rebellion*, Prospectus Collection, American Antiquarian Society.

40. Ibid.; *Nation*, May 19, 1870, 320.

41. Pollard, *First Year of the War*, 4.

42. Ibid., 4, 3.

43. *American Publishers' Circular and Literary Gazette*, April 1, 1863, 51; "Literary Notices," *Harper's New Monthly Magazine* 27 (November 1863): 849–50.

44. Pollard, *Second Year of the War*, 306–7.

45. Alexander Davidson, "How Benson J. Lossing Wrote His 'Fieldbooks' of the Revolution, the War of 1812, and the Civil War," *Papers of the Bibliographical Society of America* 32 (1938), as quoted in *The Dictionary of Literary Biography*, 30:165; Benson J. Lossing to Lyman C. Draper, May 1, 1855, as quoted in Van Tassel, *Recording America's Past*, 92–93.

46. *American Publishers' Circular and Literary Gazette*, April 1862, 47.

47. Benson J. Lossing to Helen Lossing, July 9, 1863, Benson J. Lossing Papers, Huntington Library.

48. George W. Childs to Benson J. Lossing, March 24, 1862, Benson J. Lossing Papers, Huntington Library.

49. George W. Childs to Benson J. Lossing, April 2, 1862, Benson J. Lossing Papers, Huntington Library. In the same letter Childs commented, "I suppose they will get Porte Crayon [David Strother] or J. S. C. Abbott to do it up."

50. George W. Childs to Benson J. Lossing, July 4, 1862, Benson J. Lossing Papers, Huntington Library.

51. George W. Childs to Benson J. Lossing, December 8, 1862, April 20, 1863, Benson J. Lossing Papers, Huntington Library; Rev. Thomas B. Fairchild to Benson J. Lossing, April 2, 1863, Benson J. Lossing Papers, Huntington Library.

52. George W. Childs to Benson J. Lossing, November 24, 1863, Benson J. Lossing Papers, Huntington Library.

53. Benson J. Lossing to Helen Lossing, December 12, 1864, Benson J. Lossing Papers, Huntington Library.

54. Benson J. Lossing to Helen Lossing, December 22, 1864, December 27, 1864, December 30, 1864, Benson J. Lossing Papers, Huntington Library.

55. Lossing, *Pictorial History of the Civil War in the United States of America*, 2:564.

56. Ibid., 2:3–4.

57. Godkin, *Life and Letters*, 2:33–34. *Nation*, November 23, 1865, 661.

58. Ibid.; John Lothrop Motley to George W. Childs, March 24, 1862, Dreer Collection: Callcott, *History in the United States*, 211.

59. Lossing as quoted in Van Tassel, "Benson J. Lossing," 37.

60. *Nation*, May 19, 1870, 319–20.

61. *Cincinnati Commercial Gazette*, February 15, 1865, as quoted in Stafford, "Subscription Book Publishing," 35–36.

62. Nelles, *Annie Nelles*, 313–15.

EPILOGUE

1. Lincoln used this phrase on July 4, 1861. For the idea of "a people's contest" that affected the entire home-front population in the North, see Paludan, *"People's Contest."*

2. For a fascinating account of reenactors, see Horwitz, *Confederates in the Attic.*

3. On Duyckinck's career, see especially Greenspan, "Evert Duyckinck." Inscription on flyleaf of E. A. Duyckinck's *History of the War for the Union, Civil, Military & Naval,* copy held by Main Library of University of California, Irvine.

4. See, for instance, Frank Starr's 1872 republishing of a number of Beadle's American tales. Blanck, *Harry Castlemon*, xi.

5. For a listing of the late 1865 novels in Beadle's "American Tales" series, see Johannsen, *House of Beadle and Adams*, 1:127–30.

6. Stafford, "Subscription Book Publishing," 39. See Justin M'Carthy, "'The Divine Emilye,'" *Harper's Weekly*, May 17, 1873, and "An Old Soldier," *Harper's Weekly*, July 3, 1875. On the waning of war-related fiction in *Harper's Weekly*, see Diffley, *Where My Heart Is Turning Ever*, xxvi. Livermore, *My Story of the War*, 7. Harper, *House of Harper*, 243.

7. Linderman, *Embattled Courage*, 275, 280. On the GAR, see McConnell, *Glorious Contentment*. Older histories of the GAR include Beath, *History of the Grand Army of the Republic*, and Dearing, *Veterans in Politics*.

8. The *Century* was a continuation of *Scribner's Monthly*. For publishing details of the *Century*, see Mott, *History of American Magazines, 1865–1885*, 457–80. Tooker, *Joys and Tribulations of an Editor*, 45, 46.

9. See "Camp Echoes," *Harper's Weekly*, May 28, 1892, 511, 512; "A Ballad of May," *Harper's Weekly*, May 27, 1893, 498; "Soldiers' Memorial Services," *Century* 38 (May 1889): 156; "Decoration Day," *Harper's Weekly*, June 2, 1888, 400–401; "The Blue and the Gray at Appomattox, after General Lee's Surrender, April 9, 1865," *Harper's Weekly*, May 30, 1896, 540–41; "Memorial Day: May 30, 1899," *Harper's Weekly*, May 27, 1899, 528.

10. Roosevelt, "Brotherhood and the Heroic Life," in his *Strenuous Life*, 266. Blight, " 'For Something beyond the Battlefield,' " 1162. See also Blight, *Frederick Douglass' Civil War*, and Savage, *Standing Soldiers, Kneeling Slaves*.

11. Frances Ellen Watkins Harper's *Iola Leroy or Shadows Uplifted* made an important counterclaim to the memory of the war during the "black woman's renaissance of the 1890s." See Carby, introduction to Harper, *Iola Leroy or Shadows Uplifted*, ix.

12. Optic, *Taken by the Enemy*, 5–7. For a listing of Optic's many series, with titles such as "The Starry Flag Series," "Onward and Upward Series," "The Yacht Club Series," and "The Lake Shore Series," see Jones, *"Oliver Optic" Checklist*.

13. On the plantation mythology that characterized much late-nineteenth-century popular culture, see Sundquist, *To Wake the Nations*. A partial listing of the extensive fiction of the war by Southern white women includes Emma Lyon Bryan, *1860–1865: A Romance of the Valley of Virginia* (1892); Mollie E. Moore Davis, *In War Times at La Rose Blanche* (1888); Virginia Boyle Frazer, *Brokenburne: A Southern Auntie's War Tale* (1897); Constance Cary Harrison, *Flower de Hundred* (1890), *The Carlyles* (1905), and *Belhaven Tales* (1892); Mary Johnston, *The Long Roll* (1911); Grace King, *Tales of a Time and Place* (1892); Elizabeth Avery Meriweather, *Sowing of the Swords, or, the Soul of the Sixties* (1910); Mary Noailles Murfree, *The Storm Centre* (1905); Molly Elliott Seawell, *The Victory* (1906). For a helpful listing of Civil War fiction in the late nineteenth century, see Smith, "Civil War and Its Aftermath in American Fiction." See also Lively, *Fiction Fights the Civil War*, and Menendez, *Civil War Novels*. On Southern-oriented war literature, see Silber, *Romance of Reunion;* and Hubbell, *South in American Literature*, esp. 695–740. Several African American writers published reminiscences and fiction about the Civil War in this period, including Susie King Taylor and Frances Ellen Watkins Harper. On Harper's *Iola Leroy* and African American writing in the late nineteenth century, see Bruce, *Black American Writing from the Nadir*. Faust, "Altars of Sacrifice."

14. Horwitz, *Confederates in the Attic*, 101. On the struggles by African Americans to maintain a memory of the war centered around emancipation, see Blight, "Frederick Douglass and the Memory of the Civil War." See also Blight, *Frederick Douglass' Civil War*. On the African American historians who in the late nineteenth

century sought to remind readers of African American contributions to the war effort, see Bruce, "Ironic Conception of American History." On black historians more generally during the late nineteenth century, see Bruce, "Ancient Africa and the Early Black American Historians," and Bruce, *Black American Writing from the Nadir.*

15. On the new emphasis on battle experience, see Pettegrew, "'The Soldier's Faith.'" Linderman, *Embattled Courage,* 277. On the new "cult of experience," see Wilson, *Labor of Words,* 92, 93. On the fact that Crane drew on the 1880s *Century* series "Battles and Leaders of the Civil War" rather than accounts published during the war itself for the factual underpinnings of *The Red Badge of Courage,* see Sundquist, "The Country of the Blue," in Sundquist, *American Realism,* 4.

16. Crane, *Red Badge of Courage,* 130. Wilson, *Labor of Words,* 92, 93. Roosevelt, "The Strenuous Life," as quoted in Fredrickson, *Inner Civil War,* 225. Fredrickson's chapter "The Moral Equivalent of War" remains a compelling discussion of the changing uses to which the memory of the Civil War was put in the late nineteenth century. Roosevelt, *Theodore Roosevelt,* 275.

17. On the newly masculinized literary marketplace, see especially Wilson, *Labor of Words.* On the discomfort of some older "sentimental" writers, including Elizabeth Stuart Phelps, within this newly masculinized marketplace, see Coultrap-McQuin, *Doing Literary Business.* Willa Cather, *The Kingdom of Art: Willa Cather's First Principles and Critical Statements, 1893–1896,* ed. Bernice Slote (Lincoln: University of Nebraska Press, 1966), 409, as quoted in Sharon O'Brien, "Combat Envy and Survivor Guilt: Willa Cather's 'Manly Battle Yarn,'" in Cooper et al., *Arms and the Woman,* 184. On the New Women writers, including Kate Chopin, Charlotte Perkins Gilman, and Willa Cather, see Tichi, "Women Writers and the New Woman."

18. Hemingway as quoted in Aaron, *Unwritten War,* 210. The full quotation is "There was no real literature of our Civil War, excepting the forgotten 'Miss Ravenall's [*sic*] Conversion' by J. W. De Forest, until Stephen Crane wrote 'The Red Badge of Courage.'" McPherson, foreword to Clinton and Silber, *Divided Houses,* xiv. On Crane's realism and realism more generally, see Wilson, "Stephen Crane and the Police," and Kaplan, *Social Construction of American Realism.*

BIBLIOGRAPHY

ARCHIVES AND MANUSCRIPT COLLECTIONS

American Antiquarian Society, Worcester, Mass.
   John S. C. Abbott Papers
   Broadside Collection
   Civil War Envelope Collection
   Lee and Shepard Archives
   Grenville H. Norcross Journals
   Prospectus Collection
Columbia University, New York, N.Y.
   Harper and Brothers Archives
Firestone Library, Princeton University, Princeton, N.J.
   James Perkins Walker Papers
Historical Society of Pennsylvania, Philadelphia, Pa.
   Henry C. Carey Papers
   Ferdinand J. Dreer Autograph Collection
   Society Small Collection
Houghton Library, Harvard University, Cambridge, Mass.
   James G. Gregory Catalogs
   James Russell Lowell Papers
   Charles Eliot Norton Papers
   James Parton Papers
   Ticknor and Fields Archives
   James Redpath Papers
Huntington Library, San Marino, Ca.
   James T. Fields Collection
   Charles Graham Halpine Papers
   Elizabeth Boynton Harbert Papers
   Benson J. Lossing Papers
   Nicholson Collection
   Walt Whitman Papers
Library Company, Philadelphia, Pa.
   Broadside Collection

Civil War Envelope Collection
Comic Valentine Collection
McCallister Civil War Scrapbooks
Madeira Scrapbooks
Song Sheet Collection
New-York Historical Society, New York, N.Y.
Louisa May Alcott Papers
Blashfield Papers
New York Public Library, New York, N.Y.
Robert Bonner Papers
Horace Greeley Papers
George Palmer Putnam Papers
Special Collections Library, Duke University, Durham, N.C.
Kate D. Foster Diary
Paul Hamilton Hayne Papers
Clara Victoria Dargan Maclean Papers
Sheet Music Collection
M. J. Solomons Scrapbook
Laura Waldron Papers
Schlesinger Library, Radcliffe College, Cambridge, Mass.
Briggs Family Papers
Virginia Historical Society, Richmond, Va.
McFarlane and Ferguson Papers
Virginia Military Institute, Lexington, Va.
William J. Galt Notebook
Wake Forest University, Ohio
Confederate Broadside Collection

PERIODICALS PUBLISHED DURING THE CIVIL WAR

American Literary Gazette and Publishers' Circular
American Publishers' Circular and Literary Gazette
Arthur's Home Magazine
Atlantic Monthly
Bohemian
Commonwealth
Continental Monthly
Countryman
De Bow's Review
Edgefield Advertiser
Flag of Our Union
Frank Leslie's Budget of Fun
Frank Leslie's Illustrated Newspaper
Frank Leslie's New Monthly

Harper's New Monthly Magazine
Harper's Weekly
Independent
Magnolia Weekly
Mercury (Raleigh, N.C.)
Merry's Museum
New York Illustrated News
New York Ledger
Our Young Folks
Pacific Appeal
Peterson's
Phunny Phellow
Portrait Monthly
Rebellion Record
Record (Richmond)
Round Table
Smith and Barrow's Monthly
Southern Field and Fireside
Southern Illustrated News
Southern Literary Companion
Southern Literary Messenger
Southern Monthly
Southern Punch
Spirit of the Fair
Sunday Mercury (New York)
United States Service Magazine
Vanity Fair
Weekly Southern Spy
Youth's Companion

SONGSTERS

Beadle's Dime Knapsack Songster. New York: Beadle & Co., 1861.

The Camp Fire Songster. New York: Dick & Fitzgerald, 1862.

Dawley's Ten Penny Song Books Number 1. Ballads of the War. New York: T. R. Dawley, 1864.

Democratic Campaign Songster No. 1 McClellan and Pendleton. New York: J. F. Feeks, 1864.

The Double Quick Comic Songster. New York: Dick & Fitzgerald, 1862.

The Flag of Our Union Songster. New York: T. W. Strong, 1861.

The Jack Morgan Songster. Raleigh: Branson & Farrar, 1864.

The Little Mac Songster. New York: Dick & Fitzgerald, 1862.

The New Confederate Flag Song Book. Mobile: H. C. Clarke, 1864.

The President Lincoln Campaign Songster. New York: T. R. Dawley, 1864.

The Punch Songster: A Collection of Familiar and Original Songs and Ballads
     Richmond: Punch Office, 1864.
Soldiers' and Sailors' Patriotic Songs. New York: Loyal Publication Society, 1864.
Songs for the Union. Philadelphia: A. Winch, 1861.
The Stars and Stripes Songster No. 1. New York: R. M. DeWitt, 1861.
Tony Pastor's Union Songster. New York: Dick & Fitzgerald, 1862.
Touch the Elbow Songster. New York: Dick & Fitzgerald, 1862.
The Union Song-Book. Philadelphia: Lee & Walker, 1861.
War Songs of the American Union. Boston: William V. Spencer, 1861.
Yankee Doodle Songster. Philadelphia: A. Winch, 1861.
Yankee Volunteer's Songster. Philadelphia: A. Winch, 1862.

PRIMARY SOURCES

Abbott, John S. C. *The History of the Civil War in America.* 2 vols. New York:
     Henry Bill, 1862–64.
Abrams, Alexander St. Clair. *The Trials of the Soldier's Wife: A Tale of the Second
     American Revolution.* Atlanta: Intelligencer Steam Power-Presses, 1864.
Addey, Markinfield. *"Little Mac," and How He Became a Great General: A Life of
     George Brinton McClellan, for Young Americans.* New York: James G. Gregory,
     1864.
Agents' Companion. Philadelphia: Jones Brothers & Co., [1866–69?].
Alcott, Louisa May. *Hospital Sketches.* Boston: James Redpath, 1863. Reprint,
     edited by Bessie Z. Jones, Cambridge, Mass.: Belknap Press, 1960.
―――. *Journals of Louisa May Alcott.* Edited by Joel Myerson and Daniel
     Shealy. Boston: Little, Brown, 1989.
―――, *Little Women.* Boston: Roberts Bros., 1868.
―――. *On Picket Duty.* Boston: James Redpath, 1863.
―――. *Selected Letters of Louisa May Alcott.* Edited by Joel Myerson and Daniel
     Shealy, associate editor Madeleine B. Stern. Boston: Little, Brown, 1987.
Alexander, Charles Wesley. See Bradshaw, Wesley.
Alger, Horatio. *Frank's Campaign: Or, What Boys Can Do on the Farm for the
     Camp.* Boston: Loring, 1864.
American Annual Cyclopaedia and Register of Important Events. New York:
     D. Appleton and Co., 1864.
Arp, Bill [Charles H. Smith]. *Bill Arp, So Called: A Side Show of the Southern
     Side of the War.* New York: Metropolitan Record Office, 1866.
Austin, Jane Goodwin. *Dora Darling: The Daughter of the Regiment.* Boston: J. E.
     Tilton and Co., 1864.
Barber, Joseph. *War Letters of a Disbanded Volunteer: Embracing His Experiences as
     Honest Old Abe's Bosom Friend and Unofficial Adviser.* New York: Frederic A.
     Brady, 1864.
[Barrow, Sarah L.]. *Red, White, and Blue Socks.* New York: Leavitt and Allen,
     1863.

Bell, James Madison. *The Poetical Works of James Madison Bell*. Freeport, N.Y.: Books for Libraries Press, 1970.

Bill, Ledyard, ed. *History of the Bill Family*. New York: Ledyard Bill, 1867.

——. *Pen-Pictures of the War: Lyrics, Incidents, and Sketches of the Rebellion*. New York: Ledyard Bill, 1864.

[Boykin, Edward M.]. *The Boys and Girls Stories of the War*. Richmond: West & Johnston, [1863?].

Bradshaw, Wesley [Charles Wesley Alexander]. *The Angel of the Battle-Field: A Tale of the Rebellion*. New York: American News Co., 1865.

——. *The Captivity of General Corcoran*. Philadelphia: Barclay & Co., 1863.

——. *General Sherman's Indian Spy*. Philadelphia: C. W. Alexander, 1865.

——. *Pauline of the Potomac, or General McClellan's Spy*. Philadelphia: Barclay & Co., 1862.

——. *The Picket Slayer*. Philadelphia: Alexander & Co., 1863.

——. *The Volunteers' Roll of Honor*. Philadelphia: Barclay & Co., 1863.

Breckenridge, Lucy. *Lucy Breckenridge of Grove Hill: The Journal of a Virginia Girl, 1862–1864*. Edited by Mary D. Robertson. 1979. Reprint, Columbia: University of South Carolina Press, 1994.

Brockett, Linus P., and Mary C. Vaughan, *Woman's Work in the Civil War: A Record of Heroism, Patriotism, and Patience*. Philadelphia: Zeigler, McCurdy, and Co. 1868.

Browning, Elizabeth Barrett. *Poems by Elizabeth Barrett Browning*. 4 vols. New York: J. Miller, 1862.

Brownlow, William G. *Sketches of the Rise, Progress, and Decline of Secession; with a Narrative of Personal Adventures among the Rebels*. Philadelphia: George W. Childs, 1862.

Buntline, Ned [Edward Zane Carroll Judson]. *The Rattlesnake; or, the Rebel Privateer*. New York: Frederic A. Brady, 1862.

——. *Sadia: A Heroine of the Rebellion*. New York: Frederic A. Brady, 1864.

Burnett, Alf. *Incidents of the War: Humorous, Pathetic, and Descriptive*. Cincinnati: Rickey & Carroll, 1863.

Burns, Jeremiah. *The Patriot's Offering; or the Life, Services, and Military Career of the Noble Trio, Ellsworth, Lyon, and Baker*. New York: Baker and Godwin, 1862.

The Camp Follower. Augusta, Ga.: Stockton & Co., 1864.

The Camp Jester or, Amusement for the Mess. Augusta, Ga.: Blackmar & Bro., 1864.

Carleton [Charles Carleton Coffin]. *Following the Flag*. Boston: Ticknor and Fields, 1864.

——. *My Days and Nights on the Battle-field: A Book for Boys*. Boston: Ticknor and Fields, 1863.

Castlemon, Harry [Charles Austin Fosdick]. *Frank before Vicksburg*. Cincinnati: R. W. Carroll, 1865.

——. *Frank in the Woods*. Cincinnati: R. W. Carroll, 1865.

——. *Frank on a Gunboat*. Cincinnati: R. W. Carroll, 1864.

——. *Frank the Young Naturalist*. Cincinnati: R. W. Carroll, 1864.

————. *Marcy the Blockade-Runner* Philadelphia: Henry T. Coates, 1891.

————. *Marcy the Refugee.* Philadelphia: Porter & Coates, 1892.

————. *Rodney the Overseer.* Philadelphia: Henry T. Coates, 1892.

————. *Rodney the Partisan.* Philadelphia: Henry T. Coates, 1890.

————. *Sailor Jack the Trader.* Philadelphia: John C. Winston Co., 1893.

————. *True to His Colors.* Philadelphia: Porter & Coates, 1889.

Chesnut, Mary. *Mary Chesnut's Civil War.* Edited by C. Vann Woodward. New Haven: Yale University Press, 1981.

Child, Lydia Maria. *The Freedmen's Book.* Boston: Ticknor and Fields, 1865. Reprint, New York: Arno Press, 1968.

Confederate States Almanac for the Year of Our Lord 1864. Macon, Ga.: Burke, Boykin, & Co., 1864.

Cousin John. *The Drummer Boy: A Story of the War. (In Verse). For the Young Folks at Home.* Boston: Crosby & Nichols, 1862.

Cushman, Pauline. *The Thrilling Adventures of Pauline Cushman.* Cincinnati: Rickey & Carroll, 1864.

De Fontaine, Felix G., ed. *Marginalia; or, Gleanings from an Army Notebook.* Columbia: F. G. De Fontaine & Co., 1864.

De Leon, T. C., ed. *South Songs: From the Lays of Later Days.* 1866. Reprint, Westport, Conn.: Greenwood Press, 1977.

Delphine [Delphine P. Baker]. *Solon, or the Rebellion of '61: A Domestic and Political Tragedy.* Chicago: S. P. Rounds, 1862.

Derby, James C. *Fifty Years among Authors, Books, and Publishers.* New York: G. W. Carleton, 1884.

Dickinson, Emily. *Letters of Emily Dickinson.* Edited by Mabel Loomis Todd. Boston: Roberts Brothers, 1894.

Dodge, Mary Mapes. *The Irvington Stories.* New York: James O'Kane, 1865.

Dora, the Heroine of the Cumberland or, the American Amazon. Philadelphia: Barclay & Co., 1865.

Du Bois, W. E. B. *Black Reconstruction in America.* New York: Harcourt, Brace and Co., 1935.

————. *The Souls of Black Folk.* 1903. Reprint, New York: Vintage Books/ Library of America, 1990.

Duganne, Augustine J. H. *Ballads of the War.* New York: John Robins, 1862.

Duyckinck, Evert A. *National History of the War for the Union, Civil, Military, & Naval.* New York: Johnson, Fry & Co., 1861.

[Eastman, Mary]. *Jenny Wade of Gettysburg.* Philadelphia; J. B. Lippincott, 1864.

Edgeville, Edward. *Castine.* Raleigh: William B. Smith & Co., 1865.

Edmonds, Sarah Emma. *Unsexed: Or, the Female Soldier: The Thrilling Adventures, Experiences, and Escapes of a Woman, As Nurse and Scout, in Hospital, Camps, and Battle-field.* Philadelphia: Philadelphia Publishing Co., 1864.

Edmondston, Catherine Ann Devereux. *"Journal of a Secesh Lady": The Diary of Catherine Ann Deverux Edmondston, 1860–1866.* Edited by Beth Gilbert Crabtree and James W. Patton. Raleigh: North Carolina Division of Archives and History, 1979.

Ellet, Elizabeth. *The Women of the American Revolution.* 3 vols. New York: Baker and Scribner, 1848–50.

Estvan, B. *War Pictures from the South.* New York: D. Appleton and Co., 1864.

Evans, Augusta Jane. *Macaria; or, Altars of Sacrifice.* 1864. Reprint, edited by Drew Gilpin Faust. Baton Rouge: Louisiana State University Press, 1992.

Frank Leslie's Heroic Incidents of the Civil War in America. New York: Frank Leslie, 1862.

Fun for the Camp: A Comic Medley. Columbia, S.C.: B. Duncan, 1863.

Gilmore, James Roberts. *Personal Recollections of Abraham Lincoln and the Civil War.* Boston: L. C. Page & Co., 1898.

————. See also under Kirke, Edmund.

Godkin, Edwin Lawrence. *Life and Letters of Edwin Lawrence Godkin.* Edited by Rollo Ogden. New York: Macmillan, 1907.

Greeley, Horace. *The American Conflict: A History of the Great Rebellion in the United States of America, 1860–64.* 2 vols. Hartford: O. D. Case, 1864.

————. *Recollections of a Busy Life: Including Reminiscences of American Politics and Politicians.* New York: J. B. Ford & Co., 1868.

Greene, William S. *Thrilling Stories of the Great Rebellion.* Philadelphia: John E. Potter, 1866.

Greenwood, Grace [Sarah Jane Clarke Lippincott]. *Records of Five Years.* Boston: Ticknor and Fields, 1867.

H., Mrs. [Anna Morris Ellis Holstein]. *Three Years in Field Hospitals of the Army of the Potomac.* Philadelphia: J. B. Lippincott, 1867.

Hall, Florence Howe. *The Story of the Battle Hymn of the Republic.* New York: Harper & Bros., 1916.

[Halpine, Charles Graham]. *The Life and Adventures, Songs, Services, and Speeches of Private Miles O'Reilly. (47th Regiment, New York Volunteers).* New York: Carleton, 1864.

Hanaford, Phebe Ann Coffin, and Mary J. Webber, eds. *Chimes of Freedom and Union: A Collection of Poems for the Time, by Various Authors.* Boston: Benjamin B. Russell, 1861.

Harper, Frances E. W. *Iola Leroy or Shadows Uplifted.* 1893. Reprint, Boston: Beacon Press, 1987.

Harper, James Henry. *The House of Harper: A Century of Publishing in Franklin Square.* New York: Harper & Brothers, 1912.

Harris, Joel Chandler. *The Life and Letters of Joel Chandler Harris.* Edited by Julia Collier Harris. Boston: Houghton Mifflin, 1918.

————. *On the Plantation: A Story of a Georgia Boy's Adventures during the War.* New York: D. Appleton and Co., 1892.

Harrison, Mrs. Burton [Constance Cary]. *Recollections Grave and Gay.* New York: Charles Scribner's Sons, 1911.

[Haw, Mary Jane]. *The Rivals: A Chickahominy Story.* Richmond: Ayres & Wade, 1864.

Hazeltine, Lieut.-Col. *The Border Spy; or, the Beautiful Captive of the Rebel Camp: A Story of the War.* New York: American News Co., 1863.

————. *The Prisoner of the Mill; or, Captain Hayward's "Body-Guard."* New York: American News Co., 1864.

Headley, Joel Tyler. *The Great Rebellion: A History of the Civil War in the United States.* Hartford: Hurlbut, Williams & Co., 1862.

Headley, Rev. P. C. *The Hero Boy; or, the Life and Deeds of Lieut.-Gen. Grant.* New York: William H. Appleton, 1865.

————. *The Miner Boy and His Monitor.* New York: William H. Appleton, 1865.

————. *The Patriot Boy; or, The Life and Career of Major-General Ormsby M. Mitchel.* New York: William H. Appleton, 1864.

Heady, Morrison. See Uncle Juvinell.

The Henry Bill Publishing Company's Private Instructions to Their Agents for Selling Their Subscription Books. Norwich, Conn.: Henry Bill Publishing Co., 1874.

Herrington, W. D. *The Captain's Bride: A Tale of the War.* Raleigh: William B. Smith, 1864.

————. *The Deserter's Daughter.* Raleigh: William B. Smith, 1865.

Hills, Alfred C. *Macpherson, the Confederate Philosopher.* New York: James Miller, 1864.

Holmes, Mary J. *Rose Mather: A Tale.* New York: Carleton, 1868.

Holmes, Oliver Wendell. "The Poetry of the War." 1865 lecture, privately printed, Huntington Library.

Homer, Winslow. *Campaign Sketches.* Boston: L. Prang & Co., 1863.

Howe, Julia Ward. *Reminiscences, 1819–1899.* Boston: Houghton Mifflin, 1899.

Howe, Mary A. *The Rival Volunteers; or, the Black Plume Rifles.* New York: John Bradburn, 1864.

Incidents of American Camp Life: Being Events Which Have Actually Transpired during the Present Rebellion. New York: T. R. Dawley, 1862.

Johnson, Robert Underwood, and Clarence Clough Buel, eds. *Battles and Leaders of the Civil War.* 4 vols. New York: Century, 1887.

Kerr, Orpheus C. [Robert Henry Newell]. *The Orpheus C. Kerr Papers.* New York: Blakeman & Mason, 1862.

————. *The Orpheus C. Kerr Papers. Second Series.* New York: Carleton, 1863.

————. *The Orpheus C. Kerr Papers. Third Series.* New York: Carleton, 1865.

————. *The Orpheus C. Kerr Papers. Being a Complete Contemporaneous Military History of the Mackerel Brigade.* New York: G. W. Carleton, 1871.

Kettell, Thomas P. *History of the Great Rebellion, from Its Commencement to Its Close.* Hartford: L. Stebbins, 1865.

Kirke, Edmund [James Roberts Gilmore]. *Among the Pines: or, South in Secession-Time.* New York: Charles T. Evans, 1862.

————. *Down in Tennessee and Back by Way of Richmond.* New York: Carleton, 1864.

————. *My Southern Friends.* New York: G. P. Putnam, 1863.

Kirkland, Frazer [Richard Miller Devens]. *The Pictorial Book of Anecdotes and Incidents of the War of the Rebellion.* Hartford: Hartford Publishing Co., 1866.

Larcom, Lucy. *Life, Letters, and Diary.* Edited by Daniel Dulany Addison. Boston: Houghton Mifflin, 1895.

Leland, Charles Godfrey. *Memoirs*. New York: D. Appleton and Co., 1893.

[Lester, Charles Edward]. *The Light and Dark of the Rebellion*. Philadelphia: George W. Childs, 1863.

Letters of Major Jack Downing, of the Downingville Militia. New York: Bromley & Co., 1864.

Likins, Mrs. J. W. *Six Years Experience as a Book Agent: Including My Trip from New York to San Francisco via Nicaragua*. San Francisco: 1874. Reprint, San Francisco: Book Club of California, 1992.

The Little Drummer Boy: Clarence D. McKenzie, the Child of the Thirteenth Regiment, N.Y.S.M., and the Child of the Mission Sunday School. New York: Board of Publications of the Reformed Protestant Dutch Church, 1861.

Little Mac: How He Captured Manassas. Boston: Lee and Shepard, [ca. 1861–65].

Livermore, Mary. *My Story of the War: A Woman's Narrative of Four Years Personal Experience As Nurse in the Union Army, and in Relief Work at Home, in Hospitals, Camps, and at the Front, during the War of the Rebellion*. Hartford: A. D. Worthington and Co., 1889.

Long, R. H. *Harry Todd, the Deserter; or, the Soldier's Wife*. New York: American News Co., 1864.

Lossing, Benson J. *Pictorial History of the Civil War in the United States of America*. 3 vols., 1866–68. Vols. 1 and 2, Philadelphia: G. W. Childs, 1866; Vol. 3, Hartford: T. Belknap, 1868.

Lowell, James Russell. *The Biglow Papers. Second Series*. 1866. Reprint, Boston: Houghton Mifflin, 1885.

Lyon, Nathaniel. *The Last Political Writings of Gen. Nathaniel Lyon, U.S.A.* New York: Rudd & Carleton, 1861.

McCabe, James Dabney. *The Aid-de-Camp: A Romance of the War*. Richmond: W. A. J. Smith, 1863.

McElroy's Philadelphia City Directory. Philadelphia: E. C. & J. Biddle & Co., 1861, 1862, 1863, 1864.

McElroy's Philadelphia City Directory. Philadelphia: A. McElroy, 1865.

Magnus' Universal Picture Books. New York: Charles Magnus, [1863–64].

Manufactures of the United States in 1860; Compiled from the Original Returns of the Eighth Census. Washington, D.C.: Government Printing Office, 1865.

Mason, Emily V. *The Southern Poems of the War*. Baltimore: John Murphy & Co., 1868.

Matthews, Brander. *Pen and Ink: Papers on Subjects of More or Less Importance*. 1888. Reprint, Freeport, N.Y.: Books for Libraries Press, 1971.

Melville, Herman. *The Confidence Man: His Masquerade*. 1857. Reprint, New York: W. W. Norton, 1971.

Miriam Rivers, the Lady Soldier; or, General Grant's Spy. Philadelphia: Barclay & Co., 1865.

The Modern Niobe; or, Leoni Loudon: A Tale of Suffering and Loyalty in the Heart of Rebeldom. Philadelphia: Barclay & Co., 1864.

Moore, Frank, ed. *Anecdotes, Poetry, and Incidents of the War: North and South, 1860–1865*. New York: Frank Moore, 1866.

————. *Heroes and Martyrs: Notable Men of the Time: Biographical Sketches of the Military and Naval Heroes, Statesmen, and Orators, Distinguished in the American Crisis of 1861–1862.* New York: G. P. Putnam, 1861.

————. *Lyrics of Loyalty.* New York: G. P. Putnam, 1864.

————. *Personal and Political Ballads.* New York: G. P. Putnam, 1864.

————. *The Portrait Gallery of the War, Civil, Military, and Naval: A Biographical Record.* New York: G. P. Putnam, 1864.

————. *The Rebellion Record; a Diary of American Events, with Documents, Narratives, Illustrative Incidents, Poetry, etc.* 11 vols. New York: G. P. Putnam, 1861–63; D. Van Nostrand, 1864–68.

————. *Rebel Rhymes and Rhapsodies.* New York: G. P. Putnam, 1864.

————. *Songs and Ballads of the Southern People.* G. P. Putnam, 1864.

————. *Songs of the Soldiers* G. P. Putnam, 1864.

————. *Women of the War: Their Heroism and Self-Sacrifice.* Hartford: S. S. Scranton, 1867.

Morford, Henry. *The Days of Shoddy: A Novel of the Great Rebellion in 1861.* Philadelphia: T. B. Peterson, 1863.

————. *Shoulder-Straps.* Philadelphia: T. B. Peterson, 1863.

M.T.C. [Canby, Margaret T.]. *Flowers from the Battle-Field, and Other Poems.* Philadelphia: Henry B. Ashmead, 1864.

Nasby, Petroleum V. [David Ross Locke]. *Nasby: Divers Views, Opinions, and Prophecies of Yours Trooly Petroleum V. Nasby.* Cincinnati: R. W. Carroll, 1866.

————. *The Nasby Papers: Letters and Sermons Containing the Views on the Topics of the Day, of Petroleum V. Nasby, "Paster uv the Church uv the Noo Dispensashun."* Indianapolis: C. O. Perrine & Co., 1864.

————. *The Struggles (Social, Financial, and Political) of Petroleum V. Nasby.* Boston: I. N. Richardson and Co., 1872.

Nelles, Annie. *Annie Nelles, or the Life of a Book Agent.* Cincinnati: A. Nelles, 1868.

Notes of Hospital Life from November, 1861 to August, 1863. Philadelphia: J. B. Lippincott, 1864.

N.W.T.R. [Root, N. W. Taylor]. *Contraband Christmas.* Boston: E. P. Dutton and Co., 1864.

Optic, Oliver [William Taylor Adams]. *Brave Old Salt; or, Life on the Quarterdeck.* Boston: Lee and Shepard, 1867.

————. *Fighting Joe; or, the Fortunes of a Staff Officer.* Boston: Lee and Shepard, 1866.

————. *The Sailor Boy; or, Jack Somers in the Navy.* Boston: Lee and Shepard, 1863.

————. *The Soldier Boy; or, Tom Somers in the Army.* Boston: Lee and Shepard, 1863.

————. *Taken by the Enemy.* Boston: Lothrop, Lee and Shepard Co., 1888.

————. *The Yankee Middy; or, the Adventures of a Naval Officer.* Boston: Lee and Shepard, 1865.

————. *The Young Lieutenant; or, the Adventures of an Army Officer*. Boston: Lee and Shepard, 1865.

Palmer, Sarah L. *Six Months among the Secessionists: A Reliable and Thrilling Narrative of the Sufferings and Trials of Miss Sarah L. Palmer, a Native of Pennsylvania, who, at the opening of the Great Southern Rebellion, was teaching School in Knoxville, the home of Parson Brownlow*. Philadelphia: Barclay & Co., 1862.

Patriotic and Heroic Eloquence: A Book for the Patriot, Statesman, and Student. New York: J. G. Gregory, 1861.

Pearson, Emily C. *The Poor White; or, The Rebel Conscript*. Boston: Graves and Young, 1864.

Penniman, Major [Charles Wheeler Denison]. *The Tanner-boy and How He Became Lieutenant-General*. Boston: Roberts Brothers, 1864.

————. *Winfield, the Lawyer's Son, and How He Became a Major-General*. Philadelphia: Ashmead & Evans, 1865.

Phelps, Elizabeth Stuart. *Chapters from a Life*. Boston: Houghton Mifflin, 1897.

————. *The Gates Ajar*. 1868. Reprint, edited by Helen Sootin Smith. Cambridge, Mass.: Belknap Press, 1964.

Pollard, Edward A. *The First Year of the War*. Richmond: West & Johnston, 1862.

————. *The Second Year of the War*. New York: Charles B. Richardson, 1863.

————. *The Southern History of the War: The First Year of the War*. New York: C. B. Richardson, 1863.

————. *The Two Nations: A Key to the History of the American War*. Richmond: Ayres & Wade, 1864.

Preston, Margaret J. *Beechenbrook: A Rhyme of the War*. Baltimore: Kelly & Piet, 1867.

————. *The Life and Lettters of Margaret Junkin Preston*. Edited by Elizabeth Preston Allan. Boston: Houghton Mifflin, 1903.

The Punch Songster: A Collection of Familiar and Original Songs and Ballads. Richmond: Punch Office, 1864.

Putnam, George Haven. *George Palmer Putnam: A Memoir. Together with a Record of the Earlier Years of the Publishing House Founded by Him*. New York: G. P. Putnam's Sons, 1912.

The Rebel Pirate's Fatal Prize; or, the Bloody Tragedy of the Prize Schooner Waring. Philadelphia: Reichner & Co., 1862.

Reed, William Howell. *Hospital Life in the Army of the Potomac*. 1866. Reprint, Boston: William Howell Reed, 1891.

Reid, Mayne. *The Boy Hunters, or Adventures in Search of a White Buffalo*. Boston: Ticknor, Reed, and Fields, 1853.

Reynolds, Major W. D. *The Lady Lieutenant: A Wonderful, startling and thrilling narrative of the adventures of Miss Madeleine Moore, who, in order to be near her lover, joined the Army, was elected lieutenant, and fought in western Virginia under the renowned General McClellan and afterwards at the great Battle of Bull's Run*. Philadelphia: Barclay & Co., 1862.

————. *Miss Martha Brownlow, or the Heroine of Tennessee. A truthful and graphic account of the many perils and privations endured by Miss Martha Brownlow, daughter of the celebrated Parson Brownlow*. . . . Philadelphia: Barclay & Co., 1863.

Richards, Caroline Cowles. *Village Life in America 1852–1872 including the Period of the American Civil War as Told in the Diary of a School-Girl*. New York: Henry Holt and Co., 1913.

Robinson, J. H. *Milrose; or, the Cotton-Planter's Daughter*. New York: Frederic A. Brady, 1862.

————. *Mountain Max; or, Nick Whiffles on the Border: A Tale of the Bushwhackers in Missouri*. New York: Frederic A. Brady, 1861.

————. *The Round Pack: A Tale of the Forked Deer*. New York: Frederic A. Brady, 1862.

————. *Scotto, the Scout; or, the Union Rangers: A Tale of the Great Rebellion*. New York: Frederic A. Brady, 1861.

Roger Deane's Work. Boston: Graves and Young, 1863.

Roosevelt, Theodore. *The Strenuous Life*. New York: Century Co., 1901.

————. *Theodore Roosevelt: An Autobiography*. 1913. Reprint, New York: Charles Scribner's Sons, 1927.

Ropes, Hannah. *Civil War Nurse: The Diary and Letters of Hannah Ropes*. Edited by John R. Brumgardt. Knoxville: University of Tennessee Press, 1980.

Rouse, E. S. S. *The Bugle Blast; or, Spirit of the Conflict. Comprising Naval and Military Exploits, Dashing Raids, Heroic Deeds, Thrilling Incidents, Sketches, Anecdotes* . . . Philadelphia: J. Challen & Son, 1864.

Ruth: A Song in the Desert. Boston: Gould & Lincoln, 1864.

Sargent, Epes. *Peculiar: A Tale of the Great Transition*. New York: Carleton, 1864.

Schmucker, Samuel M. *A History of the Southern Rebellion*. New York: J. W. Bradley, 1862.

A Selection of War Lyrics. New York: James G. Gregory, 1864.

Shea, John Gilmary, ed. *The Fallen Brave: A Biographical Memorial of the American Officers Who Have Given Their Lives for the Preservation of the Union*. New York: Charles B. Richardson & Co., 1861.

[Shepperson, William G., ed.]. *War Songs of the South*. Richmond: West & Johnston, 1862.

Simmons, Flora. *The Spirit of Washington: Or, McClellan's Vision: A Wonderful Revelation of the Present Rebellion*. Rochester, N.Y.: C. D. Tracy, 1863.

Simms, William Gilmore. *The Letters of William Gilmore Simms*. Edited by Mary C. Simms Oliphant et al. 5 vols. Columbia: University of South Carolina Press, 1955.

————. *The Letters of William Gilmore Simms*. Edited by Mary C. Simms Oliphant and T. C. Duncan Eaves. Vol. 6, Supplement. Columbia: University of South Carolina Press, 1982.

————, ed. *The War Poetry of the South*. New York: Richardson & Co., 1866.

Sojers' Comic Almanac for 1863. New York: T. W. Strong, [1862].

Squier, E. G. *Frank Leslie's Pictorial History of the War of 1861*. New York: Frank Leslie, 1861.

Stearns, Amanda Akin. *The Lady Nurse of Ward E*. New York: Baker & Taylor, 1909.

Stephens, Ann S. *Pictorial History of the War for the Union: A Complete and Reliable History of the War from Its Commencement to Its Close*. New York: John G. Wells, 1863.

Stone, Kate. *Brokenburn: The Journal of Kate Stone, 1861–1868*. Edited by John Q. Anderson. 1955. Reprint, Baton Rouge: Louisiana State University Press, 1995.

Storke, Elliot Gray. *The Great American Rebellion*. Auburn, N.Y.: New York Publishing Co., 1863.

Strong, George Templeton. *The Diary of George Templeton Strong*. Edited by Allan Nevins and Milton Thomas. 4 vols. New York: Macmillan, 1952.

Thayer, William M. *The Pioneer Boy, and How He Became President*. Boston: Walker, Wise, and Co., 1863.

———. *A Youth's History of the Rebellion, from the Capture of Roanoke Island to the Battle of Murfreesboro*. Boston: Walker, Wise, and Co., 1864.

Thomas, Ella Gertrude Clanton. *The Secret Eye: The Journal of Ella Gertrude Clanton Thomas, 1848–1889*. Edited by Virginia Ingraham Burr. Chapel Hill: University of North Carolina Press, 1990

Timrod, Henry. *The Essays of Henry Timrod*. Edited by Edd Winfield Parks. Athens: University of Georgia Press, 1942.

———. *The Last Years of Henry Timrod, 1864–1867*. Edited by Jay B. Hubbell. Durham, N.C.: Duke University Press, 1941.

———. *The Uncollected Poems of Henry Timrod*. Edited by Guy A. Cardwell Jr. Athens: University of Georgia Press, 1942.

Tomes, Robert. *The War with the South: A History of the War of 1861*. New York: Frank Leslie, 1863.

Tooker, L. Frank. *The Joys and Tribulations of an Editor*. New York: The Century Co., 1923.

Tousey, Sinclair. *A Business Man's View of Public Matters*. New York: American News Co., 1865.

Tramp, Tim. *War Life: Illustrated by Stories of the Camp and Field*. New York: Callender, Perce & Welling, 1862.

Trowbridge, John Townsend. *Cudjo's Cave*. Boston: J. E. Tilton and Co., 1863.

———. *The Drummer Boy*. Boston: J. E. Tilton and Co., 1863.

———. *The Ferry Boy and the Financier*. Boston: Walker, Wise, and Co., 1864.

———. *My Own Story with Recollections of Noted Persons*. Boston: Houghton Mifflin, 1903.

———. *The Three Scouts*. Boston: J. E. Tilton and Co., 1865.

Turner, Joseph Addison. *Autobiography of "The Countryman," 1866*. Edited by Thomas H. English. Atlanta: Library, Emory University, 1943.

Tuthill, Mrs. L. C. *I Will Be a Soldier*. Boston: Crosby & Nichols, 1863.

Uncle Buddy's Gift Book for the Holidays, Containing a Variety of Tales, Translations, Poetry, Chronology, Games, Anecdotes, Conundrums, etc., etc. Augusta, Ga.: Blome & Tehan, 1863.

Uncle Juvinell [Morrison Heady]. *The Farmer Boy, and How He Became Commander-in-Chief.* Edited by William M. Thayer. Boston: Walker, Wise, and Co., 1864.

Union and Patriotic Album Illustrated Envelope Holder. Boston: J. M. Whittemore, 1861.

Victor, Metta V. *Maum Guinea, and Her Plantation "Children;" or, Holiday-Week on a Louisiana Estate: A Slave Romance.* New York: Beadle & Co., 1861. Reprint, Freeport, N.Y.: Books for Libraries Press, 1972.

———. *The Unionist's Daughter: A Tale of the Rebellion in Tennessee.* New York: Beadle & Co., 1862.

Victor, Orville. *The History, Civil, Political & Military, of the Southern Rebellion.* 4 vols. New York: James D. Torrey, 1861.

———. *Incidents and Anecdotes of the War.* 1862.

The War and Its Heroes. First Series. Richmond: Ayres & Wade, 1864.

Ward, Artemus [Charles Farrar Browne]. *Artemus Ward: His Book.* New York: Carleton, 1862.

———. *Artemus Ward (His Travels) among the Mormons.* Edited by E. P. Hingston. London: John Camden Hotten, 1865.

Warren, J. Thomas. *Old Hal Williams, the Spy of Atlanta: A Tale of Sherman's Georgia Campaign.* New York: American News Co., 1865.

White, Richard Grant. *National Hymns. How They Are Written and How They Are Not Written: A Lyric and National Study for the Times.* New York: Rudd & Carleton, 1861.

———, ed. *Poetry Lyrical, Narrative, and Satirical of the Civil War.* 1866. Reprint, New York: Arno Press, 1972.

Whitman, Walt. *Collected Writings of Walt Whitman: The Correspondence.* Vol. 1, *1842–1867.* Edited by Edwin Haviland Miller. General editors Gay Wilson Allen et al. New York: New York University Press, 1961.

———. *The Complete Writings of Walt Whitman.* Edited by Richard Maurice Bucke et al. New York: G. P. Putnam's Sons, 1902.

———. *Specimen Days.* In *Leaves of Grass and Selected Prose*, edited by John Kouwehhoven. New York: Modern Library, 1950.

———. *Walt Whitman: Leaves of Grass: Comprehensive Reader's Edition.* Edited by Harold W. Blodgett and Sculley Bradley. New York: New York University Press, 1965.

———. *Walt Whitman's Civil War.* Edited by Walter Lowenfels. New York: DeCapo Press, 1960.

———. *Walt Whitman's Drum-Taps (1865) and Sequel to Drum-Taps (1865–6): A Facsimile Reproduction.* Edited by F. DeWolfe Miller. Gainesville, Fla.: Scholars' Facsimiles & Reprints, 1959.

Willett, Edward. *Bob Brant, Patriot and Spy: A Tale of the War in the West.* New York: American News Co., 1864.

———. *Crazy Dan; or, Fight Fire with Fire: A Tale of East Tennessee.* New York: American News Co., 1864.

———. *Kate Sharp; or The Two Conscripts.* New York: American News Co., 1865.

———. *Old Bill Woodworth, the Scout of the Cumberland.* New York: American News Co., 1864.

———. *The Vicksburg Spy; or, Found and Lost: A Story of the Siege and Fall of the Great Rebel Stronghold.* New York: American News Co., 1864.

Winner, Sep. *He's Gone to the Arms of Abraham: Comic War Ballad.* Philadelphia: Sep. Winner, 1863.

Winthrop, Theodore. *Canoe and Saddle.* Boston: Ticknor and Fields, 1862.

———. *Cecil Dreeme.* Boston: Ticknor and Fields, 1861.

———. *Edwin Brothertoft.* Boston: Ticknor and Fields, 1862.

———. *John Brent.* Boston: Ticknor and Fields, 1862.

———. *Life in the Open Air, and Other Papers.* Boston: Ticknor and Fields, 1862.

SECONDARY SOURCES

Aaron, Daniel. *The Unwritten War: American Writers and the Civil War.* New York: Knopf, 1973.

Abrams, M. H., et al., eds. *The Norton Anthology of English Literature.* Vol. 2. Rev. New York: W. W. Norton, 1968.

Allen, Gay Wilson, et al., eds. *American Poetry.* New York: Harper & Row, 1965.

Altschuler, Glenn C., and Stuart M. Blumin. "The Limits of Political Engagement in Antebellum America: A New Look at the Golden Age of Participatory Democracy." *Journal of American History* 84 (December 1997): 855–85.

———. " 'Where Is the Real America?': Politics and Popular Consciousness in the Antebellum Era." *American Quarterly* 49 (June 1997): 225–67.

American Historians, 1607–1865: Dictionary of Literary Biography. Vol. 30. Edited by Clyde N Wilson. Detroit: Gale Research Co., 1984.

Anderson, Benedict. *Imagined Communities: Reflections on the Origin and Spread of Nationalism.* London: Verso, 1983.

Andrews, J. Cutler. *The South Reports the Civil War.* Princeton: Princeton University Press, 1970.

Appleby, Joyce. "Reconciliation and the Northern Novelist." *Civil War History* 10 (June 1964): 117–29.

Ashcroft, Bill, Gareth Griffiths, and Helen Tiffin, eds., *The Post-Colonial Studies Reader.* New York: Routledge, 1995.

Attie, Jeanie. *Patriotic Toil: Northen Women and the American Civil War.* Ithaca, N.Y.: Cornell University Press, 1998.

Austin, James C. *Artemus Ward.* New York: Twayne, 1964.

———. *Fields of the Atlantic Monthly.* San Marino, Calif.: Huntington Library, 1953.

———. *Petroleum V. Nasby.* New Haven: Twayne, 1965.

Baker, Jean. *Affairs of Party: The Political Culture of Northern Democrats in the Mid-Nineteenth Century.* Ithaca, N.Y.: Cornell University Press, 1983.

Barnhill, Georgia. "Pictorial Histories of the United States." *Visual Resources* 11 (1995): 5–19.

Baym, Nina. *American Women Writers and the Work of History, 1790–1860.* New Brunswick, N.J.: Rutgers University Press, 1995.

———. *At Home with History: History Books and Women's Sphere before the Civil War: The James Russell Wiggins Lectures in the History of the Book in American Culture.* Worcester, Mass.: American Antiquarian Society, 1992.

———. *Woman's Fiction: A Guide to Novels by and about Women in America, 1820–1870.* Ithaca, N.Y.: Cornell University Press, 1978.

Beath, Robert. *History of the Grand Army of the Republic.* New York: Bryan, Taylor & Co., 1889.

Bederman, Gail. *Manliness and Civilization: A Cultural History of Gender and Race in the United States, 1880–1917.* Chicago: University of Chicago Press, 1995.

Bernstein, Iver. *The New York City Draft Riots: Their Significance for American Society and Politics in the Age of the Civil War.* New York: Oxford University Press, 1990.

Billings, John Davis. *Hardtack and Coffee: The Unwritten Story of Army Life.* 1888. Reprint, edited by Richard Harwell, Chicago: R. R. Donnelly & Sons Co., 1960.

Blair, Walter. *Native American Humor (1800–1900).* New York: American Book Co., 1937.

Blanck, Jacob. *Harry Castlemon: Boys' Own Author.* New York: R. R. Bowker, 1941.

Blight, David W. "'For Something beyond the Battlefield': Frederick Douglass and the Struggle for the Memory of the Civil War." *Journal of American History* 75 (March 1989): 1156–78.

———. *Frederick Douglass' Civil War: Keeping Faith in Jubilee.* Baton Rouge: Louisiana State University Press, 1989.

Blumin, Stuart M. *The Emergence of the Middle Class: Social Experience in the American City, 1760–1900.* New York: Cambridge University Press, 1989.

Bold, Christine. "Popular Forms I." In *The Columbia History of the American Novel,* edited by Emory Elliott, 285–305. New York: Columbia University Press, 1991.

Bodnar, John, ed. *Bonds of Affection: Americans Define Their Patriotism.* Princeton: Princeton University Press, 1996.

Bremner, Ellen. "Orpheus C. Kerr." *Civil War History* 2 (September 1956): 121–29.

Brodhead, Richard H. *Cultures of Letters: Scenes of Reading and Writing in Nineteenth-Century America.* Chicago: University of Chicago Press, 1993.

Brooks, Peter. *The Melodramatic Imagination: Balzac, Henry James, Melodrama, and the Mode of Excess.* New Haven: Yale University Press, 1976.

Bruce, Dickson D., Jr. "Ancient Africa and the Early Black American Historians, 1883–1915." *American Quarterly* 36 (Winter 1984): 684–99.

————. *Black American Writing from the Nadir: The Evolution of a Literary Tradition, 1877–1915*. Baton Rouge: Louisiana State University Press, 1989.

————. "The Ironic Conception of American History: The Early Black Historians, 1883–1915." *Journal of Negro History* 49 (Spring 1984): 53–62.

Bullock, Penelope L. *The Afro-American Periodical Press, 1838–1909*. Baton Rouge: Louisiana State University Press, 1981.

Callcott, George H. *History in the United States, 1800–1860*. Baltimore: Johns Hopkins University Press, 1970.

Carby, Hazel V. Introduction to *Iola Leroy or Shadows Uplifted*, by Frances E. W. Harper. Boston: Beacon Press, 1987.

————. *Reconstructing Womanhood: The Emergence of the Afro-American Woman Novliest*. New York: Oxford University Press, 1987.

Casper, Scott E. *Constructing American Lives: Biography and Culture in Nineteenth-Century America*. Chapel Hill: University of North Carolina Press, 1999.

Chartier, Roger. *Cultural History: Between Practices and Representations*. Ithaca, N.Y.: Cornell University Press, 1988.

Charvat, William. *Literary Publishing in America, 1790–1850*. Philadelphia: University of Pennsylvania Press, 1959.

————. *The Profession of Authorship in America, 1800–1870: The Papers of William Charvat*. Edited by Matthew J. Bruccoli. Columbus: Ohio State University Press, 1968.

Christie, Anne M. "Bill Arp." *Civil War History* 2 (September 1956): 103–19.

Clinton, Catherine. *Tara Revisited: Women, War, and the Plantation Legend*. New York: Abbeville Press, 1995.

Clinton, Catherine, and Nina Silber, eds., *Divided Houses: Gender and the Civil War*. New York: Oxford University Press, 1992.

Cmiel, Kenneth. *Democratic Eloquence: The Fight over Popular Speech in Nineteenth-Century America*. New York: Morrow, 1990.

Colby, Elbridge. *Theodore Winthrop*. New York: Twayne, 1965.

Conningham, Frederic A. *Currier and Ives Prints: An Illustrated Checklist*. New York: Crown Publishers, 1970.

Cooper, Helen M., et al., eds. *Arms and the Woman: War, Gender, and Literary Representation*. Chapel Hill: University of North Carolina Press, 1989.

Cott, Nancy. *The Bonds of Womanhood: "Woman's Sphere" in New England, 1780–1835*. New Haven: Yale University Press, 1977.

Coulling, Mary Price. *Margaret Junkin Preston: A Biography*. Winston-Salem, N.C.: John F. Blair, 1993.

Coulter, E. Merton. *The Confederate States of America, 1861–1865*. Baton Rouge: Louisiana State University Press, 1950.

————. *William G. Brownlow: Fighting Parson of the Southern Highlands*. Chapel Hill: University of North Carolina Press, 1937.

Coultrap-McQuin, Susan. *Doing Literary Business: American Women Writers in the Nineteenth Century*. Chapel Hill: University of North Carolina Press, 1990.

Crandall, Marjorie Lyle. *Confederate Imprints: A Checklist Based Principally on the Collection of the Boston Atheneum.* Boston: Boston Atheneum, 1955.

Cullen, Jim. *The Civil War in Popular Culture: A Reusable Past.* Washington, D.C.: Smithsonian Press, 1995.

Dannett, Sylvia G. L. *Noble Women of the North.* New York: Thomas Yoseloff, 1959.

Davidson, Alexander. "How Benson J. Lossing Wrote His 'Fieldbooks' of the Revolution, the War of 1812, and the Civil War." *Papers of the Bibliographical Society of America* 22 (1937).

Davidson, Cathy. *Revolution and the Word: The Rise of the Novel in America.* New York: Oxford University Press, 1986.

———, ed. *Reading in America: Literature and Social History.* Baltimore: Johns Hopkins University Press, 1989.

Dearing, Mary R. *Veterans in Politics: The Story of the G.A.R.* Baton Rouge: Louisiana State University Press, 1952.

Denning, Michael. "The End of Mass Culture." In *Modernity and Mass Culture,* edited by James Naremore and Patrick Brantlinger, 253–68. Bloomington: Indiana University Press, 1991.

———. *Mechanic Accents: Dime Novels and Working-Class Culture in America.* London: Verso, 1987.

Detlefsen, Ellen Gay. "Printing in the Confederacy, 1861–1865: A Southern Industry in Wartime." D.L.S. diss., Columbia University, 1975.

Diffley, Kathleen. *Where My Heart Is Turning Ever: Civil War Stories and Constitutional Reform, 1861–1876.* Athens: University of Georgia Press, 1992.

Douglas, Ann. *The Feminization of American Culture.* New York: Knopf, 1977.

Ellinger, Esther Parker. "The Southern War Poetry of the Civil War." Ph.D. diss., University of Pennsylvania, 1918.

Elshtain, Jean Bethke. *Woman and War.* New York: Basic Books, 1987.

Erkkila, Betsy. *Whitman the Political Poet.* New York: Oxford University Press, 1989.

Fahs, Alice. "Publishing the Civil War: The Literary Marketplace and the Meanings of the Civil War in the North, 1861–1865." Ph.D. diss., New York University, 1993.

Faust, Drew Gilpin. "Altars of Sacrifice: Confederate Women and the Narratives of War." *Journal of American History* 76 (March 1990): 1200–1228.

———. *The Creation of Confederate Nationalism: Ideology and Identity in the Civil War South.* Baton Rouge: Louisiana State University Press, 1988.

———. *Mothers of Invention: Women of the Slaveholding South in the American Civil War.* Chapel Hill: University of North Carolina Press, 1996.

———. *A Sacred Circle: The Dilemma of the Intellectual in the Old South, 1840–1860.* Baltimore: Johns Hopkins University Press, 1977.

Fellman, Michael. *Inside War: The Guerrilla Conflict in Missouri during the American Civil War.* New York: Oxford University Press, 1989.

Fliegelman, Jay. *Prodigals and Pilgrims: The American Revolution against*

Patriarchal Authority, 1750–1800. New York: Cambridge University Press, 1982.

Foner, Eric. *Reconstruction: America's Unfinished Revolution, 1863–1877.* New York: Harper & Row, 1988.

Forgie, George B. *Patricide in the House Divided: A Psychological Interpretation of Lincoln and His Age.* New York: Norton, 1979.

Fox, Richard Wightman, and T. J. Jackson Lears, eds. *The Culture of Consumption: Critical Essays in American History, 1880–1980.* New York: Pantheon, 1983.

Fredrickson, George M. *The Black Image in the White Mind: The Debate on Afro-American Character and Destiny, 1817–1914.* New York: Harper & Row, 1971.

———. *The Inner Civil War: Northern Intellectuals and the Crisis of the Union.* New York: Harper & Row, 1965.

Freidel, Frank. *Union Pamphlets of the Civil War, 1861–1865.* Cambridge: Harvard University Press, 1967.

Gallagher, Gary. *The Confederate War: How Popular Will, Nationalism, and Military Strategy Could Not Stave Off Defeat.* Cambridge: Harvard University Press, 1997.

Gallman, J. Matthew. *Mastering Wartime: A Social History of Philadelphia during the Civil War.* Cambridge: Cambridge University Press, 1990.

Garmon, Gerald M. *John Reuben Thompson.* Boston: Twayne, 1979.

Gillman, Susan. "The Mulatto, Tragic or Triumphant?: The Nineteenth-Century American Race Melodrama." In *The Culture of Sentiment: Race, Gender, and Sentimentality in Nineteenth-Century America,* edited by Shirley Samuels, 221–43. New York: Oxford University Press, 1992.

Gilmore, Michael T. *American Romanticism and the Marketplace.* Chicago: University of Chicago Press, 1985.

Gilmore, William. *Reading Becomes a Necessity of Life: Material and Cultural Life in Rural New England, 1780–1835.* Knoxville: University of Tennessee Press, 1989.

Ginzberg, Lori D. *Women and the Work of Benevolence: Morality, Politics, and Class in the Nineteenth-Century United States.* New Haven: Yale University Press, 1990.

Goodrich, Lloyd. *The Graphic Art of Winslow Homer.* New York: New York Museum of Graphic Art, 1968.

Gould, Stephen Jay. *The Mismeasure of Man.* New York: W. W. Norton, 1981.

Grant, Robert W. *The Handbook of Civil War Patriotic Envelopes and Postal History.* Hanover, Mass.: Robert W. Grant, 1977.

Greenbie, Marjorie Barstow. *Lincoln's Daughters of Mercy.* New York: G. P. Putnam's Sons, 1944.

Greenspan, Ezra. "Evert Duyckinck and the History of Wiley and Putnam's Library of American Books, 1845–1847." *American Literature* 64 (December 1992): 677–93.

————. *Walt Whitman and the American Reader.* New York: Cambridge University Press, 1990.

Grier, Katherine C. *Culture and Comfort: People, Parlors, and Upholstery, 1850–1930.* Rochester, N.Y.: Strong Museum, 1988.

Grimsted, David. *Melodrama Unveiled: American Theater and Culture, 1800–1850.* Chicago: University of Chicago Press, 1968.

Gross, Robert. *Printing, Politics, and the People: The 1989 James Russell Wiggins Lecture in the History of the Book in American Culture at the American Antiquarian Society.* Worcester, Mass.: American Antiquarian Society, 1989.

Hackenberg, Michael, ed. *Getting the Books Out: Papers of the Chicago Conference on the Book in Nineteenth-Century America.* Washington, D.C.: Library of Congress, 1987.

Hall, David D. *Worlds of Wonder, Days of Judgment: Popular Religious Belief in Early New England.* New York: Knopf, 1989.

Hall, David D., and John Hench, eds. *Needs and Opportunities in the History of the Book: America, 1639–1876.* Worcester, Mass.: American Antiquarian Society, 1987.

Halttunen, Karen. *Confidence Men and Painted Women: A Study of Middle-Class Culture in America, 1830–1870.* New Haven: Yale University Press, 1982.

Hanchett, William. *Irish: Charles G. Halpine in Civil War America.* Syracuse, N.Y.: Syracuse University Press, 1970.

Harrison, John M. *The Man Who Made Nasby, David Ross Locke.* Chapel Hill: University of North Carolina Press, 1969.

Harwell, Richard Barksdale. *Confederate Belles-Lettres: A Bibliography and a Finding List of the Fiction, Poetry, Drama, Songsters, and Miscellaneous Literature Published in the Confederate States of America.* Hattiesburg, Miss.: Book Farm, 1941.

————. *More Confederate Imprints.* Richmond: Virginia State Library, 1957.

Heaps, Willard A., and Porter W. Heaps. *The Singing Sixties: The Spirit of Civil War Days Drawn from the Music of the Times.* Norman: University of Oklahoma Press, 1960.

Henry E. Huntington Library and Art Gallery. *Confederate Imprints in the Henry E. Huntington Library Unrecorded in Previously Published Bibliographies of Such Material, by Willard O. Waters.* Chicago: University of Chicago Press, 1930.

Higonnet, Margaret Randolph, et al., eds. *Behind the Lines: Gender and the Two World Wars.* New Haven: Yale University Press, 1987.

Horwitz, Tony. *Confederates in the Attic: Dispatches from the Unfinished Civil War.* New York: Pantheon, 1998.

Howe, Daniel Walker, ed. *Victorian America.* Philadelphia: University of Pennsylvania Press, 1976.

Hubbell, Jay B., ed. *The Last Years of Henry Timrod, 1864–1867.* Durham, N.C.: Duke University Press, 1941.

————. *The South in American Literature, 1607–1900.* Durham, N.C.: Duke University Press, 1954.

Hunt, Lynn. *The Family Romance of the French Revolution.* Berkeley: University of California Press, 1992.

————, ed. *The New Cultural History.* Berkeley: University of California Press, 1989.

Hynes, Samuel. *A War Imagined: The First World War and English Culture.* New York: Atheneum, 1991.

Ignatiev, Noel. *How the Irish Became White.* New York: Routledge, 1995.

Ingraham, Charles A. *Elmer E. Ellsworth and the Zouaves of '61.* Chicago: University of Chicago Press, 1925.

Jackson, David K. *The Contributors and Contributions to the Southern Literary Messenger (1834–1864).* Charlottesville, Va.: Historical Publishing Co., 1936.

Johannsen, Albert. *The House of Beadle and Adams and Its Dime and Nickel Novels: The Story of a Vanished Literature.* 2 vols. Norman: University of Oklahoma Press, 1950.

Johannsen, Robert W. *To the Halls of the Montezumas.* New York: Oxford University Press, 1985.

Jones, Dolores Blythe. *An "Oliver Optic" Checklist: An Annotated Catalog-Index to the Series, Nonseries Stories, and Magazine Publications of William Taylor Adams.* Wesport, Conn.: Greenwood Press, 1985.

Joyce, Donald F. *Black Book Publishers in the United States: A Historical Dictionary of the Presses, 1817–1990.* New York: Greenwood Press, 1991.

Kaplan, Amy. *The Social Construction of American Realism.* Chicago: University of Chicago Press, 1988.

Kaser, David. *Books and Libraries in Camp and Battle.* Westport, Conn.: Greenwood Press, 1984.

Kelley, Mary. *Private Woman, Public Stage: Literary Domesticity in Nineteenth-Century America.* New York: Oxford University Press, 1984.

————. "Reading Women/Women Reading: The Making of Learned Women in Antebellum America." *Journal of American History* 83 (September 1996): 401–24.

Kelly, James, comp. *The American Catalogue of Books, (Original and Reprints), Published in the United States from Jan., 1861, to Jan., 1866, with Date of Publication, Size, Price, and Publisher's Name.* New York: Peter Smith, 1938.

Kelly, Patrick J. *Creating a National Home: Building the National Veterans' Welfare State, 1860–1900.* Cambridge: Harvard University Press, 1997.

Kelly, R. Gordon, ed. *Children's Periodicals of the United States.* Westport, Conn.: Greenwood Press, 1984.

Kennerly, Sarah Law. "Confederate Juvenile Imprints: Children's Books and Periodicals Published in the Confederate States of America, 1861–1865." Ph.D. diss., University of Michigan, 1956.

Kerber, Linda K. "'History Can Do It No Justice': Women and the Reinterpretation of the American Revolution." In *Women in the Age of the American Revolution,* edited by Ronald Hoffman and Peter J. Albert, 3–42. Charlottesville: University Press of Virginia, 1989.

————. *Women of the Republic: Intellect and Ideology in Revolutionary America.* Chapel Hill: University of North Carolina Press, 1980.

Kessler-Harris, Alice. *Out to Work: A History of Wage-Earning Women in the United States.* New York: Oxford University Press, 1982.

Laderman, Gary. *The Sacred Remains: American Attitudes toward Death, 1799–1883.* New Haven: Yale University Press, 1996.

Leonard, Elizabeth D. *All the Daring of a Soldier: Women of the Civil War Armies.* New York: W. W. Norton, 1999.

————. *Yankee Women: Gender Battles in the Civil War.* New York: W. W. Norton, 1994.

Levine, Lawrence. *Highbrow/Lowbrow: The Emergence of Cultural Hierarchy in America.* Cambridge: Harvard University Press, 1988.

Linderman, Gerald F. *Embattled Courage: The Experience of Combat in the American Civil War.* New York: Free Press, 1987.

Lipsitz, George. "Listening to Learn and Learning to Listen: Popular Culture, Cultural Theory, and American Studies." *American Quarterly* 42 (December 1990): 615–36.

————. *Time Passages: Collective Memory and American Popular Culture.* Minneapolis: University of Minnesota Press, 1990.

Lively, Robert A. *Fiction Fights the Civil War: An Unfinished Chapter in the Literary History of the American People.* Chapel Hill: University of North Carolina Press, 1957.

London, Lawrence. "Confederate Literature and Its Publishers." In *Studies in Southern History,* edited by J. Carlyle Sitterson. James Sprunt Historical Publications, 39. Chapel Hill: University of North Carolina Press, 1957.

Longfellow, Samuel, ed. *Life of Henry Wadsworth Longfellow.* Boston: Ticknor and Co., 1886.

Lott, Eric. *Love and Theft: Blackface Minstrelsy and the American Working Class.* New York: Oxford University Press, 1993.

Lucid, Robert F. "Anecdotes and Recollections." *Civil War History* 2 (September 1956): 29–48.

McClintock, Megan. "Civil War Pensions and the Reconstruction of Families." *Journal of American History* 83 (September 1996): 456–80.

McConnell, Stuart. *Glorious Contentment: The Grand Army of the Republic, 1865–1900.* Chapel Hill: University of North Carolina Press, 1992.

————. "Reading the Flag: A Reconsideration of the Patriotic Cults of the 1890s." In *Bonds of Affection: Americans Define Their Patriotism,* edited by John Bodnar, 102–19. Princeton: Princeton University Press, 1996.

McDade, Thomas M. "Lurid Literature of the Last Century: The Publications of E. E. Barclay." *American Book Collector* 8 (September 1957): 15–25.

McDade, Thomas, comp. "List of Imprints of the E. E. Barclay Co." 1957. American Antiquarian Society.

McFeely, William S. *Frederick Douglass.* New York: W. W. Norton, 1991.

McGlinchee, Claire. *James Russell Lowell.* New York: Twayne, 1967.

McPherson, James M. *Battle Cry of Freedom: The Civil War Era.* New York: Oxford University Press, 1988.

————. *For Cause and Comrades: Why Men Fought in the Civil War.* New York: Oxford University Press, 1997.

————. *The Negro's Civil War: How American Blacks Felt and Acted during the War for the Union.* 1965. Reprint, New York: Ballantine Books, 1991.

————. *Ordeal by Fire: The Civil War and Reconstruction.* Rev. ed. New York: McGraw-Hill, 1992.

Marten, James. *The Children's Civil War.* Chapel Hill: University of North Carolina Press, 1998.

————, ed. *Lessons of War: The Civil War in Children's Magazines.* Wilmington, Del.: Scholarly Resources, 1999.

Massey, Mary Elizabeth. *Bonnet Brigades: American Women and the Civil War.* New York: Knopf, 1966; reprinted as *Women in the Civil War.* Lincoln: University of Nebraska Press, 1994.

Masur, Louis P., ed. *"The Real War Will Never Get in the Books": Selections from Writers during the Civil War.* New York: Oxford University Press, 1993.

Meigs, Cornelia, ed. *A Critical History of Children's Literature.* London: Macmillan, 1969.

Menendez, Albert J. *Civil War Novels: An Annotated Bibliography.* New York: Garland, 1986.

Mitchell, Reid. *Civil War Soldiers: Their Expectations and Their Experiences.* New York: Viking, 1988.

————. *The Vacant Chair: The Northern Soldier Leaves Home.* New York: Oxford University Press, 1993.

Moore, Rayburn S. *Paul Hamilton Hayne.* New York: Twayne, 1972.

Moss, Elizabeth. *Domestic Novelists in the Old South: Defenders of Southern Culture.* Baton Rouge: Louisiana State University Press, 1992.

Moss, William. *Confederate Broadside Poems: An Annotated Descriptive Bibliography.* Westport, Conn.: Meckler, 1988.

Mott, Frank Luther. *A History of American Magazines, 1850–1865.* Cambridge: Harvard University Press, 1938.

————. *A History of American Magazines, 1865–1885.* Cambridge: Harvard University Press, 1957.

Mukerji, Chandra, and Michael Schudson, eds. *Rethinking Popular Culture: Contemporary Perspectives in Cultural Studies.* Berkeley: University of California Press, 1991.

Nardin, James T. "The War in *Vanity Fair.*" *Civil War History* 2 (September 1956): 67–85.

Nevins, Allan. *Ordeal of the Union.* 4 vols. 1971. Reprint, New York: Collier Books, 1992.

Noel, Mary. *Villains Galore.* New York: Macmillan, 1954.

Nord, David. *The Evangelical Origins of Mass Media in America, 1815–1835.* Columbia: University of South Carolina Press, 1984.

Paludan, Phillip Shaw. *"A People's Contest": The Union and Civil War, 1861–1865.* New York: Harper & Row, 1988.

Parrish, T. Michael, and Robert M. Willingham Jr. *Confederate Imprints: A Bibliography of Southern Publications from Secession to Surrender.* Austin, Tex.: Jenkins Publishing Co., 1984.

Penn, I. Garland. *The Afro-American Press and Its Editors.* New York: Arno Press, 1969.

Pettegrew, John. "'The Soldier's Faith': Turn-of-the-Century Memory of the Civil War and the Emergence of Modern American Nationalism." *Journal of Contemporary History* 31 (January 1996): 49–73.

Pickard, Samuel T. *Life and Letters of John Greenleaf Whittier.* Boston: Houghton Mifflin, 1894.

Pickering, Sam. "A Boy's Own War." *New England Quarterly* 48 (September 1975): 362–77.

Poovey, Mary. *Uneven Developments: The Ideological Work of Gender in Mid-Victorian England.* Chicago: University of Chicago Press, 1988.

Pressly, Thomas J. *Americans Interpret Their Civil War.* Princeton: Princeton University Press, 1954.

Rable, George C. *Civil Wars: Women and the Crisis of Southern Nationalism.* Urbana: University of Illinois Press, 1989.

Radway, Janice A. *A Feeling for Books: The Book-of-the-Month Club, Literary Taste, and Middle-Class Desire.* Chapel Hill: University of North Carolina Press, 1997.

————. *Reading the Romance: Women, Patriarchy, and Popular Literature.* Chapel Hill: University of North Carolina Press, 1984.

Raymond, Ida [Mary T. Tardy]. *Southland Writers: Biographical and Critical Sketches of the Living Female Writers of the South.* 2 vols. Philadelphia: Claxton, Remsen & Haffelfinger, 1869.

Reed, John Q. "Artemus Ward." *Civil War History* 2 (September 1956): 87–101.

Reynolds, David S. *Beneath the American Renaissance: The Subversive Imagination in the Age of Emerson and Melville.* New York: Knopf, 1988.

————. *Walt Whitman's America: A Cultural Biography.* New York: Knopf, 1995.

Roediger, David. *The Wages of Whiteness: Race and the Making of the American Working Class.* New York: Verso, 1991.

Romero, Lora. "Domesticity and Fiction." In *The Columbia History of the American Novel,* edited by Emory Elliott, 110–29. New York: Columbia University Press, 1991.

Rose, Anne C. *Victorian America and the Civil War.* Cambridge: Cambridge University Press, 1992.

Rose, Willie Lee. *Rehearsal for Reconstruction: The Port Royal Experiment.* 1964. Reprint, New York: Oxford University Press, 1976.

Rourke, Constance. *American Humor.* New York: Harcourt, Brace, 1931.

Royster, Charles. *The Destructive War: William Tecumseh Sherman, Stonewall Jackson, and the Americans.* New York: Knopf, 1991.

Rubin, Joan Shelley. *The Making of Middlebrow Culture.* Chapel Hill: University of North Carolina Press, 1992.

St. Armand, Barton Levi. *Emily Dickinson and Her Culture: The Soul's Society.* New York: Cambridge University Press, 1984.

Savage, Kirk. *Standing Soldiers, Kneeling Slaves: Race, War, and Monument in Nineteenth-Century America.* Princeton: Princeton University Press, 1997.

Scarry, Elaine. *The Body in Pain: The Making and Unmaking of the World.* New York: Oxford University Press, 1985.

Scharnhorst, Gary, with Jack Bales. *The Lost Life of Horatio Alger, Jr.* Bloomington: Indiana University Press, 1985.

Schultz, Jane E. "The Inhospitable Hospital: Gender and Professionalism in Civil War Medicine." *Signs* 17 (Winter 1992): 363–92.

Sedgwick, Ellery. *The Atlantic Monthly, 1857–1909: Yankee Humanism at High Tide and Ebb.* Amherst: University of Massachusetts Press, 1994.

Seitz, Don Carlos. *Artemus Ward (Charles Farrar Browne): A Biography and Bibliography.* New York: Harper & Brothers, 1919; New York: Beekman, 1974.

Sicherman, Barbara. "Sense and Sensibility: A Case Study of Women's Reading in Late Victorian America," in *Reading in America: Literature and Social History,* edited by Cathy Davidson, 201–25. Baltimore: Johns Hopkins University Press, 1989.

Silber, Nina. *The Romance of Reunion: Northerners and the South, 1865–1900.* Chapel Hill: University of North Carolina Press, 1993.

Simkins, Francis Butler, and James Welch Patton. *The Women of the Confederacy.* Richmond: Garrett and Massie, 1936.

Sizer, Lyde Cullen. "'A Revolution in Woman Herself': Northern Women Writers and the American Civil War, 1850–1872." Ph.D. diss., Brown University, 1994.

Smith, Carl. *Urban Disorder and the Shape of Belief: The Great Chicago Fire, the Haymarket Bomb, and the Model Town of Pullman.* Chicago: University of Chicago Press, 1995.

Smith, Rebecca Washington. "The Civil War and Its Aftermath in American Fiction, 1861–1899." Ph.D. diss., University of Chicago, 1937.

Sollors, Werner. "'Never Was Born': The Mulatto, an American Tragedy?" *Massachusetts Review* 27 (Summer 1986): 293–316.

Stafford, Marjorie. "Subscription Book Publishing in the United States, 1865–1930." M.A. thesis, University of Illinois at Urbana, 1943.

Stansell, Christine. *City of Women: Sex and Class in New York, 1789–1860.* New York: Knopf, 1982.

Starr, Louis M. *Bohemian Brigade: Civil War Newsmen in Action.* 1954. Reprint, Madison: University of Wisconsin Press, 1987.

Steele, Joan. *Captain Mayne Reid.* Boston: Twayne, 1978.

Steinmetz, Lee. *The Poetry of the American Civil War.* East Lansing: Michigan State University Press, 1960.

Stern, Madeleine B. *Imprints on History: Book Publishers and American Frontiers.* Bloomington: Indiana University Press, 1956.

————. *Publishers for Mass Entertainment in Nineteenth Century America*. Boston: G. K. Hall & Co., 1980.

————, ed. *Behind a Mask: The Unknown Thrillers of Louisa May Alcott*. New York: Morrow, 1975.

————. *A Double Life: Newly Discovered Thrillers of Louisa May Alcott*. Boston: Little, Brown, 1988.

————. *Plots and Counterplots: More Unknown Thrillers of Louisa May Alcott*. New York: Morrow, 1976.

Stevenson, Louise L. *The Victorian Homefront: American Thought and Culture, 1860–1880*. New York: Twayne, 1991.

Stoddard, Henry Luther. *Horace Greeley: Printer, Editor, Crusader*. New York: G. P. Putnam's Sons, 1946.

Sullivan, Larry E., and Lydia Cushman Schurman. *Pioneers, Passionate Ladies, and Private Eyes: Dime Novels, Series Books, and Paperbacks*. New York: Haworth Press, 1996.

Sundquist, Eric J. *To Wake the Nations: Race in the Making of American Literature*. Cambridge, Mass.: Harvard University Press, 1993.

————, ed. *American Realism: New Essays*. Baltimore: Johns Hopkins University Press, 1982.

Sutton, Walter. *The Western Book Trade: Cincinnati as a Nineteenth-Century Publishing and Book-Trade Center*. Columbus: Ohio State University Press, 1961.

Sweet, Timothy. *Traces of War: Poetry, Photography, and the Crisis of the Union*. Baltimore: Johns Hopkins University Press, 1990.

Taylor, William R. *Cavalier and Yankee: The Old South and American National Character*. New York: George Braziller, 1961.

Tebbel, John. *A History of Book Publishing in the United States*. New York: R. R. Bowker, 1972.

Tichi, Cecelia. "Women Writers and the New Woman." In *Columbia Literary History of the United States*, edited by Emory Elliott, 589–606. New York: Columbia University Press, 1988.

Toll, Robert C. *Blacking Up: The Minstrel Show in Nineteenth Century America*. New York: Oxford University Press, 1974.

Tompkins, Jane. *Sensational Designs: The Cultural Work of American Fiction, 1790–1860*. New York: Oxford University Press, 1985.

Trachtenberg, Alan. *Reading American Photographs: Images as History, Mathew Brady to Walker Evans*. New York: Hill and Wang, 1989.

Traubel, Horace. *With Walt Whitman in Camden, January 21 to April 7, 1889*. Philadelphia: University of Pennsylvania Press, 1953.

Tryon, William S. *Parnassus Corner: A Life of James T. Fields, Publisher to the Victorians*. Boston: Houghton Mifflin, 1963.

Tryon, William S., and William Charvat, eds. *The Cost Books of Ticknor and Fields and Their Predecessors*. New York: Bibliographic Society of America, 1949.

Van Deusen, Glyndon G. *Horace Greeley: Nineteenth Century Crusader.* Philadelphia: University of Pennsylvania Press, 1953.

Van Tassel, David D. "Benson J. Lossing: Pen and Pencil Historian." *American Quarterly* 6 (Spring 1954): 32–44.

———. *Recording America's Past: An Interpretation of the Development of Historical Studies in America, 1607–1884.* Chicago: University of Chicago Press, 1960.

Warner, Michael. *The Letters of the Republic: Publication and the Public Sphere in Eighteenth-Century America.* Cambridge, Mass.: Harvard University Press, 1990.

Weiss, William R., Jr. *The Catalog of Union Civil War Patriotic Covers.* N.p: William R. Weiss, 1995.

Westbrook, Robert B. "'I Want a Girl, Just like the Girl That Married Harry James': American Women and the Problem of Political Obligation in World War II." *American Quarterly* 42 (December 1990): 587–614.

Wharton, H. M. *War Songs and Poems of the Southern Confederacy, 1861–1865.* Philadelphia, Pa.: John C. Winston Co., 1904.

Wheelwright, Julie. *Amazons and Military Maids: Women Who Dressed as Men in the Pursuit of Life, Liberty, and Happiness.* London: Pandora Press, 1989.

Whipple, Edwin P. *Recollections of Eminent Men [With Other Papers].* Boston: Ticknor and Co., 1886.

Whites, LeeAnn. *The Civil War as a Crisis in Gender: Augusta, Georgia, 1860–1890.* Athens: University of Georgia Press, 1995.

Wiley, Bell Irvin. *The Life of Billy Yank: The Common Soldier of the Union.* Indianapolis: Bobbs-Merrill, 1951. Reprint, Baton Rouge: Louisiana State University Press, 1978.

———. *The Life of Johnny Reb, the Common Soldier of the Confederacy.* Indianapolis: Bobbs-Merrill, 1943.

Wilson, Christopher P. *The Labor of Words: Literary Professionalism in the Progressive Era.* Athens: University of Georgia Press, 1985.

———. "Stephen Crane and the Police." *American Quarterly* 48 (June 1996): 273–315.

Wilson, Edmund. *Patriotic Gore: Studies in the Literature of the American Civil War.* New York: Oxford University Press, 1966.

Wood, Ann Douglas. "The War within a War: Women Nurses in the Union Army." *Civil War History* 18 (September 1972): 197–212.

Wright, Lyle H. *American Fiction 1851–1875: A Contribution toward a Bibliography.* San Marino, Calif.: Huntington Library, 1978.

Young, Agatha. *The Women and the Crisis: Women of the North in the Civil War.* New York: McDowell, Oblensky, 1959.

Young, Elizabeth. "A Wound of One's Own: Louisa May Alcott's Civil War Fiction." *American Quarterly* 48 (September 1996): 439–74.

Zboray, Ronald. *A Fictive People: Antebellum Economic Development and the American Reading Public.* New York: Oxford University Press, 1994.

Ziff, Larzer. "Songs of the Civil War." *Civil War History* 2 (September 1956): 7–28.

INDEX

Aaron, Daniel, 1, 2, 15, 151

Abbott, John S. C., 57; *History of the Civil War in America*, 287–97, 300, 301, 302, 306, 307–8; *Kings and Queens, or Life in the Palace*, 289–90

Abbott and Company, 43

Adams, Franklin P., 312

Adams, William Taylor. *See* Optic, Oliver

"Address" (broadside), 128

African Americans: as soldiers, 2, 13, 162–63, 165–68, 170, 171–76, 178, 180–81, 183–85, 192–93, 214, 219, 280, 294, 315, 317; women, 2, 162–63, 185, 186, 188–89, 248, 316; and emancipation, 4, 13, 151, 154, 158–62, 165, 176, 178, 187–88, 192, 194, 247, 248, 249; and minstrelsy, 13, 14, 152, 154, 157, 162, 163, 168, 215, 224, 247, 280; stereotypes of, 14, 162, 166, 168, 184–85, 280; and Whitman, 117–18; and war humor, 151, 156, 157, 160, 165, 167, 180–81, 194, 212, 214–15, 217–19, 224; as contraband, 151–52, 154–56, 158, 162, 164, 168, 173, 185, 194, 214–15, 217–18, 280, 294; and heroism, 163–65, 169, 174, 175–76, 180, 193, 316; and sensational war literature, 178–80, 247–49, 251, 353–54 (n. 54); and African colonization, 215, 217; and juvenile war literature, 280–81; and postwar literature, 316. *See also* Race; Slavery

Agent's Companion, 295, 296

Alcott, Louisa May, 3, 21, 84, 169, 172, 230–31, 281; *Hospital Sketches*, 98, 112–13, 114, 115, 116, 117, 118, 140; "The

Brothers," 169, 172, 173, 174, 175; "M. L.," 191–92; "Nelly's Hospital," 273, 274; *Little Women*, 316

Alexander, Charles Wesley, 230, 241, 244; "General McClellan's Dream," 241; *General Sherman's Indian Spy*, 241; "Jeff Davis' Confession!," 241; *The Picket Slayer*, 241; *The Volunteer's Roll of Honor*, 241; *Washington's Vision*, 241; *Angel of the Battlefield*, 241, 248

Alger, Horatio, Jr., 258, 285; "Mother, May I Go?," 108; *Frank's Campaign*, 268–69, 280

"All Quiet on the Potomac" (poem), 5–6, 30

American Annual Cyclopaedia, 57, 281

American Anti-Slavery Society, 4

American News Company, 226, 228, 229, 249

American Publishers' Circular and Literary Gazette, 10, 52, 160

American Revolution, 14

American Union, 229

Anderson, E. A., 69

Anderson, Robert, 68

Anthony, E., 43

Appleton, William H., 356 (n. 21): "Young American's Library of Modern Heroes" series, 267, 272

Arkansas, 29

Arp, Bill. *See* Smith, Charles Henry

Arthur, T. S.: "Blue Yarn Stockings," 125–26

Arthur's Home Magazine, 56, 120–21, 126, 128

Ashmead and Evans, 267
Atlanta Confederacy, 30
Atlanta Intelligencer, 30
Atlanta Southern Confederacy, 90
Atlantic Monthly: and Alcott, 3, 21, 169,
172; Southern readership of, 25, 37;
and Northern publishing industry, 42;
subscriptions for soldiers, 53; and war
romances, 56; and Whitman, 66; and
war songs, 78; and Winthrop, 86–87;
and feminized war literature, 124, 140,
141; and African Americans, 152, 159;
and sensational war literature, 229; and
patriotism, 267; and war humor, 348
(n. 8)
Austin, Jane Goodwin: *Fairy Dreams*,
275; *Dora Darling, the Daughter of the
Regiment*, 275–80
"Away with the Stripes" (poem), 70
Ayres and Wade, 31

Bagby, George William, 8, 35, 40, 196, 200
Bailie, Charles, 31
Baker, George H., 61
Ballantyne, R. M., 285; *The Young Fur
Traders*, 268
Bancroft, George, 308
Barber, Joseph, 223
Barclay, E. E.: *The Lady Lieutenant*, 239–
41, 253
Barclay, Erastus, 230
Barclay and Company, 230, 241
Barney, Hiram, 68, 69
Barrick, J. R., 71
"Battle Cry of Freedom" (song), 109–10
Beadle and Company, 228, 229, 230, 238,
257, 299, 312
"Beautiful Lines" (poem), 99
Belisle, D. W.: "The Dying Soldier to His
Mother," 100
Belknap, T., 307
Bennett, A. L., 296
Bill, Gurdon, 290, 291, 292
Bill, Henry, 290, 291, 292; *Practical Instruc-
tions*, 295

Bill, Ledyard, 57, 287, 289, 290, 291, 292
Billings, John, 229
Biographies, 59
"Birds of a Feather" (cartoon), 219
Blashfield, Edwin, 229
Blight, David, 315
Blunt, E. K.: "The Southern Cross," 79
Bob Brant, Patriot and Spy, 226
Bohemian, 39
Bold, Christine, 230
Bone, John Henry, 40
Bonner, Robert, 46
"Bonnie Blue Flag, The" (poem), 30
Border Spy, The, 226
Boston Advertiser, 114
Boston Transcript, 52, 93
Bowling Green (Kentucky) Daily Courier, 30
Boynton, Elizabeth, 180, 193
Boys and Girls Stories of the War, The, 282,
283
"Boy Soldier, The" (story), 260, 263
Boys' war novels. *See* Juvenile war litera-
ture
Braddon, M. E.: *Eleanor's Victory*, 6
Brady, Frederic A., 230
Brady, Matthew, 36
"Brave at Home, The" (poem), 135
"Brave Kentucky Girl, A" (story), 272
Breckinridge, Lucy, 31
Broadsides, 1, 196, 201, 208, 222
Brockett, Linus P.: *Woman's Work in the
Civil War*, 313
Brooks, Peter, 129
Brooks, Sarah Warner: "On! Brothers,
On!," 66
Brown, John, 251
Brown, William Wells: *Clotelle*, 169, 345
(n. 32); *The Black Man*, 169, 345–46
(n. 32)
Browne, Charles Farrar, 195–96, 202, 204,
211, 215, 217, 220–23; "The War Fever
in Baldinsville," 211–12
Browning, Elizabeth Barrett: "Parting
Lovers," 135
Brownlow, Susan, 234, 235, 236, 237

Brownlow, William G.: *Sketches of the Rise, Progress, and Decline of Secession*, 234; *Parson Brownlow's Book*, 234–35

Bugle Horn of Liberty, 39, 196

"Bull Run" (broadside), 89

Bulwer-Lytton, Robert: *A Strange Story*, 6

Burke, Boykin and Company, 22

Butler, Benjamin, 151, 152, 220, 306

Butler, Charles William, 86

Calvinism, 95

Camp Jester or, Amusement for the Mess, 196

"Can the Glory of War Atone for Its Misery?," 90

Carby, Hazel, 190

Carleton, G. W., 193, 267

Carroll, R. W., 269

Cary, Alice, 53

Cary, Constance, 37, 134; "Implora Place," 138

Cary, Hetty, 80

Cary, Phoebe: "An Incident at Fort Wagner," 172

Case, O. D., 297, 299

Castlemon, Harry, 258, 269, 312; *Frank on a Gunboat*, 268, 269, 271, 312; *Frank the Young Naturalist*, 269, 270; *Frank before Vicksburg*, 269, 312; *Frank on the Lower Mississippi*, 270, 312

Cather, Willa, 317–18

Century, 314, 316, 317; "Battles and Leaders of the Civil War" series, 314, 317

Charleston Courier, 23, 25, 217

Charleston Mercury, 30

Chase, Salmon, 266

Chesnut, Mary, 17, 19, 30

Children, 1, 14, 16, 91, 165, 258–60, 263, 264, 318. *See also* Juvenile war literature

Childs, George W., 56–57, 114, 288, 304, 305–6, 307

Childs, J. Ward: "Pompey's Contraband Song," 150

"Christmas Day, A.D. 1861," 90

Christy, George, 168, 219

Cincinnati Commercial Gazette, 309

Civil War: cultural meanings of, 2, 15, 289; democratization of, 4, 16, 241, 311, 318; as organized war, 10–11, 286, 321 (n. 20); reconceptualization of, 314

Clancy, John: "A Northern Rally," 66

Clarke, James Freeman, 78

Clarke, Mary Bayard, 89; "The Battle of Manassas," 91

Cobb, Sylvanus, 26

Coffin, Charles Carleton, 14; *My Days and Nights on the Battlefield*, 258, 262, 272

Commercial literary culture: and war histories, 4, 6, 10, 55, 56, 59, 208, 288–91, 298, 301, 305–6, 308; and Northern literature, 4–5, 10, 18, 20, 42–44, 46–57, 59, 74; and Southern literature, 5, 20–21, 34–41, 323 (n. 14); and sensational war literature, 6, 7, 55, 226–30; and war romances, 6, 15, 16, 55, 56, 59; and war humor, 6, 55–56, 59, 205, 207–10, 224; and patriotism, 15, 18, 60, 74, 208, 209; and democratization of war, 16, 311; and collectibility, 51, 52; and juvenile war literature, 57, 59, 267–68, 270, 271, 281, 356–57 (n. 21); and illustrations, 59–60; and death, 86, 87; and sentimental war literature, 114–15; and feminized war literature, 129; and broadsides, 208; and subscription histories, 295; and postwar period, 312–13; and gender, 317–18

Commonwealth, 112, 191

Confederate Spirit and Knapsack of Fun, 39

Congdon, Charles, 91

"Conscript's Lament, The" (song), 201

Continental Monthly, 110–11, 136, 158–61, 229

"Contraband of War" (cartoon), 156

"Contraband's Return, The" (poem), 185–86

Conway, Moncure, 191

Cooper, James Fenimore, 245

Cooper and Pond, 43

"Cotton States' Farewell to Yankee Doodle, The" (poem), 81

Countryman, 31, 124

Fairchild, Thomas B., 306

Fanny Campbell, the Female Pirate Captain, 230

Faust, Drew Gilpin, 9, 129, 142, 143

"Feeding the Negro Children under Charge of the Military Authorities at Hilton Head, South Carolina" (cartoon), 165

Female Warrior, The, 230

Feminized war literature: and relationship between individual and nation, 2, 12, 123–24, 149; and war poetry, 106, 120, 122, 124–25, 128, 129–30, 135–36, 138, 144, 145; and hospitals, 110, 112; and women's role in war, 120–21, 122; and mothers, 121–22, 128, 129; and patriotism, 122, 123, 128–29, 130, 133, 141, 146, 340 (n. 18); and sentimentalism, 122, 123, 129, 339 (n. 7); and flag, 123–24; and chastisement of soldiers, 124–26, 128; and home-front experiences, 128–29; and economic consequences of war, 132–34; and suffering, 134–38, 142, 146–48, 341 (n. 29), 342 (n. 33); and war work, 139–43, 146; and sensational war literature, 232; and juvenile war literature, 273, 274; and postwar literature, 317

Fern, Fanny: "Soldiers' Wives," 134

Ferry Boy and the Financier, The, 267

Fields, James T., 20, 21, 53, 54–55, 86–87, 159

Flag of Our Union, 3, 42, 47, 148

Flag of Our Union Songster, The, 55

"Flag of Secession, The" (song), 71

Forbes, Edwin, 13, 168

Fosdick, Charles Austin, 258

Foster, Kate D., 30

Frank Leslie's Budget of Fun, 26, 56, 196, 205

Frank Leslie's Heroic Incidents of the Civil War in America, 56

Frank Leslie's Illustrated Newspaper: and genres, 6–7; Southern imitations of, 8, 26; and illustrations, 13, 36, 46, 49, 164;

and African Americans, 13, 151, 156, 157, 162, 163–68, 193, 280; Southern competition for, 31; and war poetry, 34, 106–7; and *Southern Illustrated News*, 37–38; and Northern publishing industry, 42; Southern readership of, 44, 46, 48; and cultural politics of war, 47; and war romances, 56; and sentimental war literature, 115; and feminized war literature, 132; and war humor, 157, 209

Frank Leslie's Pictorial History of the War of 1861, 51, 52–53, 56

Frank Leslie's Pictorials of Union Victories, 56

Frank Leslie's Portrait Pictorial, 56

Frank Leslie's War Chart, 56

Frank Leslie's War Maps, 56

Frazer, Virginia Boyle, 316

Fredrickson, George, 94, 166; *The Inner Civil War*, 10–11

"Frightened Contraband, A" (story), 215

Fugitive Slave Act, 48

Galt, William, 30

"Game of Secession, The" (game), 60

"Game of the Rebellion, The" (game), 60, 257

"Gathering of the Southern Volunteers, The" (song), 72

Gender: and popular war literature, 1, 2; and normative roles, 14; and war poetry, 65–67, 83, 106, 107–8; and sentimental war literature, 107–8, 112; and wounds, 137; and North/South differences, 142; and sensational war literature, 230–32, 235, 240, 245, 248, 252–53, 254; and juvenile war literature, 273, 282–83; and democratization of war, 311; and veterans-oriented literature, 315; and postwar literature, 316, 317–18. *See also* Feminized war literature; Women

Gilmore, James Roberts, 158, 281; *Among the Pines*, 159–62

"Give to the Soldiers" (article), 273

"Go, My Boy, Where Duty Calls You" (poem), 122

structions to Their Agents for Selling Their Subscription Books, 295–96

Herald, 26, 164

Hero Boy, The, 267, 272

Herrington, W. D.: Deserter's Daughter, The, 250; Captain's Bride, The, 250, 253–54

"He's Gone to the Arms of Abraham" (song), 201–2

Higginson, Thomas Wentworth, 159, 166, 279–80; Outdoor Papers, 20

"Highly Intelligent Contraband, The" (cartoon), 217

Hill, Theo H., 70

Holcombe, William H., 27; "Jackson, the Alexandria Martyr," 88

Holmes, Oliver Wendell: "The Poetry of War," 1, 100–101, 311; and war songs, 4–5, 77, 80; and all-consuming nature of war, 17; and newspapers, 19; and South, 25, 38; and war poetry, 53, 64, 100–101, 103, 105, 108; on soldiers as boys, 109

Holstein, Anna Morris Ellis: Three Years in Field Hospitals of the Army of the Potomac, 115

"Home Again—Back from the Yankee Camp" (cartoon), 220

Home Journal, 26

Homer, Winslow, 13, 168; Campaign Sketches, 59; Life in Camp cards, 59–60; "News from the War," 138

Hooker, A. S.: "Hospital Heroes," 115

Hope, James Barron: "Oath of Freedom— A National Hymn," 76

Horwitz, Tony, 316

"How a Man Feels When He Is Shot" (article), 260

Howe, Julia Ward: "The Battle Hymn of the Republic," 77, 78, 79, 80

Hugo, Victor: Les Mis,rables, 6

"Humorous Anecdotes of the War" (book proposal), 200

Hundley, Mrs. E. D., 71

Hunter, David, 162

"Hurrah for Jeff. Davis" (broadside), 89

Hutton and Freligh, 31

Hynes, Samuel, 224

"I Am Not Sick, I'm over Forty-five" (broadside), 222

Identity: and public literary culture, 4; cultural politics of, 14; and perception of war, 18; and war songs, 76; and war poetry, 80–81; and sentimental war literature, 94, 103; and African Americans, 158, 169, 171, 176, 189; and sensational war literature, 239–40, 247; and juvenile war literature, 278; and postwar literature, 317

"I Have Kissed Him, and Let Him Go" (song), 129–30

Illustrated envelopes, 13, 43–44, 44, 83, 84, 151, 151–52

Illustrated weeklies, 1, 2, 6–7, 13. See also specific titles

Illustrations: and Frank Leslie's Illustrated Newspaper, 13, 36, 46, 49, 164; and Southern Literary Messenger, 26; and Southern Illustrated News, 35, 36; and Southern Monthly, 35–36; and print culture, 59–60; and dying-soldier poetry, 83, 106; and Ellsworth, 84; and feminized war literature, 134; and African Americans, 156–57, 164, 166–68, 169, 170–71, 175, 193–94; and slavery, 171–72; and children, 264; and war histories, 304

"In an Ambulance" (story), 274

Independent, 42, 72

Individual and nation: and war humor, 2, 11; and feminized war literature, 2, 12, 123–24, 149; and sentimental war literature, 11, 12, 93–95, 109, 118, 119; and sensational war literature, 11, 13–14, 236, 245, 246–47; popular war literature, 11, 14, 16, 18, 60; and war poetry, 12, 93–94, 103; and African Americans, 13, 164, 176; and juvenile war literature, 13–14, 266–68, 271, 285–86; and war's meaning, 16, 18, 94; and Northern publishing industry, 43; individualized nationalism, 111–12; and heroism, 164

"Intelligent Contraband, The" (song), 154–55

"In Western Missouri" (story), 247

"Is That Mother Bending o'er Me?" (song), 108

Jackson, James W., 88

Jackson, Stonewall, 35, 89, 124

"Jackson, Our First Martyr" (poem), 88

James, Henry: "The Story of a Year," 131

James, Henry, Sr., 115

James, U. P., 230

"Jessie Underhill's Thanksgiving" (story), 130–31

"John Brown's Body" (song), 77–78, 79, 80

Johnson and Fry, 57, 305

Journal of Commerce, 22–23, 48

"Just before the Battle, Mother" (song), 108, 111

Justina, the Avenger, 228

Juvenile war literature: as popular war literature, 1, 16; and boys' war novels, 2, 11, 13, 57, 258; and adventure stories, 2, 13, 268–71, 278, 279, 285, 286, 312; and commercial literary culture, 57, 59, 267–68, 270, 271, 281, 356–57 (n. 21); and readers, 256–58, 355 (n. 1); and drummer boys, 258, 259, 262–64; and biographies, 266, 267–68, 285; and mothers, 270–71; and girls, 272–77, 282–83; and African Americans, 280–81; republishing of, 312

Kate Sharp; or, The Two Conscripts, 231–32, 257

Kentucky, 48, 56, 233, 234

Kerr, Orpheus C. *See* Newell, Robert Henry

Ketchum, Annie Chambers: "Battle-Call," 64, 65

Kettell, Thomas B.: *History of the Great Rebellion*, 290, 301–2

Killum, John: "Old Betsy," 81

Kimball, Augusta Cooper: "My Country," 67–68

Kingston, W. H. G., 279

Kirke, Edmund, 159

Knickerbocker, 158, 159

Knoxville Whig, 234

Ku Klux Klan, 82

Larcom, Lucy, 53; "The Nineteenth of April, 1861," 43, 63

Last Political Writings of General Nathaniel Lyon, U.S.A., 87–88

"Lauriger Horatius" (song), 80

"Leaf from a Summer, A" (story), 131

Lee and Shepard, 271–72

Leland, Charles Godfrey, 55, 158–59; "Northmen, Come Out!," 66

Leonard, Agnes: "After the Battle," 6

Lester, Charles Edward, 114, 115–16

Life and Adventures, Songs, Services, and Speeches of Private Miles O'Reilly, 219

Life of James W. Jackson, the Alexandria Hero, 88–89

Lincoln, Abraham: and Emancipation Proclamation, 165, 191, 295, 297; and African Americans, 192; and war humor, 195–96, 202, 205, 212, 218, 220, 221, 223, 350 (n. 47); and juvenile war literature, 266, 267; on Civil War as "a People's contest," 311; tributes to, 313

Linderman, Gerald, 316–17

Little Drummer Boy, The, 259

"Little Hero, The" (story), 282

"Little Incendiary, The" (article), 252

"Little Soldiers" (illus.), 272

"Little Soldiers, The" (story), 260

"Little Starlight" (story), 176, 178, 185

Livermore, Mary, 313

Livingston, Cora: "The Confederate Flag," 70

Lloyd, H. H., and Company, 44

Locke, David Ross, 196, 202, 204, 212–14, 218, 220, 221, 223; "Letters of a Straight Democrat," 212

London, Jack, 317

ment in Action," 166; "The Drummer Boy of Our Regiment," 264

Natchez Courier, 30

Nation, 300, 302, 307, 308, 309

National Anti-Slavery Standard, 4

National Hymn Committee, 72–74

Nationalism: and Southern literature, 5, 9, 11, 15, 23–24, 25, 27, 29, 33, 60, 65, 70, 80–81, 316; and Northern literature, 11, 194; and popular war literature, 16; and religion, 68–69; individualized nationalism, 111–12; and sensational war literature, 245; and juvenile war literature, 266, 267–68, 270, 285; and war histories, 302, 308

Nationhood: and popular war literature, 11, 12, 18, 23; and print culture, 51; and war poetry, 63, 65, 68, 70, 86; and African Americans, 154, 168, 281; and war histories, 300

"Ned Arlington; or Harper's Ferry Scenes" (story), 251–52

"Negro in the War, The" (illus.), 193

Nelles, Annie, 310

Newell, Robert Henry, 56, 74–75, 195, 196, 202, 204–11, 213, 214, 221, 222

New Orleans Delta, 23, 24

New Orleans Picayune, 30

Newspapers: and war-related literature, 1; war poetry in, 3, 4, 11, 29–30, 33–34, 53, 61, 73, 79, 80, 83, 88, 91, 186, 324 (n. 29); and readers, 19–20; and National Hymn Committee, 74; and war humor, 202, 209, 217; and commercial literary culture, 207; and war histories, 288, 292–93, 303, 307

New York Evening Post, 72

New York Herald, 218

New York Illustrated News, 231

New York Ledger, 25–26, 39, 41, 42, 46–47, 56, 134

New-York Mercury, 64, 74, 84, 202, 204–5, 226, 245

New York Times, 52, 111, 117, 121, 122, 226, 235

New York Tribune, 22, 67, 79, 217, 228, 297

New York Weekly, 42

Nick Nax, 26

Norcross, Grenville, 257, 259, 260, 263, 271–72, 281

Norfolk Day Book, 30

Norris, Frank, 317

North: and cultural politics of war, 1, 9, 18; public literary culture of, 4; publishing industry of, 5, 21, 24, 42–44, 49–51, 56, 57, 59, 60, 226, 257; literary sensibilities of, 6, 9; and homogeneity and difference, 10; and Southern writers, 34; and illustrations, 36, 37

North American Review, 257, 279, 307

Northern literature: and race, 2, 13, 151–52, 154, 156, 158–76, 178–81, 185, 192–94; and commercial literary culture, 4–5, 10, 18, 20, 42–44, 46–57, 59, 74; and sensational war literature, 7, 178–79, 227, 230–41, 244–51, 253, 254; and readers, 8, 37, 44, 48–49; and war poetry, 10, 47, 53–54, 59, 61, 62, 65–70, 71, 74, 83, 89–90, 91, 93, 98, 99, 100, 118; and nationalism, 11, 194; and Southern literature, 22, 23–28, 37, 41, 53; and patriotism, 47–48, 54; and war humor, 56, 195–96, 202, 204–15, 217, 218, 219, 223; and war histories, 56–57, 288–304; and sentimental war literature, 93, 98, 99, 100, 118; and feminized war literature, 120, 122, 123, 128, 129, 132–33, 135, 138, 139–42, 146, 148; and mulattoes, 190–92; and juvenile war literature, 256–81, 282, 283

Norton, Charles Eliot, 56, 307

Notes of Hospital Life, 110, 111, 116

Officers' journals, 59

Old Bill Woodworth, 226, 257

Old Hal Williams, 257

"Old Year's Dirge, The" (poem), 144

"One of Many" (story), 135

"On the Kentucky Border" (story), 233

Optic, Oliver, 270, 280; *The Soldier Boy,*

Punch Songster, The, 195, 201
Putnam, George Palmer, 50, 51, 52

Race: and Northern literature, 2, 13, 151–
52, 154, 156, 158–76, 178–81, 185, 192–
94; and Southern literature, 2, 27–28,
190, 255, 283; and popular literature, 4,
16; and illustrations, 13; and mulattoes,
190–92, 248–49; and war humor, 214,
215, 217, 218, 219, 220–21, 224; and sensational war literature, 240; and juvenile
war literature, 280, 283; and war histories, 293–94; and democratization of
war, 311; and veterans-oriented literature, 315; and postwar literature, 316.
See also African Americans; Slavery
Raleigh Standard, 91
Rambler, 31
Rand, Edward Sprague, Jr.: "A Tale of
1861," 287
Randall, James R.: "My Maryland," 30, 77,
79–80, 81
Randolph, J. W., 22
Readers: and popular war literature, 1,
7, 18, 19–21; and Southern literature,
8, 18, 22–31, 33, 37, 48; and Northern
literature, 8, 37, 44, 48–49; reader-
response theory, 8–9, 21; impact of war
on, 18, 22–23, 25, 47, 60; and news-
papers, 19–20; and illustrations, 36, 37;
and Victorian culture, 46; and juvenile
war literature, 256–57, 355 (n. 1); and
war histories, 295, 310
Realism, 317–18
Rebellion Record, 51, 52, 53, 69, 235, 287
"Red, White, and Blue" (story), 130
"Redemption" (poem), 79
Redpath, James, 112, 114, 156, 228–29;
"Books for the Camp Fires," 8, 169,
229
Reed, William Howell, 110, 111, 115, 117
Reid, Mayne, 267, 269, 279, 285; *The Boy
Hunters*, 268, 269
Religion: and nationalism, 68–69; and war
songs, 78–79; and war poetry, 83, 95;

and sentimental war literature, 95, 96,
113; and feminized war literature, 141,
142, 143, 146–48; and drummer boys,
258, 259, 264; and women, 270; and
juvenile war literature, 281
"Returned Prodigal, The" (cartoon), 220
Reynolds, David S., 226
Richards, Caroline Cowles, 43, 93
Richardson, Charles B.: *The Fallen Brave*,
54–55
Richmond Daily Dispatch, 29, 30, 63–64,
102, 119, 128
Richmond Daily Examiner, 30, 302
Richmond Enquirer, 91
Richmond Type Foundry, 21
Richmond Whig, 30, 37, 88, 185
Roberts Brothers, 267
Robinson, John Hovey: *The Round Pack*,
226, 245, 248, 249; *Nick Whiffles*, 246;
*Mountain Max; or, Nick Whiffles on the
Border*, 246–47
Rogers, Cornelia D.: "Ah! He Kissed Me
When He Left Me," 120, 129
Rogers, M. Louise: "Our Country," 144
Roosevelt, Theodore: *Autobiography*, 285;
"Brotherhood and the Heroic Virtues,"
314–15; "The Strenuous Life," 317
Ropes, Hannah, 114
Ross and Tousey, 43
Round Table, 15, 131, 132, 249
Royster, Charles, 7, 119
Ruth: A Song in the Desert, 147

"Sambo's Right to be Kilt" (poem), 165,
218, 219
Sargent, Epes: *Peculiar, A Tale of the Great
Transition*, 192–93, 316
Savage, John: "The Muster of the North,"
62–63
Savage, Kirk, 169, 315
Savannah Republican, 30
Sawyer, Charles Carroll: "Who Will Care
for Mother Now?," 6, 108; "Mother
Would Comfort Me," 105, 210
Scarry, Elaine, 136

"Scene in a Yankee Barber Shop" (cartoon), 217–18

"Scene in the Parlor of Mr. Barnwell's House at Beaufort, South Carolina" (illus.), 156–57

Scott, Walter, 257, 304

Scotto, the Scout, 232, 247–48

"Scout of Albado, The" (story), 183–84, 250, 252–53

Sensational war literature: as popular war literature, 1, 16; and commercial literary culture, 6, 7, 55, 226–30; and women, 7, 13–14, 227, 230–41, 244–45, 251, 252–53, 255; and relationship between individual and nation, 11, 13–14, 236, 245, 246–47; and African Americans, 178–80, 247–49, 353–54 (n. 54); and feminized war literature, 232; and flag, 235, 236; and heroic scouts, 245–46; and juvenile war literature, 277, 279; and war histories, 299–300; republishing of, 312

Sentimental war literature: as popular war literature, 1; and relationship between individual and nation, 11, 12, 93–95, 109, 118, 119; and war poetry, 16, 93, 95, 98–103, 105–8, 109, 116, 118–19; and patriotism, 93, 95, 122; and death, 93–94, 95, 96, 98–103, 113, 118, 119, 206–7; and mother, 103, 105–9; and illustrations, 106; and soldiers as boys, 109, 112–13, 270; and hospital setting, 110–17, 119; and heroism, 115–17, 151; and war humor, 201, 204, 205, 206–7; and sensational war literature, 232; and children, 258–59; and juvenile war literature, 277

Shakespeare, William, 164, 239

Sharper and Brothers, 38

Shaw, Robert Gould, 174

Shea, John Gilmary: *The Fallen Brave*, 86; *The Victims of the Rebellion*, 86

Shepperson, William G., 62; *War Songs of the South*, 29, 62

Sigourney, Lydia, 53

Simmons, James W.: "The Martyr of Alexandria," 88

Simms, William Gilmore, 6, 20, 34, 35, 39–40; *War Poetry of the South*, 313

Sinclair, Carrie Bell: "All Quiet along the Savannah To-night," 118, 119; "The Homespun Dress," 121

Six Months among the Secessionists, 236–37, 247

"Slave in 1863. A Thrilling Series of the Great Evil" (album cards), 171–72

Slavery: and emancipation, 4, 13, 151, 154, 157, 158–61, 165, 174, 176, 178, 180, 181, 183–84, 187–88, 193, 194; and Southern literature, 27–28, 181, 183, 185–89, 252–53; and *Harper's Weekly*, 48, 49; and sentimental war literature, 95; and African Americans as contraband, 151–52, 154–56, 158; and war songs, 157–58; and illustrations, 171–72; and sensational war literature, 179–80, 247, 251, 252–53; and war humor, 219–20; and juvenile war literature, 275–76, 280, 283; and war histories, 293, 296–98, 300; and postwar literature, 315–16. See also African Americans; Race

Smalls, Robert, 163–64, 165, 169

Smith, Charles Henry, 196, 202, 204, 220–23, 350 (n. 47); *Bill Arp, So Called: A Side Show of the Southern Side of the War*, 220

Smith, Seba, 204

Smith, William B., 39

Smith and Barrow's Monthly, 39

Social realism, 94

Sojers' Comic Almanac, 196

"Soldier Boy, The" (poem), 263–64

Soldiers: African Americans as, 2, 13, 162–63, 165–68, 170, 171–76, 178, 180–81, 183–85, 192–93, 214, 219, 280, 294, 315, 317; dying-soldier poetry, 6, 12, 16, 83, 93–94, 100–103, 105–7; and war poetry, 29, 53, 64–66, 84, 86, 88, 91, 95, 98–99, 108, 111, 116–19, 122–23, 128, 129–30, 135–36, 138, 186; and memorial volumes, 54; and war songs, 55, 79, 94,

War poetry: as popular war literature, 1, 4; and African Americans, 2, 165, 172, 185–89, 251; in newspapers, 3, 4, 11, 29–30, 33–34, 53, 61, 73, 79, 80, 83, 88, 91, 186, 324 (n. 29); and high-low dichotomy, 3, 15, 53, 311; and patriotism, 4, 6, 29, 62, 74, 86, 91, 93; and Southern literature, 5, 6, 29–30, 33, 39, 50, 53, 61–63, 65, 66–67, 70–71, 80–83, 90, 91, 93, 98, 99, 100, 107, 118; and commercial literary culture, 6, 10, 15, 208; dying-soldier poetry, 6, 12, 16, 83, 93–94, 100–103, 105–7; and Northern literature, 10, 47, 53–54, 59, 61, 62, 65–70, 71, 74, 83, 89–90, 91, 93, 98, 99, 100, 118; and flag, 11–12, 62, 68–71; and relationship between individual and nation, 12, 93–94; and sentimental war literature, 16, 93, 95, 98–103, 105–8, 109, 116, 118–19; and cultural politics of war, 47; and war songs, 55, 73; and death, 83–84, 86–90, 91, 93, 95, 98–103; and feminized war literature, 106, 120, 122, 124–25, 128, 129–30, 135–36, 138, 144, 145; and war humor, 201, 218, 222; and sensational war literature, 225–26; and juvenile war literature, 262, 263–64; and veterans-oriented literature, 314

War-related anecdote collections, 1, 14, 50

War romances: Southern imitation of Northern literature, 5, 37; and commercial literary culture, 6, 15, 16, 55, 56, 59; and feminized war literature, 131, 132; and sensational war literature, 226–27, 228; and juvenile war literature, 273

War songs: as popular war literature, 1, 3, 4; and commercial literary culture, 4, 208; and Northern literature, 6, 55, 72–79; and Southern literature, 6, 64, 71–72, 76–77, 79–80; and relationship between individual and nation, 12, 94; and African Americans, 13, 151, 154–55, 157, 160; and patriotism, 55, 62, 74; and war poetry, 55, 73; and soldiers, 55,

79, 94, 108–9; and national hymns, 68, 72–79; and flag, 71, 124; and war humor, 74–76, 196, 201, 210, 211, 213; and sentimental war literature, 94, 108–10, 111; and death, 100, 105; and feminized war literature, 124, 129; and children, 259–60

Waud, A. R., 13, 168

"We Are Coming Father Abraham, Three Hundred Thousand More" (poem), 107

Webber, Mary J.: *Chimes of Freedom and Union*, 53

Weekly Anglo-African, 152

Wells, J. G., 44

West and Johnson, 22, 31, 38, 302

Westbrook, Robert, 128

Wharton, M. B.: "Starry-Barred Banner, The," 71

"What Sensation Has Come to at Last" (cartoon), 227

"What the Boys and Girls Can Do" (article), 273

"When This Cruel War Is Over" (song), 6

White, Richard Grant, 53, 62, 68, 72–74; *National Hymns*, 73

Whitman, Sarah Helen: "After the Fight at Manassas," 89–90

Whitman, Walt, 95, 96, 98, 105–6, 110, 111, 112, 113, 114–15, 117–18; *Specimen Days*, 1; "Beat! Beat! Drums!," 17, 65; "Eighteen Sixty-one," 66; *Correspondence*, 93; *Drum-Taps*, 95; "The Sight in Camp in the Day-Break Grey and Dim," 95–96, 99; "Hospital Note Book," 105–6

Whittemore, J. M., 44

Whittier, John Greenleaf, 53; "Barbara Frietchie," 124, 340 (n. 11)

"Why It Could Not Be" (story), 190–91

Wiley, Bell Irvin, 109

Williams, Jim, 166

Willis, Richard Storrs, 74

Wilson, Edmund, 1, 15, 79

Winfield, the Lawyer's Son, and How He Became a Major-General, 267

Winthrop, Theodore, 84, 333 (n. 69); "Our